# Machine Translation Summit XVII

Volume 2: Translator, Project and User Tracks

Dublin, Ireland
19-23 August 2019

ISBN: 978-1-5108-9293-4

# Machine Translation Summit XVII

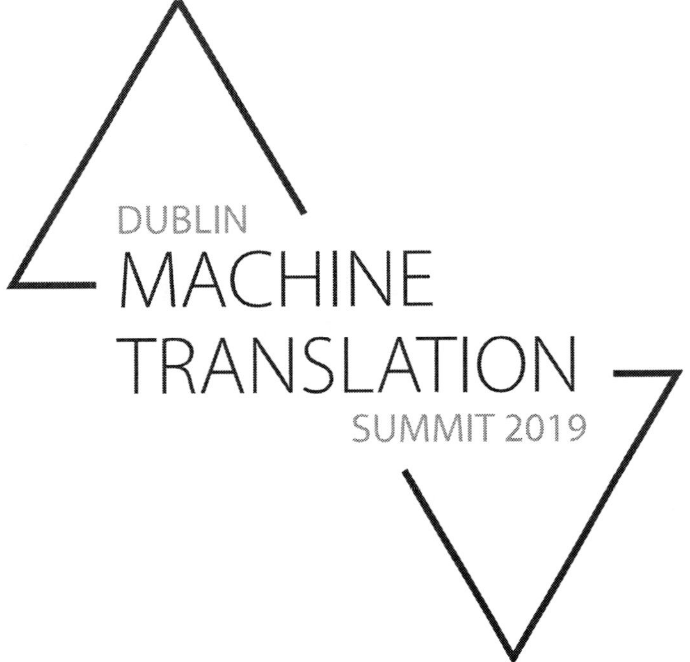



Proceedings of Machine Translation Summit XVII
Volume 2: Translator, Project and User Tracks

https://www.mtsummit2019.com

19–23 August, 2019
Dublin, Ireland

# Proceedings of Machine Translation Summit XVII
## Volume 2: Translator, Project and User Tracks

https://www.mtsummit2019.com

19–23 August, 2019
Dublin, Ireland

# Foreword by the President of the IAMT and the EAMT

*Céad míle fáilte romhaibh!*

It's a pleasure for me to warmly welcome you all to the 17th Machine Translation Summit.

Every two years, the International Association for Machine Translation (IAMT), an umbrella organization comprising the Asian Association for Machine Translation (AAMT), the Association for Machine Translation in the Americas (AMTA), and the European Association for Machine Translation (EAMT), jointly call everyone related in some way or another to machine translation and translation technologies to the most inclusive MT conference in the world, a real Summit. It brings together senior and junior researchers, developers, vendors and all kinds of users, coming from academia, industry, or even as freelancers, to share and become aware of any new developments in the field.

This is the sixth such summit held in Europe, after having visited Munich (1989), Luxembourg (1995), Santiago de Compostela (2001), Copenhagen (2007), and Nice (2013).

The organizers have assembled an excellent programme; after two days with a wide offer of tutorials and workshops, the main conference features four tracks: the research track, the users' track, a new translators' track, and the usual projects track, and includes three invited talks, poster sessions and oral sessions. Everyone will find something going on that interests them throughout the event.

Every six years, the EAMT organizes the MT Summit in Europe. The EAMT is a growing association, which organizes a yearly conference, sponsors research, development and community outreach initiatives, and annually grants a Best Thesis Award. Individuals, institutions and companies from Europe, Africa and the Middle East can join the EAMT for a modest fee and benefit from all these activities. In addition to that, EAMT members (as AMTA and AAMT members) enjoy attractive discounted fees when attending EAMT, AMTA and AAMT conferences. This is possible thanks to our members but especially to my colleagues in the EAMT Executive Committee —coming from both academia and industry— who work hard to make it all happen.

The XVII MT Summit would not be possible without the hard work of our local organizers, headed by my predecessor as EAMT president and current Executive Board member, Andy Way, who have, with the help of other MT actors from the Adapt Centre and the professional collaboration of Abbey Conference & Events, put together an excellent conference. I am very thankful for their hard work and for having put their local MT expertise at the disposal of the EAMT (and the IAMT).

*Bainigí taitneamh as*, that is, enjoy. Enjoy the programme, the company, and the city. Ten years ago, I lived here and worked here for a year and I'll miss it every day of my life. And I'll tell you something: it is especially the local people that makes Dublin —and all of Ireland— one of the best places in the world to hold a conference like our Summit. I'm sure you'll bring home sweet memories of it!


Baile Átha Cliath/Dublin, Lúnasa/August 2019


**Mikel L. Forcada**
President of the IAMT and the EAMT
Professor of Computer Languages and Systems Universitat d'Alacant
Alacant, Valencian Country, Spain.
Email: `mlf@ua.es`

# Foreword by MT Summit 2019 Conference Chair

Back in 2017, on behalf of the International Association for Machine Translation (IAMT), the European Association for Machine Translation (EAMT) entrusted me with hosting this conference that you are currently attending.

While I was grateful for the trust shown in me, as a previous IAMT/EAMT president, I was acutely aware of the need to deliver; compared to our annual EAMT conferences, MT Summits provide us with the opportunity to show our Asian and American friends and colleagues that we can put on an event that all three regional associations and the IAMT can be duly proud of; if you mess up, Europe has to wait 6 years to try to put it right!

After two years of hard work, I can say with some confidence that we have achieved this. One of the first things I did was put together a very strong support team. I would really like to thank our seven co-chairs of the four tracks, namely:

- Research track co-chairs: Barry Haddow & Rico Sennrich (University of Edinburgh, UK)

- User track co-chairs: John Tinsley (Iconic Translation Machines, Ireland) & Dimitar Shterionov (ADAPT Centre, Dublin City University, Ireland)

- Translator track co-chairs: Celia Rico (Universidad Europea de Madrid, Spain) & Federico Gaspari (ADAPT Centre, Dublin City University, Ireland)

- Projects chair: Mikel L. Forcada (Universitat d'Alacant, Spain)

I am also very grateful to Laura Rossi (Lexis Nexis, The Netherlands) and Antonio Toral (University of Groningen, The Netherlands) for acting as excellent Tutorials and Workshops Chairs, respectively. I hope you all benefited from attending these pre-conference events!

For the most part, it is these 9 individuals who have put together the programme assembled before you. Each of them will comment on their Tracks later in these proceedings, but they all deserve our heartfelt thanks, as do the panels of reviewers they assembled which helped improve all our papers. From a personal point of view, I am delighted that we have – for the first but surely not the last time – included a Translator track; I have advocated for some time now that it is only through dialogue that MT developers and the translator community can advance our field. I have been very keen to take up a number of recent opportunities to speak at translator conferences, so I am especially pleased to welcome translators to this event; thank you for coming!

I am of course grateful to everyone who submitted a paper; whether your work was selected for presentation or not, if no-one had submitted, we wouldn't have had a conference. For those of you whose work was selected for presentation, many thanks for coming to Dublin, and to DCU, which have been my home and workplace now for 28 years, half my life. All of you would have interacted via EasyChair, and I am grateful to Carol Scarton, EAMT secretary, for her effort in setting up the various accounts which enabled the submission and notification processes to run so smoothly.

When you act as IAMT/EAMT president, or edit the Machine Translation journal, or act as track chair at major conferences, sometimes you have to be a bit of a pain, because you are often asking busy people to do things, mostly for free! Having been around the block a few times, I have lots of contacts in the industry, so I made myself responsible for bringing in sponsorship. I know they will say I was close to pestering them on many occasions, but I am truly grateful for the hugely generous support we obtained from our sponsors from the translation and CAT industry:

- Silver sponsors: Microsoft, and STAR

- Bronze sponsors: Pangeanic, text & form, CrossLang, Flitto, VistaTec

- Other sponsors: Welocalize, Iconic, XTM, Unbabel, DCU, ELRA, Tilde, Springer, Apertium

I am also extremely grateful to Fáilte Ireland for their generous support of this conference, which helped my ADAPT@DCU colleagues Joss Moorkens and Sharon O'Brien present our bid in Nagoya in 2017, as well as supporting our excellent invited speakers: Laura Casanellas, Helena Moniz, and Arianna Bisazza. With many women in our team, it's extremely important to have strong female role models, and we could not have asked for better from Laura, Arianna and Helena; many thanks to all of you for agreeing to share your expertise with us!

We took the decision a while back to try to be as green a conference as possible. You will already have noticed that, in order to reduce waste, there is no delegate bag. To reduce paper, we are not producing paper proceedings, and the normal programme booklet has been replaced by a smaller 'bradge' which doubles as a name badge. We are hoping to have a tree-planting ceremony during the conference in order to reduce the carbon footprint of the Summit. To reduce transport costs, we are using onsite accommodation at DCU, and will promote the use of public transport to the off-site events. Thanks to DCU Sustainability Manager Sam Fahy for her support in these efforts.

While we decided not to produce printed proceedings, they still needed to be put together in electronic form. I am grateful to Jenny Walsh for producing such an excellent conference logo, but huge thanks are due to Alberto Poncelas for putting together the proceedings, and for helping workshop chairs to produce theirs. Alberto has also liaised with Matt Post to ensure that your papers are indexed in perpetuity on the ACL Anthology!

I have two final people to thank. Firstly, I am very grateful to Grainne McQuaid and her team in Abbey Conference and Events for their professional support of the conference. You will have met them at registration, and they are available throughout the event to ensure your needs are met. We have been engaging with them for 2 years now, and this has been a true partnership that has made this journey an enjoyable one. Secondly, I am especially grateful to my colleague Jane Dunne, for managing the planning of the conference, and for managing me too. Jane has done this over and above her work on a European project, and I could not have chosen a better, nicer person to engage with over these past two years – thank you Jane on behalf of everyone; we are all deeply grateful for your huge effort in getting us to where we all are today!

Finally, I really hope that you all enjoy the conference, that you benefit from the excellent programme that has been assembled, and that you go away from here having made new friends. I am fortunate indeed that many of my very best friends are in the MT community, and I hope to meet as many of you as possible during the event.


**Andy Way**
Chair, MT Summit 2019
Deputy Director ADAPT Centre School of Computing Dublin City University
Dublin, Ireland.
Email: `Andy.Way@adaptcentre.ie`

# Foreword by the Translator Track Program Chairs

For the first time ever, the call for papers of the 2019 edition of the MT Summit included a specific track aimed at translators, who are arguably the largest group of users of translation technologies. This exciting development built on the success of the 21st annual EAMT Conference, that was held in Alicante, Spain, roughly a year before, and featured a dedicated translator track which added an important new dimension to the multi-faceted contemporary debate on MT. The novel translator track in this year's MT Summit programme aimed at involving translators into the conversation on an equal footing with researchers, developers, vendors and users of translation technologies, as the co-chairs felt that it was high time for their voice to be heard loud and clear. With this objective in mind, specific topics of interest included in the call for papers for the translator track concerned issues that increasingly confront language and translation professionals on a daily basis, including productivity measurements and their impact on MT adoption, the role of MT in translators' work (pricing issues, post-editing tasks assignment and their acceptance among professionals), ethical and confidentiality considerations when using MT, psycho-social aspects of MT adoption, such as attitudes and (pre-)conceptions, etc. A total of 23 submissions were received for the translator track, and each of them was peer-reviewed by three independent members of the Programme Committee. After a thorough selection process, 15 papers were accepted (6 for the oral sessions and 9 for poster presentation). The Programme Committee included both academics and practitioners, also representing associations and bodies of professional translators, to reflect the key communities with a specific interest in the topics addressed by the call for papers. We were very pleased with the number and quality of the submissions to the track at its debut at the MT Summit, and were particularly delighted to receive the official support of the International Federation of Translators (FIT) for the conference, as we are convinced that this mutual recognition is essential to ensure collaboration and an open, honest debate on MT going forward. We are very grateful to the Programme Committee members for their high-quality reviews, which have been very useful to us as co-chairs to select the paper proposals that were accepted in the conference programme and to the relevant authors to improve their papers: Bogdan Babych, Valeria Barbero, Sarah Bawa-Mason, Katie Botkin, Oliver Czulo, Stephen Doherty, Ignacio Garcia, Luis González, Ana Guerberof Arenas, Adrià Martín-Mor, Joss Moorkens, Sharon O'Brien, Minako O'Hagan, Mary Phelan, Pilar Sánchez-Gijón, Mirko Silvestrini, Olga Torres-Hostench. We would also like to thank all the authors for trying their best to incorporate the reviewers' suggestions when preparing the final versions of their accepted papers that have been included in these proceedings. Finally, as regards the papers submitted to the translator track that were not accepted for the conference, we hope that the reviewers' constructive comments will be useful to improve them, so that the important and timely debate on the relationship between translators, MT and more broadly translation technologies can continue in subsequent editions of the MT Summit and at other similar conferences in the future.


**Celia Rico and Federico Gaspari**

# Foreword by the User Track Program Chairs

Firstly, we want to acknowledge what an honour it has been to serve as co-chairs of the user track for the Machine Translation Summit. Between us, in various guises, we have attended, submitted to, and presented at this conference over its history. To be involved on the other side of the fence this time has been a great experience.

Continuing with a trend started at the last MT Summit in 2017, we solicited full papers for the user track, as opposed to abstracts, so that the work might leave a longer legacy and impact beyond what is presented at the conference itself. We also requested that all submissions have at least one industry partner to encourage true user scenarios, as opposed to simulations.

The result was 24 submissions for the user track, representing 22 companies and 12 academic institutions. Ten of the submissions came from collaboration between industry and academic partners, while the rest represented applied research, applications, and use cases directly from the commercial field. There were 80 distinct authors with on average 4 authors per submission.

Geographically, the submissions originated from 12 countries from Europe, and both North and South America: Ireland (8), Spain (6), Switzerland (5), Belgium (2), Latvia (2), United States (2), Argentina (1), Austria (1), Brazil (1), Italy (1), Portugal (1), United Kingdom (1).

The 24 submissions were reviewed by an elaborate programme committee of 38 experts in the fields of localisation, machine translation and natural language processing from industry and academia. Each submission received at least 3 reviews and in some cases even 4 and 5. In these latter cases, the additional reviews helped us make more definitive decisions on borderline cases.

In total, we accepted 14 submissions for publication and presentation at the conference, resulting in an acceptance rate of 58

The range of topics covered overall reflects the fact that, now more so than ever, machine translation is in wide commercial use, with a range of applications and stories from organisations of all shapes and sizes, including big tech, service providers, SMEs, government organisations and more. Neural approaches dominate in most of the workflows, whether it is for machine translation, quality estimation, post-editing or pre- and post-processing. Great amount of research also aims at optimised performance and quality by better exploiting of data, backtranslation and reuse of translation output.

Finally, we would like to thank the authors of all submissions, our diligent programme committee, and of course the conference organisers. We hope you enjoy the proceedings.


**John Tinsley and Dimitar Shterionov**

# Organizers

**President of the IAMT and
the EAMT**
Mikel Forcada     University of Alicante
**MT Summit 2019
Conference Chair**
Andy Way     ADAPT Centre

# Programme Chairs

**Research track co-chairs**
Barry Haddow     The University of Edinburgh
Rico Sennrich     The University of Edinburgh
**User track co-chairs**
John Tinsley     Iconic Translation Machines
Dimitar Shterionov     Dublin City University
**Translator track co-chairs**
Celia Rico     Universidad Europea de Madrid
Federico Gaspari     Dublin City University
**Projects track co-chair**
Mikel L. Forcada     University of Alicante

# Program Committee

**Research Track**

| | |
|---|---|
| Alberto Poncelas | DCU |
| Aizhan Imankulova | Tokyo Metropolitan University |
| Aleš Tamchyna | Memsource a. s. |
| Alon Lavie | Carnegie Mellon University |
| Anabela Barreiro | INESC-ID |
| Andreas Maletti | Universität Leipzig |
| Andrei Popescu-Belis | HEIG-VD / HES-SO |
| Ankur Bapna | Google |
| Ann Clifton | Simon Fraser University |
| Annette Rios Gonzales | University of Zurich |
| Anoop Kunchukuttan | IIT Bombay |
| Antonio Toral | University of Groningen |
| Antonio Valerio Miceli Barone | University of Pisa |
| Arturo Oncevay | The University of Edinburgh |
| Arul Menezes | Microsoft |
| Arya McCarthy | Johns Hopkins University |
| Atsushi Fujita | National Institute of Information and Communications Technology |

| Barry Haddow | The University of Edinburgh |
| Boxing Chen | Alibaba Group |
| Carla Parra Escartín | Unbabel |
| Carolina Scarton | European Association for Machine Translation |
| Celia Rico | Universidad Europea de Madrid |
| Chenhui Chu | Osaka University |
| Chris Brockett | Microsoft |
| Christian Dugast | tech2biz |
| Christian Federmann | Microsoft |
| Christian Hardmeier | Uppsala University |
| Christoph Tillmann | IBM |
| Christos Baziotis | The University of Edinburgh |
| Colin Cherry | National Research Council Canada |
| Constantin Orasan | University of Wolverhampton |
| Cristina España-Bonet | UdS and DFKI |
| Dakun Zhang | Systran |
| Daniel Marcu | ISI/USC |
| Daniel Ortiz-Martínez | Unversitat Politecnica de Valencia |
| Dario Stojanovski | Ludwig Maximilian University of Munich |
| David Vilar | Amazon |
| Devendra Singh Sachan | CMU |
| Deyi Xiong | Tianjin University |
| Dimitar Shterionov | Dublin City University |
| Dušan Variš | Institute of Formal and Applied Linguistics; Charles University in Prague |
| Duygu Ataman | University of Trento; Fondazione Bruno Kessler; University of Edinburgh |
| Ekaterina Lapshinova-Koltunski | Saarland University |
| Ekaterina Vylomova | The University of Melbourne |
| Eleftherios Avramidis | German Research Center for Artificial Intelligence (DFKI) |
| Eva Hasler | The University of Edinburgh |
| Eva Vanmassenhove | DCU |
| Fatiha Sadat | UQAM |
| Federico Gaspari | Dublin City University |
| Felipe Sánchez-Martínez | Dep. de Llenguatges i Sistemes Informàtics. Universitat d'Alacant |
| Felix Hieber | Amazon |
| Felix Stahlberg | University of Cambridge |
| Ferhan Ture | Comcast Labs |
| Francis Tyers | Indiana University Bloomington |
| Francisco Casacuberta | Universitat Politècnica de València |
| Francisco Javier Guzman | Facebook |
| François Yvon | LIMSI/CNRS et Université Paris-Sud |
| Frederic Blain | The University of Sheffield |
| George Foster | NRC |
| Gholamreza Haffari | Simon Fraser University |
| Gonzalo Iglesias Iglesias | SDL |
| Graham Neubig | Carnegie Mellon University |
| Gregor Leusch | eBay inc |
| Hainan Xu | Johns Hopkins University |

Helena Caseli — Federal University of São Carlos (UFSCar)
Helmut Schmid — Ludwig Maximilian University of Munich
Hiroshi Echizenya — Hokkai-Gakuen University
Houda Bouamor — Carnegie Mellon University
Huda Khayrallah — Johns Hopkins University
Iacer Calixto — University of Amsterdam
Isao Goto — NHK
Jan Niehues — Maastricht University
Jesús González-Rubio — WebInterpret
Jiajun Zhang — Institute of Automation Chinese Academy of Sciences

Joachim Daiber — Apple Inc.
John Henderson — The MITRE Corporation
John Tinsley — Iconic Translation
Joke Daems — Ghent University
Jonathan Mallinson — The University of Edinburgh
Joost Bastings — University of Amsterdam
Jörg Tiedemann — University of Helsinki
José G. C. de Souza — ebay
Josep Crego — SYSTRAN
Joss Moorkens — ADAPT Centre
Juan Antonio Pérez-Ortiz — Universitat d'Alacant; Departament de Llenguatges i Sistemes Informàtics

Julia Ive — King's College London
Julia Kreutzer — Heidelberg University
Julian Schamper — DeepL GmbH
Katsuhito Sudoh — Nara Institute of Science and Technology
Ke Hu — ADAPT Centre; Dublin City University
Kenji Imamura — National Institute of Information and Communications Technology

Kenton Murray — Carnegie Mellon University School of Computer Science

Laura Jehl — Institut für Computerlinguistik; Universität Heidelberg

Laurent Besacier — Laboratoire d'Informatique de Grenoble
Lemao Liu — NICT
Lexi Birch — The University of Edinburgh
Lieve Macken — Ghent University
Linfeng Song — University of Rochester
Luisa Bentivogli — FBK
Maja Popovic — ADAPT Centre; DCU
Manny Rayner — University of Geneva
Mara Chinea Rios — Universitat Politècnica de València
Marc Dymetman — Xerox Research Centre Europe
Marcello Federico — Amazon AI
Marcin Junczys-Dowmunt — Microsoft
Marco Turchi — Fondazione Bruno Kessler
Marianna Apidianaki — CNRS
Marija Brkic — Department of Informatics; University of Rijeka
Marion Weller-Di Marco — University of Amsterdam
Mark Fishel — University of Tartu

| Markus Freitag | Google AI |
| Marta R. Costa-Jussà | Institute For Infocomm Research |
| Martin Popel | UFAL; Faculty of Mathematics and Physics; Charles University |
| Martin Volk | University of Zurich |
| Masaaki Nagata | NTT |
| Masao Utiyama | NICT |
| Mathias Müller | University of Zurich |
| Matīss Rikters | Tilde |
| Matt Post | Johns Hopkins University |
| Matteo Negri | Fondazione Bruno Kessler (FBK-irst) |
| Matthias Huck | Ludwig Maximilian University of Munich |
| Mattia Antonino Di Gangi | Fondazione Bruno Kessler; University of Trento |
| Maximiliana Behnke | The University of Edinburgh |
| Mercedes García-Martínez | Pangeanic SL |
| Meriem Beloucif | The Hong Kong University of Science and Technology |
| Michael Carl | Kent State University |
| Michel Simard | National Research Council Canada (NRC) |
| Miguel Domingo | Universitat Politècnica de València |
| Mihael Arcan | Insight Centre for Data Analytics; National University of Ireland Galway |
| Mihaela Vela | Universität des Saarlandes |
| Miloš Stanojević | The University of Edinburgh |
| Miquel Esplà | Universitat d'Alacant |
| Mireia Farrús | Universitat Pompeu Fabra |
| Mirjam S. Maučec | FERI; University of Maribor |
| Myle Ott | Facebook |
| Nicola Ueffing | eBay |
| Nikolay Bogoychev | The University of Edinburgh |
| Niyu Ge | |
| Nizar Habash | Columbia University |
| Núria Bel | Universitat Pompeu Fabra |
| Orhan Firat | Google |
| Ozan Çağlayan | Le Mans University |
| Parnia Bahar | RWTH Aachen University |
| Patrick Simianer | Lilt. |
| Paul Michel | Carnegie Mellon University - LTI |
| Pavel Pecina | Charles University In Prague |
| Petra Barančíková | Charles University in Prague |
| Philip Williams | The University of Edinburgh |
| Philipp Koehn | Johns Hopkins University |
| Praveen Dakwale | Informatics Institute; University of Amsterdam |
| Preethi Raghavan | IBM TJ Watson Research |
| Qun Liu | Huawei Noah's Ark Lab |
| Rabih Zbib | Raytheon |
| Rachel Bawden | The University of Edinburgh |
| Raj Dabre | IIT Bombay |
| Rajen Chatterjee | Apple Inc. |
| Rebecca Knowles | Johns Hopkins University |
| Rebecca Marvin | Johns Hopkins University |

Rico Sennrich                     The University of Edinburgh
Roland Kuhn                       National Research Council of Canada
Roman Grundkiewicz                The University of Edinburgh; School of
                                  Informatics
Rudolf Rosa                       Charles University
Saab Mansour                      RWTH Aachen University
Sadao Kurohashi                   Kyoto University
Sameen Maruf                      Monash University
Sameer Bansal                     The University of Edinburgh
Samuel Läubli                     University of Zurich
Sarah Ebling                      University of Zurich
Sergio Penkale                    Lingo24
Shahram Khadivi                   eBay
Shankar Kumar                     Google
Sharon O'Brien                    Dublin City University
Sheila Castilho                   Dublin City University/ADAPT Centre
Stephan Peitz                     Apple
Surafel Melaku Lakew              University of Trento
Tamer Alkhouli                    RWTH Aachen University
Taro Watanabe                     NICT
Teresa Herrmann                   Fujitsu
Tim Anderson                      Wright-Patterson Air Force Research
                                  Laboratory
Tomáš Musil                       Charles University in Prague
Toshiaki Nakazawa                 The University of Tokyo
Tsuyoshi Okita                    Kyushu Institute of Technology
Ulrich Germann                    The University of Edinburgh
Víctor M. Sánchez-Cartagena       Transducens Research Group; Departament de
                                  Llenguatges i Sistemes Informàtics; Universitat
                                  d'Alacant
Viktor Hangya                     Ludwig Maximilian University of Munich
Vincent Vandeghinste              Instituut voor de Nederlandse Taal, Centre for
                                  Computational Linguistics, KU Leuven
Vishal Chowdhary                  Microsoft
Vu Hoang                          The University of Melbourne
Wei Wang                          Google
Xing Niu                          University of Maryland
Yinfei Yang                       Redfin Inc.
Yuki Arase                        Osaka University
Yunsu Kim                         RWTH Aachen University
Yvette Graham                     Dublin City University

**Translator Track**

Adrià Martín-Mor                  UAB
Alberto Poncelas                  DCU
Ana Guerberof Arenas              DCU/ADAPT Centre
Bogdan Babych                     University of Leeds
Carolina Scarton                  European Association for Machine Translation
Celia Rico Perez                  Universidad Europea de Madrid
Federico Gaspari                  Dublin City University
Ignacio Garcia                    University of Western Sydney
Joss Moorkens                     Dublin City University

Katie Botkin — MultiLingual magazine
Mary Phelan — Dublin City University
Minako O'Hagan — The University of Auckland
Mirko Silvestrini — UNILINGUE
Olga Torres-Hostench — Universitat Autònoma de Barcelona
Oliver Czulo — Universität Leipzig
Pilar Sanchez-Gijón — Autonomous University of Barcelona
Sarah Bawa-Mason — University of Portsmouth/Institute of Translation and Interpreting
Sharon O'Brien — Dublin City University
Stephen Doherty — The University of New South Wales
Valeria Barbero — MT Summit

**User Track**

Alberto Poncelas — DCU
Aljoscha Burchardt — DFKI
Alon Lavie — Carnegie Mellon University
Bram Bulté — Katholieke Universiteit Leuven
Bruno Pouliquen — World Intellectual Property Organization
Carlos Collantes Fraile — TransPerfect / Universidad Complutense de Madrid
Carmen Heger — SZ
Carolina Scarton — European Association for Machine Translation
Chao-Hong Liu — ADAPT Centre, Dublin City University
Charlotte Tesselaar — LexisNexis Univentio
Chris Wendt — Microsoft
Christian Federmann — Microsoft
Christian Eisold — berns language consulting GmbH
Dag Schmidtke — Microsoft
Daniel Stein — eBay Inc.
David Vilar — Amazon
Declan Groves — Microsoft
Dimitar Shterionov — Dublin City University
Eva Martínez Garcia — Vicomtech / Universitat Politècnica de Catalunya
Eva Vanmassenhove — DCU
Evgeny Matusov — eBay
Félix Do Carmo — ADAPT Centre
Fred Blain — The University of Sheffield
Gema Ramírez-Sánchez — Prompsit Language Engineering, S.L.
Guodong Xie — ADAPT Centre, Dublin City University
Heidi Depraetere — Cross Language NV
Jean Senellart — SYSTRAN
John Tinsley — Iconic Translation Machines
José G. C. de Souza — eBay Inc.
Keith J. Miller — The MITRE Corporation
Kim Harris — text&form GmbH
Laurent Chevrette — Mondzo
Maxim Khalilov — Unbabel
Mercedes García-Martínez — Pangeanic SL
Nathalie DeSutter — Untranslate
Nicola Ueffing — eBay

Olga Beregovaya — Welocalize
Patrik Lambert — Pompeu Fabra University
Phil Ritchie — Vistattec
Raj Pate — CDAC
Rohit Gupta — Iconic Translations Machines Ltd.
Saša Hasan — Apple
Silvio Picinini — eBay
Steve Richardson — The Church of Jesus Christ of Latter-day Saints
Thierry Etchegoyhen — Vicomtech-IK4
Tony O'Dowd — Xcelerator Machine Translations Ltd.
Yury Sharshov — LexisNexis Univentio

**Project Track**

Alberto Poncelas — DCU
Carolina Scarton — The University of Sheffield
Mikel Forcada — University of Alicante

# Contents


**Competitiveness Analysis of the European Machine Translation Market**    1
*Andrejs Vasiļjevs, Inguna Skadiņa, Indra Sāmīte, Kaspars Kauliņš, Ēriks Ajausks,
Jūlija Meļņika and Aivars Bērziņš*

**Improving CAT Tools in the Translation Workflow: New Approaches and Evaluation**    8
*Mihaela Vela, Santanu Pal, Marcos Zampieri, Sudip Naskar and Josef van Genabith*

**Hungarian translators' perceptions of Neural Machine Translation in the European Commission**    16
*Ágnes Lesznyák*

**Applying Machine Translation to Psychology: Automatic Translation of Personality Adjectives**    23
*Ritsuko Iwai, Daisuke Kawahara, Takatsune Kumada and Sadao Kurohashi*

**Evaluating machine translation in a low-resource language combination: Spanish-Galician.**    30
*María Do Campo Bayón and Pilar Sánchez-Gijón*

**MTPE in Patents: A Successful Business Story**    36
*Valeria Premoli, Elena Murgolo and Diego Cresceri*

**User expectations towards machine translation: A case study**    42
*Barbara Heinisch and Vesna Lušicky*

**Does NMT make a difference when post-editing closely related languages? The case of Spanish-Catalan**    49
*Sergi Alvarez, Antoni Oliver and Toni Badia*

**Machine Translation in the Financial Services Industry: A Case Study**    57
*Mara Nunziatini*

**Pre-editing Plus Neural Machine Translation for Subtitling: Effective Pre-editing Rules for Subtitling of TED Talks**    64
*Yusuke Hiraoka and Masaru Yamada*

**Do translator trainees trust machine translation? An experiment on post-editing and revision**    73
*Randy Scansani, Silvia Bernardini, Adriano Ferraresi and Luisa Bentivogli*

**On reducing translation shifts in translations intended for MT evaluation**    80
*Maja Popovic*

**Comparative Analysis of Errors in MT Output and Computer-assisted Translation: Effect of the Human Factor**    88
*Irina Ovchinnikova and Daria Morozova*

A Comparative Study of English-Chinese Translations of Court Texts by Machine and Human Translators and the Word2Vec Based Similarity Measure's Ability To Gauge Human Evaluation Biases ........ 95
*Ming Qian, Jessie Liu, Chaofeng Li and Liming Pals*

Translating Terminologies: A Comparative Examination of NMT and PBSMT Systems ........ 101
*Long-Huei Chen and Kyo Kageura*

NEC TM DATA PROJECT ........ 109
*Alexandre Helle and Manuel Herranz*

APE-QUEST ........ 110
*Joachim Van den Bogaert, Heidi Depraetere, Sara Szoc, Tom Vanallemeersch, Koen Van Winckel, Frederic Everaert, Lucia Specia, Julia Ive, Maxim Khalilov, Christine Maroti, Eduardo Farah, Artur Ventura*

PRINCIPLE: Providing Resources in Irish, Norwegian, Croatian and Icelandic for the Purposes of Language Engineering ........ 112
*Andy Way and Federico Gaspari*

iADAATPA Project: Pangeanic use cases ........ 114
*Mercedes García-Martínez, Amando Estela, Laurent Bié, Alexandre Helle and Manuel Herranz*

MICE ........ 116
*Joachim Van den Bogaert, Heidi Depraetere, Tom Vanallemeersch, Frederic Everaert, Koen Van Winckel, Katri Tammsaar, Ingmar Vali, Tambet Artma, Piret Saartee, Laura Katariina Teder, Artūrs Vasiļevskis, Valters Sics, Johan Haelterman and David Bienfait*

ParaCrawl: Web-scale parallel corpora for the languages of the EU ........ 118
*Miquel Esplà, Mikel Forcada, Gema Ramírez-Sánchez and Hieu Hoang*

Pivot Machine Translation in INTERACT Project ........ 120
*Chao-Hong Liu, Andy Way, Catarina Silva and André Martins*

Global Under-Resourced Media Translation (GoURMET) ........ 122
*Alexandra Birch, Barry Haddow, Ivan Tito, Antonio Valerio Miceli Barone, Rachel Bawden, Felipe Sánchez-Martínez, Mikel L. Forcada, Miquel Esplà-Gomis, Víctor Sánchez-Cartagena, Juan Antonio Pérez-Ortiz, Wilker Aziz, Andrew Secker, Peggy van der Kreeft*

Neural machine translation system for the Kazakh language ........ 123
*Ualsher Tukeyev and Zhandos Zhumanov*

Leveraging Rule-Based Machine Translation Knowledge for Under-Resourced Neural Machine Translation Models ........ 125
*Daniel Torregrosa, Nivranshu Pasricha, Maraim Masoud, Bharathi Raja Chakravarthi, Juan Alonso, Noe Casas and Mihael Arcan*

Bootstrapping a Natural Language Interface to a Cyber Security Event Collection System using a Hybrid Translation Approach ........ 134
*Johann Roturier, Brian Schlatter and David Silva Schlatter*

Improving Robustness in Real-World Neural Machine Translation Engines    142
*Rohit Gupta, Patrik Lambert, Raj Patel and John Tinsley*

Surveying the potential of using speech technologies for post-editing purposes in the context of international organizations: What do professional translators think?    149
*Jeevanthi Liyanapathirana, Pierrette Bouillon and Bartolomé Mesa-Lao*

Automatic Translation for Software with Safe Velocity    159
*Dag Schmidtke and Declan Groves*

Application of Post-Edited Machine Translation in Fashion eCommerce    167
*Kasia Kosmaczewska and Matt Train*

Morphological Neural Pre- and Post-Processing for Slavic Languages    174
*Giorgio Bernardinello*

Large-scale Machine Translation Evaluation of the iADAATPA Project    179
*Sheila Castilho, Natália Resende, Federico Gaspari, Andy Way, Tony O'Dowd, Marek Mazur, Manuel Herranz, Alex Helle, Gema Ramírez-Sánchez, Víctor Sánchez-Cartagena, Mārcis Pinnis and Valters Šics*

Collecting domain specific data for MT: an evaluation of the ParaCrawl pipeline    186
*Arne Defauw, Tom Vanallemeersch, Sara Szoc, Frederic Everaert, Koen Van Winckel, Kim Scholte, Joris Brabers and Joachim Van den Bogaert*

Monolingual backtranslation in a medical speech translation system for diagnostic interviews - a NMT approach    196
*Jonathan Mutal, Pierrette Bouillon, Johanna Gerlach, Paula Estrella and Hervé Spechbach*

Improving Domain Adaptation for Machine Translation with Translation Pieces    204
*Catarina Silva*

Raising the TM Threshold in Neural MT Post-Editing: a Case Study on Two Datasets    213
*Anna Zaretskaya*

Incremental Adaptation of NMT for Professional Post-editors: A User Study    219
*Miguel Domingo, Mercedes García-Martínez, Álvaro Peris, Alexandre Helle, Amando Estela, Laurent Bié, Francisco Casacuberta and Manuel Herranz*

When less is more in Neural Quality Estimation of Machine Translation. An industry case study    228
*Dimitar Shterionov, Félix Do Carmo, Joss Moorkens, Eric Paquin, Dag Schmidtke, Declan Groves and Andy Way*

# Competitiveness Analysis of
# the European Machine Translation Market


**Andrejs Vasiļjevs, Inguna Skadiņa, Indra Sāmīte, Kaspars Kauliņš, Ēriks
Ajausks, Jūlija Meļņika, Aivars Bērziņš**
Tilde, Vienibas gatve 75a, Riga, LV 1004, Latvia
`firstname.lastname@tilde.lv`



## Abstract

This paper presents the key results of a
study on the global competitiveness of the
European Machine Translation market in
comparison to North America and Asia.
The study focuses on seven dimensions
that have been selected to characterize the
machine translation market. The study
concludes that while Europe still has
strong positions in Research and Innovation, it lags behind North America and
Asia in Industry and Investments, and is
also weaker than North America in Infrastructure, Data availability, and Market
visibility.


## 1 Introduction

The aim of this study was to analyze a
competitiveness of the European machine
translation (MT) market in comparison to North
America (Unites States and Canada) and Asia
(China, Japan, India, South Korea and Singapore).

This research is a part of a wider undertaking to
identify possible shortcomings and opportunities
for the European Language Technology (LT) market and identify potential actions that need to be
addressed at the European Union level.

The analysis is based on an extensive desk research of various studies, policy papers, and
online information sources. The quantitative foundation of the analysis is based on the surveys and
interviews done by and analysed under the leader-
ship of IDC in the framework of the SMART project[1]. It is also an aggregation and analysis of data
collected from previous studies on MT and the
broader localization and translation sector, and

overall economic indicators (e.g., World Economic Forum, 2017; Common Sense Advisory
(Lommel et al., 2016); TAUS (Massardo, 2016;
Seligman, 2017; TAUS, 2017); CRACKER
(2015; SRIA, 2017) and META-NET (2015)).

The study focuses on seven dimensions that can
characterize the machine translation market as
part of the broader language technology market:
Research, Innovation, Investment, Market dominance, Industry, Infrastructure, and Open Data.
These dimensions were analysed for global competitiveness, highlighting the most important
achievements and gaps in the LT ecosystem between Europe and its largest global competitors –
North America and Asia. To characterise each dimension, a number of criteria were analysed. Using these results, we have ranked the markets
within each dimension on a scale from 1 (weakest)
to 3 (strongest).

The full report of the findings from the study
has been submitted to the European Commission.
In this paper we have summarized the key findings of this report.

## 2 Competitiveness of European MT Research

The following criteria were used as quantitative
indicators: number of research centres, number of
research publications, organizational infrastructure (e.g. associations, networks and research
infrastructures).

We analysed publicly available information
about research centres in different countries. Since
information about the size of research institutions
(e.g. number and qualification of researchers, research budget, number of projects) is not available
in public sources, research institutions are not
weighted for their size.

---



[1] Study on service portfolio development and
implementation of the "service desk" component of
the CEF Automated Translation platform, SMART
2016/0103 Lot 1

## 2.1 Research Centres

The recent Wikipedia article "List of research laboratories for machine translation" lists 113 institutions, from which 91 are in scope of our study. This list includes academic, governmental, and corporate sites. This list confirms a strong research capacity in Europe, as it has 47 academic research centers compared to only 18 in America and 9 in Asia (see Table 1).

| | ACADEMIC | GOVERN-MENTAL | CORPO-RATE | TOTAL |
|---|---|---|---|---|
| EUROPE | 47 | 1 | 6 | 54 |
| ASIA | 9 | 4 | 1 | 14 |
| AMERICA | 18 | 1 | 4 | 23 |
| TOTAL | 74 | 6 | 11 | 91 |

**Table 1.** Number of research laboratories for machine translation in different regions

The higher number of European research centres compared to the number of North American research centres is also reflected in the membership of the European Association of Machine Translation (EAMT)[2] that lists 43 R&D groups and 16 corporate members. The American Association of Machine Translation (AMTA) lists 15 academic research organizations and 6 industrial research labs[3]. The Asia-Pacific Association for MT has 32 corporate members and over 66 individual members[4].

## 2.2 Publications

In this study, we researched publications in the Scopus database[5]. The research publications include both academic and industry researchers. However, it could be that industry research is underrepresented, since not all industry research results are made public. Although research papers in the fields of our study are collected by several online repositories - SCOPUS, Web of Science (WoS), DBPL, Google Scholar, arXiv, CiteSeer — only Scopus and WoS provide the information and analytical tools that were needed for this study. Both Scopus and WoS are well established academic citation indexes that are widely used to assess the outcome and impact of scientific work. However, Scopus has better coverage for our study.

To calculate the regional distribution of publications, the methodology used by Scopus to count the distribution of publications between countries

was applied, i.e., if authors of the same publication represent different regions, then this publication is counted for each region that the authors represent

We analysed the publications in the Scopus database retrieved by querying for "machine translation" in title, abstract, and keywords. Figure 1 shows the number of publications for the time period from 2000-2017 (7008 in total) clearly demonstrating the increase of interest in this topic in the first decade of this century and the relatively stable number of publications in this decade.

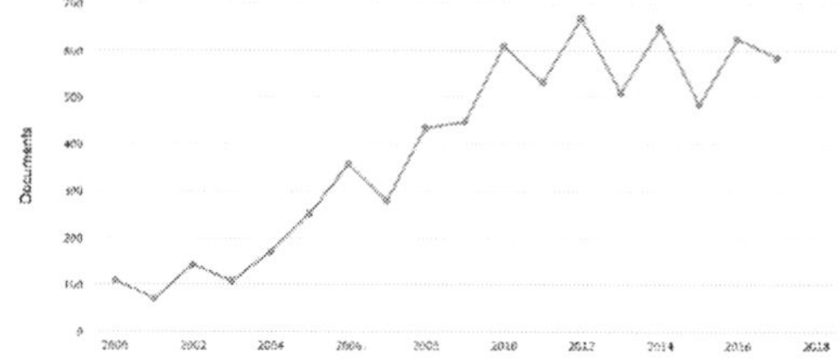

**Figure 1** Number of publications for "machine translation" (2000-2017)

When querying for "machine translation" for the years 2010-2018, we found 4931 publications, 4723 of these publications are from the countries/regions addressed in this study (on July 10, 2018). Publications on CAT tools were not included and analysed in this study, because the number of publications on CAT tools alone[6] in the Scopus DB for 2010-2018 is very small (only 149 additional publications or about 3% were found).

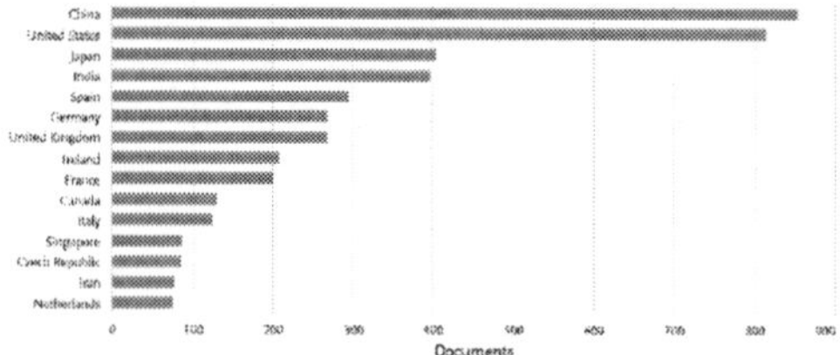

**Figure 2.** Number of MT related publications in Scopus database: top 15 countries (2010-June 2018)

Figure 2 shows the 15 countries that have the highest number of publications for the years 2010-2018. We can see that the leader is China (854 publications), followed by the United States (814 publications), and Japan (403 publications). The list of the top 15 countries includes such European countries as Spain (293 publications), Germany (266 publications), UK (266 publications), Ireland

---

[2] http://www.eamt.org/, retrieved on 12.07.2018
[3] https://amtaweb.org/resources, retrieved on 12.07.2018
[4] http://www.aamt.info/english/about/01.php, retrieved on 12.07.2018

[5] The Scopus database can be found in https://www.scopus.com/
[6] Publications that do not mention "machine translation" in title, abstract, or keywords

(208 publications), France (200 publications), Italy (124 publications), Czech Republic (85 publications), and the Netherlands (75 publications).

When the number of publications is compared between North America, Asia and Europe, the leader is Asia with 1932 publications, followed by Europe with 1752 publications and North America with 975 publications (Figure 3).

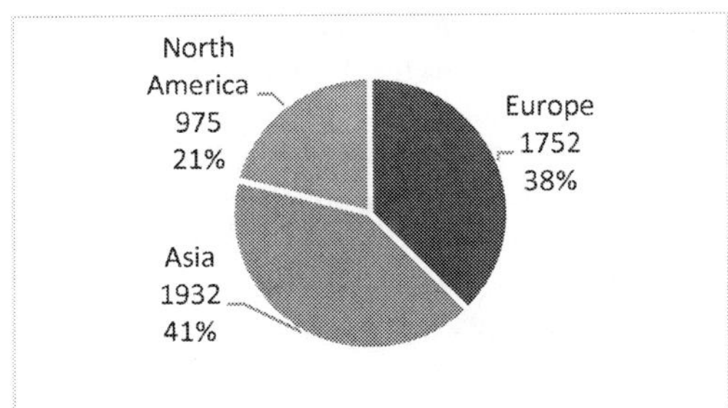


**Figure 3**. Distribution of publications between regions (2010-2018)

When top 20 authors are compared, half (10) of the most prolific authors are currently working in Europe, 9 in Asia and only one in America (Table 2).

| AUTHOR NAME | NUMBER OF PUB. | COUNTRY | REGION |
| --- | --- | --- | --- |
| 1.Way, A. | 75 | Ireland | Europe |
| 2.Sumita, E. | 67 | Japan | Asia |
| 3.Liu, Q. | 55 | Ireland | Europe |
| 4.Casacuberta, F. | 45 | Spain | Europe |
| 5.Specia, L. | 44 | UK | Europe |
| 6.Zhao, T. | 40 | China | Asia |
| 7.Utiyama, M. | 35 | Japan | Asia |
| 8.Xiong, D. | 35 | China | Asia |
| 9.Zhang, M. | 34 | China | Asia |
| 10.Zhou, M. | 34 | US | America |
| 11.Ney, H. | 31 | Germany | Europe |
| 12.Yvon, F. | 31 | France | Europe |
| 13.Neubig, G. | 29 | Japan | Asia |
| 14.Zong, C. | 29 | China | Asia |
| 15.Liu, Y. | 28 | China | Asia |
| 16.Turchi, M. | 28 | Italy | Europe |
| 17.Van Genabith, J | 28 | Germany | Europe |
| 18.Costa-Jussà, M.R | 27 | Spain | Europe |
| 19.Finch, A. | 26 | Japan | Asia |
| 20.Toral, A. | 26 | Netherlands | Europe |

**Table 2.** Authors publishing on MT (2010 - June 2018) with more than 25 publications (top 20) according to Scopus: distribution between countries and regions

When results are compared by organizations, there are 8 institutions from Europe, 4 from Asia, and 3 from America among the published top 15 (see Figure 4).

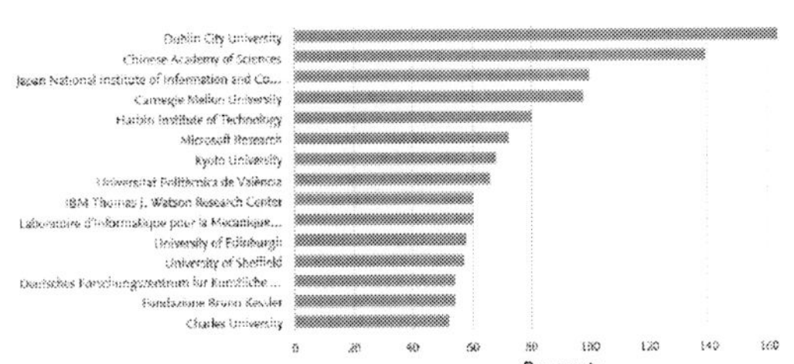


**Figure 4.** Top 15 organizations that published papers on machine translation (2010-June 2018) in Scopus

When only industry and privately financed organisations are compared, global companies — *Microsoft (132)*, *IBM (76)* and *Google (43)* with headquarters in US, together with DFKI (54) and FBK (54) form the top 5 (see Figure 5).

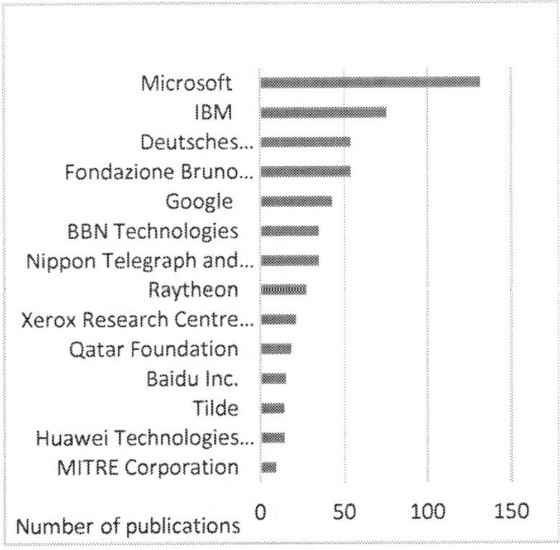


**Figure 5.** Industry and privately financed organisations that published on MT (2010-June 2018) in Scopus

We also analysed conference proceedings from ACL, COLING, EACL, NAACL and NIPS[7] - five important computational linguistics conferences by querying for "machine translation". We found more recent (2015-2017) papers from United States (68) and China (42), but fewer from Germany (34), United Kingdom (27), Ireland (21) and other European countries. While US authors have more publications as authors from each single EU or Asian country, European countries are still leaders, when the regional distribution of publications are compared.

## 3 Innovation

As proxies for innovation by region, we analysed the market of origin of the most popular tools,

---

[7] ACL (2010-2017), COLING (2010, 2012, 2013, 2014, 2016), EACL (2010, 2012, 2013, 2014, 2017), NAACL (2010, 2012, 2013, 2015, 2016), NIPS (2010-2017) proceedings were indexed in Scopus by the time of this study.

emergence of start-ups in the respective industry across regions, and known implementation of the latest technique in each respective area.

### 3.1 Market of origin of the translation automation tools

Parallel to MT technologies, we have witnessed dynamic innovation in computer assisted translation (CAT) tools that play a major role in automating professional translation. Despite a huge improvement in the quality of machine translation thanks to the advances in neural MT (e.g. Bojar et al., 2018), recent research has shown that MT systems are still not able to produce translations of sufficient quality at the sentence level and even more so on document level. Often machine translation output still requires post-editing by a human to correct errors and improve the quality of the translation (Läubli et al., 2018; Hassan et al., 2018; Toral et. al., 2018).

CAT incorporates this manual editing stage into translation software, making translation an interactive process between human and computer. 11 out of the 24 recognized CAT tools that are used by the majority of translation companies have been developed in Europe.

### 3.2 Translation technology start-ups

Another indicator of innovation is the emergence of start-up companies that introduce new technologies, innovative ways of addressing business needs, and novel business models. For this analysis we collected a list of translation technology start-ups from AngelList[8] – a U.S. website for startups and angel investors – and assigned their regional attribution based on the location of their headquarters. Europe is the leader in the number of emerging start-ups (54) closely followed by North America (51), leaving Asia in a distant third position (28).

### 3.3 Adoption of Neural MT

In recent years, Neural MT (NMT) has become a global trend in MT development that has created opportunities for new services. Global adoption of NMT is led by Google (Wu et al., 2016) and Facebook but European companies and public sector have been quick to follow. In a few months from the first release of the Chinese-English NMT by Google there were numerous NMT systems launched by European companies Tilde (Pinnis et al, 2017), KantanMT, SDL, and DeepL. The European Commission also is on the fast track to adopt NMT by replacing the MT@EU statistical MT systems with the NMT systems on the eTranslation platform[9].

## 4 Investments

Based on data from translation industry research by Common Sense Advisory (2017) and the Slator 2018 Language Service Provider Index (2018), Table 3 lists the top 20 global translation companies by turnover. Nearly all the top 20 are investing in MT by either developing their own or buying existing MT service providers. Many have the latest NMT technologies illustrating how very important cutting-edge technologies are in the language services sector.

| COMPANY | COUNTRY | ACTIVITIES & ACQUISITIONS | TURNOVER[10] |
|---|---|---|---|
| Lionbridge | US | Bought CLS Communication (2014)<br>Bought by H.I.G. (2016)<br>In-house NMT | $590m |
| TransPerfect | US | Investments in in-house MT | $615m |
| HPE ACG | FR | In-house to HP | No info |
| LanguageLine Solutions | US | Sold to Teleperforma (FR) for $1.5 b (2016) | $451m |
| SDL | GB | Aquired Language Weaver for $42.5 (2010)<br>In-house NMT | $388.5m<br>$56 m LT turnover |
| RWS Group | GB | Uses SDL MT | $221.5m |
| Welocalize | US | Uses 3rd party MT (Microsoft, Iconic MT etc.) | $200 m |
| STAR Group | CH | In-house MT | $166.2m |
| Amplexor | LU | Aquired Sajan for $28.5 (2017) | $175.6m |
| Moravia | CZ | In-house MT<br>Acquired by RWS (2015) | $100m |
| Hogarth Worldwide | GB | No info | $177m |
| CyraCom International, Inc. | US | Interpreting, looking for early stage investment | $161m |
| RR Donnelley Language Solutions | US | In spin-off mode | $93m |
| Semantix | SE | No info | $107m |
| Honyaku Center Inc. | JP | Acquired Media Research Inc for $4.8 (2017) | $26m |
| Pactera Technology International Ltd | CN | Sold for $675m to HNA EcoTech (2016) | $85.2m |
| Ubiqus | FR | Interpretation, no known MT | $82.6 |
| Keywords Studios | GB | Games, audio | $180.1m |
| United Language Group (ULG) | US | ULG purchased Lucy MT for an undisclosed amount (2017) | $79m |
| Logos Group | IT | No information on MT available | No info |

---

[8] https://angel.co/
[9] https://ec.europa.eu/cefdigital/wiki/display/CEFDIG-ITAL/eTranslation

[10] https://slator.com/features/the-slator-2018-language-service-provider-index/

| Capita Translation and Interpreting | GB | Acquired through merger SmartMate MT | $178m |

**Table 3**. Top 20 global translation companies: Activities and acquisitions

## 5 Market Dominance

Market dominance is defined as a measure of the strength of a brand, product, service, or firm, relative to competitive offerings, including the extent a product, brand, or firm controls a product category in a given geographic area. We analysed the market dominance in all three regions by comparing total web traffic (e.g. number of times a unique IP address has opened the webpage of the said company) received by the dedicated web domains of the largest providers of MT services. Based on this analysis, North America clearly dominates the market in terms of attracting customers to their services. With their relatively few companies, but clearly dominating presence and market penetration, the Asian MT companies are snapping at the heels of the North American companies. There is a greater number of European companies, but their market presence is more fragmented resulting in a weaker market position.

As the largest MT companies (with their respective brands and services) are headquartered in the US, the MT landscape is dominated by North American providers. The North American MT industry clearly outperforms European and also Asian businesses in terms of their market power and dominance. North American MT providers also have strong market position in Asia and Europe. In Asian markets they face strong local competition from Baidu, Tencent, Sogou and others.

The global MT market has a very high degree of concentration – 20% of the market players[11] account for more than 80% of the revenue. A majority of companies earn on MT less than a million euros annually, indicating that MT market is underdeveloped overall and even more so in the markets outside North America.

According to TAUS estimations (TAUS, 2017), more than 40% of the global MT market is dominated by "a small set of very big "Internet" companies including Google, Amazon, Microsoft, Yandex, Facebook and Baidu, who offer free MT service either to all-comers or to their global customers (Amazon), and/or in certain cases a paying service to enterprises and other large-scale users".

As a result of the dominance by large players both in B2B and B2C markets, smaller MT developers and service providers including a majority of European based companies face challenges in gaining market visibility and increasing their brand awareness.

Free online MT as a service, e.g. Google Translate, freetranslation.com (powered by Microsoft), Reverso, has a major impact on the MT market. In terms of the perceived value – MT services have been commoditized, even devalued, with a concurrent strong impact on the perceived quality expectations by both individual consumers as well as businesses. "Large players such as Google, Microsoft and Apple have some positive effects, as they strongly contribute to create or increase market awareness. On the other hand, they are tough competitors as they offer mass market free software which is difficult to compete with, especially for SMEs."[12]

## 6 Industry

Industry in the context of this study is defined as the commercial machine translation product developers and service providers.

The criteria for measuring the Industry dimension is the market capitalization and estimates of market revenues of the companies that can be identified as being engaged in language services and specifically in MT development and implementation (Table 4).

| COMPANY | COUNTRY | INDUSTRY | MARKET CAP 2018 ($B) | IN-HOUSE MT |
|---|---|---|---|---|
| Apple | US | Tech | 851 | MT |
| Alphabet | US | Tech | 719 | MT |
| Microsoft | US | Tech | 703 | MT |
| Amazon | US | Consumer Services | 701 | MT |
| Tencent | China | Tech | 496 | MT |
| Berkshire Hathaway | US | Financials | 492 | |
| Alibaba | China | Consumer Services | 470 | MT |
| Facebook | US | Tech | 464 | MT |

**Table 4.** Top Global Companies by Market Capitalization and their activities in MT, as of March 31, 2018

---

[11] "mix of big Internet, pure-play MT and Large LSP/MLV companies such as Google, Systran, Microsoft, SDL" (TAUS, 2017)

[12] IDC 2018 for SMART 2016-0103 Lot 1

Table 4 shows the impact of MT on the global economy, by highlighting that 7 of the largest 8 companies by market cap have a notable presence in this technology sector. In addition, comparing independent estimations, we can assume that the global MT market in 2017 was worth $300m – $350m with an annual growth rate close to 20%.

According to the IDC study[13], the estimated European market for translation technologies is EUR 67m ($78.3m). This would lead to an estimation of the share for European MT market in a range of 22%-26% or about a quarter of the global market.

## 7  Infrastructure

Europe is lagging behind other global economic powers in providing computing power for computing intensive applications such as MT. Although Europe consumes 29% of global HPC resources it supplies less than 5% of them.

According to estimations by the European Commission, Europe needs to invest close to $800bn in its digital infrastructure to catch up with the United States and China.[14] Although this estimate includes investments in fibber-optics networks, 5G networks and other ICT infrastructure, a substantial part of these investments is needed to meet European demand for high performance computing power.

## 8  Data for Machine Translation

Availability of data is crucial as almost all contemporary machine translation systems are based on data-driven techniques.

As indicators for data availability, we analysed the availability of open data, access to proprietary data resources, and legal regulations of data usage. Europe outperforms North America and Asia in terms of developed and freely accessible language resources that play an essential role in the development of machine translation systems.

EU institutions have released massive volumes of freely available language resources that contain data for more than 24 EU languages and exceed 5 billion words. The European Open Data Portal[15] provides access to diverse language resources. It also contains a dedicated repository of public sector language resources for MT created and populated by the European Language Resource Coordination Action[16], funded by the EU Connecting Europe Facility programme (Lösch et al., 2018).

In North America and Asia open data initiatives have been primarily concerned with structured data from registers and databases as well as machine generated data mostly in numerical format. Open data repositories in North America and Asia (e.g. US Government open data, Japan government open data portal) provide only few if any language resource.

In regard to proprietary data and user generated content, global online US and Asia companies have a strong advantage versus European players. Global dominance of companies like Facebook, Google, and Amazon in their primary business activities in the fields of social media, internet search and e-commerce allow them to harvest unmatchable amounts of data that they can use in other areas of their activities like MT.

This is also true for Chinese firms like Alibaba and Tencent, which have become similarly dominant in their home market (Giles, 2018).

European copyright regulation is much more restrictive for data usage comparing to the United States. Lack of the fair use principle makes huge volumes of copyright protected data unavailable for use by European researchers and machine translation developers (Hugenholtz, 2013; Von Lohmann, 2017). At the same time US businesses and research institutions reap an advantage by applying the fair use exception and using this data.

## 9  Summary

Figure 6 summarizes the global position of the European MT market using a simple 3 point score representational graph.

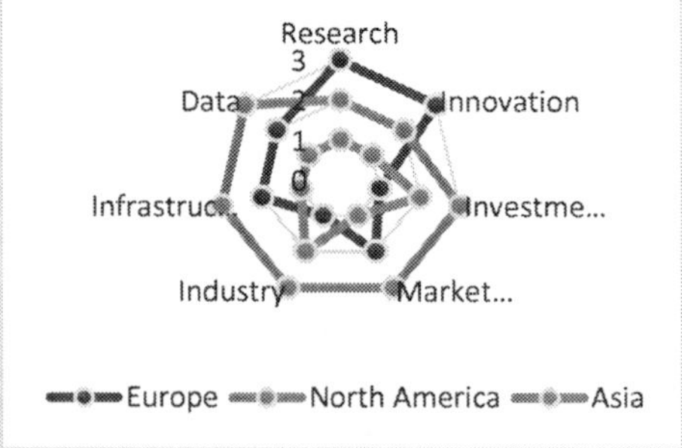


**Figure 6.** Comparative position of European machine translation market versus North America and Asia regions (1 – weakest, 3 - strongest).

---

## References

Bojar, O., Federmann, C., Fishel, M., Graham, Y., Haddow, B., Koehn, P., Monz, C. 2018. Findings of the 2018 Conference on Machine Translation (WMT18). *Proceedings of the Third Conference on Machine Translation (WMT)*, Volume 2: Shared Task Papers, 272-303.

Common Sense Advisory. 2017. *The Top 100 LSPs in 2017. Extract from "Who's is Who in Language Services and Technology: 2017*. Cambridge, Massachusetts: Common Sense Advisory.

CRACKER and LT-Observatory. 2015. *Strategic Agenda for the Multilingual Digital Single Market: Technologies for Overcoming Language Barriers towards a truly integrated European Online Market*. http://www.cracking-the-language-barrier.eu/wp-content/uploads/SRIA-V1.0-final.pdf

Crego, J., Kim, J., Klein, G., Rebollo, A., Yang, K., Senellart, J., … & Enoue, S. 2016. SYSTRAN's Pure Neural Machine Translation Systems. *arXiv preprint arXiv:1610.05540*

Giles M. 2018. It's Time to Rein in the Data Barons. *MIT Technology Review*, June 19, 2018

Hassan, H., Aue, A., Chen, C., Chowdhary, V., Clark, J., Federmann, C., … & Liu, S. 2018. Achieving Human Parity on Automatic Chinese to English News Translation. *arXiv preprint arXiv:1803.05567*.

Hugenholtz, P. B. 2013. Fair use in Europe. *Communications of the ACM*, 56(5), 26-28.

Lommel, A. R., and DePalma, D. A. 2016. *Europe's Leading Role in Machine Translation: How Europe is Driving the Shift to MT*. Cambridge, Massachusetts: Common Sense Advisory.

Läubli S., Sennrich, R., Volk, M. 2018. Has Machine Translation Achieved Human Parity? A Case for Document-level Evaluation. *Proceedings of the 2018 Conference on Empirical Methods in Natural Language Processing*, 4791–4796.

Lösch, A., Mapelli, V., Piperidis, S., Vasiļjevs, A., Smal, L., Declerck, T., Schnur, E., Choukri, K. and Van Genabith, J. 2018. European Language Resource Coordination: Collecting Language Resources for Public Sector Multilingual Information Management. *Proceedings of the Eleventh International Conference on Language Resources and Evaluation (LREC 2018)*, 1339-1343.

Massardo, I., van der Meer, J., and Khalilov, M. 2016. *TAUS Translation Technology Report*. TAUS.

META-NET. 2015. Strategic Research Agenda for the Multilingual Digital Single Market. http://www.meta-net.eu/projects/cracker/multimedia/mdsm-sria-draft.pdf.

Pinnis, M., Krišlauks, R., Miks, T., Deksne, D. and Šics, V. 2017. Tilde's Machine Translation Systems for WMT 2017. *Proceedings of the Second Conference on Machine Translation*, Volume 2: Shared Task Papers, 374-381.

Seligman, M., Waibel, A., and Joscelyne, A. 2017. *TAUS Speech-to-Speech Translation Technology Report*. TAUS.

Slator. 2018. The Slator 2018 Language Service Provider Index: Slator.

Strategic Research and Innovation Agenda. 2017. *Language Technologies for Multilingual Europe: Towards a Human Language Project*. Retrieved from: http://cracker-project.eu/wp-content/uploads/SRIA-V1.0-final.pdf

TAUS. Joscelyne, A. (Ed.), 2017. TAUS Machine Translation Market Report. TAUS.

Toral, A., Castilho, S., Hu, K., & Way, A. 2018. Attaining the Unattainable? Reassessing Claims of Human Parity in Neural Machine Translation. *arXiv preprint arXiv:1808.10432*.

Von Lohmann, F. 2017. Fair use as innovation policy. *Copyright Law* (pp. 169-205). Routledge.

World Economic Forum. 2017. Schwab, K. (Ed.), *The Global Competitiveness Report 2017-2018*. Geneva: World Economic Forum.

Wu, Y., Schuster, M., Chen, Z., Le, Q. V., Norouzi, M., Macherey, W., … & Klingner, J. 2016. Google's neural machine translation system: Bridging the gap between human and machine translation. *arXiv preprint arXiv:1609.08144*

# Improving CAT Tools in the Translation Workflow: New Approaches and Evaluation

Mihaela Vela[1], Santanu Pal[1,2], Marcos Zampieri[3] Sudip Kumar Naskar[4]
Josef van Genabith[1,2]

[1]Saarland University, Germany, [2]DFKI, Germany
[3]University of Wolverhampton, UK, [4]Jadavpur University, India
m.vela@mx.uni-saarland.de

## Abstract

This paper describes strategies to improve an existing web-based computer-aided translation (CAT) tool entitled *CATaLog Online*. *CATaLog Online* provides a post-editing environment with simple yet helpful project management tools. It offers translation suggestions from translation memories (TM), machine translation (MT), and automatic post-editing (APE) and records detailed logs of post-editing activities. To test the new approaches proposed in this paper, we carried out a user study on an English–German translation task using *CATaLog Online*. User feedback revealed that the users preferred using *CATaLog Online* over existing CAT tools in some respects, especially by selecting the output of the MT system and taking advantage of the color scheme for TM suggestions.

## 1 Introduction

The use of computer software is an important part of the modern translation workflow (Zaretskaya et al., 2015; Schneider et al., 2019). A number of tools are widely used by professional translators, most notably CAT tools and terminology management software. These tools increase translators' productivity, improve consistency in translation and, in turn, reduce the cost of translation (Zampieri and Vela, 2014). The most important compo- nent in state-of-the-art CAT tools are transla- tion memories (TM). The translators can ei- ther accept, reject or modify the suggestions received from the TM engine. As the pro- cess is done iteratively, every new translation increases the size of the translation memory making it more useful for future translations.

The idea behind TMs is relatively simple, however, the process of matching and retrieval of source and target segments is not trivial. In this paper we discuss new approaches to im- prove TM retrieval and CAT tools interfaces. With our contribution we aim to make TM suggestions more useful and accurate

(i) by presenting new retrieval strategies for the TM suggestions, and

(ii) by making the translator's job easier in terms of presenting the translation sug- gestions in the CAT tool.

To achieve these goals, we use a new web-based CAT tool called *CATaLog Online* (Pal et al., 2016a)[1], which builds on an existing desktop CAT *CATaLog* (Nayek et al., 2015) but is en- hanced with with a new interface layout.

The remainder of this paper is structured as follows: Section 2 presents related work on CAT tools and TMs, Section 3 describes the main functions of *CATaLog Online* includ- ing similarity matching, color coding scheme, and strategies to improve TM search efficiency. Section 4 presents the results obtained in the user studies carried out, and finally Section 5 presents the conclusions of this paper and av- enues for future research.



---

[1]Available at `http://santanu.appling.uni-saarland.de/MMCAT/`

## 2   Related Work

Most professional translators today use the so-called computer-aided translation (CAT) tools (van den Bergh et al., 2015; Schneider et al., 2019). General-purpose CAT tools offer a variety of features, most commonly TM, MT, a glossary and terminology management, concordance search to display words in context, quality estimation (QE) check, QE scores, auto-completion suggestions, and several administrative features to organize projects.

In the translation and localization industry, translators are more and more acting as post-editors, working with pre-translated texts from TM or MT output. This has turned CAT tools an essential part of the translators' workflow. A number of studies on translation process were carried out to investigate translators' productivity, cognitive load (CL), effort, time, quality, etc.

Guerberof (2012) and Zampieri and Vela (2014) report on studies comparing the productivity and quality of human translations using MT and TM output, showing the gain in productivity when post-editing MT segments in comparison to using TM segments or when translating from scratch. The incorporation of MT output into the CAT tools allows also for a different kind of MT evaluation. Zaretskaya et al. (2016a,b) approached post-editing and MT output from a different perspective, namely by using post-editing indicators and the post-editing environment (a CAT tool) to reason about the difficulty of MT output. In her overview on the existing methods for measuring post-editing effort (identified by temporal, technical and cognitive indicators) Koponen (2016), concluded that determining the amount of cognitive effort still poses questions. She further argued that accurate measurements would influence productivity, but the individual experience of the post-editors as well as their work conditions are also criteria to be considered.

TM as a feature is still valued higher than MT, with 75% of translators believing it to increase throughput and preserve consistency, while 40% think MT usage is problematic due to the amount of errors (Moorkens and O'Brien, 2017). The retrieval of TM matches in most commercial and many research sys-tems are based on string matching mechanisms that do not exploit semantic similarity (Gupta et al., 2015, 2016) and post-editing effort (Koponen, 2012), and the presentation of TM matches to users touches upon a research topic in human–computer interaction (HCI) – information visualisation – that has received little attention in both translation studies (TS) and natural language processing (NLP). O'Brien (2012) views translation as a form of human-computer interaction showing how the translation profession has changed over time, also due to the newest developments in the area of machine translation and the integration of the MT output into CAT tools for post-editing. This view is mirrored in recent research, dealing with cognitive load in the translation and post-editing process. Vieira (2014) uses a psychology-motivated definition of cognitive load, while Herbig et al. (2019) propose a model that uses a wide range of physiological and behavioral sensor data to estimate perceived cognitive load during post-editing of machine MT.

These findings suggest that a) MT is definitively suitable to be integrated into a TM, b) even a slightly better MT output integrated into a translation environment can improve the translation performance and c) post-editing indicators should consider - if possible - also the personal performance of each translator.

## 3   *CATaLog Online*: System Description

This section describes the *CATaLog Online*, a novel and user-friendly web-based CAT tool, its main functionalities and novel features that distinguish it from other CAT tools. *CATaLog Online* offers translations from three engines – TM (Nayek et al., 2015), MT (Pal et al., 2015a) and APE (Pal et al., 2015b), from which users can choose the most suitable translation and post-edit. Users can upload their own translation memories to the platform or can make use of the background translation memory, if any, integrated into the tool for the language pair. Instead of using the background MT tools, users can also upload the translations produced by third-party MT systems.

**TM Search and Segment Retrieval**
*CATaLog Online* combines elements of both

TER and Needleman-Wunsch algorithm to design its similarity and retrieval metric. We take the alignment computed by TER but calculate the similarity score using the intuition of the Needleman-Wunsch algorithm by penalizing edit operations and rewarding matches. A detailed description of TM retrieval implemented in *CATaLog Online* can be found in Nayek et al. (2015).

**Color Coding** To make that decision process easy, *CATaLog Online* color codes the matched and unmatched parts in both source and target sides of the TM suggestions. Green portions imply that they are matched fragments and red portions imply mismatches.

Ideally, the TM suggestion translation having the maximum number of green words should be the ideal candidate for post-editing.

**Improving Search Efficiency** Comparing every input sentence against all the TM source segments makes the search process very slow, particularly for large TMs. To improve search efficiency, *CATaLog Online* uses the Nutch[2] information retrieval (IR) system. Nutch follows the standard IR model of Lucene[3] with document parsing, document Indexing, TF-IDF calculation, query parsing and finally searching/document retrieval and document ranking. In our implementation, each document contains (a) a TM source segment, (b) its corresponding translation and (c) the word alignments.

**Machine Translation and Automatic Post Editing** Along with TM matches, *CATaLog Online* provides MT output (Pal et al., 2015a) to the translator, an option provided by many state-of-the-art CAT tools (e.g. MateCat (Federico et al., 2014)). Besides the retrieved TM segment and the MT output *CATaLog Online* provides also a third option to the translator: the output of an automatic post-editing system meant to be post-edited as the MT output. The APE system is based in an OSM model (Pal et al., 2016b) and proved to deliver competitive performance in previous editions of the Automatic Post Editing (APE) shared task at WMT Bojar et al. (2016).

**Editing Logs** For a given input segment, *CATaLog Online* provides four different options: TM, MT, APE and translation from scratch; the translator either chooses the best translation suggestion among these options or translates from the scratch. For both post-editing and translation the CAT tool the user activities are logged and can be downloaded in XML format. In addition to these logs, the translator can also download the alignments between source and target text.

**Data** The data used for building the internal TM in *CATaLog Online* as well as MT and APE system consists of the EuroParl corpus and the news and common crawl corpus collected during the 2015 WMT shared. task[4]

## 4 User Studies with *CATaLog Online*

We conducted experiments with Translation Studies students and professional translators to evaluate *CATaLog Online*. The data used in the evaluation process was translated from English into German. The goals of our user studies are:

(i) to compare *CATaLog Online* and a similar CAT tool, MateCAT, in terms of human post-editing performance;

(ii) to compare the efficiency of the three proposed solutions (TM, MT and APE) in a real translation environment.

The comparison between MateCat and *CATaLog Online* was carried out by students performing post-editing on English to German MT output. The 16 students participating in this evaluation were undergraduate students enrolled on a Translation Studies program, attending a translation technologies class, including sessions on MT and MT evaluation. All of them were native speakers of German, with no professional experience, but with good or very good knowledge of English (B2 and C1 level[5]).

Half of the students were asked to perform post-editing of the MT output in MateCat, the

---

[2]http://nutch.apache.org/
[3]http://lucene.apache.org/

[4]http://www.statmt.org/
[5]Linguistic competence categories as in the Common European Framework: https://www.coe.int/en/web/common-european-framework-reference-languages/level-descriptions

other half in *CATaLog Online*. Each student was presented with a set of 30 sentences (news in English and the corresponding German MT output) and was asked to perform post-editing on the German MT output. From the set of 30 sentences, 20 sentences were randomly chosen, 10 sentences were common to all students, allowing the direct comparison between Mate-Cat and *CATaLog Online*.

MateCat captures information about the number of words, the post-editing time and effort, but is also tracking the changes between the MT output and the final post-edited version of the MT output. *CATaLog Online* captures information about post-editing time, and also keeps track of the changes, counting the number of insertions, deletions, substitutions, and shifts.

Since post-editing time (measured in seconds) is the information captured by both tools, we are using it for the comparison between Matecat and *CATaLog Online*. This contrasting listing of the post-editing times holds just for the 10 sentences in common, where we can be sure that the sentences have the same length.

Table 1 shows the post-editing time in seconds, proving that the sentences in MateCat were edited faster than in *CATaLog Online*. The notation S1 to S16 stands for each of the 16 evaluators. One reason for this result, also commented by the evaluators, might be the different design of the editing interface. Mate-Cat provides a plain, simple interface, whereas *CATaLog Online*'s interface is quite colorful containing more than just editing window.

|  | **MateCat** |  |  | ***CATaLog Online*** |
|---|---|---|---|---|
| Stud1 | 1112 | Stud9 |  | 3079 |
| Stud2 | 1086 | Stud10 |  | 2623 |
| Stud3 | 1304 | Stud11 |  | 1761 |
| Stud4 | 2602 | Stud12 |  | 5499 |
| Stud5 | 2176 | Stud13 |  | 1788 |
| Stud6 | 876 | Stud14 |  | 5773 |
| Stud7 | 901 | Stud15 |  | 3040 |
| Stud8 | 823 | Stud16 |  | 4178 |

**Table 1:** Direct comparison of MateCat and *CATaLog Online* by post-editing time (in seconds) for the 10 sentences in common.

The second experiment is addressing the quality of the proposed translation solutions in *CATaLog Online*. Users are provided with the following translations:

- the translation from *CATaLog Online*'s TM,

- the output of the integrated machine translation system,

- the output of the integrated automatic post-editing system

In order to evaluate the three proposed solutions (TM, MT and APE) in a real translation environment, the same 16 students from the post-editing task were asked to select the most helpful translation. The experimental design was similar to the one above. Each student was presented 30 English news sentences in *CATaLog Online*, 10 being in common to all students, and asked to opt for the most appropriate German translation. In the evaluation phase of this experiment, we noticed that the students' decision for the MT or APE system is based on chance, since the MT output and the output from the APE system are very similar to each other. As a consequence, we excluded the APE output from the list of possible translations and repeated the experiment with three professional translators. The professional translators were native speaker of German with at least two years of experience in translation. Before translating they were provided with guidelines and a short introduction into working with *CATaLog Online*. The translators were asked to perform English to German translation of 200 news sentences with *CATaLog Online* by choosing between:

(a) the output of *CATaLog Online*'s MT system (MT),

(b) the suggestions from *CATaLog Online*'s internal translation memory (TM),

(c) translating from scratch without any suggestion (None).

The selection of the first two possibilities (a) or (b) assumes that translators will edit suggestions proposed by the tool, while for (c) he/she will have to do the translation from scratch.
From the set of 200 sentences each translator received, 100 were repeated, allowing us to measure the agreement between the three translators. Since *CATaLog Online* is providing an extensive editing log, we collected in-

| | **200 sentences** | | | **100 sentences** | | |
|------|-----|-----|-----|-----|-----|-----|
| | T1 | T2 | T3 | T1 | T2 | T3 |
| MT | 160 | 169 | 161 | 74 | 85 | 82 |
| TM | 1 | 16 | 0 | 1 | 7 | 0 |
| None | 39 | 15 | 39 | 25 | 8 | 18 |

**Table 2:** Selection of suggestions by translators in *CATaLog Online*.

formation concerning the engine used in translation (MT, TM, or translation from scratch), the number of deletions, insertions, substitutions and shifts as well the edit time (in seconds) for each segment.

The first analysis of the logs shows that all three translators have a tendency in choosing first the suggestion made by the MT system and perform further editing on it. Table 2 gives an overview of the selected suggestions and shows that the MT system achieves a selection rate of around 80%. The remaining sentences are either translated from scratch or by using the suggestions provided by the TM. The selection suggestions are similar for both the 200 sentenced and the 100 sentences in common.

For the 100 sentences in common, we measured pairwise inter-rater agreement between translators by computing Cohen's $\kappa$ Cohen (1960) for different variables. We concentrated on the suggestions used in the translation process (MT, TM, or translation from scratch), editing time, as well as the overall number of edits.

From Table 3, we observe that translators agree only in terms of overall number of edits. Editing time and the selection of a specific suggestion (MT, TM, or translation from scratch) are parameters on which the translators do not agree. We computed Pearson's correlation coefficient $\rho$, to test whether the total number of edits (with a low $\kappa$) is influencing the post-editing time (with a high $\kappa$). We achieved a $\rho$ value of 0.10, not allowing us for a clear interpretation concerning correlation.

Figure 1, depicts a slight tendency that a higher number of edits requires more edit time. We also notice cases in which a high number of edits do not require much editing time and vice versa. It seems that a higher number of edits does not necessary mean a longer editing time, this being an indicator for the fact that post-editing time is a subjective measure and should be treated carefully.

Taking a closer look at the type of edits performed during editing, we notice that the edits with the highest frequency are substitutions, followed by insertions, deletions and shifts. Concluding on the user studies described in this section, we show that translators have a clear preference in choosing the output of the MT system for performing their translation task, even if they do not make the same decision for the same segments. In terms of editing time, the data shows that in this setting, time is a translator-dependent variable, influencing the low correlation coefficient with the number of edits. This aspect has to be taken into consideration when measuring post-editing/translation effort by post-editing/translation time, since time is a subjective measure for effort depending on the experience level, working conditions as well as personal abilities.

### 4.1 User Feedback

The professional translators participating in our experiment were asked to rate *CATaLog Online* by comparing it to other CAT tools in terms of usability. The main positive and negative impressions are summarized below.

**Positive Feedback** Translators reported that the unique coloring system in *CATaLog Online* - offered by none of the existing TM based CAT tools - helped them to complete the editing of suggestions from the TM. They also found the proposed MT suggestions as really helpful and referred positively to the arrangement of the suggestions in *CATaLog Online*.

**Negative Feedback** The lack of certain functionalities like a spell-checker, keyboard shortcuts, a concordancer was rated negatively by the translators. Although they rated positively the color coding, the interface was considered to be overloaded.

### 4.2 Limitations

Finally, based on the experiments carried out and the feedback from participants we believe that the current version of *CATaLog Online* has the following limitations:

- Currently, the tool cannot handle document formatting such as bold/italic fonts, bullets;

| | Selected suggestions | | | Editing time | | | Number of edits | | |
|---|---|---|---|---|---|---|---|---|---|
| | T1 | T2 | T3 | T1 | T2 | T3 | T1 | T2 | T3 |
| T1 | - | 0.08 | 0.20 | - | -0.16 | -0.06 | - | 0.49 | 0.42 |
| T2 | 0.08 | - | 0.05 | -0.16 | - | -0.13 | 0.49 | - | 0.26 |
| T3 | 0.20 | 0.05 | - | -0.06 | -0.13 | - | 0.42 | 0.26 | - |

**Table 3:** Cohen's $\kappa$ measuring agreement for the selected suggestion, editing time and number of edits.

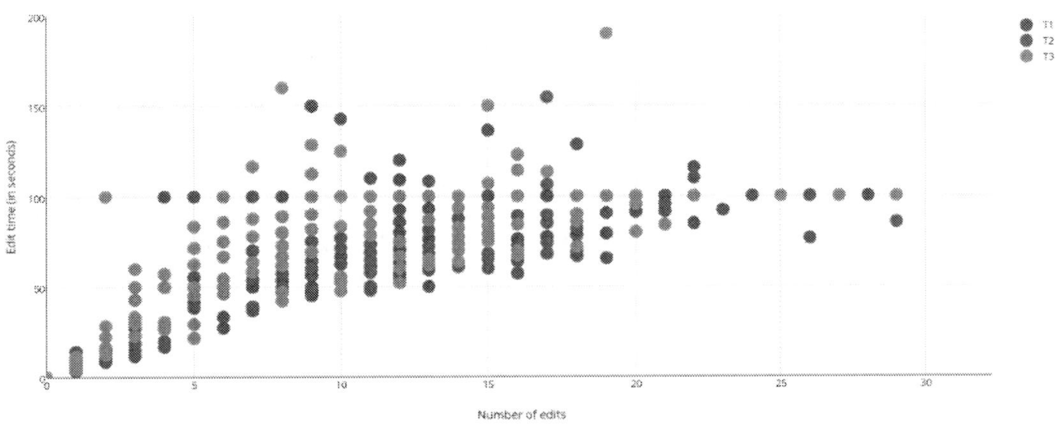

**Figure 1:** Correlation between the overall number of edits and edit time.

- It does not handle stemming;

- The current experiment does not consider individual edit operations in terms of coherence and cohesion of the whole segment which calls for a controlled experiment towards this specific objective by defining different test set for each individual edit operations.

## 5 Conclusions and Future Work

The paper presents strategies to improve a new free open-source CAT tool and post-editing interface, *CATaLog Online*, based on several experiments carried out and presented in this paper. The tool offers translation suggestions from TM, MT and APE. The tool is specifically designed to improve post-editing productivity and user experience with CAT. A novel feature in the tool is a new intra-segment color coding scheme that highlights matching and irrelevant fragments in suggested TM segments. The feedback from the translators show that color coding the TM suggestions makes the decision process easier for the user as to which TM suggestion to choose and work on. It also guides the translators as to which fragments

to post-edit on the chosen TM translation. The similarity metric employed in the tool makes use of TER, Needleman–Wunsch algorithm and Lucene retrieval score to identify and re-rank relevant TM . The tool keeps track of all the post-editing activities and records detailed logs in well structured XML format which is beneficial for incremental MT/APE and translation process research. The *CATaLog Online* user evaluation showed that translators have a clear preference in choosing the output of the MT system for performing their translation task. They also evaluated positively the color scheme for the TM suggestions as well as the arrangement of the suggestions within the tool. The informal feedback revealed that features like spell-checker, quality assessment (QA) features and keyboard shortcuts could improve the tool further.

## Acknowledgments

We would like to thank the participants of this user study for their valuable contribution. We further thank the MT Summit anonymous reviewers for their insightful feedback.

This research was funded in part by the German research foundation (DFG) under grant number GE 2819/2-1 (project MMPE) and People Programme (Marie Curie Actions) of the European Union's Framework Programme (FP7/2007-2013) under REA grant agreement no 317471. We are also thankful to Pangeanic, Valencia, Spain for kindly providing us with professional translators for these experiments.

## References

Bojar, O., Chatterjee, R., Federmann, C., Graham, Y., Haddow, B., Huck, M., Jimeno Yepes, A., Koehn, P., Logacheva, V., Monz, C., Negri, M., Neveol, A., Neves, M., Popel, M., Post, M., Rubino, R., Scarton, C., Specia, L., Turchi, M., Verspoor, K., and Zampieri, M. (2016). Findings of the 2016 Conference on Machine Translation. In *Proceedings of WMT*.

Cohen, J. (1960). A Coefficient of Agreement for Nominal Scales. *Educational and Psychological Measurement*, 20(1):37–46.

Federico, M., Bertoldi, N., Cettolo, M., Negri, M., Turchi, M., Trombetti, M., Cattelan, A., Farina, A., Lupinetti, D., Martines, A., et al. (2014). The Matecat Tool. In *Proceedings of COLING*.

Guerberof, A. (2012). *Productivity and Quality in the Post-Edition of Outputs from Translation Memories and Machine Translation*. PhD thesis, Rovira and Virgili University Tarragona.

Gupta, R., Orăsan, C., Zampieri, M., Vela, M., van Genabith, J., and Mitkov, R. (2016). Improving Translation Memory Matching and Retrieval Using Paraphrases. *Machine Translation*, 30(1):19–40.

Gupta, R., Orăsan, C., Zampieri, M., Vela, M., and van Genabith, J. (2015). Can Translation Memories Afford not to Use Paraphrasing? In *Proceedings of EAMT*.

Herbig, N., Pal, S., Vela, M., Krüger, A., and van Genabith, J. (2019). Multi-modal Indicators for Estimating Perceived Cognitive Load in Post-editing of Machine Translation. *Machine Translation*.

Koponen, M. (2012). Comparing Human Perceptions of Post-editing Effort with Post-editing Operations. In *Proceedings of WMT*.

Koponen, M. (2016). Is machine Translation Post-editing Worth the Effort? A Survey of Research into Post-editing and Effort. *Journal of Specialised Translation*, 25:131–141.

Moorkens, J. and O'Brien, S. (2017). Assessing User Interface Needs of Post-editors of Machine Translation. In *Human Issues in Translation Technology*, pages 127–148. Routledge.

Nayek, T., Naskar, S. K., Pal, S., Zampieri, M., Vela, M., and van Genabith, J. (2015). CATaLog: New Approaches to TM and Post Editing Interfaces. In *Proceedings of NLP4TM*.

O'Brien, S. (2012). Translation as Human–computer Interaction. *Translation Spaces*, 1:101–122.

Pal, S., Naskar, S., and van Genabith, J. (2015a). UdS-Sant: English–German Hybrid Machine Translation System. In *Proceedings of WMT*.

Pal, S., Vela, M., Naskar, S. K., and van Genabith, J. (2015b). USAAR-SAPE: An English–Spanish Statistical Automatic Post-Editing System. In *Proceedings of WMT*.

Pal, S., Zampieri, M., Naskar, S. K., Nayak, T., Vela, M., and van Genabith, J. (2016a). CATaLog Online: Porting a Post-editing Tool to the Web. In *Proceedings of LREC*.

Pal, S., Zampieri, M., and van Genabith, J. (2016b). USAAR: An Operation Sequential Model for Automatic Statistical Post-editing. In *Proceedings of WMT*.

Schneider, D., Zampieri, M., and van Genabith, J. (2019). Translation Memories and the Translator: A Report on a User Survey. *Babel*, pages 734–762.

van den Bergh, J., Geurts, E., Degraen, D., Haesen, M., van der Lek-Ciudin, I., and Coninx, K. (2015). Recommendations for Translation Environments to Improve Translators' Workflows. In *Proceedings of Translating and the Computer*.

Vieira, L. (2014). Indices of Cognitive Effort in Machine Translation Post-editing. *Machine Translation*, 3(28):187–216.

Zampieri, M. and Vela, M. (2014). Quantifying the Influence of MT Output in the Translators' Performance: A Case Study in Technical Translation. In *Proceedings of HaCaT*.

Zaretskaya, A., Pastor, G. C., and Seghiri, M. (2015). Translators' Requirements for Translation Technologies: Results of a User Survey. In *Proceedings of New Horizons is Translation and Interpreting Studies*.

Zaretskaya, A., Vela, M., Pastor, G. C., and Seghiri, M. (2016a). Comparing Post-Editing Difficulty of Different Machine Translation Errors in Spanish and German Translations from English. *International Journal of Language and Linguistics*, 3(3).

Zaretskaya, A., Vela, M., Pastor, G. C., and Seghiri, M. (2016b). Measuring Post-editing Time and Effort for Different Machine Translation Errors. *New Voices in Translation Studies*, 15:63–92.

# Hungarian translators' perceptions of neural machine translation in the European Commission

**Ágnes Lesznyák**
European Commission
Directorate-General for Translation
agnes.lesznyak@ec.europa.eu

## Abstract

This paper summarises findings from structured interviews with Hungarian translators in the European Commission's Directorate-General for Translation on their experiences with neural machine translation as a translation aid since 2017. The translators have widely divergent views on the use and usefulness of neural machine translation and varying practices when it comes to integrating it into their work. The paper concludes that human factors play a crucial role in the success of application and argues that translators' attitudes and intriguing cognitive processes merit greater scientific attention.

## 1 Introduction

With the emergence of neural technology, the quality of machine translation (MT) output has improved rapidly in recent years, in particular for languages with more complex morphology, such as Hungarian. Nevertheless, human intervention is still indispensable for checking and improving texts where the accuracy of information transfer is vital, such as in the legal domain, or texts intended for publication (Ive et al. 2018; Way 2018; Knowles et al. 2019).

Research in this area has focused mainly on aspects of post-editing (PE), the traditional treatment applied by translators to improve the quality of MT output.[1] A number of studies (e.g. Plitt and Masselot 2010; Koponen 2012;

Guerberof 2014; Koehn and Germann 2014) have found that PE productivity and effort differ greatly between individual translators dealing with MT output. However, human factors such as professional translators' views and practices, have attracted relatively little academic attention.

In a groundbreaking study, Cadwell et al. (2017) investigate what influences the adoption of MT by professional translators in two different institutional settings, one being the European Commission's Directorate-General for Translation (DGT). They conclude that translators' sense and level of 'agency' have a crucial impact on their attitudes towards MT.

The changing nature of MT output (due to rapid technological development) may also influence translators' perceptions and work processes. Since neural machine translation (NMT) is a recent development, the body of relevant research is necessarily small (Castilho et al. 2019).

By reporting on the experience of professional translators working in DGT's Hungarian Language Department, we want to raise awareness of aspects of interaction with NMT that are highly relevant for practitioners and may require further scientific insight, in order to prompt greater acceptance and more efficient use of this tool.

## 2 Background

### 2.1 eTranslation

eTranslation[2], the successor to the European Commission's MT service MT@EC, has been developed by the DGT in the framework of the Connecting Europe Facility. It offers statistical (SMT) and neural machine translation (NMT) into all the 24 official languages of the European Union, plus Icelandic and Norwegian. At the time of writing, it can be used by officials in the

---



[1] For an overview of the practice of and research into PE, see Koponen (2016).

[2] https://ec.europa.eu/cefdigital/wiki/display/CEFDIGITAL/What+is+eTranslation

EU institutions and all EU Member States, Iceland and Norway. It is intended mainly as a component of digital services, but it also offers stand-alone services for the translation of documents and text snippets[3] and is provided as an integrated service for use by DGT translators (see section 2.2). eTranslation guarantees data confidentiality and security.

Following a test phase in early 2017, the general roll-out of NMT in DGT began with the launch of eTranslation in November 2017.

The emergence of neural technology represented a breakthrough for MT in language pairs involving Hungarian (Tihanyi and Oravecz 2017). As the level of quality of SMT did not allow for efficient PE, DGT's Hungarian translators had only used it sporadically. Therefore, working with NMT output was most Hungarian translators' first encounter with MT in their professional activity.

### 2.2  NMT in DGT's internal workflow

DGT offers translation services to other Commission Directorates-General, who send translation requests to a central DGT service that pre-processes texts automatically using various applications. Relevant segments and documents are extracted from predefined databases and a normative memory, and subsequently made available to translators as tmx files. Since July 2018, this pre-processing has involved MT into all EU languages (except Irish). The resulting tmx file can be imported, together with other tmx files, into the CAT tool.

DGT guidelines for the use of MT set out minimum requirements in terms of translators' technical knowledge and the amount of MT output they are expected to post-edit in order to familiarise themselves with the technology.

Beyond this, individual translators decide whether to use MT output for any given assignment. In principle, they have three options:
- pre-translate the whole document with the pre-processed tmx files provided (including MT) and then post-edit the text; or
- insert the MT.tmx automatically (auto-populate) and post-edit it segment by segment; or
- use the predictive typing function to insert chunks offered from the MT.tmx.

### 3  Interviews

DGT's Hungarian Language Department employs 49 translators and 9 assistants[4]. The translators are supported by a terminologist and a language technology coordinator. The language department also has a quality officer responsible for quality management[5].

DGT translators have a variety of professional backgrounds. Many Hungarian translators have studied languages and been formally trained as translators. However, some have a degree in law, economics or engineering, plus a post-graduate diploma or several years of professional experience in translation.

Between June 2018 and January 2019, the quality officer carried out structured interviews for internal quality management purposes with 38 translators working in the department.[6] By that time translators had been able to use NMT in their daily work for 8 to 14 months, mainly in translating from English into Hungarian. The interviews were not intended as a survey that would produce quantifiable results. Rather, the aim was to explore translators' views on NMT, their work practices (cf. above options) and practical issues that had arisen. The findings would feed into follow-up quality assurance action.

Translators were interviewed in Hungarian and were asked the following questions:
- When is it worth using NMT?
- How do you use NMT?
- Which language version do you read first?
- In what way is NMT different from translation memories (TMs) containing human translation? What deserves special attention?
- What are the advantages of using NMT?
- As a reviser, are you aware of whether a translation was made using NMT?

Translators were also encouraged to raise and discuss any topics that they considered relevant to the use of NMT. Therefore, the interviews differed considerably in length, from around 20 to 90 minutes.

The interviewer made notes of the translators' answers[7] and analysed and summarised them in a

---



[4] The figures reflect the situation in April 2019. The number of translators and assistants in active service are subject to constant change.

[5] On quality management and the role of quality officers see Drugan et al. (2018).

[6] Time and workload constraints meant that it was not possible to talk to all the translators. No assistants were interviewed, as they do not work with NMT.

[7] For reasons of collegiality, it was not considered

report. The results were shared and discussed with the translators in a half-day workshop. This made it possible to double check the interpretation of the data collected.

For obvious methodological reasons this paper makes no claims of generalizable findings. Where ratios are mentioned, this is to highlight recurring themes in translators' reports. Issues referred to only once may turn out to be just as relevant for the translation process. The themes identified here should be verified in future research.

## 4 Discussion

The interviews showed that the translators' views on NMT are highly divergent and their work practices vary widely a year after the introduction of NMT into the workflow. They expressed conflicting opinions on how useful NMT was, when it was worth using and how it could be used efficiently. Their observations were so disparate that the interviewer sometimes wondered whether they referred to the same tool.

The differences were reflected not only in the details, but also in the translators' overall opinions as to the benefits of NMT. Some see NMT as a very useful, positive development, while others (having tested it on a number of documents) have stopped using it or use it only sparingly. These findings are in line with those of Cadwell et al. (2016), who found no consensus among DGT translators on some central questions relating to the use of MT.

In the following sections, we summarise and discuss recurring themes from the interviews.

### 4.1 Factors influencing the usefulness of NMT output

Two factors in particular seem to determine whether Hungarian translators in DGT consider NMT useful: relevance, and the quality of the NMT output, which is perceived as correlating with segment length. The latter will be discussed in section 4.2.

The question of relevance of MT output is critical for DGT translators: very often, EU documents relate closely to previous documents, such as legal bases, or concurrently translated other texts. In such cases, consistency between texts is paramount: translators must re-use previous translations and not translate the new document from scratch. As a result, they may prefer TMs

---



originating in DGT's multilingual database (Euramis) and judge NMT output counterproductive or a distraction in certain situations.

When gauging the usefulness of an NMT.tmx file, translators rely on 'match rates': some import the file only if the match rate for the document is under a certain percentage, typically 50% or 30%. Cadwell et al. (2016) report that DGT translators working into different languages seem to differ in this respect: while those translating to some languages use NMT output when the retrieval rate is low, others do so when it is high. The reason for this apparent disagreement may lie in the types of document translated by individual translators and an inherent contradiction in MT. Generally, NMT output seems to be useful when there is no TM available and translators would have to translate from scratch. However, NMT works better for high-retrieval, i.e. recurring documents since they were included in the training corpus of the engine with high probability. Recurrence means that there are TMs available which may or may not have priority over MT, depending on the document type. NMT output may be useful for high retrieval documents if there is no obligation to edit fuzzy matches from TMs. Therefore, this apparent disparity may require finer analysis.

Some translators import the NMT.tmx file and take a decision on the usefulness of the NMT output at segment level. They typically use NMT for 'empty' segments, i.e. where reference TMs do not return any hits under a certain match rate. This approach allows them to respect the 'relevance' principle and use NMT at the same time.

Some translators highlighted the usefulness of NMT for urgent assignments, despite the risk of the MT output not being sufficiently post-edited. They argued that a greater risk in such situations is not to have a translation at all, i.e. not to comply with the service provision requirement.

The domain and the genre of a document does not seem to directly influence the perceived usefulness of NMT in the DGT working environment. Interestingly, the interviewees held opposing views as to the usefulness of NMT for particular document types such as press material, Commission communications and legal acts, and used the same arguments for and against NMT. There are many possible explanations for this. One may be translators' varying sensitivity to or awareness of different types of error in NMT output (see section 4.2). Another may lie in their working methods. Very few reported unprompted that they do a complete read-through of their translations. We have reports in another context that this is not done in times of high workload. There is some evidence (e.g. Dragsted 2006) that CAT tools direct translators' attention to the segment level. Läubli et al. (2016) report that the document-level (as opposed to segment-level) presentation of NMT output influences human raters' perception of quality.

One interesting factor mentioned by some translators as having an impact on the usefulness of NMT was their familiarity with the source language or the domain in question. They rely on NMT more when working from a language in which they do not feel confident or in a domain with which they are not familiar. This is in line with the findings of Moorkens et al. (2018). In their study, translators with less experience found MT suggestions more useful. Although the Hungarian translators reporting this benefit of MT had sufficient translation experience, they felt a certain lack of language or domain competence in the situation in question.

The next section will discuss translators' perceptions of NMT output and of the treated (i.e. pre-revision) product.

### 4.2 Typical errors and quality issues

The interviewees said that the unpredictable quality of NMT output is a key factor discouraging them from using it. Quality varies widely from one segment to another: some need hardly any intervention, while others have to be re-translated. Therefore, NMT output always has to be checked thoroughly and very often requires significant PE. This may explain why translators develop certain 'control' practices (see section 4.3).

As mentioned above, segment length seems to be a decisive determinant of the quality of Hungarian NMT output. The interviewees mostly agree that short segments are of much better quality than longer ones – the former only need to be revised, whereas the latter often have to be deleted and translated from scratch. The borderline between 'short' and 'long' seems to be around 30–40 words.

A correlation between sentence length and quality has previously been reported for other language pairs (for an overview, see Castilho et al. 2018). Koehn and Knowles (2017) found that NMT outperformed SMT up to a sentence length of about 60 words, but beyond that the quality fell off. The fact that 200-word sentences are not uncommon in certain types of EU document may place a serious constraint on the usefulness of NMT in the Commission.

Translators see longer sentences as problematic not only because of the potential for lower NMT quality but because their complexity prevents a quick assessment of their correctness. It takes too much time and cognitive effort to analyse the components and decide what can be used. In such cases, it seems more efficient to re-translate the segment.

Translators' responses as regards recurring errors identified in NMT output confirm the relevant findings in the literature (see e.g. Eisold 2017; Van Brussel et al. 2018; Yamada 2019). Below, we discuss these errors in the case of Hungarian.

Mistranslation and deceptive fluency emerged as the two main issues. The sources of the errors were not easy to identify, but problems mentioned included incorrect word order; misplaced attributes; inversion of subject and object; and wrong ordering of clauses. Elliptical sentences and non-literal meaning also seem frequently to give rise to mistranslations.

While these error types call for close attention to the text, intensive PE is needed to correct other typical errors, such as incorrect information structure and missing referential elements and sentence connectors. Translators have to convert sentence-level MT into a coherent text.

On the other hand, morphological errors seem to be rare in eTranslation's Hungarian NMT output. Errors mentioned were incorrect endings, definite articles and possessive structures, and non-concordance between subject and object.

A typical recurring error in the Hungarian NMT output is the translation of proper names into fictional words. Since this is a new phenomenon for translators and a challenge for automatic quality checks, this type of error constitutes a risk in the translation process. It may have serious consequences if it prevents the reader from identifying a unique referent.

A source of serious concern for many translators was incorrect or inconsistent terminology, and in general, the context-independent translation of vocabulary. This tendency in the NMT output is a serious obstacle to efficient work, since terms have to be checked one by one in a termbase. As DGT translates many legal texts, this type of error presents a high risk and increases the need for thorough quality control.

When asked about the quality of translations submitted for revision, the majority of the translators[8] maintained that they clearly recognised NMT chunks and segments even if 'automated translation' was not explicitly signaled in the CAT tool. Only three said they could not tell whether NMT had been used. When asked about 'tell-tale signs', some cited cases of colleagues who had worked reliably for years suddenly starting to translate less accurately and produce highly amateur solutions. However linguistic perfection may also be a give-away if readers realise that a text does not follow the institutional style they are used to. There were also complaints about the readability of translations, unclear references and missing logical links, i.e. document-level errors.

These remarks may indicate that revisers encounter more, or other types of, errors than before the introduction of NMT. Several said that pre-revision translations have been of a lower quality, requiring more intervention and effort from revisers. This may lead to tensions between colleagues concerned.

Generally, the errors that revisers identified as revealing the use of NMT were the same as those detected in the NMT output itself. This may suggest that at least some errors filter through to the quality check phase, indicating flaws at the translation stage.

Therefore, in the next section we discuss how translators interact with NMT output.

### 4.3 Technical aspects of NMT use

DGT's Hungarian translators have developed divergent practices to integrate NMT into their individual workflow in what they consider an efficient and safe way. They have shown astounding creativity in adapting a technical tool to their professional convictions and practices.

In general, we can say that many translators do not post-edit MT, but insert chunks from the NMT.tmx into their translations, in much the same way as they use other reference material. This is because they consider PE a high-risk activity: they report that if the NMT output is inserted automatically into a segment, they tend to be deceived by its linguistic fluency and oversee errors. If they first take the time to read and understand the source language sentence and create a mental structure of the equivalent sentence in Hungarian, they can safely insert elements (or whole sentences) of the NMT output. Some do not even copy/paste chunks, but re-type

them. They report processing information in their head while they are typing. Others use the CAT tool's predictive typing function to prompt suggestions in context. These findings confirm the conclusion of Cadwell et al. (2016) that, for some DGT translators, the job means 'being in control of the final outcome'.

Other translators auto-populate and post-edit their text segment by segment with NMT output when no other TM is available. But permutations of these methods were also reported.

Very few translators pre-translate the whole text with the various reference materials and post-edit the translation as a whole.

Those who pre-translate or auto-populate segment by segment reported some emerging practices to improve the efficiency of their work. They systematically delete sentences that exceed 30–40 words; they do not understand at first reading; or contain references to legal acts. However, some translators consciously try to retain long sentences and to find useful chunks.

Over time, many translators have developed a conscious strategy as to whether to read the source segment or the NMT output first. A minority read the latter first, in order to decide whether it is of sufficient quality. If so, they go on to read the source sentence and compare the meaning. They then decide whether to delete the NMT output in part or in full.

The majority read the source sentence first. They argue that this prevents them from being influenced by a wrong or unfortunate rendering of the source sentence before they have understood its meaning or formed a mental structure of the target sentence. They say that NMT output can be very misleading and, once read, is difficult to depart from.

Some interviewees were not able to say which language version they read first. They had either never reflected on the issue or assumed that they read both versions in parallel or in batches alternately.

Only one translator indicated that she read the NMT output as if she was revising a translation, whereas several stated explicitly that they do not read NMT output as a text to be revised.

In the final section we discuss the benefits and drawbacks that the translators identified when using NMT.

### 4.4 Advantages and risks

Two advantages of using NMT that translators mention repeatedly are that it speeds up their work and reduces typing effort.

---

[8] All translators in the Hungarian department carry out revision tasks.

However, the question of time gain is highly controversial among translators. Around half of the interviewees report that using NMT allows them to produce translations more quickly. In fact, for some, speed is the only advantage. Some add that the time gained is mitigated by a loss in quality: NMT allows them to produce lower quality more quickly.

The other half were either unsure as to whether they work faster with NMT, saying that this varies greatly depending on the document, or suggest that NMT use might speed up translation but slow down revision (for revisers' comments, see section 4.2).

Nearly half report that NMT reduces typing effort. Some stress that they either cannot touch-type or are slow typers and benefit from being able to insert whole chunks into their texts. However, some emphasise that they prefer typing: while they are typing, they are mentally preparing their translation. For them, typing is not an additional chore to translation but integral into the complex cognitive process of translation.

The perceptions of greater speed and less typing effort may be interrelated: because translators are doing less typing, they may feel that they are processing their text faster. Nevertheless, the claim of greater speed has not been tested.

A very interesting set of themes that arose from the interviews were the perceived psychological and cognitive benefits of using NMT. A quarter of the interviewees said that they found it reassuring not to have a blank segment and to have to start a translation from scratch. Some mention that the NMT output is a source of inspiration, especially when they are tired or do not know how to deal with a construction. Cadwell et al. (2016) found this to be an unusual reason for using MT.

Several translators reported that they had sometimes been highly impressed by the eloquent solutions that NMT offers.

We can only speculate as to the reasons for the readiness of DGT translators to embrace MT. One explanation may be that, as institutional translators, they are used to integrating translations from different sources.

A further benefit that was mentioned is that PE requires less cognitive effort than translation: it is easier to find and correct errors in an existing text than to create a new text. However, by no means all translators share this view. Some find PE more cognitively demanding than translation. They also argue that accepting NMT solutions is less demanding than improving them. This drives translators into a passive role which may affect their translation skills in the long run. Cadwell et al. (2016) report that some DGT translators reject MT because of its potentially detrimental effect on their abilities.

As a disadvantage of using NMT, some translators mentioned that they might tend to skim the NMT output, instead of reading it in the depth required to judge whether it correctly renders the meaning of the original.

In this context, it was also claimed that PE was killing translators' creativity. The word 'creativity' seemed to be used here in the sense of being able to produce a new text, a process accompanied by attention, focus and an active mindset, as opposed to a passive attitude that soon leads to a lack of attention. This sense of 'creation' is a source of motivation for some translators, which they will lose if they are only required to 'clean up' a text. Herbig et al. (2019) emphasise the need to improve translators' motivation by appropriately addressing cognitive load in the PE process, in order to avoid exhaustion and boredom, the effects of which may lead to higher translation costs.

Finally, some translators note that, in the absence of explicit expectations, the availability of NMT output (of 'good enough' quality) makes it possible to produce a translation with minimal human intervention. This constitutes a high risk for the quality of the product.

## 5    Conclusions

Overall, many of the translators interviewed consider NMT useful, but the majority have reservations about it in their daily work. This is partly because the quality of NMT output varies greatly from segment to segment and cannot be predicted reliably. Translators tend to recognise typical errors and see NMT as a tool that helps them do their work. However, many also see significant drawbacks and know that MT is not a substitute for human translation. As a result, they have developed working methods that compensate for the perceived disadvantages and give them 'control'. In practice, these methods mean that these translators translate rather than post-edit. Unfortunately, some of the working methods create new risks. A number of errors in the NMT output do not seem to be effectively corrected in the PE/translation phase, which puts pressure on revisers. These phenomena need to be analysed for quality assurance purposes.

The wide range of (sometimes conflicting) views among translators may not be new or unique to the use of NMT, but may be a result of reflection on new circumstances. Having to adapt to a new tool makes one more aware of differences that already existed and may play a more significant role in the future.

## References


Cadwell, Patrick, Sharon O'Brien and Carlos S. C. Teixeira. 2017. Resistance and accommodation: factors for the (non-)adoption of machine translation among professional translators. *Perspectives*, 26(3):301-321.

Cadwell, Patrick, Sheila Castilho, Sharon O'Brien and Linda Mitchell. 2016. Human factors in machine translation and post-editing among institutional translators. *Translation Spaces*, 5(2):222-243.

Castilho, Sheila, Joss Moorkens, Federico Gaspari, Rico Sennrich, Andy Way and Panayota Georgakopoulou. 2018. Evaluating MT for massive open online courses. *Machine Translation,* (2018)32:255-278.

Dragsted, Barbara. 2006. Computer-aided translation as a distributed cognitive task. *Pragmatics & Cognition,* 14(2):443-464.

Drugan, Joanna, Ingemar Strandvik and Erkka Vuorinen. 2018. Translation quality, quality management and agency: principles and practice in the European Union institutions. In Joss Moorkens, Sheila Catilho, Stephen Doherty and Federico Gaspari (eds.), *Translation quality assessment: from principles to practice.* Berlin: Springer, 39-68.

Eisold, Andreas. 2017. Zur Rolle der Terminologie in der maschinellen Übersetzung. Jörg Porsiel, (ed.) *Maschinelle Übersetzung: Grundlagen für den professionellen Einsatz*, Bundesverband der Dolmetscher und Übersetzer, 109-125.

Guerberof Arenas, Ana. 2014. Correlations between productivity and quality when post-editing in a professional context. *Machine Translation,* 28:165-186.

Herbig, Nico, Santanu Pal, Mihaela Vela, Antonio Krüger and Josef van Genabith. 2019. Multi-modal indicators for estimating perceived cognitive load in post-editing of machine translation. *Machine Translation,* (2019). https://doi.org/10.1007/s10590-019-09227-8

Ive, Julia, Aurélien Max and François Yvon. 2018. Reassessing the proper place of man and machine in translation: a pre-translation scenario. *Machine Translation,* 32(4):279-308.

Knowles, Rebecca, Marina Sanchez-Torron, and Philipp Koehn. 2019. A user study of neural interactive translation prediction. *Machine Translation,* (2019). https://doi.org/10.1007/s10590-019-09235-8

Koehn, Philipp and Ulrich Germann. 2014. The impact of machine translation quality on human post-editing. *Proceedings of the EACL 2014 Workshop on Humans and Computer-assisted Translation,* Gothenburg, Sweden. Association for Computational Linguistics, 38-46.

Koehn, Philipp and Rebecca Knowles. 2017. Six challenges for neural machine translation. *Proceedings of the First Workshop on Neural Machine Translation*, Vancouver, Canada, August 4, 2017. 28–39.

Koponen, Maarit. 2016. Is machine translation post-editing worth the effort? A survey of research into post-editing and effort. *The Journal of Specialised Translation*, 25:131-148.

Läubli, Samuel, Rico Sennrich, Martin Volk 2018. Has machine translation achieved human parity? A case for document-level evaluation. *Proceedings of the 2018 Conference on Empirical Methods in Natural Language Processing*, Brussels, Belgium, 4791–4796.

Moorkens, Joss, Antonio Toral, Sheila Castilho and Andy Way. 2018. Translators' perceptions of literary post-editing using statistical and neural machine translation. *Translation Spaces* 7:2, 240–262.

Plitt, Mirko, and François Masselot. 2010. A Productivity test of statistical machine translation post-editing in a typical localisation context. *The Prague Bulletin of Mathematical Linguistics,* 93:7-16.

Tihanyi László and Csaba Oravecz. 2017. First experiments and results in English-Hungarian neural machine translation. *Proceedings of the 13th Conference on Hungarian Computational Linguistics (MSZNY 2017),* Szeged, Hungary, 275-286.

Yamada, Masaru. 2019. The impact of Google Neural Machine Translation on post-editing by student translators. *The Journal of Specialised Translation*, 31:87-106.

Van Brussel, Laura, Arda Tezcan, and Lieve Macken. 2018. A fine-grained error analysis of NMT, PBMT and RBMT output for English-to-Dutch. *Proceedings of the Eleventh International Conference on Language Resources and Evaluation*, May, 3799-3804.

Way, Andy. 2018. Traditional and emerging use-cases for machine translation. In: Joss Moorkens, Sheila Castilho, Federico Gaspari, Stephen Doherty (eds.) *Translation Quality Assessment: From principles to practice.* Springer, Berlin, 159–178.

# Applying Machine Translation to Psychology: Automatic Translation of Personality Adjectives

**Ritsuko Iwai[1,2], Daisuke Kawahara[1], Takatsune Kumada[1,2], Sadao Kurohashi[1]**
[1]Kyoto University / Yoshida Honmachi, Sakyo-ku, Kyoto-shi, 606-8501, Kyoto, JAPAN
[2]RIKEN BSI-TOYOTA Collaboration Center / Hirosawa 1-1, Wako-shi, Saitama, 351-0198, JAPAN
`{ritsuko.iwai,dk,t.kumada,kuro}@i.kyoto-u.ac.jp`

## Abstract

We introduce our approach to apply machine translation to psychology, especially to translate English adjectives in a psychological personality questionnaire. We first extend seed English personality adjectives with a word2vec model trained with web sentences, and then feed the acquired words to a phrase-based machine translation model. We use Moses trained with bilingual corpora that consist of TED subtitles, movie' subtitles and Wikipedia. We collect Japanese translations whose translation probabilities are higher than .01 and filter them based on human evaluations. This resulted in 507 Japanese personality descriptors. We conducted a web-survey ($N$=17,751) and finalized a personality questionnaire. Statistical analyses supported the five-factor structure, reliability and criterion-validity of the newly developed questionnaire. This shows the potential applicability of machine translation to psychology. We discuss further issues related to machine translation application to psychology.

## 1 Introduction

This study introduces an example of the application of machine translation (MT) to psychology for academic research purposes. Translation is a critical part in psychological studies using questionnaires. Developing psychologically equivalent questionnaires across languages and cultures involves careful consideration and requires good knowledge of both the source and target languages and familiarity in psychological theories and concepts. The construction process requires conceptual equivalence as well as semantic equivalence (Herdman et al., 1998). Considering a typical phrase in an English questionnaire, "he is open to experiences," for example, it is not difficult to understand with a proficiency in English, but it is a difficult task to translate this description of personality in simple and intuitively understandable words (semantic equivalence), because "open" in Japanese is not used with abstract words. In addition, the translated items must reflect similar psychological concepts among Japanese respondents (conceptual equivalence).

The lists of English personality adjectives are generally difficult to translate because of their semantic ambiguities. For example, a typical personality adjective, "complex," has four meanings in the online Cambridge English dictionary[1] : Having a lot of different but related parts, being difficult to understand because of relatedness of parts, building, and bad feeling. In addition, multiple translations are listed in the Weblio English-Japanese dictionary[2] for each meaning. In the Japanese version of the Ten Item Personality Inventory (TIPI-J; Oshio et al., 2012), "complex" is translated as "変わった考えを持つ"/having unique ideas. It is difficult to judge to what extent the translation reflects on "complex." Furthermore, "変わった" has nuances of odd and strange in Japanese.

Therefore, it is often difficult to find adequate words that satisfy both conceptual and semantic equivalence. To resolve the issue, we use word embeddings and phrase-based statistical machine translation to translate English personality adjectives into Japanese. We regard a bag of personali-



---

[1] https://dictionary.cambridge.org
[2] https://ejje.weblio.jp

ty related words as covering the concepts. The translated results should reflect the equivalent concepts and semantics.

## 2 Related Work

### 2.1 Big-Five

Big-Five is one of the most widely used frameworks to understand human universal personality (e.g., McCrae and Costa, 1997). It assumes that human individual differences in personality are describable in five broad traits; Extraversion (extraverted, sociable, and talkative), Agreeableness (cooperative, agreeable, and warm), Conscientiousness (self-disciplined, well-prepared, and self-motivated), Neuroticism (anxious and emotional), and Openness-to-Experiences (analytic, creative, and curious)[3].

The framework comes from the lexical approach. Researchers collected adjectives that describe human personality from dictionaries, repeated human evaluations and identified the five-factor structure (e.g., Goldberg, 1992; Norman, 1963).

### 2.2 Translation of Big-Five Questionnaires into Japanese

For Japanese, two previous studies were devoted to obtaining adequate translations of personality adjectives. Wada (1996) listed all the translations of the 300 English personality-like adjectives in Adjective Checklist (Gough and Heilbrun, 1983), referring to an English-Japanese dictionary. She constructed the Big Five Scale (BFS) with 60 items evaluated by university students. Another study was conducted by Oshio et al. (2012). They translated the Ten Item Personality Inventory and evaluated the items five times by means of respondent surveys (TIPI, Gosling et al., 2003). They also asked the original authors if the backward translation appropriately reflected the five original personality concepts. The final Japanese version of the TIPI (TIPI-J) used relatively long and explanatory phrases as translations of simple English adjectives.

### 2.3 Automatic Translation of Personality Adjectives

Ueda et al. (2016) introduced an approach to acquire the Japanese translations of English personality adjectives. They used 20 personality

adjectives derived from TIPI (Gosling et al., 2003) and acquired words related to these adjectives, using a word2vec model trained with 50 million web-sentences. Having personality adjectives in a bilingual corpus, they searched for bilingual corpora and combined the three bilingual corpora, 0.2 million TED subtitles, 1.2 million movie subtitles, and 0.4 million Wikipedia sentences. Iwai et al. (2017) selected 109 candidates from the list by Ueda et al. (2016) and conducted a web-survey with 500 young and 500 older adults. They identified the five-factor structure in both young and older samples. Although they planned to use four words per trait, they found only three words for EX and AG, and two words for CO. The numbers were unsatisfactory to construct a personality questionnaire. In this study, we improve the procedure to acquire the translation candidates and finalize the 20-item personality questionnaire.

## 3 Automatic Translation of Personality Adjectives

In this section, we introduce our method to translate psychological questionnaires.

### 3.1 Preparation for Bilingual Corpus

As a previous study (Ueda et al., 2016), to limit the scope to daily life contexts, we combine the bilingual corpora of TED talks, movie subtitles, and Wikipedia. The size is, however, slightly larger than Ueda et al. (2016), 2.1 million sentences, 0.3 million sentences more; TED[4] (0.2 million sentences), movie subtitles[5] (1.5 million sentences), and Wikipedia (0.4 million sentences, Chu et al., 2016).

### 3.2 Acquisition of Words Similar to Personality Adjectives.

In addition to TIPI (Gosling et al., 2013), we prepare the personality adjectives derived from Goldberg (1992) (Table 1). We feed the English personality adjectives to the word2vec[6] model trained with 50 million English web-sentences. The adjectives are, however, abstract and polysemous, and not necessarily limited to describe personality. We, thus, combine from two to four words to generate the averaged vectors within the same trait, in addition to feeding one adjective to

---

[3] In the following sections, Extraversion is abbreviated as EX, Agreeableness as AG, Conscientiousness as CO, Neuroticism as NE, and Openness-to-Experiences as OP.

[4] https://wit3.fbk.eu
[5] http://diates.lingfil.uu.se
[6] https://code.google.com/p/word2vec

Table 1 *Examples of Personality Adjectives, Related Words, and Phrase-Based Translations*

| Trait | +/- | English | Sim. | Japanese | Prob. | Method |
|---|---|---|---|---|---|---|
| EX | | courageous | .682 | 勇敢だ* | .364 | combination |
| | + | playful | .695 | ふざける | .333 | combination |
| | | talkative | 1.000 | 話し好きだ | .308 | combination |
| | | disconcert | .546 | 当惑* | 1.000 | combination |
| | - | timid | 1.000 | 臆病だ | .375 | individual |
| | | timid | 1.000 | 内気だ | .250 | individual |
| AG | | respectful | .690 | 尊敬 | .333 | combination |
| | + | merciful | .290 | 慈悲深い | .235 | individual |
| | | dignify | .667 | 威厳 | .200 | combination |
| | | arrogant | .731 | 傲慢だ | .235 | combination |
| | - | cynical | .764 | 皮肉だ | .231 | combination |
| | | selfish | 1.000 | 利己的だ | .229 | individual |
| CO | | honest | .657 | 正直だ | .274 | combination |
| | + | trustworthy | .696 | 信頼できる | .254 | combination |
| | | conscientious | 1.000 | 誠実だ | .308 | combination |
| | | insensitive | .712 | 無神経だ | .500 | combination |
| | - | insensitive | .712 | 鈍感だ | .500 | combination |
| | | foolish | .731 | 愚かだ | .345 | combination |
| NE | | unhappy | .755 | 不幸だ | .234 | combination |
| | + | apprehensive | .747 | うろたえる | .200 | combination |
| | | emotional | 1.000 | 感情* | .199 | combination |
| | | restful | .694 | 安らかだ | 1.000 | combination |
| | - | carefree | .668 | のんきだ | .345 | combination |
| | | tolerable | .731 | 我慢 | .345 | combination |
| OP | | inventive | .736 | 独創的だ* | .143 | combination |
| | + | creative | 1.000 | 創造的だ* | .115 | combination |
| | | intelligent | 1.000 | 知的だ* | .111 | combination |
| | | unsophisticated | 1.000 | 浅い | .250 | individual |
| | - | vulgar | .728 | 下品だ | .222 | combination |
| | | simplistic | .783 | 単純だ | .158 | combination |

Note: + = positive; - = negative; Sim. = similarity values of word embeddings; * = the translations that are in Iwai et al. (2017); Prob.=translation probabilities; Sim. 1 = the words in the previous studies (Goldberg, 1992; Gosling et al., 2003); Individual=single word; Combination=combined vectors.

the model and list the related words when cosine similarities are higher than .2. In the case of related words with multiple factors, each word is associated with the trait that has the highest similarity. "Arrogant", for example, is similar to both AG minus and CO minus. In this case, the similarity to AG minus is higher (.783) than CO minus (.354), as such, we associate "arrogant" with AG minus.

As a result, we acquired a total of 200 unique candidate words in total. The list includes the words that are not in either Goldberg (1992) or Gosling et al. (2003), such as courageous, playful, and thoughtful.

### 3.3 Automatic Translation

Referring to Ueda et al. (2016), we also use the phrase-based statistical machine translation system, Moses[7]. Table 1 indicates examples of translation results. Using the bilingual corpora in section 3.1, we developed a phrase table and extracted 728 unique translations of the personality adjectives-related words in the table with more than a .01 translation probability.

**Filtering:** We filter translations and merge variant expressions by using a Japanese morpheme analyzer JUMAN++[8] and a Japanese dependency and case structure analyzer KNP[9]. For filtering, we refer to parts of speech and information in JUMAN++ dictionaries and collect the translations under the conditions of content words, either adjectives, verbs or nouns and are not humans, because conjunctions and dummy nouns are also in the table. Furthermore, this procedure makes it possible to merge expression varieties such as 落ち着く and 落ち着いている into 落ち着く. The procedures result in 631 translations.

**Human evaluations:** In spite of filtering, the automatic filtering fails to exclude translations unrelated to personality. Such translation errors include mainly those presumingly caused by alignment errors. The errors, for example, are 綿花/cotton as the translation of *"indifferent,"* 耳/ear for *"stubborn,"* and 訪米/visit to the United States for *"anxious"*. As a result, we regard 507 translations as personality descriptors (80.3 %).

**Comparisons with previous studies:** Merging the 109 personality descriptors in Iwai et al. (2017) and the above 507 ones results in a total

of 559 unique personality descriptors. A total of 52 personality descriptors are unique in Iwai et al. (2017) and 450 are unique in the current list while 57 personality descriptors are in common. Newly-acquired translations include 積極/ "active" and 陽気だ/ "cheerful" while おとなしい/ "silent" and 内向的だ/ "introverted," for example, do not appear at this time.

The personality descriptor rate is similar to the previous study by Iwai et al. (2017) (81.0%). However, we acquire more varieties of personality descriptors that were not enough in the previous studies.

## 4 Development and Evaluations of a Japanese Personality Questionnaire

To select the twenty-items, we conducted a web-survey and statistical analysis to identify the five-factor structure, calculate reliability, and examine validity. Exploratory Factor Analysis (EFA) is a statistical approach to extract common factors across measured variables based on correlation coefficients (Fabrigar et al., 1999). In constructing a psychological questionnaire, it is important to evaluate reliability and validity. Reliability indicates how responses are reliably produced. Internal consistency assumes that a person tends to similarly answer items within the same trait, which Cronbach's α indicates (Cronbach, 1951). Furthermore, a psychological questionnaire must measure the targeted concepts, which is named as validity. One method to assess validity is criterion-validity. Criterion-validity investigates correlations between the latent variables in the newly constructed questionnaire and the corresponding latent variables in a "criterion" questionnaire. The correlations are expected to be high between similar latent variables and low between unrelated latent variables. We use TIPI-J (Oshio et al., 2012) for this validity evaluation.

### 4.1 Web-Survey

**Participants:** We conducted a web-survey on registrants of the Human Information Database by NTT Data Institute of Management Consulting, Inc in October 2016 ($N$=17,751, *Female*=11,037, *Mean*=49.8 years old, *SD*=13.4).

**Tested Items:** To conduct a web-survey, two psychologists (the first and the third authors) selected and modified the translations into questionnaire-item formats. We had limited resources and only 51 items were testable. In addition to the 18 items from Iwai et al. (2017), we, thus,

---

[7] http://www.statmt.org/moses/

[8] http://nlp.ist.i.kyoto-u.ac.jp/EN/index.php?JUMAN++

[9] http://nlp.ist.i.kyoto-u.ac.jp/EN/index.php?KNP

reviewed the list carefully and selected 33 items acquired from the list in Section 3.3. We basically attempted to choose words that are not in Iwai et al. (2017) and from EX plus (e.g., 陽気だ/ "cheerful" and 積極/ "active"), AG minus (e.g., 横柄だ/ "arrogant" and 傲慢だ/ "arrogant"), CO plus (e.g., 公正だ/ "fair" and 正直だ/ "honest"), NE minus (e.g., 安らかだ/ "peaceful" and のんきだ/ "carefree"), and OP minus (e.g., 単純だ/ "simplistic" and 浅い/ "unsophisticated").

OP minus translations are especially difficult. The OP minus adjectives mainly consist of the adjectives with an "un" prefix. As a result, we have a very limited number of candidate words in OP minus. "浅い," an example of translation of "unsophistication," literally means shallow, is modified into 興味が浅い/ "have an shallow interest."

Participants completed the 51 items, using a seven-point scale from 1= strongly disagree to 7 =strongly agree.

**Ten Item Personality Inventory-Japanese (TIPI-J):** Participants also completed another Big-Five questionnaire, TIPI-J (Gosling et al., 2003; Oshio et al., 2012) using a seven-point scale (EX: $M$= 7.4, $SD$=2.3, $\alpha^{10}$=.49; AG: $M$= 9.5, $SD$=2.0, $\alpha$=.37; CO: $M$= 8.2, $SD$= 2.2, $\alpha$=.51; NE: $M$= 7.9, $SD$=2.1, $\alpha$=.46; OP $M$= 8.0, $SD$=2.1, $\alpha$=.39).

### 4.2    Results

**Selection of twenty-items:** We repeated the exploratory factor analysis (EFA) using a maximum likelihood with robust standard errors method with a geomin rotation[11] to select the twenty items (four items for each factor). Based on the first EFA with the 51 items, we eliminated the 9 items that loaded highly on multiple factors. Next, we conducted the second EFA with the 41 items, reviewed the loading matrix, and selected four items for each trait based on the following standards: An item (1) which loading was over |.50| and (2) the secondary loading did not exceed |.35|. In the cases that a trait failed to acquire four items in reference on the standards, we selected the items by loading. Selecting AG items, however, was not straightforward.  Although  "安らか/peaceful" indicated high load ing in AG, the word caused confusion because it is often used to describe facial expressions or

Table 2 *The Final 20-Items*

| Traits | Items |
| --- | --- |
| EX | 陽気だ (N), 活発だ(C), 積極 (N), 話し好きだ (N) |
| AG | 穏やかだ (N), 協力 (C), 温和だ (O), 同調 (O) |
| CO | 無神経だ (N), 鈍感だ (N), 無責任だ (C), いい加減だ (N) |
| NE | 心配 (C), 自責 (O), 混乱 (C), 感情 (C) |
| OP | 分析 (C), 考察 (O), 独創 (C), 知性 (O), |

Note: O = the words that appear only in Iwai et al. (2017); N = the words that appear only in this study; C = the words in common between Iwai et al. (2017) and the current study.

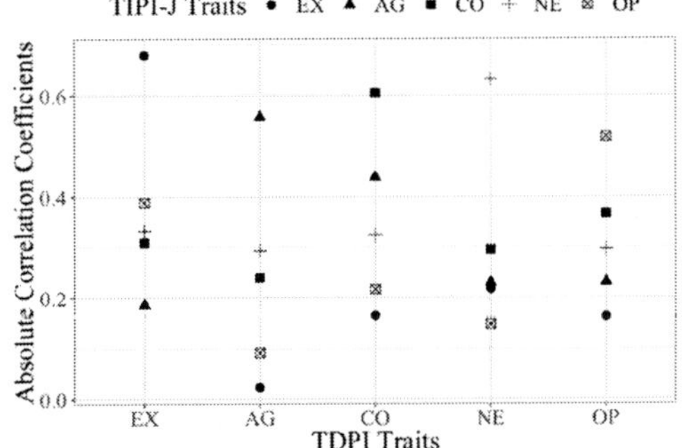


*Figure 1* Correlation coefficients between Trait Descriptors Personality Inventory (TDPI) and Ten Item Personality Inventory-Japanese (TIPI-J).

mood, rather than personality.  "協力的 /cooperative" seemed more acceptable among the other candidates in terms of semantics. We, thus, conducted the two patterns of EFA using the 20 items. The model fit indices were slightly better in the  "安らか/peaceful"  version but had very small differences (CFI[12] = .978 vs. .972, TLI[13]=.958 vs. 947, RMSEA[14]=.029 vs. .033)[15] and the factor loading patterns were similar. We, thus, decided to finalize the 20-items including  "協力的." Table 2 indicates the twenty-words in the items. We name the questionnaire as Trait Descriptors Personality Inventory (TDPI).

**Descriptive Statistics and Reliability:** We calculated descriptive statistics for each trait and internal consistency (EX: $M$= 15.9, $SD$=4.2,

---

[10]  $\alpha$= Cronbach $\alpha$

[11] For details about EFA rotations, please refer to Browne (2001).

[12] Comparative Fit Index

[13] Tucker Lewis Index

[14] Root Mean Square Error of Approximation

[15] The model fit indices are considered as excellent when CFI and TLI > .950, RMSEA < .03 and good when CFI and TLI > .900, RMSEA < .05 (Marsh et al., 2009).

$\alpha$=.82;AG: *M*= 17.8, *SD*=2.0, $\alpha$=.78;CO: *M*= 17.9, *SD*= 4.2, $\alpha$=.79;NE: *M*= 15.9, *SD*=4.2, $\alpha$=.66;OP *M*= 17.8, *SD*=3.4, $\alpha$=.74). Cronbach's $\alpha$s were substantial. The means of correlation coefficients between the traits were quite low (the mean *r*=.22), which indicates that each trait was differentiated from other traits.

**Criterion-validity.** We calculated correlation coefficients of trait scores in TDPI with those in TIPI-J (Figure 1). The means of correlation coefficients between the same traits were high (*r* =.58 ~.68). On the other hand, the means of not-corresponding correlation coefficients were low (*r*=.25). The results indicate that the two questionnaires measure similar psychological factors and differentiate the similar factors from the factors that are hypothesized as different ones.

# 5   Discussion

The results of the web-survey show applicability of MT to psychological studies, i.e., using MT to extracting candidate entries. However, we find three issues which need to be considered.

## 5.1   Limited Resources

The translation probability has a limited role in the procedure. Overall, translation probabilities are relatively low. Only 138 of 631 translations indicate more than a .1 translation probability. Furthermore, most of the errors are alignment errors. Such errors imply that the bilingual corpus does not include enough translations of personality descriptors. The present study focuses on personality. However, there are many psychological questionnaires with English adjectives such as values (Schwartz et al., 2003) and interpersonal relationships (Fletcher et al., 2003). We expect that such contextual matters and not enough resources are the shared issue for those who are interested in using MT in practical usage.

## 5.2   Replicability and Stability

While this study indicates applicability to questionnaire development in psychology, it entails the issue of replicability and stability due to choices of a mono-lingual corpus for word embeddings. Our study uses the same size corpus for word embeddings as Iwai et al. (2017) did. However, 47.2 % of the translations are not replicated in the current study. Out of the final 20 items, the 5 items are in the previous study, the 7 items only from this study, and 8 items are in common.

Inconsistent replicability is not due to translation. Our procedure is phrase-based and we use the extended bilingual corpus of Iwai et al. (2017). Even if we ignore translation probabilities and review all the results, many of them are not in the list. This indicates that different personality adjectives-related words were fed into Moses, because all the phrases in English are aligned to the particular phrases in Japanese. However, the translations peculiar in the previous studies are also good as personality descriptors and some of them remain as the final items.

As the current study suggests, it is better to acquire substantial candidates with limited resources as in Section 5.1 and it is better to repeat the procedures.

## 5.3   Expert Knowledge

The two previous issues are all solved by using the psychologists' expert knowledge. The previous studies (Iwai et al., 2017; Ueda et al., 2016) and this study demonstrate that word embeddings and MT allow researchers to collect personality-related English words and Japanese translation candidates and such candidates are tolerable to use as psychological items with expert knowledge. On the other hand, it is still just at the beginning of the step to implement MT into psychological studies. It is highly appreciated that the manual parts are reduced and replaced with technical improvements in NLP and MT.

# 6   Conclusions

MT allowed us to collect candidates of Japanese personality descriptors. We manage to construct a new personality questionnaire that consists of only MT-extracted words. To the best of our knowledge, this is the only personality measurement developed using Natural Language Processing (NLP) techniques such as word embeddings and phrase-based statistical MT. The questionnaire is practically usable in psychological studies. The study provides evidence to extend applicability of MT to another research field. On the other hand, the expert knowledge is critical, at least, in the target language and culture, to design a questionnaire and items. Such experts' efforts are expected to be reduced with more adequate parallel corpora and further examination to justify word embeddings.

## References

Michael W. Browne. 2001. An Overview of Analytic Rotation in Exploratory Factor Analysis. *Multivariate Behavioral Research*, 36(1):111–150.

Chenhui Chu, Toshiaki Nakazawa, and Sadao Kurohashi. 2016. Integrated Parallel Sentence and Fragment Extraction from Comparable Corpora. *ACM Transactions on Asian and Low-Resource Language Information Processing*, 15(2):10–22.

Lee J. Cronbach. 1951. Coefficient Alpha and the Internal Structure of Tests. *Psychometrika*, 16(3):297–334.

Leandre R. Fabrigar, Duane T. Wegener, Erin J. Strahan, and Robert C. MacCallum. 1999. Evaluating the Use of Exploratory Factor Analysis in Psychological Research. *Psychological Assessment*, 4(3):272–299.

Garth J. O. Fletcher, Jeffry A. Simpson, and Geoff Thomas. 2000. The Measurement of Perceived Relationship Quality Components: A Confirmatory Factor Analytic Approach. *Personality and Social Psychology Bulletin*, 26(3):340–354.

Lewis R. Goldberg. 1992. The Development of Markers for the Big-Five Factor Structure. *Psychological Assessment*, 4(1):26–42.

Samuel D. Gosling, Peter J. Rentfrow, and William B. Swann Jr. 2003. A Very Brief Measure of the Big-Five Personality Domains. *Journal of Research in Personality*, 37(6):504–528.

Harrison G. Gough and Alfred B. Heilbrun. 1983. *The Adjective Check List Manual*. Consulting Psychologists Press, Palo Alto, 1983 edition.

Michael Herdman, Julia Fox-Rushby, and Xavier Badia. 1998. A Model of Equivalence in the Cultural Adaptation of HRQoL Instruments: The Universalist Approach. *Quality of Life Research*, 7(4):323–335.

Ritsuko Iwai, Takatsune Kumada, Daisuke Kawahara, and Sadao Kurohashi. 2017. Translating Big-Five Personality Constructs from English to Japanese, Using Statistical Machine Translation. Poster session presented at *the18th Annual Meeting of Society for Personality and Social Psychology*, San Antonio, U.S.A.

Herbert W. Marsh, Bengt Muthén, Tihomir Asparouhov, Oliver Lüdtke, Alexander Robitzsch, Alexandre J. S. Morin, and Ulrich Trautwein. 2009. Exploratory Structural Equation Modeling, Integrating CFA and EFA: Application to Students' Evaluations of University Teaching. *Structural Equation Modeling: A Multidisciplinary Journal*, 16(3):439–476.

Robert R. McCrae and Paul T. Jr. Costa. 1997. Personality Trait Structure as a Human Universal. *American Psychologist*, 52(5):509–516.

Atsushi Oshio, Shingo Abe, and Pino Cutrone. 2012. Development, Reliability, and Validity of the Japanese Version of Ten Item Personality Inventory (TIPI-J). *The Japanese Journal of Personality*, 21(1):40–52.

Shalom H. Schwartz, Gila Melech, Arielle Lehmann, Steven Burgess, Mari Harris, and Vicki Owens. 2001. Extending the Cross-Cultural Validity of the Theory of Basic Human Values with a Different Method of Measurement. *Journal of Cross-Cultural Psychology*, 32(5):519–542.

Shinpei Ueda, Daisuke Kawahara, Sadao Kurohashi, Ritsuko Iwai, and Takatsune Kumada. Automatic Translation of English Personality Adjectives into Japanese. In *Proceedings of 22nd Annual Meeting of Natural Language Processing*, Sendai, Japan 282–285.

Sayuri Wada. 1996. Construction of the Big Five Scales of Personality Trait Terms and Concurrent Validity with NPI. *The Japanese Journal of Psychology*, 67(1):61–67.

# Evaluating machine translation in a low-resource language combination: Spanish-Galician


**María do Campo Bayón**
Grup Tradumàtica
Universitat Autònoma de Barcelona
`maria.docampo@e-campus.uab.cat`

**Pilar Sánchez-Gijón**
Grup Tradumàtica
Dept. de Traducció i d'Interpretació i
d'Estudis de l'Àsia Oriental
Universitat Autònoma de Barcelona
`pilar.sanchez.gijon@uab.cat`



## Abstract

This paper reports the results of a study designed to assess the perception of adequacy of three different types of machine translation systems within the context of a minoritized language combination (Spanish-Galician). To perform this evaluation, a mixed design with three different metrics (BLEU, survey and error analysis) is used to extract quantitative and qualitative data about two marketing letters from the energy industry translated with a rule-based system (RBMT), a phrase-based system (PBMT) and a neural system (NMT). Results show that in the case of low-resource languages rule-based and phrase-based machine translations systems still play an important role.


## 1 Introduction

In the last couple of years, Neural Machine Translation is gaining more attention in the translation industry and becoming more popular thanks to the considerably good results obtained in certain language combinations. Nevertheless, low-resource languages and minoritized languages represent some challenges for machine translation (MT) usage and training. This paper describes the process followed to test and evaluate three different MT systems in a closely related language combination such as Spanish-Galician.

## 2 Aim of this study

This study aims to determine which type of MT system (RBMT, PBMT or NMT) is perceived as more adequate in the context of a minoritized language such as Galician in an MT+Post-editing (PE) workflow. For that purpose, the quality of all three raw outputs was established with the following metrics:

- Evaluating which type of MT system obtains better results applying the BLEU metric.
- Evaluating which type of MT system obtains better results in a human evaluation (quality perception survey conducted among professional post-editors).
- Evaluating which type of MT system obtains better results following an error analysis framework (MQM).

## 3 Background

### 3.1 NMT Evaluation

With the outbreak of NMT, many studies have tried to shed some light on the real and the perceived quality of this kind of MT systems. Shterionov et al. (2018) show that a few translators see NMT as a booster of their productivity. Some translators even see (N)MT as a handicap for their productivity while others perceive it the other way around (Sánchez-Gijón et al., 2019). In terms of NMT quality perception, Castilho et al. (2017) conclude that raw NMT segments may not be preferred by translators. In the same paper, they concluded that, compared to PBMT, NMT represents a step forward but it implies also some limitations. The same idea of strengths and weaknesses on NMT with respect to PBMT can be found in Popovic, 2017. Most of these studies describe tests involving language combinations of high-resource languages. This paper approaches this topic from the perspective of a low-resource language: Galician.

### 3.2 MT in Galician

As a minoritized language, Galician represents a serious challenge to develop MT systems due to the lack of technological and data resources. In recent years, there has been an enormous effort, mainly from the academic community, to develop Natural Language Processing (NLP) resources and compile corpora such as GalNet, the Galician WordNet (Gomez Guinovart & Solla Portela, 2017), SemCor (Solla Portela & Gomez Guinovart, 2017), several terminology projects (Solla Portela & Gomez Guinovart, 2015), big corpus annotation (Gomez Guinovart & Lopez Fernández, 2009), Freeling (Padro & Stanilovsky, 2012) and Linguakit (Gamallo & Garcia, 2017).

There are also some MT systems specifically created for Galician: the RBTA MT system of the *Centro Ramón Piñeiro para a Investigación en Humanidades* (Diz Gamallo, 2001), OpenTrad Apertium (Armentano-Oller & Forcada, 2006) and Carvalho PBMT system (Pichel Campos et al., 2009).

Nevertheless, the need to keep investigating in NLP and Deep Learning (DL) in Galician is very clear in order to develop the corpora and the strategies needed to train phrase-based and neural systems and obtain better results (Agerri et al., 2018: 2322).

## 4 Methodology

The investigation is divided into three different phases. The first one consisted of choosing the source document to be processed by the three different MT systems. Two marketing letters of approximately 500 words in total with specific terminology from the energy industry were chosen. After that, RBMT (OpenTrad Apertium) and PBMT (ModernMT v. 2.5) systems were created and trained. In the case of Apertium, the stable version of the pair Spanish-Galician was downloaded into an Ubuntu environment and trained with specific terminology of the source field. Similarly, a new engine was created in MMT v. 2.5 and trained with a thematic translation memory (TM) of 4315 translation units and a parallel corpus of 6 million words from the legal and administrative field. Lastly, regarding NMT system, due to the lack of enough high-quality training data, we selected Google Neural Spanish-Galician engine to perform the texts.

Once all three MT systems in the language combination Spanish-Galician were available, a set of 32 Spanish segments was translated with each of them. The quality of the raw MT segments obtained was measured in the next phase of the investigation following different approaches.

The second phase of the investigation involved the evaluation of the quantitative data results obtained applying the automatic metric Bilingual Evaluation Understudy, abbreviated as BLEU (Papineri et al., 2001). Then, a survey was designed to compile qualitative information about the quality perception of Spanish-Galician post-editors. For that purpose, a sample of 14 segments from the whole set was used. 69 professional translators with experience in Spanish-Galician post-editing were selected from the CPSL Language Solutions resource database and Proz portal. Finally, 15 people participated in that survey. To complete the qualitative results, an error analysis was performed following the MQM framework. Once all the individual results were analysed, a global evaluation was performed to triangulate the resulting data.

## 5 Results

### 5.1 Automatic evaluation

The BLEU score on the whole set of segments is as follows:

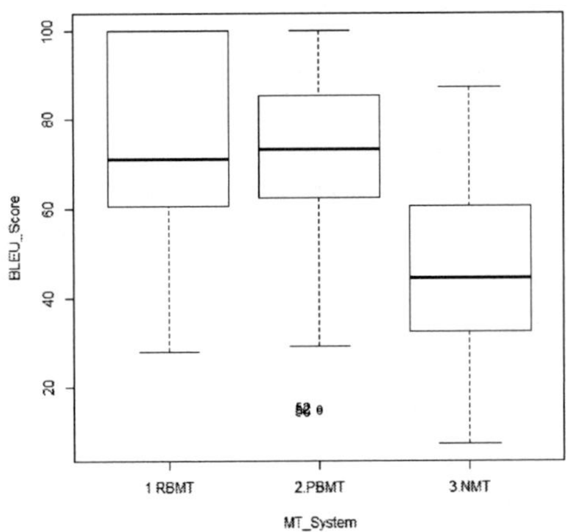

*Figure 1. BLEU Score*

RBMT and PBMT segments show higher scores than NMT. There is not significant difference between RBMT and PBMT scores, but differences are significant between these two systems and NMT:

|      | RBMT   | PBMT   | NMT     |
|------|--------|--------|---------|
| RBMT | 1      | 0.831  | **<0.0001** |
| PBMT | 0.831  | 1      | **0.000**   |
| NMT  | **<0.001** | **0.0004** | 1       |

*Figure 2. p-values per pairs*

Finally, 14 of the source segments contains more than 30 words. These segments were identified as long segments and analysed separately. This is the BLUE score obtained in the subset of 14 long segments analysed by post-editors:

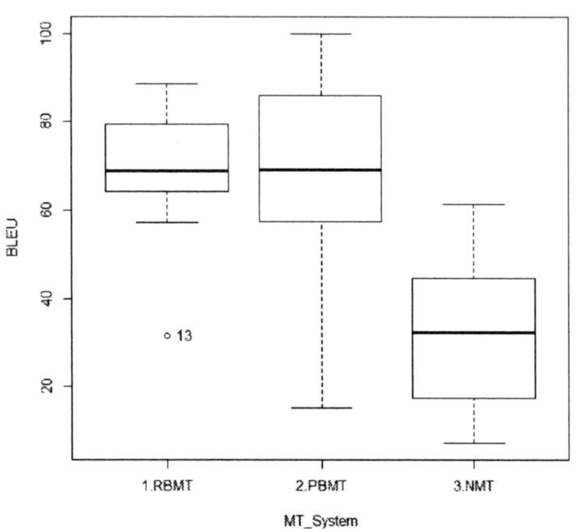

*Figure 3. BLEU Score of long segments*

RBMT segments show higher and more homogeneous scores than NMT and PBMT. Differences between NMT and both PBMT and RBMT are significant. Differences between PBMT and RBMT are not significant:

|      | RBMT   | PBMT   | NMT     |
|------|--------|--------|---------|
| RBMT | 1      | 1.000  | **0,0002** |
| PBMT | 0.831  | 1      | **0.004**  |
| NMT  | **0.0002** | **0.004** | 1       |

*Figure 4. p-values per pairs in long segments*

## 5.2 Human evaluation

The human evaluation was designed to gather two different pieces of information segment by segment: ranking of MT system and which MT system is considered good enough to be post-edited. 14 translated segments, one by each MT system, were selected as sample. Equal translation results from different MT systems or too bad translations were excluded from the survey in order not to distort the survey results.

### 5.2.1 Global evaluation

Human evaluators were asked to answer 2 questions. In each question, they had to rank the three different raw machine translations as 1st, 2nd and 3rd place. Then, they had to specify if they would use or not the machine translation to post-edit (binary response). In relation with BLEU scores, the results of usable/not usable segments show that RBMT and PBMT would be used to be post-edited.

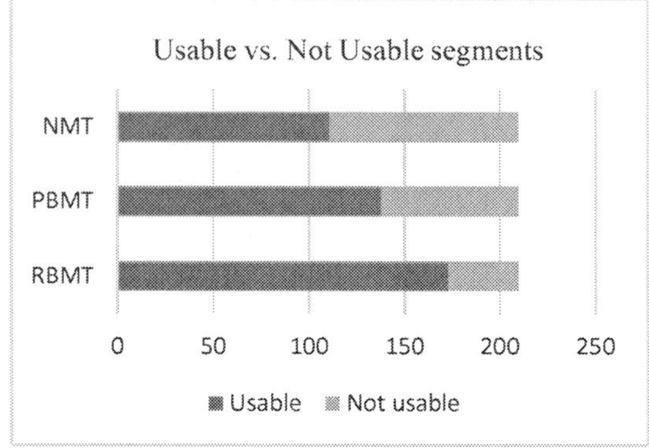

*Figure 5. Segments usable vs. not usable to post-edit*

To analyse this data, the non-parametric statistical test Cochran 's Q test is applied.

| Variable | Categories | Frequencies | %      |
|----------|------------|-------------|--------|
| RBMT     | 0          | 37          | 17.619 |
|          | 1          | 173         | 82.381 |
| PBMT     | 0          | 72          | 34.286 |
|          | 1          | 138         | 65.714 |
| NMT      | 0          | 99          | 47.143 |
|          | 1          | 111         | 52.857 |

| | |
|---|---|
| C (Observed value) | 42.014 |
| C (Critical value) | 5.991 |
| FD | 2 |
| **p-value** | **<0.0001** |
| Alfa | 0.05 |

*Figure 6. Cochran's Q test results*

Differences are significant (p-value < 0.0001). Proportions among the three groups are statistically significant (Marascuilo procedure):

| Contrast | Value | Critical Value | Significance |
|----------|-------|----------------|--------------|
| \|p(RBMT − p(PBMT)\| | 0.167 | 0.103 | Yes |
| \|p(RBMT − p(NMT)\|  | 0.295 | 0.106 | Yes |
| \|p(PBMT − p(NMT)\|  | 0.129 | 0.116 | Yes |

*Figure 7. Marascuilo procedure results*

And the proportions show that the three groups are different:

| Sample | Proportion | Groups | | |
|---|---|---|---|---|
| NMT | 0.529 | A | | |
| PBMT | 0.657 | | B | |
| RBMT | 0.824 | | | C |

*Figure 8. Proportions of MT systems*

Regarding the ranking, these are the results from each segment. As Figure 9 shows, RBMT and PBMT are better positioned that NMT. Post-editors also agreed that all segments selected as 1st place would be used to post-edit.

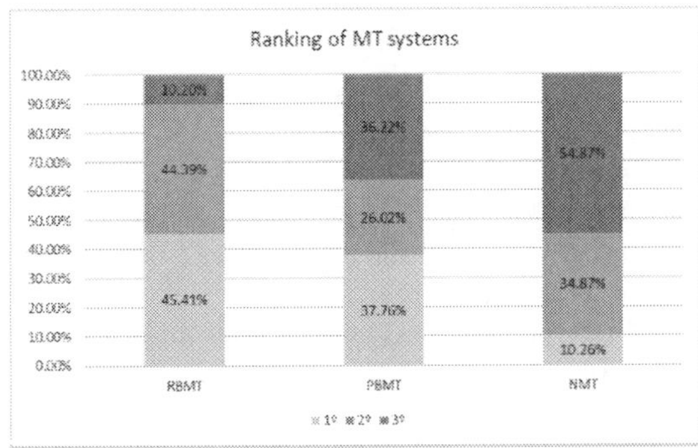

*Figure 9. Ranking of MT systems*

To establish whether these differences among MT systems are significant, the Kruskal-Wallis test was applied. Comparing results per pairs, in all cases p-value was under 0.05, meaning that differences are significant.

### 5.2.2 Long segments

Four of the source segments contains more than 30 words. These segments were identified as long segments and analysed separately.

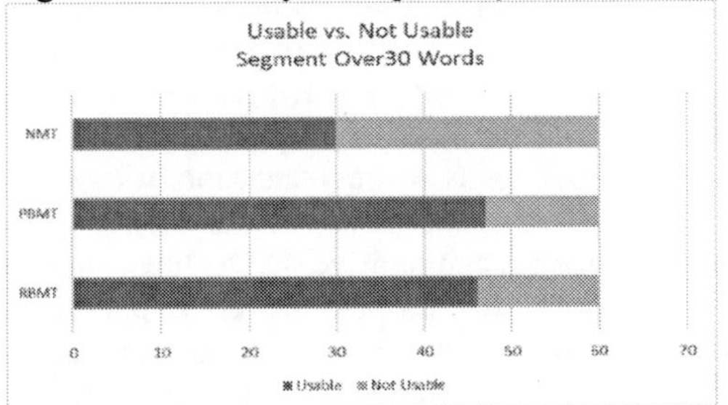

Figure 10. Usable vs. not usable in long segments

To analyse this data, the non-parametric statistical test Cochran 's Q test is applied.

| Variable | Categories | Frequencies | % |
|---|---|---|---|
| RBMT | 0 | 14 | 23.333 |
| | 1 | 46 | 76.667 |
| PBMT | 0 | 13 | 21.667 |
| | 1 | 47 | 78.333 |
| NMT | 0 | 30 | 50.000 |
| | 1 | 30 | 50.000 |

| | |
|---|---|
| C (Observed value) | 15.167 |
| C (Critical value) | 5.991 |
| FD | 2 |
| **p-value** | **0.001** |
| Alfa | 0.05 |

*Figure 11. Cochran's Q test results in long segments*

Differences are significant (p-value = 0.001). Proportions are statistically significant, but not among all three groups (Marascuilo procedure):

And the proportions show that there are differences between NMT and the other two MT systems:

| Contrast | Value | Critical Value | Significance |
|---|---|---|---|
| \|p(RBMT − p(PBMT)\| | 0.017 | 0.187 | No |
| \|p(RBMT − p(NMT)\| | 0.267 | 0.207 | Yes |
| \|p(PBMT − p(NMT)\| | 0.283 | 0.205 | Yes |

*Figure 12. Marascuilo procedure results in long segments*

| Sample | Proportion | Groups | |
|---|---|---|---|
| NMT | 0.500 | A | |
| PBMT | 0.767 | | B |
| RBMT | 0.783 | | B |

*Figure 13. Proportions in long segments*

Usable scenario in long segments differs from the whole document. Figure 14 shows which segment from each MT system would be chosen to be post-edited in 1st, 2nd and 3rd place.

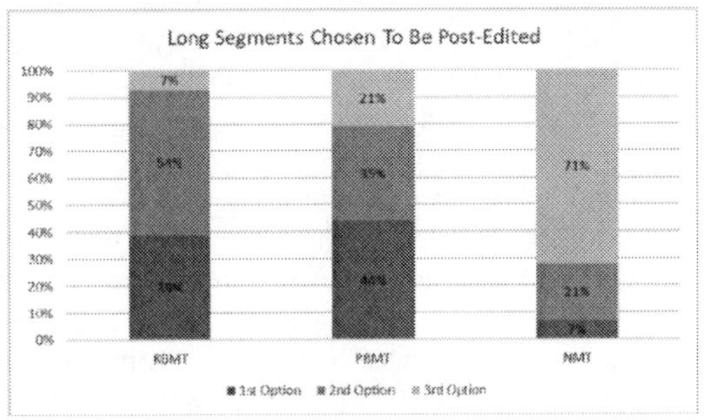

*Figure 14. Ranking of MT systems in long segments*

To establish whether these differences among MT systems are significant, the Kruskal-Wallis test was applied. Comparing results per pairs, the p-value was under 0.05 only between NMT and the other to MT systems:

|      | RBMT | PBMT | NMT |
|------|------|------|-----|
| RBMT |      | No   | **Yes** |
| PBMT | No   |      | **Yes** |
| NMT  | **Yes** | **Yes** |  |

*Figure 15. Statistical differences in long segments*

### 5.3 Error analysis

A Multidimensional Quality Metrics (MQM) customized framework was used to identify the errors made by each MT system. Only relevant types of errors from accuracy, fluency, style and terminology were selected. Figure 16 shows the total number of errors obtained per segment in each MT system:

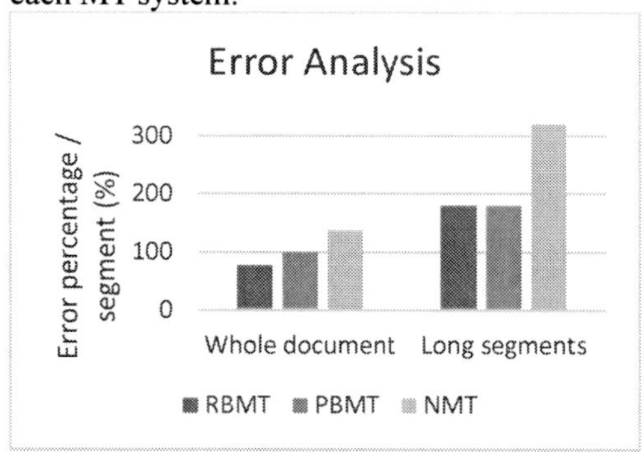


*Figure 16. Error percentage per segment*

Regarding the type of errors, there's a clear prevalence in all MT systems of mistranslations, gender and number agreement errors, function-words errors, word-order errors and unidiomatic expressions. Also, PBMT and NMT made more addition, omission, orthography, typography and part-of-speech errors, and domain terminology inconsistencies. RBMT and NMT registered verb concordance errors and awkward constructions. Finally, the only system with register errors was NMT.

The clearest example of error in RBMT is the wrong identification of the preposition *para* (*for*, in English) and the undefined feminine form of the article: *una* (*a* in English). RBMT interprets these words as verbs so they are translated as *parar* (*stop*) and *unir* (*join*). PBMT sometimes makes errors in verbal constructions such as the wrong translation of *hemos venido* by *comezamos viñesen (we started coming* instead of *we have come*).

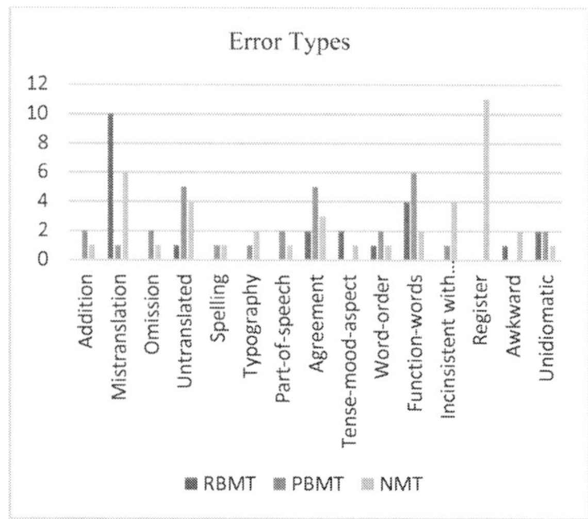


*Figure 17. Error types*

Finally, a repetitive error in NMT is the change of register. In this phrase, not only the verbal form is incorrect but also changes from the second person plural to the singular even if it is the same in the source text:

Spanish: Instala ahora el gas y disfruta de todas sus ventajas […] en todos los rincones de tu casa

*Galician:* Agora *instálalle* [incorrect verbal construction] *o gas e goce* [second person plural] *de todas as súas* [second person plural] *[…] en todos os recunchos da túa* [second person singular] *casa.*

## 6    Conclusions

The main conclusion is that although NMT seems promising in frequent language combinations, especially if English is involved, it is not obtaining the desired results in low-resource languages such as the pair Spanish-Galician. NMT has not yet unseated RBMT and PBMT, performing, in fact, worse than these systems.

This small study reveals that more tests should be done to replicate results and evaluate special needs to have a competitive NMT. Subsequent investigations must consolidate error patterns of each system to address some of the most prominent issues. Thus, there's a clear need to work in the access to the resources and parallel data needed to train MT systems, especially in PBMT and NMT.

Consequently, any future lines of investigation in MT and minoritized languages should be focused on searching and optimizing NLP and text resources.

## Acknowledgement

This work was supported by the ProjecTA-U project "Machine Translation Users", grant number FFI2016-78612-R [MINECO / FEDER, UE].

## References

Agerri, R., Gómez Guinovart, X., Rigau, G. & Solla Portela, M. A. 2018. Developing New Linguistic Resources and Tools for the Galician Language. *Proceedings of the 11th Language Resources and Evaluation Conference (LREC'18)*: 2322-2325.

Armentano-Oller, C. & Forcada, M. L. 2006. Open-source machine translation between small languages: Catalan and Aranese Occitan. *Strategies for developing machine translation for minority languages (5th SALTMIL workshop on Minority Languages)*. May 22-28, p. 51-54.

Armentano-Oller, C., Carrasco, R. C., Corbí-Bellot, A. M., Forcada, M. L., Ginestí-Rosell, M., Ortiz-Rojas, S. et al. 2006. Open-source Portuguese-Spanish machine translation. In *Computational Processing of the Portuguese Language: 7th Workshop on Computational Processing of Written and Spoken Portuguese*, PROPOR. Lecture Notes in Artificial Intelligence 3960. Springer-Verlag, 50–59.

Burchardt, A. & Lommel, A. 2014. *Practical Guidelines for the Use of MQM in Scientific Research on Translation Quality*. Available at <http://www.qt21.eu/downloads/MQM-usage-guidelines.pdf >.

Castilho, S., Moorkens, J., Gaspari, F., Calixto, I., Tinsley, J., & Way, A. 2017. Is Neural Machine Translation the New State of the Art? In *The Prague Bulletin of Mathematical Linguistics*, 108:1, 109–120. <https://doi.org/10.1515/pralin-2017-0013>.

Diz Gamallo, I. 2001. The importance of MT for the survival of minority languages: Spanish-Galician MT system. *Proceedings of MT Summit VIII*, November 2001, Spain.

Gamallo, P. & Garcia, M. 2017. Linguakit: a multilingual tool for linguistic analysis and information extraction. *Linguamática*, 9(1): 19–28.

Gómez Guinovart, X. & López Fernández, S. 2009. Anotación morfosintáctica do Corpus Técnico do Galego. *Linguamática*, 1(1): 61–71.

Gómez Guinovart, X. & Solla Portela, M. A. 2017. Building the galician wordnet: methods and applications. *Language Resources and Evaluation*, 52 (1): 317–339.

Iglesias, G., Rodríguez Liñares, L., Rodríguez Banga, E., Campillo Díaz, F. L. & Méndez Pazó, F. 2010. Perspectivas de la traducción automática castellano-gallego mediante técnicas estadísticas y por transferencia. *IV Jornadas en Tecnología del Habla*, November 8-10 of 2006, Zaragoza. pp. 111-116.

Padró, L. & Stanilovsky, E. 2012. Freeling 3.0: Towards wider multilinguality. In Nicoletta Calzolari et al. (Eds.). *Proceedings of the Eighth International Conference on Language Resources and Evaluation (LREC-2012)*, pp. 2473–2479, Istanbul, Turkey.

Papineni, K., Roukos, S., Ward, T. & Zhu, W. 2001. *BLEU: A Method for Automatic Evaluation of Machine Translation*, IBM Research Report RC22176 (W0109−022).

Popović, M. 2017. Comparing Language Related Issues for NMT and PBMT between German and English. *The Prague Bulletin of Mathematical Linguistics*, 108(1): 209-220.

Pichel Campos, J. R., Malvar Fernández, P., Senra Gómez, O., Gamallo Otero, P. & García González, A. 2009. Carvalho: English-Galician SMT system from EuroParl English-Portuguese parallel corpus. *Procesamiento del Lenguaje Natural*, 23: 379-381.

Sánchez-Gijón, P., Moorkens, J., & Way, A. (2019). Post-editing neural machine translation versus translation memory segments. *Machine Translation*, 31-59. <https://doi.org/10.1007/s10590-019-09232-x>.

Shterionov, D., Superbo, R., Nagle, P., Casanellas, L., O'Dowd, T. & Way, A. (2018). Human versus automatic quality evaluation of NMT and PBSMT. *Machine Translaiton*, 32, 217–235. <https://doi.org/10.1007/s10590-018-9220-z>.

Solla Portela, M. A. & Gómez Guinovart, X. 2015. Termonet: Construcción de terminologías a partir de WordNet y corpus especializados. *Procesamiento del Lenguaje Natural*, 55:165–168.

Solla Portela, M. A. & Gómez Guinovart, X. 2016. Dbpedia del gallego: recursos y aplicaciones en procesamiento del lenguaje. *Procesamiento del Lenguaje Natural*, 57:139–142.

Solla Portela, M. A. & Gómez Guinovart, X. 2017. Diseño y elaboración del corpus SemCor del gallego anotado semánticamente con wordnet 3.0. *Procesamiento del Lenguaje Natural*, 59:137–140.

# MTPE in Patents: A Successful Business Story


**Valeria Premoli**
Aglatech14 S.p.A
vpremoli@aglatech14.it

**Elena Murgolo**
Aglatech14 S.p.A
emurgolo@aglatech14.it

**Diego Cresceri**
Creative Words
diego.cresceri@creative-words.com



## Abstract

This paper illustrates how we successfully implemented MTPE in our workflow and how the decision of having our own engine turned out to be decisive. After having compared different solutions, we decided to choose an MT provider that could train an engine on our behalf with our material (TMs and glossary in the field of mechanics) to translate patents upon customers' request. After the training, we tested the new engine to evaluate the MT output. Because the quality was so good, we decided to create an in-house team of post-editors, coordinated by one of our senior translators. Due to the increasing request from some of our customers, we needed also some external post-editors to count on, so we contacted an LSP specialized in post-editing and we offered them training in patents post-editing. The challenge for the future is to involve more freelancers and to be able to overcome the resistance that many of them still have towards Machine Translation.


## 1   Introduction

Up until a few years ago, machine translation (Machine Translation, MT) technology was still at a stage in which its commercial deployment was not possible. In most fields, Rule-based and Statistical MT, up to Hybrid MT, were not precise enough and the post-editing phase was always deemed too time-consuming and resource-intensive to be used in LSPs and companies in general. This scenario changed completely with the introduction of Neural MT.

Suddenly, language providers around the world found themselves facing a growing request for post-editing services, especially in the areas where light post-editing was a feasible option.

However, in the field of Intellectual Property, customers still tend to request Human Translation, probably worried that MTPE will not meet the required standards in terms of accuracy and precision.

Only relatively recently, about two years ago, we were asked to start post-editing texts in the mechanics field and we were faced with a new challenge, since at the time we had never done MTPE and we didn't know how to proceed.

We committed to find the best way to satisfy our customers' needs and decided to create our own customized engine.

The challenges we had in front of us were the selection of an MT provider that could provide an engine with a good enough output to be implemented without causing production losses; the training of an in-house team, the so-called "Tech Team", to make the most of this new technology; and the training of external resources to face the growing volumes of MTPE requests.

## 2   Data Collection

Our company is specialized in the translation of patents. The two main areas in which we work are Mechanics and Life Sciences, with many subfields such as Automotive, Biology, Medical devices, Chemistry and so on. Some of our customers started to express an interest in MT and asked us if we were able to offer Post-Editing services in order to reduce costs and above all turnaround times.

Therefore, we decided to explore the options offered by the market. Our first choice has been to train our own engine with a popular MT provider. At that time, though, we were completely new to this and we didn't have the required knowledge to do that, also because we didn't have a person that could work full-time on this project. We decided then to opt for a provider that could train an engine on our behalf using the materials we could provide. The mechanics field has been our first choice because the volumes we received from said customers were high and we thought that the training of new resources could be easier in this field than in the Life Sciences one. We collected all the material we had in order to send it to the provider, and then exported all the Translation Memories concerning such field in .tmx format (Automotive, Devices, Mechanics, Electronic Consumer, Electronics, Medical Devices). Due to the amount of TUs provided, we were offered the opportunity to go for a PNMT specialization. Besides the Translation Memories, we also exported our Termbase (which covers different domains) filtering only the mechanics related terms. The engine has been trained within a month and after this period we have been able to deploy it and to start using it in a test phase, called Proof of Concept.

## 3 PoC

Once the new engine had been trained with the material we provided and with few additional documents, the service provider offered us a two-week testing period (PoC – Proof of Concept). The two main objectives were to test the environmental setup of the CAT tool integrated API, and the quality of the trained engine.

We received a short briefing at the beginning of the test period and were in regular contact with the support team of the service provider. Then, we scheduled a wrap-up call to report our findings, after which the engine was fully deployed for the mechanical and electrotechnical patents that required MT translation and post-editing.

### 3.1 Connecting the Engine

The plug-in for our CAT tool of choice is structured to combine TMs' results up to a certain fuzzy threshold, which can be set by the user based on the particular requirements of each project, and the automatic translation of all remaining segments, namely those with either no results from the TMs or with fuzzy percentages inferior to such threshold.

The results, be it fuzzy matches or automatic translation, is applied to the file to be translated after a pre-translation to be launched either during the creation of the project or in a second, separate step. The text will then appear in the CAT's editor as a fully translated text with different colour coding to show the origin of each translated segment (fuzzy or AT).

One of the main problems is that, in case of a mismatch between the threshold of look-up match for the TM concordance search and the value for MT translation, the CAT is unable to insert the AT during the pre-translation step. Although the issue was partially solved by matching the two values, the solution was only satisfactory to a limited extent, and it appears to have been solved only in later versions of the plug-in.

### 3.2 MT Output Evaluation

The crucial issue during the PoC was to establish whether the MT raw output's quality was high enough to constitute a solid base for a substantial increase in productivity.

To this end, two translators with previous patent translation and proofreading experience were appointed to the testing, one full-time, the other on a 4-hours-a-day basis.

A feedback form was provided to monitor the type, frequency, and severity of the mistakes in the output. It was mainly focused on finding out what kind of mistakes were present in the translation and which of these could have a feasible solution to be implemented on our side, or by the service provider.

Severity was scaled from 0 to 3 (0 = Not understandable, 1= hardly understandable, 2= understandable, 3= good).

As it turned out, the quality was very high, with only ten not understandable segments in the course of nine projects (about 48,000 words), and six hardly understandable ones. These fifteen segments received a low score because of grammatical errors of various kind (concordance masculine-feminine, singular-plural, etc.), because of a too literal translation, or because the machine "guessed" words it had never encountered before, creating non-existing, half translated compounds.

We found very few punctuation mistakes, mostly added spaces.

All in all, however, the most troubling issue was, and still is, the fact that single terms are not translated consistently throughout the translation. In the strictly regulated field of patents, where the consistency of the translation is of the foremost importance, also from a legal point of view, the translation of a single term with different equivalents in the target language leads to a huge waste of time and cognitive resources on the part of the post-editor.

Moreover, since Italian is an inflecting language, the replacement of such wrongly translated words turned out to be very time-consuming.

Unfortunately, this issue still has no satisfactory solution, even though Glossaries offer a partial improvement (however, glossaries seem to work on a 'search and replace' basis, namely the engine translates the whole text, automatically choosing the Italian equivalent, and then forces the term from the glossary of choice on the target text, thus creating masculine-feminine concordance mistakes. Also, once a term was inserted in a glossary, the machine was not able to automatically apply the respective singular or plural forms or to decline verbs).

## 4 Tech Team

To maximise the engine's profitability, it was decided to create an in-house team of full-time post-editors to process all the PE requests from various clients.

### 4.1 Recruitment of the Team

The choice of the team in such a project is crucial. As a future-oriented company, we are aware that MT and PE in our industry are not only the future, but already the present. At the same time, we understand that many freelancers are reluctant to try it out and fear that machines will take their place. This is why we have decided to create an in-house team with new people, instead of outsourcing post-editing (at least during this first phase). We decided to look for newly graduated, tech-oriented translators, with the idea that they could have fewer prejudices and less resistance towards Machine Translation. We re-allocated one internal resource, who, together with three other people we hired, formed the so-called "Tech Team", namely a group of full-time in-house post-editors. Also, one of the in-house translators was appointed as coordinator for the project and had the task of coordinating the post-editing team and manage any possible technical issue that came up, possibly by keeping in contact with the provider's support service.

### 4.2 Training

The initial training of our internal team was a practical explanation by the two translators who had tested the engine during the PoC step.

Based on actual projects to be then delivered to clients, the new post-editors were shown both the technical aspects of the CAT tool interface, and the linguistic issues connected with the MT output.

All our in-house PE staff was simultaneously trained in post-editing and in patent translation, creating a very practical learning environment. Instead of generic notions about PE in general, they learned "on the field" how to apply their linguistic and proofreading skills to such a technical field.

After a couple of months of use, we scheduled a training session by an external expert who, based on the results of a few short tests carried out by the in-house post-editors, created a training program for the company's management and employees.

The test that the in-house post-editors performed was a Human Evaluation Test, focused on fluency and accuracy, scored based on type and frequency of errors. The results showed an outstanding performance by the MT engine.

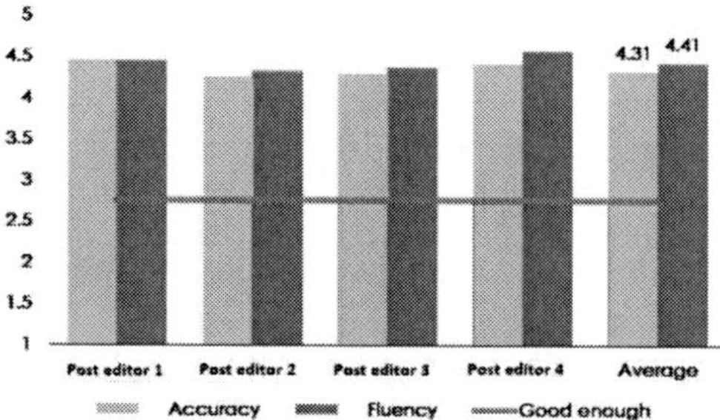


Figure 1. Fluency and Accuracy Performance of the Mechanical Engine.

As we expected, terminology errors were the most frequent, followed by mistranslations and inconsistencies.

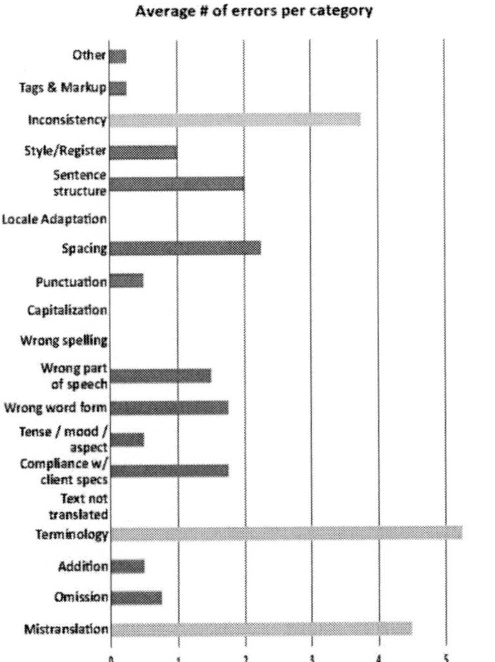



Figure 2. Average # of errors per category.

Training started from a base level, explaining what MT is and how it integrates into the business' workflow, to a practical module containing Post-editing guidelines.

## 5 External Post-Editors

### 5.1 Training on Patents

As volumes became higher and the request for PE translations from some customers increased, we decided to look for external post-editors. We already knew an Italian company whose core business is post-editing, so we decided to involve them in our project. It turned out to be a win-win situation: we got the expertise in MTPE and we offered them training in patent translation. Our Recruitment Specialist, who used to be an internal translator and now recruits and qualifies new resources, prepared a training session to explain what a patent is and which are the characteristics of patents in relation to the translation.

The difficult part for them was to learn how to post-edit patents, because you have to maintain consistency in the terminology and you need to remain extremely literal. Nothing should be deleted, all the words of the source text should be translated in the target, paying attention for example to definite and indefinite articles.

We have fully reviewed all the translations received from said other company in order to send feedback that could help them improve and learn how to post-edit patents.

### 5.2 External Resources: Partner LSP

A third-party company was contacted that had been providing post-editing services in a variety of verticals since early 2017. Given the specific nature of the first MTPE projects (big volumes, low quality expected), they had created a team of newly graduated linguists, who they then trained remotely on post-editing. Such LSP was approached to provide post-editing services for patents, and they thought it could be a good fit provided that they could be given specific training on patent translation. They selected an initial team of 12 of their best post-editors (based on their willingness to participate, knowledge of technical translation, and availability) and asked them to join for a live training by our Recruitment Specialist. The training consisted of some theoretical information about patents' structure, terminology and style, which are quite peculiar. After the onsite training, a trial period was agreed, in order for the team to get up to speed and fully understand the requirements. Transparency on the post-editors' background, full cooperation on their training and open feedback were paramount in the success of this initiative. After the initial 12 post-editors, more linguists have been successfully added to the team, with training provided remotely.

### 5.3 External Resources: Freelancers

When the LSP was approached and asked to provide a team of post-editors, they were chosen from an existing database of newly graduated linguists that were then specifically trained on post-editing. When the team was originally formed, different recruiting methods had been used, including direct contact with universities and use of social media (posts and job offers on Facebook proved effective considering the age of the target required). In most cases, the job offer was accepted with no reluctancy from the young professionals that had little or no previous on-field experience with translation. However, when respondents had previous (5+ years) experience on the market, they tended to consider post-editing more as a low-level, degrading task and reacted with strong criticism to the job offer, with some extreme occasions where the LSP was even considered fraudulent and scammy.

When we tried to involve our existing freelancers in this process we faced more difficulties. We especially noticed a certain amount of distrust towards the quality of the output and the compensation rates. To ease the passage to PE and to avoid confusion as much as possible, we still continue paying our freelancers on a word count basis, calculating a discount grid based on CAT analysis. Both fuzzy matches and MT-translated words are calculated as percentages from the full rate. Many "old-style" translators still think that MT is something bad because they don't know how to use it effectively to transform it into a super-efficient tool. They see it as something that can reduce their income, because MTPE rates are lower, but without considering it a way to boost their productivity. We have seen that the reality in our case is different, and we tried to use the data we collected during the training in order to convince them. When we showed the good output of our engine and the productivity of our in-house post-editors, some of our freelancers were positively surprised and decided at least to try. As we did with the third-party company, we always sent exhaustive feedback after our revision step and, in the end, some of them accepted to work in this way from time to time. We still face some reluctance, but we are working hard to change their minds and demonstrate that MT could be a good choice in some cases.

## 6 Resources' Reluctancy

One of the main challenges we face today is to overcome the reluctancy of freelance translators to work with MT. As the number of clients requiring post-editing services increases, and with the growing interest of the industry towards MT, AI, and PE, we felt the need to keep up with the new developments of technology and with the changes that it is bringing about in the translation market. To that end, we believe that our freelancers need to know exactly what post-editing is and how to take advantage of machine translation as a productivity tool, in order to translate faster but with the same quality.

To better understand the mindset of the freelancers we want to involve in post-editing, we recently conducted an anonymous survey, asking 71 professional translators in our database to answer a few short questions about MT and PE.

Figure 3. Age range of the respondents.

64,79% of the respondents had already worked in post-editing, while 35,21% of the people involved only had experience with "human" translation so far, mainly because they've never been asked to do that (80,77%). Only 4 participants stated they were completely against post-editing. When asked why, they answered that the rates are too low and the output quality too low to be a valid aid in the translation process. A few also claimed that, after many years of experience, they do not believe that the productivity increase would be enough to justify the lower rates, especially since they believe they are still faster at translating in the traditional way.

Less than half of the respondents (43,66%) had never taken part in a training session on post-editing but most of them would be interested in attending in the future (81,25%). This latter figure is of particular interest because it shows that providing training solutions could help overcome the distrust towards MT and PE.

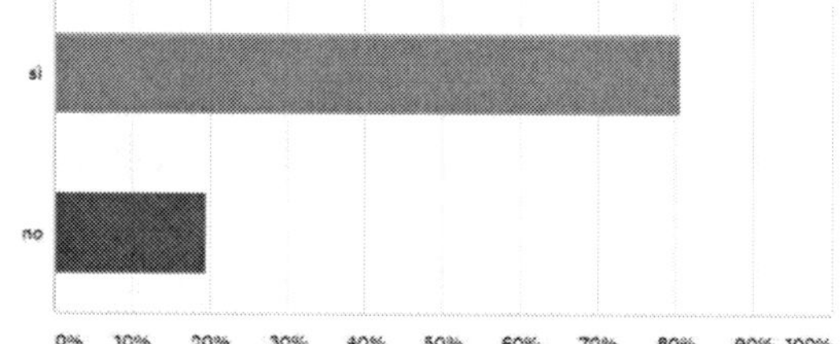

Figure 4. Percentage of translators who would like to attend MTPE training in the future.

Based on these findings we organised two training sessions, one in Milan and one in Bologna. The 44 freelancers who attended the sessions received a specific training encompassing a general introduction on MT and its history, and an in-depth explanation about the different types of post-editing (particularly, full and light post-editing) and the typical errors found in MT pre-translated texts. Afterwards, they took part in a practical session led by our in-house post-editors where they had the chance to put into practice all the information previously received. We then sent a follow-up survey, the results of which showed that most people, that is 25 out of 30 respondents, were very satisfied and willing to start post-editing for us in the near future.

To ease the transition to the new tasks, we felt that reassuring them that they will continue receiving "human" translation jobs would be helpful to help them break the proverbial ice. They were also given a chance to talk with our internal post-editors and to ask them for tips and tricks to tackle any typical MT error, and to further discuss how to take full advantage of these new tools.

Considering these results and the many opinions gathered talking to freelancers and other professionals working in LSPs, we believe that providing training to demonstrate how useful MT can be and how to get the most out of its integration in the workflow, instead of simply forcing translators to become full-time post-editors, and supporting the transition with feedback after each job is a good way to help them overcome their initial fear and resistance.

## 7 Conclusion

Post-editing is the future in our industry. In most industry-specific conferences MT is one of the main topics and it is clear that LSPs should be able to meet the requests of the market in order to remain competitive and to be able to satisfy their customers.

Our experience, at the moment, is limited, for various reasons, the most relevant being the fact that our use of MTPE is bound to the request thereof by a customer. Most clients are still reluctant to the use of MT, therefore we focused on the fields in which such requests are more common.

This means that, for now, we can only offer our clients MTPE services in very specific subjects, namely mechanical and chemical patents from English into Italian, at least in case we have to pre-translate the text with our engine.

This being said, the results are still very satisfying: last year we MT-processed about 5.5 million words, 2 million of which were post-edited by external resources (12 translators and 1 reviewer) and the remaining 3.5 million by our 4 in-house post-editors.

Since many of our customers are now asking PE for different fields of application and different language combinations, for example German or French into Italian, we are planning to explore new possibilities, such as new customised engines. It shall also be interesting to consider training our own engine on the premises, in the beginning surely with the support of a specialised service provider, and see how this technology can help us face turnaround times that are becoming tighter and tighter.

The hardest thing to overcome will surely be the reluctance of many translators to get involved in PE projects, so one of our goals is to convince them to try out this working mode and become full-fledged post-editors. The key to this is to have them understand that MT can be a tool that can help them boost their productivity while maintaining high standards of quality.

This kind of reluctance and suspicion was expressed also by some in-house translators, who were used to "old-style" translation. After attending the same training session as our freelancers and after being shown the actual potential of MT, they post-edited their first texts. When we asked again, they stated that their productivity actually increased thanks to the good output of the engine.

Based on our experience so far, we strongly believe that a key factor to succeed is to present PE not as the substitution of Humans by Machines, the reduction of translators' usefulness to the confines of accessories to the computer, or the conversion of people themselves to automatons.

At the same time, we are committed to train and involve newly graduates and young translators or post editors who, with their fresh approach to technology, will help shape the "augmented translators" of the future.

MTPE must be understood as a positive and handy new skill that will allow linguists to work at their full-potential and take maximum advantage from this increasingly tech-dominated world.

We believe that, even though the request for patent post-editing is still low when compared to the request for human translation, the future of translation will turn out to be increasingly technological and MT-centred.

# User expectations towards machine translation: A case study


**Barbara Heinisch**
Centre for Translation Studies
University of Vienna
Austria
barbara.heinisch@univie.ac.at

**Vesna Lušicky**
Centre for Translation Studies
University of Vienna
Austria
vesna.lusicky@univie.ac.at



## Abstract

Neural machine translation (NMT) systems have emerged as powerful platforms for providing fluent translations in a variety of languages and domains. The widespread adoption of NMT has heightened the need for studying the results and impact of these systems. Although acceptance of machine translation has been analyzed, the expectations of users towards NMT have not received much attention yet. This paper investigates the expectations of novice translators enrolled on a postgraduate program in specialized translation. In addition, it examines the confirmation or disconfirmation of expectations towards machine translation (MT) output among this user group. A three-step mixed-method approach was applied: a quantitative questionnaire and two recurrent (pre-trial and post-trial) evaluations of raw MT outputs. The evaluations consisted of the identification and classification of errors in NMT output according to the Multidimensional Quality Metrics. The respondents expected the MT output to be of rather low quality, but the quality of NMT output was not as high as the participants expected. Compared to the expected frequency of error types in the MT output, the reported frequency differed significantly. This paper argues that the users' experience and expectations have an impact on the use and evaluation of machine translation.




## 1 Introduction

Language technology applications have become a ubiquitous service used by various user groups to overcome language barriers. While certain types of technology, such as translation memory systems, are specialized tools used by translators only, machine translation (MT) systems are also used by non-translators. If the exposure of MT users was somewhat limited to gist translation in the past, users are increasingly implementing MT in professional and other scenarios. The acceptance of MT tools and services is attested by the high number of users of generic online MT services (Way, 2018). Based on their prior experiences, users develop and form expectations towards MT.

Expectations are beliefs about attributes or performance of a product or service in the future (Olson et al., 1979). Users' expectations may have an influence on the intended use and evaluation of MT. Expectations also provide the frame of reference for satisfaction (Higgs et al., 2005). Satisfaction with a service is crucial when introducing or evaluating MT. Expectations are dynamic constructs, a synergy of users' pre-trial perceptions and beliefs about performance or attributes of a product or a service. Although there is some ambiguity regarding the definition and operationalization of expectations, the service quality literature differentiates several categories of expectations, most frequently: forecast, normative, ideal and minimum tolerable. The four categories cover different dimensions of expectations: forecast describes users' perception of what will occur; normative describes users' perception of what should occur; ideal describes the highest level attainable in a category; and minimum tolerable describes the minimum baseline for normative and ideal

(Higgs et al., 2005). Users' expectations and the type of expectations depend on internal and external cues, such as users' prior experience and information on products.

Users' (quality) expectations towards MT output and resulting implications for MT use are an under-explored topic in MT research (Way, 2018). So far, expectations were addressed in relation to the estimation of the quality of post-editing effort (Specia et al., 2009). Way (2018) gives an overview of what level of quality can be expected from MT. Existing research recognizes the critical role played by adoption (Cadwell et al., 2018) and acceptance of MT (Moorkens & Way, 2016; Koskinen & Ruokonen, 2017). Gaspari et al. (2015) also attempted to map the expectations, requirements and needs of the translation industry concerning translation quality and MT.

With the widespread application of neural machine translation (NMT) as the MT approach of choice in generic as well as specialized MT systems, the question of pre-trial user expectations should be addressed, especially user expectations based on previous use and information obtained on the service. They may have implications for the users' intended purpose of MT use and their satisfaction with the service. The notion of expectations should also be considered in human evaluation of MT output: the types of expectations and a potential negative bias may influence the results of human evaluations of MT output.

There is a growing body of literature that recognizes the importance of quality assessment of MT output. For MT developers, scale and robustness are major concerns, but end-users are also interested in receiving good-enough or high-quality translations (Way, 2018). The concept of fitness-for-purpose of translation has been widely recognized, but the assessment methods vary in operationalization and theoretical framework. The quality of MT output is either assessed automatically or by humans. First, automatic evaluation is usually based on evaluation metrics such as BLEU (Papineni et al., 2002), NIST, WNMf or METEOR (Anastasiou & Gupta, 2011). Metrics such as BLEU compare the MT output string with a human translation which is seen as "gold standard". However, these metrics ignore the source sentence as a reference and the fact that there might be more than one correct translation (Way, 2018). Second, human evaluation (also) requires the use of evaluation criteria (a brief overview of evaluation criteria provide Fiederer & O'Brien (2009)). When comparing raw MT output with human translations, the purpose of MT, e.g. whether MT is used to get the gist of a text or for publication purposes, is usually not taken into account. Only the latter would usually require post-editing.

A series of error typologies have been developed to assess the quality of machine-translated content. The Multidimensional Quality Metrics (MQM) error typology (Lommel et al., 2014) has been increasingly used and expanded for the evaluation of NMT (Klubička et al., 2018). The MQM framework provides a comprehensive typology of quality issues. This error typology contains standardized names and definitions of errors and has the flexibility of several assessment layers and their granularity. The MQM issues are organized in eight major dimensions: Accuracy, fluency, terminology, locale convention, style, verity, design, and internationalization (Lommel et al., 2014).

By the nature of design, the assessment of the quality of MT output is a post-trial evaluation and does not consider pre-trial expectations.

## 2 Research design and method

The research reported in this paper has several objectives. First, the research investigates the expectations of a group of postgraduate specialized translation students towards MT. This paper explores how previous experience with MT influences their expectations towards the overall quality of and error types found in MT output. Second, it seeks to examine the confirmation or disconfirmation of these expectations by an evaluation of two MT outputs.

This study makes a contribution to research on expectations towards MT by demonstrating that experience and expectations influence the use of MT systems and the evaluation of MT output. We applied a mixed-method approach, combining a quantitative questionnaire as well as MT output evaluation, i.e. error identification, error classification and correction of MT output.

### 2.1 Questionnaire

A questionnaire consisting of three parts with closed and open questions was distributed among the user group. The first part was designed to ascertain the respondents' translation experience, working languages (A, B and C language (AIIC, 2018)) and professional experience.

The second part of the questionnaire addressed the respondents' prior experience in MT use, including the frequency of and reasons for MT use. The participants were asked to state whether they use MT for professional, study or private purposes, which MT systems they use and for which types of text. This part also elicited information on the respondents' forecast, normative and ideal expectations towards MT. The participants were asked to rank the quality-related issues and their frequency they would expect in MT output according to the MQM. All respondents had to state the most frequent errors they expect in MT output.

The third part of the questionnaire elicited information on the quality expectations and expected errors when using an MT system for two different texts. The students were asked to read the English source text. Afterwards they had to state their expectations towards the quality of the related MT output utilizing a five-point grade system (excellent, good, satisfactory, sufficient, useless). They had to rank the expected errors in the MT output according to the MQM. Second, they had to download a spreadsheet containing the MQM and TAUS Dynamic Quality Framework (DQF) (Görög, 2014). They compared the source and target text and identified (and corrected) errors in the MT output. Each error was assigned to an MQM error (sub)category and an error severity level on a five-point scale in the spreadsheet. The completed spreadsheets served as basis for the third step, which consisted in ranking the error types found in the MT output according to their frequency. By using the TAUS DQF and MQM for the error identification and classification task, we could compare their expectations with the evaluation result.

The questionnaire was circulated in early 2019. 79 students enrolled on a master's program in translation and focusing on specialized translation were recruited for this study. 32 individuals were excluded from the study because English was none of their working languages or they did not complete all the tasks.

## 2.2 Evaluation of MT output

The objective of the participants' evaluation of MT output in the third part of the questionnaire was to collect the error issues detected in raw MT output by the respondents. The evaluation was used for contrastive analysis of users' expectations towards error issues in MT output and the actual errors detected. It helped analyze the confirmation or disconfirmation of expectations.

The quality of the raw MT output was evaluated by the students based on the MQM error typology and the TAUS DQF. Prior to evaluation, they were familiarized with both frameworks.

The students were given two English source texts and their German MT outputs. The MT outputs used for evaluation were excerpts from British newspaper articles on a topic related to Austria. They comprised about 200 words each and were translated from English to German with the EU Council Presidency Translator (2019) platform. The study participants were provided with the source texts and the raw MT output as well as the MQM and TAUS DQF spreadsheet for both texts. The sentences in German were evaluated at the segment level in accordance with the MQM.

## 3 Results

### 3.1 Profile of the respondents

Of the final cohort of 47 respondents, 8 already worked as professional translators and 39 were novice translators. The majority (68%) of the respondents worked with German as A language, ahead of Italian (11%) and Russian, Hungarian, Polish, English and French. More than half of the participants (60%) stated that English was their B language, with German, Russian, Croatian and Japanese being the B language of the remaining respondents. The C languages were quite diverse, ranging from English (38%), French, Spanish, Slovakian, Italian, German to Greek and Romanian. Six respondents stated that they do not work with a C language. When asked about their translation experience, the majority (79%) indicated that they had translated more than 15 texts during their studies. The 8 students (17%) who had already worked as professional translators were active in the fields of engineering, social sciences and humanities.

### 3.2 Experience in MT use

About 62% of the respondents already had experience in MT use. Almost all of them (93%) reported that they use MT as part of their studies. More than two-thirds (69%) indicated that they use MT for private purposes and 31% of the respondents for professional purposes. When asked about the frequency of MT use in a professional, private or study context, 41% of the students indicated that they use MT for study purposes on a weekly basis and the remainder several times a year (19%) or several times a month (15%). For private purposes, they commented to use MT several times a year (31%), on a weekly basis (21%), on a daily basis (3%) or never (14%). For professional purposes, the respondents indicated that they never use MT (55%) or they use it several times a month (17%), on a daily basis (14%), several times a year or on a weekly basis (7% each).

Those experienced in MT use translated documents, e.g. reports or files (79%), ahead of websites (34%) or correspondence, e.g. e-mails (24%). Most of them reported that they use MT for translations from German into English and vice versa. They listed DeepL (69%) and Google Translate (59%) when asked about the MT system of choice. Another system mentioned was eTranslation. Among the MT systems which the respondents already tested but did not use frequently were Google Translate, the Facebook translator, Bing, Yandex and Babel.

The reasons for using MT included saving time (69%), getting the gist of a text (66%), consulting a reference (55%), avoiding repetitive work (31%), avoiding typing (21%) and avoiding research (3%).

### 3.3 Expectations towards MT quality

The participants expected MT to provide a raw translation, i.e. a first draft they can post-edit (53%) or a gist translation (38%) when using MT for study purposes. Only 5 respondents (11%) would want MT to provide immediately usable translations in a study context. For professional and private purposes, 21 respondents (45%) expected MT output to produce texts which can be used immediately without post-editing, i.e. they expected a final translation. For professional purposes, 15 respondents (32%) reported that they would use MT output as a draft translation. For private purposes, 24 respondents (51%) would use MT output only as a gist translation. This means that draft translations were more important in a study context, whereas gist purposes (to understand the meaning of the text) and final translations were more relevant in a private context.

When asked to rank their general expectations towards working with an MT system, 81% of the respondents ranked fast translation first. Proper functioning and intuitive use of the MT system ranked second among 60% of the respondents, whereas intuitive use still ranked third among 28% of the respondents. On ranks 4 to 6 the respondents predominately listed translation of different file formats, status feedback and accessibility of the MT system.

In response to the question about the expected quality-related issues in MT output, nearly a third (30%) of those surveyed ranked accuracy first while nearly one quarter (23%) ranked fluency first. Just over a third of those who responded ranked accuracy second, while approximately a fifth (21%) ranked fluency second. Terminology (30%) and style (23%) were the two main aspects on the third rank while locale conventions and style (23% each) had the highest number of responses on the fourth rank. Design and verity were mentioned predominantly on ranks 6 and 7.

### 3.4 Expectations towards error types and their (dis)confirmation

After having read the first source text (ST1), the respondents rated the expected quality of the related MT output (O1) with a grade ranging from excellent to useless. Almost half (49%) of the respondents expected the quality of the MT output to be sufficient, while 40% of those surveyed expected satisfactory MT output. Only a small number of the participants expected good quality (4%) or useless translations (6%). After having read O1 and after having identified, categorized and corrected the errors in the raw MT output, the participants rated the quality of O1 as follows: Sufficient (40%), useless (28%), satisfactory (23%) and good (9%). Thus, the number of useless grades increased significantly while the number of satisfactory and sufficient grades decreased.

The expected errors and their frequency in O1 were primarily related to fluency (38% on the first rank), accuracy (28% on the first rank, 32% on the second rank), style (23% on second rank) and terminology (21% on third rank). When compared to the errors reported, accuracy errors increased and fluency and verity errors decreased on rank 1, while fluency errors increased, and accuracy and terminology errors decreased on rank 2. Style errors increased slightly on rank 3 while locale convention errors increased on rank 4.

For the second source text (ST2), the students predominantly expected the MT output (O2) to be of sufficient quality (55%) or useless (26%). The other students reported that O2 would have satisfactory (13%) or good quality (6%). Compared to their expectations, they rated the actual translation to be of lower quality. The participants stated that O2 was useless (36%) or of sufficient quality (49%). This demonstrates that they expected the MT output to be of higher quality than later reported.

When asked about the expected error types in O2, well over half (64%) of the respondents ranked accuracy errors first and more than half (57%) ranked fluency errors second. Well under half of those surveyed (40%) ranked style errors third. After completing the MQM table, there was a significant increase in fluency errors and decrease of accuracy errors on rank 1 as well as a significant increase in fluency errors on rank 2 and a slight increase in terminology errors. On rank 3, the students reported a higher number of accuracy errors and a smaller number of locale convention errors than expected.

Thus, both accuracy and fluency were the MQM error categories listed the most in all analyzed areas, i.e. the overall quality of MT output, the expected error types and the error types found. However, the data showed a slight shift of the accuracy and fluency categories between the expected and actual error types in both texts.

In summary, the majority of the participants expected the MT output to be of sufficient or inferior quality. Partly, the translations for both texts did not meet their expectations since they assessed the MT output of higher quality before and of lower quality after the evaluation.

There was a disconfirmation of the respondents' expectations towards the error types in MT output. For O1, the participants expected a higher frequency of fluency errors (on the first rank) before the evaluation. However, they reported a higher frequency of accuracy errors after the evaluation (62% on the first rank).

The expected error types in O2 mentioned by the students may be influenced by the outcome of the analysis of the error issues found in O1. As mentioned before, after having analyzed O1, the majority of the errors reported were related to accuracy (62% on the first rank). This is also reflected in the expected error issues reported for O2. Here, accuracy errors were expected by 64% of the respondents (on the first rank). There was a higher confirmation of their expectations towards the translation quality of O2. For O2, there were slightly more fluency and less accuracy errors (on the first rank) reported than expected.

This demonstrates that the participants in this study have rather low expectations towards the quality of the MT output. These expectations have been partly met, since the quality of both target texts translated with the MT system was reported to be lower than expected. This might also be the reason why the participants expected the second text to be of a slightly lower quality than the first one. This also means that there was a minor discrepancy between the pre-trial expectations and the errors found by the participants during evaluation. Moreover, this user group expected a higher frequency of some error types compared with the reported post-trial frequency.

## 4    Discussion

We focused on postgraduate translation students due to the documented competence profile of this user group. Their competence profile included translation, technological and revision competence (EMT, 2009). Therefore, we assumed that the students had a basic knowledge of MT systems, their advantages and disadvantages as well as post-editing. It was necessary to familiarize them with the rather complex MQM framework which required a certain amount of time.

Although this study is limited to a small number of participants, one NMT engine, the text type newspaper article and a certain language pair and direction, it revealed that participants use MT regularly or have used it at least once, especially freely available systems. DeepL was the most frequently used system among the translation students, ahead of Google Translate. We also saw that the users' previous experience with MT systems has an impact on future expectations towards similar systems. This is in accordance with Anastasiou & Gupta (2011), assuming that freely available, easily accessible MT which produces good-enough quality translations continues to be the MT system of choice for casual users who wish to translate websites or use MT for private purposes.

The expectations towards working with the MT system among the analyzed user group were that the system should work fast, function properly and can be used intuitively.

The majority of the respondents had considerable experience of MT use for study or private purposes. Almost half of the students (45% each) reported that they expect MT output, in professional and private contexts, to be useable immediately without any further editing. However, when they used MT as part of their studies, more than half of the respondents expected a raw translation they can post-edit rather than an immediately usable translation. Gist translations were more important in a private context. A possible explanation for this might be that the majority had already used MT output as a draft translation they post-edited. Based on our experience, translation students aim for producing high-quality translations. Therefore, they adapt the MT output to meet their ideal expectations. For private purposes, however, they seem to use MT output not as a pre-translation they can work on, but for languages they might not understand. Here, it might be more important to get the gist of the text rather than high accuracy and fluency. Thus, their expectations fall into the category of minimum tolerable. This finding seems to be consistent with other research which found a dance of agency (Cadwell et al., 2018).

One interesting finding is that the students expected the MT output to be of rather low quality although they had used (general-purpose) MT before. This finding is contrary to previous studies which have suggested that those students expressing higher skepticism towards MT had the least exposure to it (Fulford, 2002) and that a negative attitude towards MT seems to be related to a lack of knowledge and (practical) experience (Gaspari, 2001). However, these studies focused on the students' opinions or attitudes, whereas this study addressed their previous MT experience in relation to their expectations as well as the confirmation or disconfirmation of their expectations. A possible explanation for the rather low expectations towards the quality of MT output is that students may be aware of the limitations of MT systems since they use it in their studies.

When we asked the students about their expectations towards the MT output quality, accuracy and fluency were ranked high. This suggests that accuracy and fluency made up translation quality for them. This finding was also reported by another study, where translators expected an MT engine to suggest correct translations, which may refer to correct target-language syntax as well as grammar and semantic equivalence to the source text (Lagoudaki, 2008).

With a small sample size and a focus on translation students (and not professional translators), caution must be applied, as the findings might not be generalizable to other user groups. However, MT-related tasks require other competences than the traditional profile of professional translators and additional competences than those acquired in translator training (Pym, 2013). Professional translators may also have limited practical exposure to MT and post-editing (Blagodarna 2018). In addition, a major issue with conceptualizing expectations is the sources of information or lack thereof used to form expectations: marketing communication by developers, mass media, training settings, word-of-mouth referrals, and prior experience with similar products. Service quality is not static but should be considered as a dynamic process (Boulding et al., 1993). Therefore, this study can only provide a small insight into user expectations of translation students at a certain point in time. In addition, students may not have identified all errors in the raw MT output. They may also lack critical evaluation of the MT output and would rather search for errors that human translators usually make (Sycz-Opoń &

Gałuskina, 2017). Moreover, our analysis does not take account of intra-annotator or inter-annotator agreement when identifying and categorizing the errors of the MT output.

The aim of (neural) MT is to reach the fluency of human translations (Way, 2018). However, accuracy, e.g. whether the MT output imparts the meaning of the source text, seems to be a major concern of translation students for the texts analyzed in this study. NMT engines provide fluent and easily readable translations. However, these fluent translations may mislead users to think that the content is translated correctly, although the message may be completely wrong.

## 5    Conclusion

Translation should fulfil a specific purpose for the intended recipient in a certain context (Reiss & Vermeer, 1984). Therefore, this paper highlights the importance of paying attention to user expectations and not only to MT (quality) evaluation (by users). This article attempts to show that user expectations are crucial in translation, including processes in MT since they may help predict user interventions, such as pre- and post-editing. This paper argues that users' past experiences, expectations and (dis)confirmation of expectations frame human evaluation of MT. Therefore, users' expectations should be factored in when introducing MT services and novel approaches to MT.

## Acknowledgment

This work has been partly funded by the European Union's Connecting Europe Facility under grant agreement no. INEA/CEF/ICT/A2016/1297953.

## References

AIIC. 2018. *Working languages.* Retrieved from https://aiic.net/page/4004/what-are-working-languages-to-a-conference-interpreter/lang/1

Anastasiou, Dimitra and Rajat Gupta. 2011. Comparison of crowdsourcing translation with Machine Translation. *Journal of Information Science,* 37(6):637–659. https://doi.org/10.1177/0165551511418760

Blagodarna, Olena. 2018. Insights into post-editors'profiles and post-editing practices. *Tradumàtica: tecnologies de la traducció,* (16):35–51.

Boulding, William, Ajay Kalra, Richard Staelin, and Valarie A. Zeithaml. 1993. A Dynamic Process Model of Service Quality: From Expectations to

Behavioral Intentions. *Journal of Marketing Research*, 30(1):7–27. https://doi.org/10.2307/3172510

Cadwell, Patrick, Sharon O'Brien, and Carlos C. S. Teixeira. 2018. Resistance and accommodation: factors for the (non-) adoption of machine translation among professional translators. *Perspectives*, 26(3):301–321. https://doi.org/10.1080/0907676X.2017.1337210

EMT. 2009. *Competences for professional translators, experts in multilingual and multimedia communication.* Retrieved from https://ec.europa.eu/info/sites/info/files/emt_competences_translators_en.pdf

EU Council Presidency Translator. 2019. *EU Council Presidency Translator.* Retrieved from: https://translate2018.eu/

Fiederer, Rebecca and Sharon O'Brien. 2009. Quality and Machine Translation: A realistic objective? *JoSTrans.* (11):52–74. Retrieved from http://www.jostrans.org/issue11/art_fiederer_obrien.pdf

Fulford, Heather. 2002. Freelance translators and machine translation: An investigation of perceptions, uptake, experience and training needs. In *6th European Association of Machine Translation*, 117–122. Retrieved from http://www.mt-archive.info/EAMT-2002-Fulford.pdf

Gaspari, Federico. 2001. Teaching Machine Translation to Trainee Translators: A Survey of Their Knowledge and Opinions. In *Proceedings of the MT Summit VIII,* Santiago de Compostela, Spain, 35–44.

Gaspari, Federico, Hala Almaghout, and Stephen Doherty. 2015. A survey of machine translation competences: Insights for translation technology educators and practitioners. *Perspectives*, 23(3):333–358. https://doi.org/10.1080/0907676X.2014.979842

Görög, Attila. 2014. Dynamic Quality Framework: quantifying and benchmarking quality. *Tradumàtica: tecnologies de la traducció,* (12):443–454. https://doi.org/10.5565/rev/tradumatica.66

Higgs, Brownyn, Michael Jay Polonsky, and Mary Hollick. 2005. Measuring expectations: forecast vs. ideal expectations. Does it really matter? *Journal of Retailing and Consumer Services*, 12(1):49–64. https://doi.org/10.1016/j.jretconser.2004.02.002

Klubička, Filip, Antonio Toral, and Víctor M. Sánchez-Cartagena. 2018. Quantitative fine-grained human evaluation of machine translation systems: a case study on English to Croatian. *Machine Translation*, 32(3):195–215.

Lagoudaki, Elina 2008. The value of machine translation for the professional translator. *Proceedings of the 8th Conference of the Association for Machine Translation in the Americas*, 262–269.

Lommel, Arle, Hans Uszkoreit, and Aljoscha Burchardt. 2014. Multidimensional quality metrics (MQM): A framework for declaring and describing translation quality metrics. *Tradumàtica: tecnologies de la traducció,* (12):455–463.

Moorkens, Joss and Andy Way. 2016. Comparing Translator Acceptability of TM and SMT outputs. In *Proceedings of the 19th Annual Conference of the European Association for Machine Translation*, 141–151.

Olson, Jerry and Philip A. Dover. 1979. Disconfirmation of consumer expectations through product trial. *Journal of Applied Psychology* (64):179–189. https://doi.org/10.1037/0021-9010.64.2.179

Papineni, Kishore, Salim Roukos, Todd Ward, and Wei-Jing Zhu. 2002. BLEU: A Method for Automatic Evaluation of Machine Translation. In *Proceedings of the 40th Annual Meeting of the Association for Computational Linguistics (ACL),* Philadelphia, 311–318. https://doi.org/10.3115/1073083.1073135

Pym, Anthony. 2013. Translation skill-sets in a machine-translation age. *Meta: Journal des traducteurs/Meta: Translators' Journal*, 58(3):487-503.

Reiss, Katharina and Hans J. Vermeer. 1984. *Grundlegung einer allgemeinen Translationstheorie. Linguistische Arbeiten: Vol. 147.* Tübingen, Max Niemeyer.

Koskinen, Kaisa and Minna Ruokonen. 2017. Love letters or hate mail? Translators' technology acceptance in the light of their emotional narratives. In Dorothy Kenny (ed.). *Human issues in translation technology*, Routledge, 26-42.

Specia, Lucia, Craig Saunders, Marco Turchi, Zhuoran Wang, and John Shawe-Taylor. 2009. Improving the confidence of machine translation quality estimates. *Proceedings of the Twelfth Machine Translation Summit (MT Summit XII)*, 136–143.

Sycz-Opoń, Joanna and Ksenia Gałuskina. 2017. Machine Translation in the Hands of Trainee Translators – an Empirical Study. *Studies in Logic, Grammar and Rhetoric*, 49(1):195–212. https://doi.org/10.1515/slgr-2017-0012

Way, Andy. 2018. *Quality expectations of machine translation.* Retrieved from http://arxiv.org/pdf/1803.08409v1

# Does NMT make a difference when post-editing closely related languages? The case of Spanish-Catalan


**Sergi Alvarez**
Universitat Pompeu Fabra
salvarezvid@uoc.edu

**Antoni Oliver**
Universitat Oberta de Catalunya
aoliverg@uoc.edu

**Toni Badia**
Universitat Pompeu Fabra
toni.badia@upf.edu



## Abstract

In the last years, we have witnessed an increase in the use of post-editing of machine translation (PEMT) in the translation industry. It has been included as part of the translation workflow because it increases productivity of translators. Currently, many Language Service Providers offer PEMT as a service.

For many years now, (closely) related languages have been post-edited using rule-based and phrase-based machine translation (MT) systems because they present less challenges due to their morphological and syntactic similarities. Given the recent popularity of neural MT (NMT), this paper analyzes the performance of this approach compared to phrase-based statistical MT (PBSMT) on in-domain and general domain documents. We use standard automatic measures and temporal and technical effort to assess if NMT yields a real improvement when it comes to post-editing the Spanish-Catalan language pair.


## 1 Introduction

Machine translation (MT) between (closely) related languages presents less challenges and has received less attention than translation between distant languages because it shows a smaller number of translation errors. For a long time now, post-editing of machine translation (PEMT) has been included as a regular practice for these language combinations because it increases productivity and reduces costs (Guerberof, 2009a).

Catalan and Spanish are closely-related languages derived from Latin. They share many morphological, syntactic and semantic similarities. This yields good results for rule-based and statistical-based systems. These systems are currently being used for post-editing both general and in-domain texts in many different companies and official organizations.

The quality of the MT output is one of the main elements that determines the post-editing effort. The higher the MT quality, the more effective post-editing can be. However, automatic metrics generally used to assess the quality of MT do not always correlate to the required post-editing effort (Koponen, 2016). Nor does translators' perception tend to match PE effort (Koponen, 2012; Moorkens et al., 2018). Research in this field has mainly focused on measuring the post-editing effort related to MT output quality (Guerberof, 2009a; Guerberof, 2009b; Specia, 2011; Specia, 2010), productivity (O'Brien, 2011; Parra Escartín and Arcedillo, 2015; Plitt and Masselot, 2010; Sanchez-Torron and Koehn, 2016), translator's usability (Castilho et al., 2014; Moorkens and O'Brien, 2013) and perceived post-editing effort (Moorkens et al., 2015).

Regarding post-editing effort, all research uses the three separated, but inter-related, dimensions established by Krings (2001): temporal, technical and cognitive. Temporal effort measures the time spent post-editing the MT output. Technical effort makes reference to the insertions and deletions applied by the translator and is usually measured with keystroke analysis with HTER (Snover et al., 2006). Cognitive effort relates to the cognitive processes taking place during post-editing and has been measured by eye-tracking or think-aloud protocols. Krings (2001) claimed that post-editing effort could be determined as a combination of all three dimensions. Even though no current measure includes them all, cognitive effort correlates with technical and temporal PE effort (Moorkens et al.,

2015).

In recent years, neural MT has gained popularity because the results obtained in terms of quality have been very successful as evidenced in WMT 2016 (Bojar et al., 2016), WMT 2017 (Bojar et al., 2017), and WMT 2018 (Bojar et al., 2018). These results have initiated a shift from statistical machine translation (SMT) to neural machine translation (NMT) in many translation industry scenarios. Google, for example, which first used rule-based MT, and then (phrase-based) SMT, has very recently replaced some of their statistical MT engines by NMT engines (Wu et al., 2016).

As NMT is becoming more popular among language service providers and translators, it is essential to test if it can really improve the post-editing process compared to phrase-based SMT (PSMT). Recent research (Bentivogli et al., 2016; Castilho et al., 2017) has shown an improved quality of NTM for post-editing certain language pairs, such as German, Greek and Portuguese (Castilho et al., 2017). But as far as we know, post-editing closely related languages has been scarcely analyzed before. We carry out two sets of experiments. The first experiments compare the post-editing of NMT and PBSMT output for general news texts from Spanish into Catalan. The second batch of experiments focus on in-domain formal documents and study the post-editing of NMT and PBSMT output for Spanish to Catalan UE documents. The latter texts tend to have more fixed syntactic structures than the former, but present a larger use of technical content and terminology. In both sets of experiments we compare post-editing temporal and technical effort with automatic metrics. We also carry out a manual analysis of the machine translation outputs.

Given the similarities between Spanish and Catalan, we want to test if NMT improves temporal or technical post-editing effort for these two languages. This leads us to the main questions that this paper tries to solve:

- Which MT method (PBSMT or NMT) yields better results for post-editing Spanish into Catalan?
- How do post-editing measures correlate with automatic metrics?
- How does the domain and the formality of the texts affect the post-editing performance between Spanish and Catalan?

## 2  Related Work

MT systems between related languages have always been considered less complex. In fact, rule-based MT and SMT have yielded better results for these language combinations (Vicic and Kubon, 2015; Kolovratník et al., 2009). In the last few years, there has been an increasing attention on NMT and recent research has tried to analyze if there is a real improvement in quality, both using automatic metrics and human evaluation. Bentivogli et al. (2016) write one of the first research papers comparing how NMT and SMT affect post-editing. They post-edit NMT and SMT outputs of English to German translated TED talks to analyze both results. They conclude that one of the main strengths of NMT is reordering of the target sentence. In general terms, NMT decreases the post-editing effort, but degrades faster than SMT with sentence length.

Wu (2016) compares BLEU (Papineni et al., 2002) and human scores for machine-translated wikipedia entries to evaluate the quality of NMT and SMT. This paper and others (Junczys-Dowmunt et al., 2016; Isabelle et al., 2017) confirm that there is an improvement in the global quality of the translated output using NMT systems.

Toral and Sánchez-Cartagena (2017) take the study by Bentivogli et al. (2016) and increase the initial scope by adding different language combinations and metrics. Although they conclude that NMT produces a better quality than previous systems, the improvement is not always clear for all language combinations.

Castilho et al. (2017) report on a comparative study of PBSMT and NMT. It analyzes four language pairs and different automatic metrics and human evaluation methods. In general, NMT produces better results, although the paper highlights some strengths and weaknesses. It pays special attention to post-editing and uses the PET interface (Aziz et al., 2012) to compare educational domain output from both systems using different metrics. One of the conclusions is that NMT reduces word order errors and improves fluency for certain language pairs, so that fewer segments require post-editing. However, the PE effort is not reduced when working with NMT output.

Koponen et al. (2019) present a comparison of PE changes performed on NMT, RBMT and SMT output for the English-Finnish language combina-

| Corpus | Segments | Tokens es | Tokens ca |
|---|---|---|---|
| DOGC | 6,943,595 | 155,233,465 | 157,000,914 |
| General | 4,163,009 | 93,489,848 | 93,538,673 |

**Table 1:** Size of the training corpora

| System | BLEU | NIST | WER |
|---|---|---|---|
| NMT Marian Admin. | 0.845 | 13.055 | 0.1424 |
| PBSMT Moses Admin. | 0.896 | 13.458 | 0.0881 |
| Google Translate Admin. | 0.869 | 13.279 | 0.0918 |
| NMT Marian General | 0.767 | 12.426 | 0.185 |
| PBSMT Moses General | 0.812 | 12.799 | 0.171 |
| Google Translate General | 0.826 | 12.980 | 0,121 |

**Table 2:** Automatic evaluation figures

tion. A total of 33 translation students edit in this English-to-Finnish PE experiment. It outlines the strategies participants adopt to post-edit the different outputs, which contributes to the understanding of NMT, RBMT and SMT approaches. It also concludes that PE effort is lower for NMT than SMT.

Regarding NMT for related languages, Costa-Jussà (2017) analyzes automatic metrics and human scores for NMT and SMT from Spanish into Catalan. She concludes that NMT quality results are better both for automatic metrics and human evaluation for in-domain sets, but PBSMT results are better for general domain ones. However, as far as we are concerned, there are no studies analyzing how these MT outputs affect post-editing for in-domain texts, although there have been other papers with a more linguistic approach that have studied the main linguistic issues for NMT between certain related language pairs (Popovic et al., 2016).

## 3 MT systems and training corpora

For our experiments, we have trained two statistical and two neural machine translation systems: one of each for a general domain and the other for the Administrative/Legislative domain.

### 3.1 Corpora

For the general domain we have combined three corpora: (1) a self-compiled corpus from Spanish-Catalan bilingual newspapers; (2) the GlobalVoices corpus (Tiedemann, 2012) and (3) the Open Subtitles 2018 corpus (Lison and Tiedemann, 2016).

The systems for the Administrative/Legislative

domain have been trained with the corpus from the Official Diary of the Catalan Government (Oliver, 2017). The Catalan part of the corpora has been normalized according to the new orthographic rules of Catalan. This step has been performed in an automatic way.

In Table 1 the sizes of the training corpora are shown. A small part of the corpus (1000 segments) has been reserved for optimization (statistical) and validation (neural). Another set (1000 segments) has been reserved for evaluation. So there are no common segments in the train, validation and evaluation subcorpora.

The corpora have been pre-processed (tokenized, truecased and cleaned) with the standard tools distributed in Moses[1]. The same preprocessed corpora have been used for training the statistical and the neural systems.

### 3.2 PBSMT system

For the statistical system we have used Moses (Koehn et al., 2007) and trained a system for each of the corpora. We have used a language model of order 5. For the alignment we have used mgiza with grow-diag-final-and.

### 3.3 NMT system

For the neural machine translation system we have used Marian[2] (Junczys-Dowmunt et al., 2018). We have trained the systems using an RNN-based encoder-decoder model with attention mechanism (s2s), layer normalization, tied embeddings, deep encoders of depth 4, residual connectors and

---

[1]http://www.statmt.org/moses/
[2]https://marian-nmt.github.io

| Domain | System | Mean | Std. Deviation |
|---|---|---|---|
| In-domain (UE) | Marian | 50.89 | 11.78 |
| | Moses | 73.70 | 29.60 |
| | Google | 34.68 | 10.88 |
| General domain | Marian | 33.71 | 2.75 |
| | Moses | 42.94 | 13.96 |
| | Google | 32.93 | 12.65 |

**Table 3:** Temporal post-editing effort (secs/segment)

| Domain | System | Mean | Std. Deviation |
|---|---|---|---|
| In-domain (UE) | Marian | 64.55 | 65.75 |
| | Moses | 12.09 | 10.50 |
| | Google | 2.23 | 1.38 |
| General domain | Marian | 37.99 | 31.91 |
| | Moses | 16.43 | 1.62 |
| | Google | 27.34 | 37.88 |

**Table 4:** Technical post-editing effort (keystrokes/segment)

LSTM cells (following the example of the Marian tutorial[3]).

## 4 Automatic evaluation of the MT systems

The systems have been automatically evaluated using mteval[4] to obtain the values for BLEU, NIST and WER. Table 2 includes the evaluation figures for all the MT systems used. As a reference, we also include the metrics for Google Translate[5] for the same evaluation sets.

## 5 Experiments

We have carried two sets of experiments to assess the correlation of MT metrics with the post-editing time and technical effort. The participants were students in their last year of the Degree in Translation and Language Sciences. They post-edited during a PE task organized as part of a course on Localization taught by one of the authors. They all acknowledged a C2 level of both languages. Although students may not be experienced professionals, the participants have translated into this specific language combination during their translation degree program, and have received specific PE training during the course before carrying out the PE task. For these reasons, we can consider them semiprofessionals (Englund Dimitrova, 2005).

In the first experiment, 12 participants post-edited a short text (441 words, 14 segments) from Spanish into Catalan translated with our in-domain PBSMT Moses, our in-domain NMT Marian and NMT Google Translate systems. The text was a passage from a UE document, which presented more fixed syntactic structures, but larger technical content. They had to carry the task using PET (Aziz et al., 2012), a computer-assisted translation tool that supports post-editing. It logs both post-editing time and edits (keystrokes, insertions and deletions, that is, technical effort). As it was a short text, they were asked to post-edit it without any pauses. The main characteristics of the post-editing tool were also explained before beginning the task.

In the second experiment, the same 12 participants post-edited a general domain short text (379 words, 17 segments) from Spanish into Catalan translated with our general purpose PBSMT Moses, our NMT Marian and NMT Google Translate systems. The text was a fragment from a piece of news appeared in the newspaper *El País* on April 4th, 2019. They post-edited the text with the same tool and conditions as in the first experiment.

In order to avoid bias, participants never post-edited the same text twice. We divided the 12 post-editors into groups of 4 people. All the members of each group post-edited the in-domain text translated with an MT system. They also post-edited the general text output for the same MT system.

[3]https://marian-nmt.github.io/examples/mtm2017/complex/
[4]https://github.com/odashi/mteval
[5]Translations were performed on April 9th, 2019

| Domain | System | Mean | Std. Deviation |
|---|---|---|---|
| In-domain (UE) | Marian | 42.85 | 0.71 |
| | Moses | 53.57 | 1.50 |
| | Google | 85.71 | 1.32 |
| General domain | Marian | 20.59 | 1.12 |
| | Moses | 20.58 | 1.12 |
| | Google | 39.70 | 0.83 |

**Table 5:** Percentage of unmodified segments

## 6 Results

### 6.1 Automatic measures

To assess the quality of the MT systems, we included some of the most commonly used automatic evaluation metrics. The BLEU metric (Papineni et al., 2002) and the closely related NIST (Doddington, 2002) are based on n-gram. The word error rate (WER), which is based on the Levenshtein distance (1966), calculates the minimum number of substitutions, deletions and insertions that have to be performed to convert the generated text into the reference text. For all the mea surements, our NMT Marian system had the worst rates (see Table 2). However, our PBSMT Moses model had 0.027 BLEU points more than Google Translate for in-domain texts. In the general domain, Google Translate was better rated. That is why we decided to include Google Translate as part of the post-editing tasks.

### 6.2 Post-editing time and effort

For the in-domain (Administrative/Legislative) post-editing task, our NMT Marian model was the one that took longer post-editing technical effort, although Moses was the one that took longer post-editing temporal effort. This correlates to the worst results in the automatic metrics. In fact, as we can see in the manual evaluation (see example 2, Table 6), errors include adding elements that were not found in the source segment.

Our Moses system had 0.027 BLEU points more than Google Translate in the automatic evaluation. However, post-editors spent less time post-editing the Google Translate output (see Table 3). Regarding the technical effort, Google Translate has a very low rate, which is statistically significant, and correlates to the number of unmodified segments (see Table 5). This correlates to the results obtained by Shterionov et al. (2018), where the automatic quality evaluation scores indicated that the PBSMT engines performed better, but the human reviewers showed the opposite result.

For the general post-editing task, automatic metrics correlate to temporal but not to technical effort. The Google Translate output, which showed a 0.014 increase in BLEU, was translated using far more keystrokes per segment. However, it should be noted the high standard deviation in this case, as in the case of the Marian output.

Another interesting figure is the number of unmodified segments (see Table 5). In this case Google Translate results are far better than Moses, both for in-domain and general domain, which seems to indicate that NMT produces more fluent sentences.

### 6.3 Manual analysis

The goal of the manual analysis is to complement the information provided by the measures in previous sections. Following Farrús et al. (2010), we have used a taxonomy in which errors are reported according to the different linguistic levels involved: orthographic, morphological, lexical, semantic and syntactic, and according to the specific cases that can be found in the post-editing tasks from Spanish into Catalan. Table 6 shows the error rates for all outputs. Table 7 includes several translation examples from the three systems for the general domain test set. In general, examples show the advantages of the Google Translate neural MT system compared to PBSMT output, in the following terms:

1. There is a **better use of prepositions** in the NMT versions. In this case, the Marian output generates the better version (which includes the pronoun *el* and the use of *el* before the year instead of *en*).

2. There is **a better integrity of meaning** in the Google Translate version. One of the recurrent problems of our Marian version was the addition of extra information or the mistrans-

| Domain | System | Ortogr. | Morph. | Lexical | Semantic | Syntactic | Total |
|---|---|---|---|---|---|---|---|
| In-domain (UE) | Marian | 0 | 0 | 2 | 18 | 0 | **20** |
| | Moses | 2 | 0 | 2 | 0 | 2 | **6** |
| | Google | 0 | 0 | 0 | 0 | 1 | **1** |
| General domain | Marian | 0 | 0 | 8 | 5 | 3 | **16** |
| | Moses | 9 | 12 | 2 | 0 | 5 | **28** |
| | Google | 0 | 11 | 1 | 0 | 3 | **15** |

**Table 6:** Number of errors according to the linguistic level

| 1 | ES | Se presume que Van Gogh lo pidió prestado al dueño en 1890 [...] |
|---|---|---|
| | Marian | Es presumeix que Van Gogh **el** va demanar prestat al propietari **el** 1890 [...] |
| | Moses | Es presumeix que Van Gogh **ho** va demanar prestat **el** propietari en 1890 [...] |
| | Google | Es presumeix que Van Gogh va demanar prestat **a l'amo en** 1890 [...] |
| 2 | ES | Es un Lefaucheux [...] hallado en un prado de la localidad de Auvers-sur-Oise por un campesino |
| | Marian | És **un lladre** [...] trobat en un **enclavament** de la localitat **d'arreu del món** |
| | Moses | És **un Lefaucheux** [...] trobat en un prat de la localitat **basca** d'Auvers-sud-Oise per un pagès |
| | Google | És **un Lefaucheux** [...] trobat en un prat de la localitat d'Auvers-sud-Oise per un pagès |
| 3 | ES | En 1888, intentaron trabajar juntos en Arlés, al sur de Francia. |
| | Marian | El 1888, van intentar treballar junts a **Espanya**, al sud de França. |
| | Moses | En 1888, van intentar treballar junts, a **Arle. Al sud** de França |
| | Google | En 1888, van intentar treballar junts a Arles, al sud de França. |
| 4 | ES | De la pistola no volvió a saberse nada hasta 1965 y su antigüedad está certificada. |
| | Marian | De la pistola no **es va tornar a saber res** fins al 1965 i la seva antiguitat està certificada. |
| | Moses | De la pistola no **va tornar a saber res** fins **1965.** Està certificada la seva antigui**tat i** |
| | Google | De la pistola no **va tornar a saber res** fins a 1965 i la seva antiguitat està certificada. |

**Table 7:** Translation examples

lations, like in this case. The Moses version also ads *basca* (it's the only time Moses adds extra information).

3. The Google Translate version **is more fluent**. Even though the Moses output generally includes all the source information, it sometimes truncates the sentences.

4. NMT achieves **a better syntactic organization** that produces a more understandable sentence with less mistakes.

## 7 Discussion

This paper shows a comparison between PBSMT and NMT for general and in-domain documents from Spanish into Catalan. Automatic metrics show better results for PBSMT with in-domain texts. However, Google Translate NMT system has a better rate when translating general domain sentences.

Regarding post-editing, for this study, text types, and language pair results show an improvement of unmodified segments and temporal effort for NMT systems. For the in-domain text, with a lower BLUE rate, both technical and temporal effort, as well as the number of unmodified segments and translation errors, show a clear improvement of Google Translate. The manual analysis also confirms that NMT systems tend to solve some of the usual problems of PBSMT systems when translating closely related languages. However, as it is shown in the translation from our NMT Marian system, a lower quality in NMT systems tends to produce unreliable translation outputs, which complicate the post-editing process.

We plan to improve our Marian NMT system using the subword-nmt algorithm (Sennrich et al., 2015) to minimize the effect of out-of-vocabulary words.

## Acknowledgments

The training of the neural MT systems has been possible thanks to the NVIDIA GPU grant programme.

## References

Aziz, Wilker, Sheila C. M. De Sousa, and Lucia Specia. 2012. PET: A Tool for Post-editing and Assessing Machine Translation. *Proceedings of the Eight International Conference on Language Resources and Evaluation (LREC'12)*, pages 3982–3987.

Bentivogli, Luisa, Arianna Bisazza, Mauro Cettolo, and Marcello Federico. 2016. Neural versus Phrase-Based Machine Translation Quality: a Case Study. *Proceedings of the 2016 Conference on Empirical Methods in Natural Language Processing*, pages 257–267.

Bojar, Ondrej, Rajen Chatterjee, Christian Federmann, Yvette Graham, Barry Haddow, Matthias Huck, Antonio Jimeno Yepes, Philipp Koehn, Varvara Logacheva, Christof Monz, Matteo Negri, Aurelie Neveol, Mariana Neves, Martin Popel, Matt Post, Raphael Rubino, Carolina Scarton, Lucia Specia, Marco Turchi, Karin Verspoor, and Marcos Zampieri. 2016. Findings of the 2016 Conference on Machine Translation. *Proceedings of the First Conference on Machine Translation*, 2:131–198.

Bojar, Ondřej, Rajen Chatterjee, Christian Federmann, Yvette Graham, Barry Haddow, Shujian Huang, Matthias Huck, Lmu Munich, Philipp Koehn, Jhu / Edinburgh, Qun Liu, Varvara Logacheva, Mipt Moscow, Christof Monz, Matteo Negri Fbk, Matt Post, Johns Hopkins, Univ Raphael Rubino, and Marco Turchi Fbk. 2017. Findings of the 2017 Conference on Machine Translation (WMT17). *Proceedings of the Second Conference on Machine Translation*, 2:169–214.

Bojar, Ondřej, Christian Federmann, Mark Fishel, Yvette Graham, Barry Haddow, Matthias Huck, Philipp Koehn, and Christof Monz. 2018. Findings of the 2018 Conference on Machine Translation (WMT18). *Proceedings of the Third Conference on Machine Translation*, pages 272–303.

Castilho, Sheila, Fabio Alves, Sharon O'Brien, and Morgan O Brien. 2014. Does Post-editing Increase Usability? A Study with Brazilian Portuguese as Target Language. *Proceedings European Association for Machine Translation (EAMT)*, (2010).

Castilho, Sheila, Joss Moorkens, Federico Gaspari, Rico Sennrich, Vilelmini Sosoni, Panayota Georgakopoulou, Pintu Lohar, Andy Way, Antonio Valerio Miceli Barone, and Maria Gialama. 2017. A Comparative Quality Evaluation of PBSMT and NMT using Professional Translators. *Proceedings of MT Summit XVI, vol.1: Research Track*, pages 116–131, 9.

Costa-Jussà, Marta R. 2017. Why Catalan-Spanish Neural Machine Translation? Analysis, Comparison and Combination with Standard Rule and Phrase-based Technologies. *Proceedings of the Fourth Workshop on NLP for Similar Languages, Varieties and Dialects (VarDial)*, pages 55–62.

Doddington, George. 2002. Automatic Evaluation of Machine Translation Quality Using N-gram Co-occurrence Statistics. *Proceedings of the Second International Conference on Human Language Technology Research*, pages 138–145.

Englund Dimitrova, Birgitta. 2005. *Expertise and explicitation in the translation process.* John Benjamins Publishing Company, Amsterdam.

Farrús, Mireia, Marta Costa-jussa, Jose Bernardo Mariño Acebal, and José Fonollosa. 2010. Linguistic-based evaluation criteria to identify statistical machine translation errors. *Proceedings of the 14th Annual Conference of the European Association for Machine Translation*, 01.

Guerberof, Ana. 2009a. Productivity and Quality in MT Post-editing. *Proceedings of MT Summit XII.*

Guerberof, Ana. 2009b. Productivity and Quality in the Post-editing of Outputs from Translation Memories and Machine Translation. *The International Journal of Localisation*, 7(1):11–21.

Isabelle, Pierre, Colin Cherry, and George F. Foster. 2017. A Challenge Set Approach to Evaluating Machine Translation. *CoRR*, abs/1704.07431.

Junczys-Dowmunt, Marcin, Tomasz Dwojak, and Hieu Hoang. 2016. Is Neural Machine Translation Ready for Deployment? A Case Study on 30 Translation Directions. *CoRR*, abs/1610.01108.

Junczys-Dowmunt, Marcin, Roman Grundkiewicz, Tomasz Dwojak, Hieu Hoang, Kenneth Heafield, Tom Neckermann, Frank Seide, Ulrich Germann, Alham Fikri Aji, Nikolay Bogoychev, André F. T. Martins, and Alexandra Birch. 2018. Marian: Fast Neural Machine Translation in C++. *Proceedings of ACL 2018, System Demonstrations*, pages 116–121, July.

Koehn, Philipp, Hieu Hoang, Alexandra Birch, Chris Callison-Burch, Marcello Federico, Nicola Bertoldi, Brooke Cowan, Wade Shen, Christine Moran, Richard Zens, et al. 2007. Moses: Open source toolkit for statistical machine translation. *Proceedings of the 45th annual meeting of the association for computational linguistics companion volume proceedings of the demo and poster sessions*, pages 177–180.

Kolovratník, David, Natalia Klyueva, and Ondrej Bojar. 2009. Statistical Machine Translation Between Related and Unrelated Languages. *Proceedings of the Conference on Theory and Practice of Information Technologies, ITAT 2009, Horský hotel Kralova studna, Slovakia, September 25-29, 2009*, pages 31–36.

Koponen, Maarit, Leena Salmi, and Markku Nikulin. 2019. A Product and Process Analysis of Post-editor Corrections on Neural, Statistical and Rule-based Machine Translation Output. *Machine Translation*.

Koponen, Maarit. 2012. Comparing Human Perceptions of Post-editing Effort with Post-editing Operations. *Proceedings of the Seventh Workshop on Statistical Machine Translation*, pages 181–190.

Koponen, Maarit. 2016. Is Machine Translation Post-editing Worth the Effort? A Survey of Research into Post-editing and Effort. *The Journal of Specialised Translation*, pages 131–148.

Krings, Hans P. 2001. *Repairing Texts: Empirical Investigations of Machine Translation Post-editing Process*. The Kent State University Press, Kent, OH.

Levenshtein, Vladimir Iosifovich. 1966. Binary Codes Capable of Correcting Deletions, Insertions and Reversals. *Soviet Physics Doklady*.

Lison, Pierre and Jörg Tiedemann. 2016. Opensubtitles2016: Extracting large parallel corpora from movie and tv subtitles.

Moorkens, Joss and Sharon O'Brien. 2013. User Attitudes to the Post-editing Interface. *Proceedings of Machine Translation Summit XIV: Second Workshop on Post-editing Technology and Practice, Nice, France*, pages 19–25.

Moorkens, Joss, Sharon O 'brien, Igor A L Da Silva, Norma B De, Lima Fonseca, Fabio Alves, and Norma B De Lima Fonseca. 2015. Correlations of Perceived Post-editing Effort with Measurements of Actual Effort. *Machine Translation*, 29:267–284.

Moorkens, Joss, Antonio Toral, Sheila Castilho, and Andy Way. 2018. Translators' Perceptions of Literary Post-editing using Statistical and Neural Machine Translation. *Translation Spaces*, 7:240–262.

O'Brien, Sharon. 2011. Towards Predicting Post-editing Productivity. *Machine Translation*, 25(3):197–215.

Oliver, Antoni. 2017. El corpus paral·lel del diari oficial de la generalitat de catalunya: compilació, anàlisi i exemples d'ús. *Zeitschrift für Katalanistik*, 30:269–291.

Papineni, Kishore, Salim Roukos, Todd Ward, and Wei-Jing Zhu. 2002. Bleu: a Method for Automatic Evaluation of Machine Translation. *Proceedings of 40th Annual Meeting of the Association for Computational Linguistics*, pages 311–318, July.

Parra Escartín, Carla and Manuel Arcedillo. 2015. A Fuzzier Approach to Machine Translation Evaluation: A Pilot Study on Post-editing Productivity and Automated Metrics in Commercial Settings. *Proceedings of the ACL 2015 Fourth Workshop on Hybrid Approaches to Translation (HyTra)*, 1(2010):40–45.

Plitt, Mirko and François Masselot. 2010. A Productivity Test of Statistical Machine Translation Post-Editing in a Typical Localisation Context. *The Prague Bulletin of Mathematical Linguistics NUMBER*, 93:7–16.

Popovic, Maja, Mihael Arcan, and Filip Klubicka. 2016. Language Related Issues for Machine Translation between Closely Related South Slavic Languages. *Proceedings of the Third Workshop on NLP for Similar Languages, Varieties and Dialects, VarDial@COLING 2016, Osaka, Japan, December 12, 2016*, pages 43–52.

Sanchez-Torron, Marina and Phillipp Koehn. 2016. Machine Translation Quality and Post-Editor Productivity. *Proceedings of AMTA 2016*, pages 16–26.

Sennrich, Rico, Barry Haddow, and Alexandra Birch. 2015. Neural machine translation of rare words with subword units. *arXiv preprint arXiv:1508.07909*.

Shterionov, Dimitar, Riccardo Superbo, Pat Nagle, Laura Casanellas, Tony O'Dowd, and Andy Way. 2018. Human versus automatic quality evaluation of nmt and pbsmt. *Machine Translation*, 32(3):217–235, Sep.

Snover, Matthew, Bonnie Dorr, Richard Schwartz, Linnea Micciulla, and John Makhoul. 2006. A Study of Translation Edit Rate with Targeted Human Annotation. *Proceedings of Association for Machine Translation in the Americas*, (August):223–231.

Specia, Lucia. 2010. Combining Confidence Estimation and Reference-based Metrics for Segment-level MT Evaluation. *The Ninth Conference of the Association for Machine Translation in the Americas*.

Specia, Lucia. 2011. Exploiting Objective Annotations for Measuring Translation Post-editing Effort. *Proceedings of the European Association for Machine Translation*, (May):73–80.

Tiedemann, Jörg. 2012. Parallel Data, Tools and Interfaces in OPUS. *Lrec*, 2012:2214–2218.

Toral, Antonio and Víctor M. Sánchez-Cartagena. 2017. A Multifaceted Evaluation of Neural versus Phrase-Based Machine Translation for 9 Language Directions. *CoRR*, abs/1701.02901.

Vicic, Jernej and Vladislav Kubon. 2015. A Comparison of MT Methods for Closely Related Languages: A Case Study on Czech - Slovak and Croatian - Slovenian Language Pairs. *Text, Speech, and Dialogue - 18th International Conference, TSD 2015, Pilsen,Czech Republic, September 14-17, 2015, Proceedings*, pages 216–224.

Wu, Yonghui, Mike Schuster, Zhifeng Chen, Quoc V. Le, Mohammad Norouzi, Wolfgang Macherey, Maxim Krikun, Yuan Cao, Qin Gao, Klaus Macherey, Jeff Klingner, Apurva Shah, Melvin Johnson, Xiaobing Liu, Lukasz Kaiser, Stephan Gouws, Yoshikiyo Kato, Taku Kudo, Hideto Kazawa, Keith Stevens, George Kurian, Nishant Patil, Wei Wang, Cliff Young, Jason Smith, Jason Riesa, Alex Rudnick, Oriol Vinyals, Greg Corrado, Macduff Hughes, and Jeffrey Dean. 2016. Google's Neural Machine Translation System: Bridging the Gap between Human and Machine Translation. *CoRR*, abs/1609.08144.

# Machine Translation in the Financial Services Industry: a Case Study

**Mara Nunziatini**
Welocalize Italy S.r.l.
Via Alserio 22, Milan, Italy
mara.nunziatini@welocalize.com

## Abstract

The use of Machine Translation is spreading quickly in the translation industry. While its implementation is smooth in some contexts, in the regulated services industry it certainly seems trickier. In particular, the financial services industry can be considered a less conventional scenario within which to implement MT. This paper explains how MT was successfully implemented in the workflow of a translation company specialized in financial services, and how freelance translators got positively involved in the process.

## 1 Introduction

Welocalize Italy S.r.l. is Welocalize's Italian headquarter, based in Milan. This hub used to be a translation company on its own and was recently merged into Welocalize to become its FSI-specialized translation hub. The greater part of its business, since its foundation, has always been focused on the translation of financial, tax and legal documents. In order to stay in step with competitors and trends in the translation industry, and to offer a wider range of services and more flexibility to its customers, the company started thinking of implementing Machine Translation in its workflow. In this paper we will describe how we implemented MT in this regulated sector.

## 2 Description of the Company

### 2.1 Client Base

The company's client base boasts a relevant number of faithful, long-time customers which mainly includes large Italian enterprises, SMEs and multi-national auditing companies (or their Italian subsidiaries), but also banks and lawyers.

Every year, for marketing, tax or legal purposes, these customers need to translate financial texts (mainly Financial Statements and Transfer Pricing documentation) and/or legal documents and, after years of cooperation, many clients have become familiar with the company's Project Managers and salespeople. However, in order to retain key customers, find new clients and keep up with competition, the company started facing the need of providing lower prices and shorter turnaround times, while still delivering top quality – a fundamental aspect of the FSI industry. In the meantime, the global translation industry started talking about neural MT (Castilho et al., 2017), and all the major LSPs were already implementing MT in their workflow, therefore offering more competitive prices and shorter turnaround times. Similarly, the LSP we are part of has been using MT for many years, and was already implementing neural MT (Schmidt and Marg, 2018).

### 2.2 Description of the Business

Our company's business concentrates in one peak season which approximately starts in March and ends in June, this is the time when Italian enterprises (or foreign enterprises with an Italian subsidiary) listed on the stock market publish their Financial Statements in Italian and in English, so as to reach a bigger number of stakeholders. Another busy season corresponds with the publication of half-yearly financial statements (end of summer till October, approximately).

Another relevant part of the business, but with reduced volumes compared to Financial Statements, regards Transfer Pricing documentation. For this type of content, there is not really a peak season – rather, these translation requests come in continuously, in a more or less regular fashion. Transfer Pricing documents are aimed at proving that the prices of goods and services which are exchanged among subsidiaries, affiliates or controlled companies are in line with the arm's length principles[1]. These are usually drafted in English in the case of multi-national companies and need to be translated into Italian for tax purposes.

The greater part of Financial Statements is translated from Italian into English, while the greater part of Transfer Pricing documentation is translated from English into Italian.

### 2.3 Technology Resources

As for technology resources, the company was not advanced before the merger. Only recently has this business started using CAT tools as part of the standard workflow. In fact, this hub used to implement a traditional translation and proofreading workflow with automation of processes being non-existent. Documents to be translated were sent by email to the translator, who was asked to deliver a final file in the same format and layout as the original. Besides, the Translation Management System in use offered basic functionalities only. For this reason, projects were handled without the file having been uploaded to any CAT tool, and management of resources like TMs and glossaries was completely manual, time-consuming and not so efficient.

After the merger, the use of CAT tools and bilingual files started to be implemented in the workflow, TM management became more efficient, while in the translation industry MT was a topic more and more discussed.

Thanks to implementing a new TMS and creating centralized translation memories in a more structured way, we managed to build up significant and good-quality TMs for the main subjects translated (Financial Statements, Transfer Pricing, Non-Financial Statements, etc.). These memories were very helpful when exploring the use of MT for our group.

### 2.4 External Vendors

Vendor database is not very big and mainly comprises reliable English and Italian native speakers who have been working for the company for several years already. These vendors specialize in translating financial documents and have a high productivity in terms of words translated per day, thanks to their multi-year experience and personal linguistic resources.

However, the vendor base is so small that Project Managers end up working always with the same translators, who often get fully booked, especially during peak season. The average freelancer is highly experienced in the subject matter and, due to our own processes, some of them were only recently introduced to the use of CAT tools and other automation aids. The greater part of them had never heard anything about MT.

The small vendor base started to be a blocker for the growth of the company. It is more and more difficult to find financial translators with enough experience who are reliable and affordable, so production really depends on this small base's availability. Furthermore, while the trend in the industry overall is to cut costs, these experienced freelancers tend to increase their rates.

### 3. Need to Implement MT and Challenges to Implementation

The possibility of offering MT as part of the services has begun to look attractive and indeed necessary, but is it possible to implement MT in the FSI?

### 3.1 The Importance of Quality

Financial translation requires great attention to details as even a small mistake can lead to a major problem. Financial translation requires expertise and experience, as the importance of integrity and accuracy of information in financial documents cannot be underestimated.

### 3.2 Terminology

Translating terminology, and doing so consistently, is a major challenge in the financial world. It is fundamental to ensure consistency and comparability between documents of the same company related to different periods (i.e. to compare quarterly and annual reports). Financial terms can be intricate and represent a challenge for translators who do not have understanding of or experience in financial translation. Understanding concepts in their context is very important in

---

[1] OECD Transfer Pricing Guidelines for Multinational Enterprises and Tax Administrations, July 2017.

financial translation – and we know this is one of the weak points of MT. Just to mention a couple of tricky examples, "ammortizzare" in Italian is translated "amortize" if we are talking of intangible assets, while is translated "depreciate" if we are talking about tangible assets. Another tricky one is "periodo" which is translated "year" in yearly Financial Statements but "period" in half-yearly Financial Statements. Terminology must also be compliant with IFRS[2] (International Financial Reporting Standards), i.e. a set of accounting standards developed by the IASB (International Accounting Standards Board).

Besides, date format and currency format may vary a lot depending on customer's preference (as at 31 December 2018, as of December 31, 2018…) just like currency format (EUR, €, euro, Euro).

### 3.3 Numbers Localization

In financial documents, numbers matter greatly. Besides, when doing financial translation, numbers must be localized (Italian and English use different decimal and thousand separators). An error in the positioning of a comma, an excess digit or omission of a digit mean thousands in monetary losses.

### 3.4 Timeliness

During peak season, the business becomes especially fast-paced and constrained by time, lots of requests come in every day that add on to the already booked translations. Translations need to be delivered in a very short time as it is very important that these documents do not miss any deadline. However, in most of the cases, the greater part of trusted translators and reviewers are already fully-booked. For this reason, salespeople cannot give clients the translation they want in the time they need and are left with nothing better to offer than a longer turnaround time or a lower quality.

### 3.5 Confidentiality

Financial documents need to be secure since they disclose private company information. They must remain private and handing them over to third parties poses great risks. It is extremely important that the company uses reliable tools, since the LSP must ensure that no data are shared externally.

## 4 Description of Engine Selection and MT Implementation Process

After having identified all the possible requirements and challenges, we decided to start the engine selection process with the help of the company's Machine Translation team.

Our ideal candidate was a state-of-the-art, customizable engine which is compatible with the CAT tools used internally. Besides, in order to be cost-effective for production, it must deliver good-quality output. Last but not least, the engine must by no means represent a risk for data privacy, and its price had to be in line with the company's budget. In 2018, when the implementation process began, "state-of-the-art" meant "neural".

The potential candidates identified were 3:

- Option 1: a generic financial neural machine translation engine;
- Option 2: a generic non-customizable neural machine translation system;
- Option 3: a customizable neural machine translation provider, which allowed us to create two engines (one to translate Transfer Pricing documentation from English into Italian, and another to translate Financial Statements from Italian into English).

Option 1 and 2 were the first options to come in, while Option 3 was identified only at a later stage and trained with our TMs. All the three Options are neural engines, but at a first glance we would think Option 3 would suit us best as it is customizable. However, the most important criteria to choose the best engine was the quality of the output, so we proceeded to test the quality of each engine's raw output.

### 4.1 Testing Option 1 vs. Option 2

The quality test was run on a 2500-word sample from a Financial Statements which was translated from English to Italian with both options. Quality check consisted of a full post-editing of both raw outputs by two native speaker in-house post-editors specialized in financial translation. Quality was evaluated by comparing the amount and type of changes, and the time linguists spent to fix them was calculated. As for the types of mistakes, we noticed that certain issues appeared both in Option 1 and Option 2's output. The linguists flagged

---

[2] https://www.ifrs.org/

more or less the same amount of grammar issues, untranslated content, mistranslations and inconsistent terminology in both outputs. Option 1's output showed a bigger amount of formatting issues and omissions, while Option 2's output, being Option 2 a generic engine, showed a bigger amount of key terminology issues.

To sum up, both engines proved to have pros and cons, and we decided to think of what kind of mistakes were quicker and easier to spot and fix. Formatting can be fixed pretty quickly, and terminology can also be fixed easily by connecting a glossary to the project, while omissions are the trickiest issues. For this reason, and also because Option 1 was not compatible with the CAT tools used internally, we decided that Option 2 would be a better candidate.

## 4.2 Testing Option 2 vs. Option 3

Then, Option 3 was also proposed by the company's Machine Translation team and new tests were carried out to evaluate the quality of Option 3's output compared to the two original options. The second test phase was divided into 2 steps: automatic scoring and human evaluation.

For automatic scoring, we use a proprietary tool that outputs a number of industry-standard automatic metrics, such as BLEU, GTM, Meteor, NIST, PE Distance, TER (TAUS, 2012). We typically run this tool on two sets of input: source + MT vs. human reference from a TM (during engine building), as well as source + MT vs. human post-edited reference (during pilot and production). The table below shows the results from scenario 1, i.e. the human reference was not specifically created by translators performing PE on the MT output.

| LP | MT Engine | BLEU | NIST | METEOR | GTM | Avg. PE |
|---|---|---|---|---|---|---|
| EN>IT | Option 1 | 22.68 | 5.55 | 40.56 | 54.07 | 43.30% |
| EN>IT | Option 2 | 29.79 | 6.64 | 47.78 | 60.63 | 38.18% |
| *EN>IT* | *Option 3* | *39.12* | *7.62* | *56.15* | *66.99* | *31.62%* |
| IT>EN | Option 1 | 35.42 | 7.14 | 34.42 | 66.96 | 42.90% |
| *IT>EN* | *Option 2* | *38.78* | *7.33* | *38.11* | *70* | *39.93%* |
| IT>EN | Option 3 | 36.21 | 6.98 | 35.07 | 67.18 | 42.38% |

Table 1. Results of automatic scoring.

As showed in the table, Option 1 obtained the worst score for both language pairs, Option 2 obtained the best score for Italian into English and Option 3 obtained the best score for English into Italian.

After human evaluation, Option 1 was excluded again, and Option 2 was also excluded since the quality did not prove to be significantly better than Option 3 for Italian into English. Option 3 was the preferred from a linguistic point of view, but also because it is cheaper compared to the other options, the lexical coverage is much wider, and it can be customized and updated.

## 4.3 Evaluating Option 3's raw output

We then started the third phase of the testing process. This test was aimed at analysing and scoring the accuracy and fluency of the raw output and validate the results of the automatic scoring (Marg, 2016). It also allowed us to identify the typical issues in the MT output, and to start putting together post-editing instructions. The test was performed by two linguists for each language pair (2 for Italian into English and 2 for English into Italian).

### 4.3.1 Results for English into Italian

The test for English into Italian was performed by two native in-house translators specialized in financial translation. The text translated was a piece of Transfer Pricing document. Both linguists scored accuracy and fluency consistently.

As for accuracy, the major issues concern mistranslations (calques, antonyms, positive to negative sentence or vice versa), omissions (especially missing numbers) and terminology.

As for fluency, there seemed to be a shared opinion as to the grammar mistakes (gender and number agreement, wrong and/or missing prepositions, *consecutio temporum*, translation of modal verbs) and locale adaptation (numbers and measurements were not localized).

### 4.3.2 Results for Italian into English

The test for Italian into English was performed by two external preferred native translators who specialize in financial translation (Plitt and Masselot, 2010). The text translated was a piece of Financial Statements. Also in this case, both linguists scored accuracy and fluency consistently.

As for accuracy, major issues concerned mistranslations (proper nouns and acronyms replaced by random words) and omissions. Terminology also appeared to be problematic, while numbers were not missing in MT output for this language pair.

As for fluency, major issues concerned word order (which often mirrors Italian word order), grammar (primarily verb tenses) and locale adaptation (numbers and measurements were not localized).

To sum up, some types of issues were spotted in both language pairs, while others were language pair specific.

## 5    MT into Production: Preliminary Phase

Having chosen the preferred MT engine and identified the main potential issues, we decided to run a few more tests to analyse more deeply the mistake trends for each language pair. The results of the analysis showed that, to achieve publishable quality – required for our business – a full-post editing was necessary. Originally, to reach the required quality, we implemented a TP process which envisaged a first step (Translation) and a second step (Proofreading). In the MT pilot projects, we decided to keep two steps to ensure top quality: post-editing and review – basically the translation step was replaced by post-editing.

### 5.1  Onboarding Freelance Post-Editors

We then started thinking of the new workflow and how it would merge with our existing vendor base. As mentioned above, it did not include any experienced post-editors. For this reason, we started organizing non-mandatory Machine Translation Post-Editing training for the suitable vendors in our database (Massardo et al., 2016). We sent them an invite and explained them that we were implementing MT in our workflow and they would be offered MT post-editing tasks in the near future.

We gave three training sessions: one in 2018 and two in 2019. The training we gave in 2018 was a generic MTPE training and applied to all language pairs and domains, while of the two training sessions we gave in 2019 one was focused on post-editing our engine's raw Transfer Pricing translation from English into Italian, and the other was focused on post-editing our engine's raw Financial Statements translation from Italian into English in a CAT tool environment. Apart from covering the topics already discussed in the 2018 edition, the 2019 training also focused on the most frequent mistakes delivered by our engine and on how MT was introduced in the workflow. In

March 2019 our database included a number of new post editors specialized in finance.

### 5.2  Instructions for Linguists

We decided to create an instructions file for linguists to be sent over with each project, in order to remind them the guidelines for full post-editing[3] and the most frequent known engine errors (Joscelyne, 2008).

Apart from indicating the above-mentioned most frequent mistakes for each language pair, instructions warned linguists about some strange errors delivered by the engine in very short strings only, which are always a challenge for MT. Basically, proper nouns (company names, cities…) and acronyms (GBP, HPC…) are frequently replaced by random words. Sometimes errors delivered by neural MT engines cannot be fixed by implementing changes in the engine directly, so for the time being we decided to mention this issue in the instructions.

The instructions file also included other useful key take-aways, suggestions and reminders on how to perform post-editing and review of postedited content in a CAT tool environment, like how to understand if the translation of the segment comes from TM or MT, and the indication to follow the TM as for preferred date and currency format.

## 6    MT into Production: Pilot Phase

As mentioned above, projects with PE are handled the same way of the standard TP projects, with translation being replaced by post-editing, plus three new steps: pre-editing, pretranslation with MT and post edit distance measurement, all performed by our internal staff.

After having ascertained that a project is suitable for MTPE by following some internal criteria, we start the pre-editing step, which consists of some minor interventions on the source file to facilitate machine processing, like running a spell-check and removing double spaces. We then upload the file on the CAT tool and pretranslate number-only and untranslatable-only segments. Number-only segments are automatically localized by the CAT tool – this way we reduce the risk of having them mistranslated or

---

[3] As explained in the ISO 18587:2017 standard, which provides guidelines for the process of full, human post-editing of machine translation output.

not localized. Untranslatable-only segments are short segments made up by proper names, company names, acronyms (like EBIT, EBITDA) or characters (%, €, - ...) that do not change from Italian into English and vice versa.

Then, the file is pretranslated with the project TM: the TM is leveraged down to 75% Fuzzy matches. Anything that does not have a ≥75% match in the TM is considered a New Word segment, that is sent to MT. This threshold was chosen because our internal linguists did not find Fuzzy matches below 75% to be very useful as a starting point for translation. For the time being, we like forcing post-editors to work on machine translated content, so, to reduce the temptation of writing the translation from scratch, we pretranslate with MT the matches below 75% and New Word segments. The file is then sent to post-editors along with instructions, and after post-editing is complete, the reviewer, who also received the instructions, can start working on the file.

Since one of the most delicate issues regards key terminology consistency, we associate an empty glossary to each project. Linguists are required to populate it during the translation step with key terminology which is translated wrongly or inconsistently by the MT engine. CAT tool's QA check – which is set up internally upon project creation – will automatically deliver an error message every time a term in the glossary is not translated properly. These glossaries will also be used to update the MT engine.

After the translation is delivered to the customer, we run an auto scoring test on the MT post-edited segments only to see how much of the raw output was changed, and send a survey to the linguists so that they can express their opinion on the quality of the raw output and provide suggestions for improvement. These last two steps are extremely useful for the future updating of the engine.

So far, we have run a fairly big amount of pilot projects, and the results in terms of productivity increase for both language pairs are satisfactory. Productivity increase varies depending on many factors – vendor's experience with MTPE (Guerberof, 2009) and individual speed, source file, language pair, client requirements, etc. – but on average it ranges between 20-25%. We expect this percentage to increase after engine updating and fine-tuning. We ensured that the quality of the final translation was of the same high standard as before by running the same QA processes.

## 7   Vendors' Feedback

Translators often get stressed when they hear the word "machine translation", especially the ones who are more reluctant to try out new technologies. As mentioned above, many translators of our vendor base are not familiar with CAT tools and are not willing to learn how to use them. Some of them are so experienced, productive and used to work "the old way" that they see anything technologically new as something that will affect them negatively.

To sum up, our background was not really the most suitable within which to implement MT, however, some of the freelancers were happy and curious to take part to the training and the pilot projects. They wanted to start getting familiar with machine translation, since more and more LSPs are implementing it in their workflow – this therefore means more job opportunities for them, as well as an increase in productivity.

In all the training sessions we gave, resources asked how the implementation of MT will affect their rates. We were expecting a lot of concerns on this matter (this was also flagged by O'Brien et al., 2009), so we decided to keep the rates unchanged during the pilot phase – basically matches pretranslated with MT were paid like new words for all projects. This way we managed to convince many of them to give MT a try.

As mentioned earlier, a short questionnaire was sent to all the vendors who took part to the pilot projects in order to gather feedback and suggestions. The answers show that the greater part of them feels the MT output was overall useful as a starting point for their translation, and that in most cases they used big portions of MT raw output, introducing minor changes only. Many of them stated they felt they worked faster thanks to MT and that they are willing to work on more MTPE projects. Besides, they were left some blank space where to add suggestions and a description of the most common issues they found in the raw output. Among the issues flagged by linguists, apart from the ones already discussed, the problem of aligning with client's preferred format for amounts and dates was raised, as well as the lack of creativity of the engine and misinterpretation of the meaning of some sentences.

## References

Castilho, Sheila, Joss Moorkens, Federico Gaspari, Iacer Calixto, John Tinsley and Andy Way. 2017. Is Neural Machine Translation the New State of the Art? *Prague Bulletin of Mathematical Linguistics*, 108.

Guerberof, Ana. 2009. Productivity and quality in MT post-editing. *Proceedings of MT Summit XII - Workshop: Beyond Translation Memories: New Tools for Translators MT*, Ottawa, Canada.

Joscelyne, Andrew. 2008. Post-editing: Update on Best Practices, *TAUS Report*.

Marg, Lena. 2016. *The Trials and Tribulations of Predicting Machine Translation Post-Editing Productivity.* Presented at the 2016 Language Resources Evaluation Conference (LREC). http://www.lrecconf.org/proceedings/lrec2016/pdf/8 10_Paper.pdf Accessed 16 April 2019

Massardo, Isabella, Jaap van der Meer, Sharon O'Brien, Fred Hollowood, Nora Aranberri and Katrin Drescher. 2016. *MT Post-Editing Guidelines*. TAUS Signature Editions.

O'Brien Sharon, Johann Roturier, Giselle de Almeida. 2009. Postediting Machine Translation Output Guidelines. *Proceedings of MT Summit XII – Tutorials,* Ottawa, Canada.

Plitt, Mirko and François Masselot. 2010. A productivity test of statistical machine translation post-editing in a typical localisation context. *Prague Bulletin of Mathematical Linguistics*, 93:7– 16.

Schmidt, Tanja and Lena Marg. 2018. How to Move to Neural Machine Translation for Enterprise-Scale Programs—An Early Adoption Case Study. *Proceedings of the 21st Annual Conference of the European Association for Machine Translation*, Alicante, Spain.

TAUS - Enabling better translation. 2012. Advancing Best Practices in Machine Translation Evaluation, *TAUS Labs Report*.

# Pre-editing Plus Neural Machine Translation for Subtitling: Effective Pre-editing Rules for Subtitling of TED Talks


Yusuke Hiraoka
Kansai University
yusuke@wakate-honyaku.net

Masaru Yamada
Kansai University
yamada@apple-eye.com



## Abstract

In this study, the authors developed a set of pre-editing rules for TED Talk subtitling to translate Japanese source text into English. The simplified rules optimized for NMT (@TexTra® Minnano jido hon'yaku) were intended for use by a monolingual pre-editor of content to be disseminated in English. The rules were a) insert punctuation b) make implied subjects and objects explicit, and c) write proper nouns in English. The effectiveness of the rules was evaluated by human raters and BLEU score. Quality improvement was confirmed significant on human evaluation, although in some cases no changes or even degrade in quality were observed. However, one of the main concerns about the feasibility of this approach, the 21-character limit specified in the TED subtitling guidelines, was validated. The authors hold that pre-editing plus NMT is a promising approach to translating TED Talk subtitles.


## 1 Introduction

The translation quality of neural machine translation (hereafter referred to as NMT or MT) has improved drastically when compared with that of previous systems such as statistical machine translation. NMT systems have been in practical use for the English-Japanese combination since 2016. This technological advancement is expected to help ease the effects of a worldwide shortage of translators. To fully meet the increasing translation demand of all language combinations would require approximately two billion translators (Common Sense Advisory, 2018). NMT, with its advantages in cost and delivery time, could be a solution for this excessive demand.

While post-editing has already established itself as a means of translation for specific purposes in industry, pre-editing has not yet been in practice. Research on pre-editing is also under development, especially for the English-Japanese combination. Pre-editing cost-effectiveness and effective pre-editing strategies have not yet been investigated (Miyata & Fujita, 2017).

Despite the lack of evidence or precedent supporting the adoption of pre-editing, the authors of the present study see ample potential in it, particularly monolingual pre-editing, by which a person with limited knowledge of the target language (i.e. English) would be able to publish their own content translated from their L1 (Japanese).

The development of information technology has also impacted the translation process. For instance, the source content of audiovisual translation has become multifaceted, ranging from user-generated videos such as YouTube1 to TED Talks2. This shift has led to increased demand for subtitling with low cost and quick turnaround. Ultimately, it would be ideal if content creators or non-professional fansub translators could perform pre-editing of their own content for dissemination.

Given this background, the present study will investigate the possibility of monolingual pre-editing of online audiovisual contents, specifically TED talk subtitling, by non-



1 https://www.youtube.com/
2 https://www.ted.com/

professional translators—from Japanese into English—with an aim to establish a set of effective monolingual pre-editing rules which is considered to be easily adopted by online communities.

## 2 Research question

The study aims to develop and test a set of simple, effective pre-editing rules for audio-visual contents including TED Talk subtitling to translate Japanese source text to English, using @TexTra® Minnano jido hon'yaku,3 an NNT engine developed by the National Institute of Information and Communications Technology (NICT) in Japan. The three rules are based on the previous research and are intended to be as simple and easy to follow as possible, so they can be used by monolingual users with limited knowledge of English. Therefore, the present study will examine the following question: how effective are those pre-editing rules at improving NMT quality of TED Talk subtitling?

## 3 Experiment design

### 3.1 TED subtitling

TED Talks is a free online video service led by TED, a non-profit organization, that promotes a global TED conference where a number of well-known speakers deliver presentations on "ideas worth spreading," normally in the English language. Under the umbrella of TED, the organization also holds regional conferences worldwide at which local speakers present in their native language.

The source content to be investigated in this study was a presentation from TEDxTokyo 2012 to 2013, delivered in Japanese and transcribed by volunteer TED Talk viewers. These transcriptions became the source texts fed into an NMT system to be translated into English. For analysis, this set of source texts, pre-edited by the researcher and machine-translated, was used to compare the final quality.

### 3.2 Text type of the source speech

The TED source speech content for this study is a presentation delivered in Japanese, transcribed in the original language, and then translated into multiple languages by volunteer translators in the TED translation project.

The Japanese texts used for the present study were transcriptions of excerpts from four videos shown in Appendix B. The entire text data comprise approximately 12,000 Japanese characters with 606 subtitle segments in total.

In accordance with TED subtitling guidelines, these transcribed subtitles contain sound representations (e.g. "laugh" and "applause") for enhanced accessibility to deaf and hard-of-hearing viewers which are not normally seen in professionally-produced movie subtitles. Thus, for the present investigation, these were omitted prior to the comparative analysis.

### 3.3 TED subtitles as target text

The English target text of the TED presentation to be used as a reference point for quality evaluation was translated by TED volunteer translators. It contains approximately 4,900 English words with 616 subtitle segments in total. The translation quality of volunteer created subtitles is regarded to be close to the professional quality because TED volunteer translators have to go through a rigid translation process involving multiple reviews, and they are required to follow TED-specific subtitling guidelines, including the following rules:

1. keep the subtitle reading speed at a maximum of 21 characters per second (CPS);
2. try to preserve as much meaning as possible.

These rules are different from conventional movie subtitling norms that limit characters to under 12 CPS, which is approximately half the number of characters allowed in TED subtitles. The looser character limit adopted in the TED subtitling may relate to viewers being able to rewind the video and watch portions they missed again. The liberalized character limit also allows TED subtitling to make more 'literal' translations than in conventional movie subtitling so it can better preserve the source meaning. Conventional movie subtitling with the 12-character limit normally requires editing and condensing source information to fit through 'sense-based' translation or trans-creation. Therefore, these

---

3 https://mt-auto-minhon-mlt.ucri.jgn-x.jp

TED subtitling rules—permitting more characters and more literal translation that aims to preserve the source meaning—are considered favorable for the use of MT, and worth investigating.

### 3.4 Pre-editing method

Pre-editing is generally categorized into two methods, bilingual pre-editing and monolingual pre-editing. Bilingual pre-editing allows the pre-editor to edit the source text while looking at the MT output whereas monolingual pre-editing does not. Thus, monolingual pre-editing requires no target language skill.

The focus of this research is monolingual pre-editing since part of our ultimate goal is to enable content creators or people with limited target language command (i.e. monolingual speakers) to pre-edit the source text of their own language to disseminate content. For this purpose, it is desirable to set simple pre-editing rules for pre-editors to follow.

### 3.5 Monolingual pre-editing rules

Hiraoka & Yamada (2019) previously carried out an investigation to create pre-editing rules for popular Japanese YouTube content and selected the top 19 most effective editing categories in terms of quality improvement.

From the 19 pre-editing rules, the authors of this study chose three to observe (Table 1) based on frequency (cf. Miyata & Fujita, 2017) and ease of use, considering the potential post-editor to be a non-bilingual content creator with limited knowledge of the target language and also low editing skills in the source language.

As Miyata & Fujita (2017) states, pre-editing normally requires skillful editing of the source language to identify and edit errors that violate rules provided in the specific instructions. Thus, for this investigation we have selected a very simple set of rules that monolingual speakers can follow easily without referring to the target language.

| Rule | Type | Method |
|---|---|---|
| 1 | Punctuation | Compensate missing punctuation (tôten) |
| 2 | Subject / Object | Compensate missing subject and/or object |
| 3 | Proper Noun | Write proper nouns in target language (English) |

Table1. Pre-edit Rules

As shown in Appendix C, rules include 1) inserting missing punctuations based on spaces, line breaks and segment breaks of the original source texts, 2) compensating subjects and/or objects of the sentence since the Japanese language is a pro-drop language in which certain pronouns are omitted when they are pragmatically or grammatically inferable, and 3) writing in the target language (English) in the Japanese source text.

### 3.6 Subtitle segments to be pre-edited

In order to evaluate quality improvement after application of the three pre-editing rules, the experimenters first pre-processed the existing TED subtitles by adjusting their alignments between the transcribed segments (Japanese) and human-translated ones (English) to correspond correctly .

Secondly, the adjusted segments were investigated to determine what types of pre-editing rules were needed according to the set of rules established in 3.5. Then we applied the missing rules to each segment (i.e. pre-edited) to make sure the segments satisfied all three elements compensated by the pre-editing rules. Table 2 summarizes the number of segments and which rules have been applied to them. Then we selected an equal number of segments from each 'Rules Application' category for quality evaluation, minimizing biased sampling of categories where different rules were applied.

| Rules Application | Num. of Segments |
|---|---|
| Rule 1 + 2 | 80 |
| Rule 1 + 3 | 19 |
| Rule 2 + 3 | 9 |
| Rule 1 + 2 + 3 | 5 |
| Total | 113 |

Table 2. Application of pre-editing rules

## 4 Evaluation methods

The effectiveness of the pre-editing rules was measured in terms of improvement of MT output quality given the 21-character-per-second (CPS) limitation. Since the translation target is TED subtitling, character limitation also needs to be taken into account.

## 4.1 Translation quality evaluation

Quality evaluation of MT outputs of both 'raw source' and 'pre-edited source' was carried out by human evaluators following the same guidelines. Along with it, we have also used an automatic evaluation, BLEU score, to investigate the correlation between human evaluation and BLEU.

Human evaluation was conducted by a Japanese speaker following the evaluation criteria shown in Table 3. The criteria were modified from a five-grade scale commonly used for MT system evaluation (Goto et al. 2013; Miyata & Fujita 2017). The reasons for employing the criteria in this study were 1) to minimize variations between human evaluators, and 2) to optimize for non-native English speakers.

The raters evaluated each segment using a three-point scale, with 3 indicating 'Good' and 1 indicating 'Nonsense.' For details, see Appendix A.

| Criterion | Score |
|-----------|-------|
| Good | 3 |
| Acceptable | 2 |
| Nonsense | 1 |

Table 3. Human Evaluation Criteria

Mean score of total subtitle segments are calculated and compared between MT output of the raw source and the pre-edited source for improved quality.

BLEU score was also employed to evaluate the NMT outputs of the raw and pre-edited source texts against TED human translation as a reference text.

## 4.2 Inter-rater agreement

Prior to human evaluation, the inter-rater reliability ($\kappa = 0.639$) was confirmed to be within the range of "substantial agreement" (Landis and Koch, 1977). This attests to the reliability of the quality evaluation scale.

## 5 Results of evaluation

The evaluation results confirmed that, compared to the results of MT output of the raw source text (hereafter referred to as Raw MT), the MT output of the pre-edited source text (hereafter, Pre-Edit MT) made quality improvement in the average score of both human evaluation and BLEU. It is also revealed the total number of subtitle segments that resulted in score increase to be 41%. Although some score decreases were found in the pre-edited MT, most of the segments stayed above the 'Acceptable' level on the human evaluation scale.

In addition to translation quality, we have also examined the subtitling character limitation and verified that the number of segments in both raw MT and pre-edited MT output that violate the 21-CPS rule guideline by TED was almost none. Hence, it is concluded that pre-editing with the three rules does not preclude meeting the 21-CPS requirement.

The following sections show detailed results of each aspect.

## 5.1 Characters Per Second

This section touches on whether MT can translate the pre-edited source segment in accordance with the 21-CPS limit for TED subtitles. We calculated the number of characters used in each segment and the use ratio – the actual number of characters used in the segment divided by the maximum allowable characters.

The result reveals the number of segments in the pre-edited MT that violate the 21-CPS requirement to be just one segment. The average CPS in the pre-edit MT (12.5 CPS) has increased from that of the human translation (11.6); however, the difference is not statistically significant ($p > 0.01$ in Wilcoxon signed-rank test). Hence, it is concluded that pre-edited MT subtitles would meet the 21-CPS requirement of TED.

| Data Set | Avg. CPS | 21 CPS Violation |
|----------|----------|------------------|
| Human translation | 85.7 | 0 |
| Raw MT | 90.7 | 2 |
| Pre-edited MT | 90.2 | 1 |

Table 4: Average CPS and CPS violation

### Overall translation quality

The average score of the human evaluation showed that the raw MT and the pre-edited

MT has a statistically significant difference in their translation quality.

Table 5 shows that the raw MT output scored on average 1.85 on human evaluation and 7.70 on BLEU, which means these subtitles are, on average, 'Acceptable,' a translation functioning as adequate information with audiovisual elements.

In contrast, pre-edited MT output scored 2.21 on human evaluation and 9.32 on BLEU. The improvement of 0.36 from the raw MT on human evaluation is statistically significant (p < 0.01 in Wilcoxon signed-rank test).

| Data Set | Avg. Human Evaluation Score | BLEU |
|---|---|---|
| Raw MT | 1.8 | 7.70 |
| Pre-edited MT | 2.21 | 9.32 |
| Difference | 0.36* | 1.62 |

Table 5: Evaluation average score of raw and pre-edited MT

Graph 1 shows the percentages of quality levels, such as 'Good,' 'Acceptable,' and 'Nonsense,' of raw and pre-edited MT segments. It is notable that the number of pre-edited MT segments evaluated to be 'Good' increased from 12% to 41%.

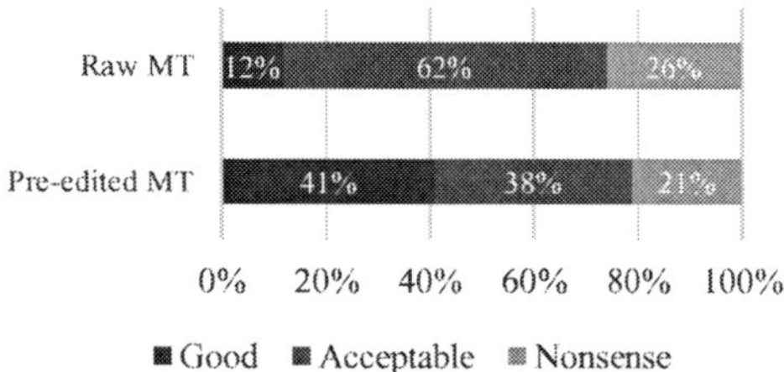


Graph 1: Quality breakdown

Graph 2 below shows the percentages of segments that changed in quality or were unaffected after pre-editing. While half of the segments maintained the same quality rating, 41% of the pre-edited MT segments were improved and only 9%, were rated of lower quality.

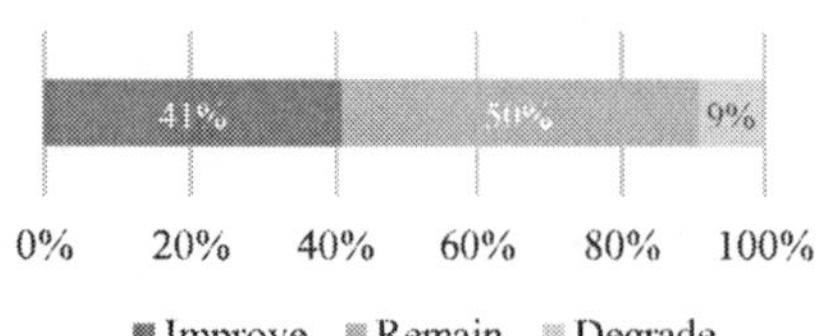


Graph 2: Percentage of quality improvement, remain, and degrade

## 5.2 Examples of pre-edited NMT output

Pre-edited segments that improved in quality

Below is an example of a segment that improved on human evaluation from 'Nonsense' (1) to 'Good' (3). Adding punctuation and subjects to each sentence— simple rules—has made the quality of the subtitles much better.

| ST / HT |
|---|
| 上司が苦しい データが苦しい 考えるのが嫌になってしまった<br>Your boss was being difficult. The data was difficult. You become sick of thinking. |

| Raw NMT (HE Score) |
|---|
| I don't like the difficulty of my boss's difficult data. (1) |

| PrE (HE Score) |
|---|
| 上司が苦しい。 データが苦しい。 私は考えるのが嫌になってしまった。<br>My boss is difficult. I have difficulty in data. I hate to think about it. (3) |

Table 5. Example of HE Increase from Nonsense to Good

### 5.2.1 Pre-edited segments that degraded.

Although there is only a small number of segments that degraded after pre-editing, the following example below dropped two points on the scale from 'Good' to 'Nonsense'.

| ST / HT |
|---|
| で 思いもよらないアイデアが出てくる<br>You can come up with ideas that you wouldn't have thought of otherwise. |

| Raw NMT (HE Score) |
|---|
| There's an unexpected idea. (3) |

| PrE (HE Score) |
|---|
| で、自分の思いもよらないアイデアが出てくる。<br>So there's an idea that I don't want to think about. (1) |

Table 6. Example of degrading

The insertion of punctuation and subject was incorporated into this segment. A subject of the sentence, "自分の" (one's own), was complemented, but how it was added was not sufficient, resulting in a nonsense translation.

If it "自分の" is replaced with "自分が" ("I" in the subject of a sentence), then the MT result improves, as shown below.

で、自分<u>が</u>思いもよらないアイデアが出てくる。
I have an idea that I can't think of.

## 6 Discussion

### 6.1 What are effective pre-editing rules for TED subtitling?

A set of pre-editing rules for TED subtitling intended for non-language expert use—insertion of punctuation, adding explicit subjects and objects, and writing proper nouns in the target language—was tested for its effect in this study. It was proven overall effective, with approximately 40% of the subtitle segments pre-edited with at least two of the rules reaching a 'Good' quality translation, although some lessening or lack of improvement in quality was also observed.

However, for practical use, implementation of these pre-editing rules in TED subtitling is, we feel, effective to improve overall readability. In addition, it is not yet clear what percentage of satisfactory MT outputs is needed to make potential audiences understand with additional audiovisual information, which may be a topic of our further research.

### 6.2 Does pre-editing affect the 'readability' of subtitles?

The readability of subtitles is another essential aspect of translation quality as regulated by the CPS rules. The result of this experiment shows pre-edited MT outputs meet the character limit requirement. Thus, for TED subtitle translation, the pre-editing rules and the pre-editing method can be effectively employed in this respect.

### 6.3 What skills are required for pre-editing in subtitling?

The editing rules were developed to be as simple as possible in order to enable monolingual speakers to perform pre-editing and disseminate their content in neural machine-translated text. However, our results could not rule out the possibility that editing performance may vary depending on pre-editor skill or knowledge. Further

investigation into variants of editing rules for different pre-editors is therefore needed, including issues as to whether training may reduce user variation. Effective intralingual subtitling is simple and well-organized rather than ones that transcribe all speech including some fillers and misstatements.

## 7 Conclusion and further research

In this study, the authors developed a set of pre-editing rules for TED Talk subtitling to translate Japanese source text into English. The simplified rules optimized for @TexTra NMT were intended for use by monolingual pre-editors who can perform pre-editing for dissemination in English. This study investigated the effectiveness of the rules and confirmed quality improvements as evaluated by human ratings and BLEU score. The difference between raw MT and pre-edited MT output was statistically significant. However, there were some cases where pre-editing MT quality did not improve or even worsened the final product. In addition, variations in pre-editing were also confirmed, which may cause additional quality losses depending on the skill of the pre-editor. Lastly, the rules examined in this study were only for Textra NMT, so their effectiveness would need to be verified for use with other NMT systems, though we believe improvements would be leveraged.

## References

Common Sense Advisory. 2018. Machine Translation for Human Innovation. Retrieved on November 17, 2018: http://www.commonsenseadvisory.com/machine_translation.aspx

Goto, Isao, Ka Po Chow, Bin Lu, Eiichiro Sumita, and Benjamin K. Tsou. 2013. Overview of the Patent Machine Translation Task at the NTCIR-10 Workshop. In *Proceedings of the 10th NII Testbeds and Community for Information access Research Conference*, pages 260-286.

Hiraoka, Yusuke and Masaru Yamada. 2019. Is Neural Machine Translation Capable of Subtitling?: Pre-editing Rules for Subtitling of TED Talks. In *Proceedings of the 25th Natural Language Processing conference*, pages 934-937.

Landis, Richard and Gary G Koch. 1977. The Measurement of Observer Agreement for Categorical Data. *Biometrics,* 33(1): 159-174.

Miyata, Rei and Atsushi Fujita. 2017. Investigating the Effectiveness of Pre-Editing Strategy and the Diversity of Pre-Edit Operations for Better Use of Machine Translation. *Invitation to Interpreting and Translation Studies*, 18: 53-72.

## Appendix

### A. Human Evaluation Criteria

**Good**

| | |
|---|---|
| 5 | Information of the original text has been completely translated. There are no grammatical errors in the translation. Word choice and phrasing are natural even from a native speaker's point-of-view. |
| 4 | Word choice and phrasing are slightly unnatural, but information of the original text has been completely translated and there are no grammatical errors in the translation. |

**Acceptable**

| | |
|---|---|
| 3 | There are some minor translation errors with less important information, but the meaning of the original text can be easily understood. |
| 2 | Important parts of the original text are omitted or incorrectly translated, but the core meaning of the original text can still be understood with some effort. |

**Nonsense**

| | |
|---|---|
| 1 | The meaning of the original text is incomprehensible. |

### B. TEDxTokyo Videos

TED presentations used for the present study were selected from the 2012 and 2013 TEDxTokyo. They are all categorized as a topic of "Business" on the TEDxTokyo website (https://www.tedxtokyo.com/).

| Title (Japanese)<br>YouTube URL | Length (mm:ss) | Presenter | Num. of Segments (original/aligned) | |
|---|---|---|---|---|
| | | | JPN | EN |
| The treasure islands of Japan (Nihon no ritō ha takarajima) https://www.youtube.com/watch?v=W_SBR3p_qyA | 8:49 | Isamoto, Atsuko | 128/61 | 130/61 |

| | | | | |
|---|---|---|---|---|
| Life balance (Raifu baransu)<br>https://www.youtube.com/watch?v=sd6OLoQW0hY | 12:14 | Komuro,<br>Yoshie | 171/103 | 233/103 |
| Changing the world with spider webs (Kumo no ito de kawaru sekai)<br>https://www.youtube.com/watch?v=ldybnuFxdiQ | 5:54 | Sekiyama,<br>Kazuhide | 199/60 | 148/60 |
| Play this word game to come up with original ideas (Atarashī aidea no tsukurikata)<br>https://www.youtube.com/watch?v=jzDwcNliXV8 | 8:41 | Takahashi,<br>Shinpei | 108/71 | 105/71 |

## C. Examples of Pre-editing

Examples of the three pre-editing rules developed in this study are illustrated below.

---

**Punctuation insertion**

---

**Examples:**

Original text

今 日本は 少子化だけじゃなくうつ病の問題 ダイバーシティ 大介護の問題 財政難 問題山積の国です。
[Back Translation: The birth rate is not the only problem we're facing. All sorts of problems such as depression diversity elderly care financial problems are piled up.]

Pre-edited text

今、日本は、少子化だけじゃなく、うつ病の問題、ダイバーシティ、大介護の問題、財政難、問題山積の国です。
[Back Translation: The birth rate is not the only problem we're facing. All sorts of problems, such as depression, diversity, elderly care, financial problems are piled up.]

**Note:**

> No clear-cut rules are available for inserting punctuation in Japanese, but the way they are added above is to clarify the word boundaries to improve machine-translatability as well as human readability, since the Japanese writing system does not require spaces between words and sometimes word boundaries are ambiguous. Therefore, inserting punctuations such as commas, performed by pre-editors, would support MT quality improvement.

---

**Subject/Object insertion**

---

**Examples:**

Original text

だから会議が長引き 貧困なアイディアが出て 売れない 帰れない。
[Back Translation: So the meeting drags on and only poor ideas come up; won't sell; can't go home;]

Pre-edited text

だから会議が長引き 貧困なアイディアが出て 商品が売れない 社員は帰れない。
[Back Translation: So the meeting drags on and only poor ideas come up; the products won't sell; the employees can't go home;]

**Note:**

- It is necessary to add explicit subjects and/or objects of a sentence since the Japanese language is a pro-drop language in which certain pronouns are omitted when they are pragmatically or grammatically inferable.

- A sentence with a verb (predicate) requires a subject and object if applicable, so they have to be added by the pre-editor.

- Insertion of a subject "I" is, for most cases, not mandatory because it is often added automatically in neural machine translation; however, it is still recommended to clarify the subject.

**Proper Noun**

**Examples:**

Original text

後 5 年で 日本の <u>団塊世代</u>は 一斉に70代に入ります。
[Back Translation: The baby boomers will be in their 70s in the next 5 years.]

Pre-edited text

後 5 年で 日本の <u>The baby boomers</u> は 一斉に70代に入ります。

**Note:**

- Machine translation is not yet good at translating proper nouns. Thus, when a proper noun is included in the original source text, one can either translate it into the target language (English) and write it in the source text or romanize it in the source text.

# Do translator trainees trust machine translation? An experiment on post-editing and revision


**Randy Scansani**
University of Bologna
Forlì, Italy
randy.scansani@unibo.it

**Silvia Bernardini**
University of Bologna
Forlì, Italy
silvia.bernardini@unibo.it

**Adriano Ferraresi**
University of Bologna
Forlì, Italy
adriano.ferraresi@unibo.it

**Luisa Bentivogli**
Fondazione Bruno Kessler
Trento, Italy
bentivo@fbk.eu



## Abstract

Despite the importance of trust in any work environment, this concept has rarely been investigated for MT. The present contribution aims at filling this gap by presenting a post-editing experiment carried out with translator trainees. An institutional academic text was translated from Italian into English. All participants worked on the same target text. Half of them were told that the text was a human translation needing revision, while the other half was told that it was an MT output to be post-edited. Temporal and technical effort were measured based on words per second and HTER. Results were complemented with a manual analysis of a subset of the observations.


## 1 Introduction

In the last few years, neural machine translation (NMT) has become the state-of-the-art paradigm in the field of machine translation (MT). This fast-paced progress has shaken the translation industry and the research world, causing different reactions. Part of the research world has responded with enthusiastic claims about the quality achieved with this new architecture (Hassan et al., 2018; Wu et al., 2016), while other studies have tempered such enthusiasm, reporting less clear-cut improvements (Toral and Sánchez-Cartagena, 2017; Castilho et al., 2017).

Companies and individual professionals have started to exploit MT more than in previous years. As testified by the 2018 Language Industry Survey[1], for the first time more than half of companies and individual language professionals have stated that they use MT in their workflow. In the same survey repeated in 2019[2], only generic MT engines (Google Translate and DeepL) were chosen among the 20 most-used tools in companies' workflow.

In this uncertain scenario, translators' opinion on MT is likely to be mixed. In the 2019 Language Industry Survey[3], MT was identified as a negative trend by 20% and as a positive one by 30% of the respondents. Lack of training in MT low output quality resulting from adoption of general purpose engines, and a potential downward trend in translation rates may all explain the negative opinion (some) translators have of MT (Läubli and Orrego-Carmona, 2017), and their limited trust, leading to non-adoption of MT suggestions (Cadwell et al., 2018). Investigating how trust towards MT influences translator trainees' behaviour towards the output, along the lines of Martindale and Carpuat (2018), is thus crucial to evaluate the likelihood that translators convincingly embrace MT.

In this contribution, we ask whether translators' trust changes based on the task they are working on, i.e. if they behave differently when they believe they are revising a human translation (HT) *vs.* post-editing an MT output. We see trust as strictly related to productivity: when post-editors/revisers do not trust a text, they are likely to carry out time-consuming and potentially unnecessary searches, or perform unnecessary edits.

In our study, 47 students from a Master's in



---

[1]A survey on trends in the language industry carried out by EUATC, Elia, FIT Europe, GALA and LINDWeb. https://bit.ly/2RpQtm2
[2]https://bit.ly/2ZknGlL
[3]https://bit.ly/2ZknGlL

translation of an Italian university, revised/post-edited the same English translation of an Italian source text composed of two academic module descriptions. Half of them were told that the translation was an MT output, while the other half was told that the text had been translated by a human translator. We measured the time each participant spent on each sentence, and the number and extent of changes they made. In what follows we summarise previous work on post-editing (PE) and trust (Sect. 2), describe the experimental setting and method (Sect. 3), outline results (Sect. 4) and draw some conclusions (Sect. 5).

## 2   Related work

### 2.1   Post-editing of MT

To the best of our knowledge, no work has been published yet on the assessment of trust towards MT as measured in a PE task. Martindale and Carpuat (2018) conducted a survey among non-professionals to understand how their trust was influenced by fluency and adequacy. The former issue is found to have a stronger negative impact on non-professional translators. More recently, Cadwell *et al.* (2018) interviewed two groups of institutional translators to investigate the reasons for adoption or rejection of MT suggestions. Both groups mentioned lack of trust toward MT as one of the reasons for rejecting MT segments.

Focusing on PE tasks in different languages, a number of papers have analysed how performance changes for different subjects or in different work environments, and using one or more effort categories among those listed by Krings (2001): temporal, technical and cognitive. Moorkens and O'Brien (2015) used edit distance and speed to compare the productivity of professionals and students in a PE (En–De) task, whose aim was to evaluate the suitability of the latter for translation user studies. Daems *et al.* (2017) examined how 10 Master's students and 13 professional translators coped with translation from scratch and PE of newspaper articles (En–Nl), measuring translation speed and cognitive load. Moorkens and O'Brien (2015) found that students have a less negative attitude towards technology, but their productivity cannot be compared to that of professionals; by contrast, according to Daems *et al.* (2017) the performance of the two groups was not as different as could be expected, and indeed students were more at ease with PE than professionals.

Yamada (2019) compared perceived cognitive effort, amount of editing and final quality between two PE tasks carried out by students, one using an NMT output and one a PBMT output (En–Ja). While the cognitive effort was similar for the NMT and PBMT tasks, NMT output required less editing effort and led to a better final quality.

Rossetti and Gaspari (2017) measured perceived and real effort of six MA students when translating with translation memories (TMs) and in a PE scenario, triangulating time measurements, think-aloud protocols (TAPs) and retrospective interviews. Results show that only suggestions coming from the TM had a positive impact on perceived task complexity and temporal effort.

Despite growing interest in PE, to the best of our knowledge trust has not been investigated in such task. Furthermore, our language combination (It–En) is relatively under-represented in PE experiments, and the text domain we are focusing on (university module descriptions) is a novel one in this scenario.

### 2.2   Trust

The notion of trust is a multifaceted one, which has been studied in a host of different fields. McKnight *et al.* (2001) report that, in three different monolingual English dictionaries, on average 17 different definitions of trust are provided. Lee and See (2004) define trust as "the attitude that an agent will help achieve an individual's goal in a situation characterised by uncertainty and vulnerability".

Even though human-machine relationships may develop in the same way as human-human ones (Madhavan and Wiegmann, 2007), the constructs developed to describe trust between human beings do not fully transfer to human-machine interactions (Lee and See, 2004). First, human beings, behave intentionally. Second, interpersonal trust depends on how both parties perceive the counterpart's behaviour, which does not happen when one of the parties involved is a machine. In this case, trust follows from observation of technology performance, from understanding of its underlying architecture, and from intended use (Lee and See, 2004). Translators' lack of trust toward MT might therefore be influenced by different factors, including inconsistency/unpredictability of its output (especially true of NMT), or misconceived expectations about its functioning.

Since several academic programs have recently

started to offer courses on MT, the next generation of translators will be the first to enter the market with some knowledge of it. Whether their trust in the technology is likely to increase as a result is still an open question.

## 3 Experimental setup

### 3.1 Goals and variables

Post-editors' productivity was analysed with respect to the following variables: *(a)* translation method (students are told that the text is an MT output *vs.* a HT); *(b)* translation correctness (the translation is correct and needs to be confirmed *vs.* it is incorrect and needs to be edited).

### 3.2 Participants

47 students of the Master's in Specialised Translation of the University of Bologna took part in the experiment. 23 participants worked on the PE task and 24 on the revision task.

Native languages of the participants working on MT were Italian (69.6%), English (4.3%) and other (26.1%). The native language of participants working on the purported revision of a HT was Italian (79.2%), English (8.3%) and other (15.5%). Although translating into English as L2 is not common practice for experiments in this field, the reality of the profession is quite different. Two surveys quoted by Pokorn (2016) revealed, respectively, that for 24% of the respondents the ability of translating into an L2 is essential or important for newly employed translators[4] and that more than 50% of 780 free-lance translators working in 80 states (including Italy) translate into L2 [5]

All students belonged to the same cohort. This allowed us to control for *(i)* their PE/translation experience; *(ii)* their knowledge of the text type and disciplinary domains of the texts; *(iii)* their knowledge of English.

Regarding *(i)*, students attended hands-on modules on CAT tools and on MT and PE as part of their syllabus. One week before the experiment, they received training on the use of MateCat,[6] the tool used for the task (see Sect. 3.3). Also, in a pre-experiment questionnaire, they were asked

| Question | Answers | MT part. | HT part. |
|---|---|---|---|
| **Professional experience with MT/PE** | None | 91.3% | 95.8% |
| | Little | 8.7% | 0% |
| | Much | 0% | 4.2% |
| **MT usefulness for translators** | Not useful | 0% | 0% |
| | Useful | 82.6% | 70.83% |
| | Very useful | 17.4% | 30.43% |

**Table 1:** Results of the questionnaire on participants' professional experience and opinion on usefulness of MT, split by type of task (HT or PE).

how much experience they had with the revision of a HT or PEMT in a professional setting. Possible answers were: *None*, *Little*, i.e. from 1 to 5 professional tasks or *Much*, i.e. more than 5 professional tasks. Results are reported in Table 1 and show that the degree of expertise is similar in both groups, since the vast majority of the participants had no or little professional experience. Regarding *(ii)*, all subjects are likely to be familiar with the text type, since course unit descriptions address students, and are unlikely to be acquainted with the domains (pharmacy and chemistry), since their academic background is in languages and linguistics. Concerning *(iii)*, all students are tested upon enrollment in the Master's, a minimum of C1 CEFR being required for admission.[7]

To collect data on participants' opinion regarding MT, in the pre-experiment questionnaire they were asked how useful they thought MT is for translators. Results in Table 1 suggest that all participants have a positive opinion on MT, confirming the results described by Daems *et al.* (2017) and Moorkens and O'Brien (2015) (see Sect. 2.1).

### 3.3 Task

The same text was used for both the MT PE task and the HT revision task. It was composed of two course unit descriptions – for a course on chemistry and one on pharmacy – written in Italian. The English version was produced with a state-of-the-art off-the-shelf NMT system, which ensures the high-quality of the target text used for the experiment.

The final version of the text was the result of a two-step procedure. First, to make sure the text could be believed to be a HT, we checked for possible mistakes typical of MT systems. To establish which sentences were (in)correct, three evaluators were asked to assign each sentence to one

---

[4] 2011 OPTIMALE survey, involving translation companies from 27 countries – including Italy. `https://bit.ly/2x3V0Bo`

[5] 2014 survey by the International Association of Professional Translators and Interpreters. `https://bit.ly/2h0bjsO`

[6] `https://www.matecat.com/`

[7] `https://bit.ly/2pVyffz`

of the following categories: *(i) correct* (the meaning of the source sentence is conveyed in the target text and no editing is required); *(ii) incorrect* (the meaning of the source sentence is conveyed in the target text but edits are required. In this case, evaluators were asked to annotate the part of the sentence that should be edited); *(iii) wrong* (the meaning of the source sentence is not conveyed in the target text). The final decision as to the correctness of each sentence was made by majority vote. None of the sentences was labelled as *wrong*.

A small amount of edits were performed in order to have half *correct* sentences and half *incorrect* ones in the data set (see Sect. 3.1). At the end of this procedure, the text consisted of 60 sentence pairs, corresponding approximately to 670 source words in total.

Participants worked in MateCat. A project – including a termbase – was assigned to each of them.

A week before, students were given basic information about the experiment.[8] After reading the instructions, students started working autonomously. In the instructions they were invited to work as they normally would. They were asked to deliver a target text of publishable quality, but encouraged to use the provided target text as much as possible and not to over-edit. Researchers were present in the lab throughout.

### 3.4 Evaluation methods

Productivity was measured in terms of HTER (Snover et al., 2006) between the original text and the participants' edited version, and in terms of words per second (WPS). The latter was obtained by converting MateCat time measurements on a segment level into seconds and dividing them by the number of words in the target text.

Two separate linear mixed models were built, one for each dependent variable, i.e. HTER and WPS. In both cases, the independent variables (or fixed effects) are categorical, i.e. translation method (MT/HT), and translation correctness (correct/incorrect). We included in the model an interaction of the two, with participant and segment as random effects.

Random effects were tested for significance using the likelihood ratio test. Following Gries (2015), a model including all fixed and random effects was built and compared using ANOVAs



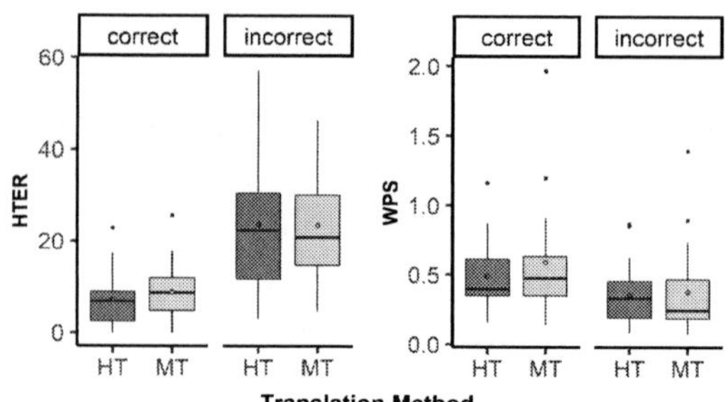

**Figure 1:** HTER (on the left) and WPS (on the right) values for individual segments split by translation method and correctness of the translation.

against different models, each excluding one of the random effects. If the difference between the two models was significant ($p < 0.05$), the random effect was kept in the model.

## 4 Results

Tables 2 and 3 summarise significance and estimates for the effects of the two linear mixed models. Figure 1 shows the distribution of HTER and WPS values for individual segments split by translation method and correctness.

### 4.1 HTER analysis

As expected, in Figure 1 HTER is higher for incorrect sentences overall. While differences between PEMT and HT revision in both cases are small, HTER values for correct MT sentences are slightly higher than values for correct HT sentences.

Moving on to results of our linear mixed model, the two random effects *participant* and *segment* do have a statistically significant impact on the HTER scores (see Table 2), i.e. the observations for the same segment or for the same participant are strongly correlated. Using a mixed model guarantees that the effect of these correlations on the dependent variable is controlled for. Translation correctness is the only fixed effect with a statistically significant impact on HTER, while neither translation method nor its interaction with translation correctness significantly impact on it.

The model thus shows that the number of edits changes significantly only between correct and incorrect sentences, while the amount of edits performed on HT and MT sentences does not differ significantly. The effect of the interaction was not significant either, i.e. no significant change in HTER scores is observed in HT revision and MT PE across translation correctness conditions.

|        | Effect      | HTER *p* value | WPS *p* value |
|--------|-------------|----------------|---------------|
| **Random** | Participant | <0.001*** | <0.001*** |
|            | Segment     | <0.001*** | <0.001*** |
| **Fixed**  | Correctness | <0.0001*** | 0.1185 |
|            | Method      | 0.6 | 0.4367 |
|            | Interaction | 0.14 | 0.4334 |

**Table 2:** Significance of random and fixed effects on the two dependent variables: HTER and WPS

| Variables | HTER | WPS |
|-----------|------|-----|
| HT correct | 7.284 | 0.492 |
| MT correct | 8.986 | 0.598 |
| HT incorrect | 25.402 | 0.470 |
| MT incorrect | 23.603 | 0.399 |

**Table 3:** Estimates of the two linear mixed models for HTER and WPS. HTER goes up when more edits are performed. WPS goes up when productivity increases.

The similarity of the HTER values is confirmed by estimates in Table 3, where HTER is only slightly higher for MT sentences (+ 1.702), while the opposite happens in incorrect sentences, where HTER is higher for HT revised sentences (+1.799). We conclude that HTER does not provide evidence of a lack of trust toward MT and that behaviours observed for both translation methods are similar.

### 4.2 Words per second analysis

Figure 1 shows that WPS is higher for correct sentences than for incorrect ones, while it is similar for PE and revision in the two conditions.

As in Sect. 4.1, the *p* values in the WPS column of Table 2 confirm the statistically significant effect of the two random effects (participant and segment) on the dependent variable. However, in this case neither the two fixed effects (translation correctness and translation method), nor their interaction have a significant effect. This means that differences in terms of WPS between correct and incorrect sentences are not statistically significant. Similarly, significant differences between HT revision and PE were not found. When considering the interaction of translation method and translation correctness, WPS does not change significantly.

Looking at Table 3 we can see that, as expected, participants were more productive on correct sentences than on incorrect ones, but values do not vary substantially. WPS is higher (+ 0.106) for correct MT sentences than for correct HT sentences, while for incorrect sentences productivity in terms of WPS is higher (+ 0.010) for HT than for MT.

Combining these results with those in Sect. 4.1, we can confirm that students did not trust MT less than HT or vice versa.

### 4.3 Qualitative analysis

Given that neither translation method nor its interaction with translation correctness were found to significantly affect technical and temporal effort, we performed a qualitative analysis on a subset of the sentences. Segments with the highest difference between MT and HT in terms of mean HTER were examined.

Concerning Example 1 in Table 4, in both revision and PE, the same number of participants made the right decision, i.e. no edits. In the HT condition most of the participants who edited the sentence only changed the preposition. In the MT condition, terms were changed as well, resulting in a higher HTER score for MT (25.6) than for HT (17.3). Simlarly in Example 2, most post-editors changed verb tenses or nominalised verbs. Mean HTER was 11.4 for MT and 6.79 for HT: most revisers did not edit the sentence.

Regarding incorrect sentences that were edited less in PE than revision, it would seem that revisers paid more attention to issues in the text than post-editors did. For example, all three occurrences of *reaction* in Example 3 should be plural and the term provided by the termbase is *Alkyl halides* rather than *Haloalkane*. 58.3% of the revisers spotted both issues, while only 34.78% of the post-editors did. As a result, mean HTER was 57.2 for HT revision and 43.4 for PE.

In Example 4, it would be sufficient to add the word *examination* at the end. However, in the HT condition most of the participants (54%) carried out a number of other edits applying to the whole sentence. Post-editors carried out unnecessary edits to a lesser extent (4.8%), such that mean HTER was 48.9 for HT and 43.8 for MT.

## 5 Discussion and limitations

In this contribution we have compared post-editor and reviser trainees' trust towards MT and HT based on HTER and WPS (see Table 2 and 3). According to two linear models, significant changes were only found between HTER on correct and incorrect sentences.

No evidence of a lack of trust towards MT emerged. This behaviour confirms the positive opinion on MT stated in the pre-experiment ques-

| Ex. | Sent. type | Text | Correctness |
|---|---|---|---|
| 1 | OUTPUT | Drugs during pregnancy, in children and in the elderly | Correct |
| | PE | Drugs in children, in the elderly and during pregnancy | |
| | REVISION | Drugs during pregnancy, for children and for the elderly | |
| 2 | OUTPUT | Finally, possible technical solutions to reduce the use of solvents and their recycling will be discussed | Correct |
| | PE | Finally, possible technical solutions for solvent usage reduction and solvent recycling will be discussed | |
| | REVISION | Finally, possible technical solutions to reduce the use of solvents and to enable their recycling will be discussed. | |
| 3 | OUTPUT | Haloalkane reactions (metal reaction, elimination reaction) | Incorrect |
| | PE | Alkyl halides reactions (metal reaction, elimination reaction). | |
| | REVISION | Alkyl halides reactions (metal reactions, elimination reactions). | |
| 4 | OUTPUT | The requirement to take the test is to have taken the Microbiology | Incorrect |
| | PE | The requirement to take the test is to have taken the Microbiology examination. | |
| | REVISION | Only the students who passed the Microbiology test can take the exam. | |

**Table 4:** Examples of correct and incorrect outputs with large HTER differences between HT and MT.

tionnaire (see Table 1). This constructive attitude and the ability to interact with technology may be the result of greater awareness of the limits and strengths of MT and PE practice, acquired as part of their academic education (see Sect. 1 and 3.2).

While not significant, differences do exist, and they can provide interesting insights for future work. In correct sentences an increase in HTER corresponds to an increase in WPS – and thus in productivity – and in incorrect sentences a decrease in HTER corresponds to a decrease in WPS. These fluctuations are to be expected, since HTER is based on the number of edits, while WPS is also related to cognitive effort. High HTER scores are often linked to simple preferential changes (see Sect. 4.3), e.g. nominalizations and stylistic vocabulary variation. Such changes may be costly in terms of HTER, but do not require long searches or sentence restructuring – which would be costly in terms of WPS as well. If segments with complex terms are thoroughly checked with a focus on terminology, edits are less costly in terms of HTER than WPS, and discrepancies arise between WPS and HTER. Since participants are not expert in pharmacy or chemistry, terminology searches would not suggest distrust, while preferential changes would. To investigate the presence of preferential changes in the edits, future work might focus on a more thorough qualitative analysis, categorizing the changes introduced in the different conditions and the attention-needing points in the raw output. A longer task would also be necessary, which would however increase fatigue and lead to possible adverse effects, especially since volunteer translator trainees are involved.

In Sect. 3.2 we have seen that students' professional experience is similar in both tasks, and that they are acquainted with the basic notions of PE practice. Their familiarity with revision is certainly greater, though, as this is a standard component in translation courses at both BA and MA level. The more limited familiarity with PE might explain the WPS values obtained, which are highest for MT correct and lowest for MT incorrect. When a mistake is spotted in an MT-translated sentence, more time is spent choosing a strategy to edit it whereas, when a sentence is correct, it is quickly confirmed, as productivity is of the essence in PE. For HT revision, WPS results are more similar in both correctness conditions than is the case in MT. The lowest productivity observed in the MT incorrect condition would suggest that there is still scope for improving translators/post-editors trust in machine translation. More studies would be needed to shed light on the complex and multidimensional nature of trust. For example, pre- and post-experiment questionnaires and interviews could better clarify what participants expect from a HT *vs.* an MT output, and why.

These observations and limitations should not hide the main finding of this study, namely that there are no significant differences between post-editors' and revisers' trust. We would like to interpret this as a sign that, after receiving training on this new technology and before entering the translation industry, a new generation of translators does not seem to be affected by prejudice against PEMT as much as one could expect.

## References

Cadwell, Patrick, Sharon OBrien, and Carlos S. C. Teixeira. 2018. Resistance and accommodation:

factors for the (non-) adoption of machine translation among professional translators. *Perspectives*, 26(3):301–321.

Castilho, Sheila, Joss Moorkens, Federico Gaspari, Iacer Calixto, John Tinsley, and Andy Way. 2017. Is neural machine translation the new state of the art? *The Prague Bulletin of Mathematical Linguistics*, 108(1):109–120. Exported from https://app.dimensions.ai on 2018/09/13.

Daems, Joke, Sonia Vandepitte, Robert Hartsuiker, and Lieve Macken. 2017. Translation methods and experience : a comparative analysis of human translation and post-editing with students and professional translators. *META*, 62(2):245–270.

Gries, Th. Stefan. 2015. The most under-used statistical method in corpus linguistics: multi-level (and mixed-effects) models. *Corpora*, 10(1):95–125.

Hassan, Hany, Anthony Aue, Chang Chen, Vishal Chowdhary, Jonathan Clark, Christian Federmann, Xuedong Huang, Marcin Junczys-Dowmunt, William Lewis, Mu Li, Shujie Liu, Tie-Yan Liu, Renqian Luo, Arul Menezes, Tao Qin, Frank Seide, Xu Tan, Fei Tian, Lijun Wu, Shuangzhi Wu, Yingce Xia, Dongdong Zhang, Zhirui Zhang, and Ming Zhou. 2018. Achieving human parity on automatic chinese to english news translation. *CoRR*, abs/1803.05567.

Krings, Hans P. 2001. *Repairing Texts: Empirical Investigations of Machine Translation Post-Editing Processes*. Kent State University Press, Kent, Ohio.

Läubli, Samuel and David Orrego-Carmona. 2017. When google translate is better than some human colleagues, those people are no longer colleagues. In *Translating and the Computer 39*, pages 56–69, London.

Lee, John D. and Katrina A. See. 2004. Trust in automation: designing for appropriate reliance. *Human Factors*, 46(1):50–80.

Madhavan, Poornima and Douglas A. Wiegmann. 2007. Similarities and differences between human-human and humanautomation trust: an integrative review. *Theoretical Issues in Ergonomics Science*, 8(4):277–301.

Martindale, Marianna J. and Marine Carpuat. 2018. Fluency over adequacy: A pilot study in measuring user trust in imperfect MT. abs/1802.06041.

McKnight, D. Harrison and Norman L. Chervany. 2001. What trust means in e-commerce customer relationships: An interdisciplinary conceptual typology. *International Journal of Electronic Commerce*, 6(2):35–59, December.

Moorkens, Joss and Sharon O'Brien. 2015. Post-editing evaluations: Trade-offs between novice and professional participants. In *Proceedings of the 18th Annual Conference of the European Association for Machine Translation*, pages 75–81, Antalya, Turkey, May.

Pokorn, Nike K. 2016. Is it so different? competences of teachers and students in 12 translation classes. *International Journal of Translation*, 18:31–48.

Rossetti, Alessandra and Federico Gaspari. 2017. Modelling the analysis of translation memory use and post-editing of raw machine translation output: A pilot study of trainee translators' perceptions of difficulty and time effectiveness. In Hansen-Schirra, Silvia, Oliver Czulo, and Hofmann Sascha, editors, *Empirical Modelling of Translation and Interpreting*, pages 41–67, Berlin. Language Science Press.

Snover, Matthew, Bonnie Dorr, Richard Schwartz, Linnea Micciulla, and John Makhoul. 2006. A study of translation edit rate with targeted human annotation. In *Proceedings of Association for Machine Translation in the Americas*, pages 223–231.

Toral, Antonio and Víctor M. Sánchez-Cartagena. 2017. A multifaceted evaluation of neural versus phrase-based machine translation for 9 language directions. In *Proceedings of the 15th Conference of the European Chapter of the Association for Computational Linguistics, EACL 2017, Valencia, Spain, April 3-7, 2017, Volume 1: Long Papers*, pages 1063–1073.

Wu, Yonghui, Mike Schuster, Zhifeng Chen, Quoc V. Le, Mohammad Norouzi, Wolfgang Macherey, Maxim Krikun, Yuan Cao, Qin Gao, Klaus Macherey, Jeff Klingner, Apurva Shah, Melvin Johnson, Xiaobing Liu, Lukasz Kaiser, Stephan Gouws, Yoshikiyo Kato, Taku Kudo, Hideto Kazawa, Keith Stevens, George Kurian, Nishant Patil, Wei Wang, Cliff Young, Jason Smith, Jason Riesa, Alex Rudnick, Oriol Vinyals, Greg Corrado, Macduff Hughes, and Jeffrey Dean. 2016. Google's neural machine translation system: Bridging the gap between human and machine translation. *CoRR*, abs/1609.08144.

Yamada, Masaru. 2019. The impact of Google Neural Machine Translation on post-editing by student translators. *The Journal of Specialised Translation*, pages 87–106, 01.

# On reducing translation shifts in translations intended for MT evaluation


**Maja Popović**
ADAPT Centre
Dublin City University
Ireland
`maja.popovic@adaptcentre.ie`



## Abstract

Automatic evaluation of machine translation (MT) is based on the idea that the quality of the MT output is better if it is more similar to human translation (HT). Whereas automatic metrics based on this similarity idea enable fast and large-scale evaluation of MT progress and therefore are widely used, they have certain limitations. One is the fact that the automatic metrics are not able to recognise acceptable differences between MT and HT. The frequent cause of these differences are translation shifts, the optional departures from theoretical formal correspondence between source and target language units for the sake of adapting the text to the norms and conventions of the target language. This work is based on the author's own translation experience related to the evaluation of MT output compared to the experience unrelated to MT. The main observation is that, although without any instructions in this direction, fewer translation shifts were performed than when translating for other purposes. This finding will hopefully initialise further systematic research both from the aspect of MT as well as from the aspect of translation studies (TS) and bring translation theory and MT closer together.


## 1 Introduction and Motivation

The notion of translation shifts (Catford, 1965; van Leuven-Zwart, 1989; van Leuven-Zwart, 1990;



Curys, 2006) is an important concept in translation theory. A shift has ocurred if the translation procedure has been "oblique" instead of "direct/literal" (Vinay and Darbelnet, 1958) so that there are "departures from formal correspondence" (Catford, 1965). A translated text in a target language can differ from the original text in the source language in many aspects and levels (such as lexical, structural, discourse, etc.) and still be perfectly acceptable. Apart from the transformations necessary for the sake of grammatical well-formedness, it is common practice to introduce optional changes to adapt the text to the norms and conventions of the target language depending on the genre, domain, register, etc. Although such changes are not strictly necessary, the professional translators are expected to deliver texts which appear natural in the target language.

These shifts, although natural and necessary in human translation (HT), pose challenges if the translations are used for automatic evaluation of machine translation (MT) systems. The vast majority of MT automatic evaluation metrics is based on similarity between MT and HT, and availability of a heterogeneous set of human reference translations is largely beneficial for metrics' performance (Albrecht and Hwa, 2008; Popović et al., 2016b). In practice, however, only one reference HT is available and its characteristics can strongly affect the results of automatic evaluation.

A lot of work has been done exploring differences between different types of texts, such as between texts originally written in a given language and texts translated into a given language ("translationese") (Baroni and Bernardini, 2006; Rabinovich and Wintner, 2015; Wintner, 2016; Daems et al., 2017), human and machine translations (Ahrenberg, 2017), as well as post-edited MT outputs (PEs) as a special case of HT (Čulo and Nitzke, 2016; Daems et al., 2017; Farrell, 2018). Overall, the main findings are that HTs differ from original language texts because the source language seems to always "leave a trace" in the translation ("shine through"); similarly, PE, although generally capable of reaching the same quality as HT, always carries a "trace" of the used MT system.

Less work can be found about relations between these facts and the evaluation of machine translation. Popović et al. (2016b) compared the use of PEs and HTs, and suggest that PEs should be used carefully for MT evaluation due to the bias of each PE towards its MT system caused by the previously mentioned system's "shining through". Two methods for reducing translation shifts in reference HTs in order to alleviate automatic MT evaluation are proposed by Ahrenberg (2006) and Fomicheva et al. (2015). Ahrenberg (2006) proposes a method to identify "simpler" HTs which have certain desirable properties and are not too complex for MT systems. Fomicheva et al. (2015) investigate rule-based paraphrasing methods to reduce shifts in HTs and generate additional reference translations. Nevertheless, there is still a lot of room for systematic and extensive experiments dealing with different HTs and their relation to the MT evaluation. For example, even though a large number of HTs intended for MT evaluation have been generated in the framework of the WMT shared tasks[1] (Bojar et al., 2018; Bojar et al., 2017) running since 2006 until the present, no information can be found about the translators, such as how many segments did each individual translate, what are their qualifications, what translation experience or credentials do they have, how are they linked to the domain(s) of the data sets, whether they were aware of the purpose of their work and whether it had any influence.

This work reports the first qualitative feedback related to this topic. The work is based on the author's translation experience related to the evaluation of MT output compared to the experience unrelated to MT. The MT-related experience covers both translation as well as post-editing of MT output in order to provide reference human translations for automatic MT evaluation and/or error analysis. The main observation is that the transla-

tion shifts tend to be diminished when translating for MT evaluation purposes thus producing less creative and more literal translations.

This finding will hopefully become an attractive direction for future work both for MT as well as for translation studies (TS) and hopefully eventually contribute to bringing translation theory and MT closer together.

## 2 Translator's Background and Experience

The author's educational background is technical and not related to translation studies. Nevertheless, she has been interested in languages and translation since childhood (probably as a result of being raised by a translator mother), and has been translating on a more or less regular basis.

Her experience unrelated to MT involves mainly translation of scientific technical texts, as well as correspondences and short summaries of literary texts, between Serbian (native language) and English or French (professional proficiency). It also includes translation between German and English (professional proficiency) of lecture scripts about Machine Learning, Pattern Recognition and Signal Processing for courses held at the RWTH Aachen University.

The author has extensive experience in human and automatic MT evaluation and error analysis, including assigning adequacy and/or fluency (related) scores, error annotation on different levels of granularity, developing automatic evaluation metrics, developing automatic error classification tools, as well as comparing automatic metrics and tools with the corresponding results of human evaluation and annotation.

Her translation and post-editing (PE) experience related to MT evaluation involves mostly the Serbian language (native proficiency) as well as Croatian (near-native proficiency) as target languages, and English, Spanish, German (professional proficiency) and Slovenian (advanced passive competence) as source languages. The translated/post-edited texts include movie subtitles, user reviews (mainly about movies), and news.

For all these tasks, the goal of the work was clear, however no external instructions were specified (such as minimal post-editing or keeping maximal similarity to the source text), but were independently defined by the author. For example, the PE2rr corpus (Popović and Arčan, 2016) con-

---

[1] http://statmt.org/wmt19/, http://www.statmt.org/wmt18/, etc.

tains post-edited MT outputs together with error annotations and was created mainly in order to enable assessment of automatic error classification tools. Some parts of this corpus (English-to-Serbian and German-to-Serbian MT outputs) were post-edited by the author, who decided to perform relatively light post-editing without taking into account preferences concerning style, lexical choice, grammatical structure, etc. The reasoning behind this decision was that state-of-the-art automatic error classification tools are certainly not able to distinguish such subtle error categories. On the other hand, some other parts of this corpus were taken from the TaraXÜ corpus (Avramidis et al., 2014) which was developed independetly and post-edited by other translators without stating any particular goal. Many of these PEs contain much more substantial changes, including separating one sentence into two or joining two sentences. The same PE guidelines were applied for identifying the main problems for MT between the closely related Croatian, Serbian and Slovenian languages (Popović et al., 2016a), where the PEs are used as reference translations. The author has also generated reference HTs for the IMDb corpus in order to enable fast development of the first English-to-Serbian MT system for IMDb reviews through the use of automatic evaluation metrics (Lohar et al., 2019). During this translation process, the author noticed that a number of translations could feel much more natural if they diverged from the close (literal) translations, however she abstained from introducing these shifts knowing that the final goal of the translation was evaluating an MT system.

An important fact is that none of the MT evaluations included comparison between MT quality and HT quality in order to estimate the remaining gap (Toral and Way, 2018), or to claim "human parity" (Hassan et al., 2018) (reassessed by Toral et al. (2018)) "cracking NMT"[2] or similar.

## 3 Observations on translation shifts

The main observation about both translation and post-editing processes is a tendency towards a balance between two antagonised aspects: maximal similarity between source and translated texts and naturalness of the generated text in the target language. On the one hand, paraphrasing the close version and shifting away from the source is normal and natural, and the most common in practice. On the other hand, keeping the close version would ensure more reliable MT evaluation results, as suggested in (Ahrenberg, 2006; Fomicheva et al., 2015). Using a close HT version as a reference enables better and easier identification of potential drawbacks of the system related to the mandatory changes due to systemic differences between the languages. Therefore the author performed less paraphrasing and fewer shifts than usual (when the purpose of translation was not related to MT evaluation). The generated translations were thus often stylistically flawed but grammatically correct and accurate.

The observed divergences between the original texts and translations can be divided in three groups. First group of divergences was completely avoided:

- merging or splitting original sentences

  Sentences within a paragraph could be sometimes organised differently than in the source language text (merging two sentences, splitting one sentence into two, or even reorganising some parts); taking into account that state-of-the-art[3] MT systems as well as automatic evaluation metrics work only on the sentence (segment, line) level, such changes would heavily affect the MT evaluation.

- adding extra information on a sentence level

  Although in some cases adding extra information to a traslated sentence contributes to the naturalness of the generated text, the translator abstained from it because it is difficult for the MT systems to generate such content properly.

The second group of shifts was applied, however less frequently than usual. These shifts were mainly introduced when a closer version, although grammatically correct, would require awkward constructions. Some of these shifts were applied more frequently than others, and the following list is roughly ranked according to the increasing frequency:

- changing passive voice into active voice

  The passive voice (which is very frequently used in English, for example "the criminal

---



[3]Some of the on-going MT research attempts to go beyond the sentence level.

was arrested by the police") was kept in the translated text whenever possible.

- replacing a pronoun with the corresponding noun

  This shift is to some extent similar to the maximally avoided "adding extra information". Nevertheless, in some cases the usage of a pronoun instead of the noun can lead to ungrammatical sentences, so this type of divergence was introduced in such cases (this can happen with the English pronoun "it" which can be rather ambiguous and often cannot be translated directly).

- changing negation structure

  Different languages have different negation rules, and preservation of the source language structure is not always possible. However, possible stylistic changes were avoided (for example, "it is not necessary" can be replaced by "it is unnecessary").

- choosing a less common lexical option

  The usage of less frequent synonyms can add subtlety to the translated text and improve its naturalness. However, the author chose a more common option in the majority of such cases.

- changing phrase order

  Whenever possible, the order of phrases in the source text was preserved in the translation (this happens often in free-word-order target languages).

The third group of shifts was not avoided:

- omitting/using pronoun in pro-drop target languages

  Pro-drop languages do not always require a personal pronoun because this information is encoded in the verb morphology. When translating into a pro-drop language, the pronouns were always used naturally, independently of the pronouns in the source language.

- changing verb tense, aspect or mood

  Different languages can have different usage of verb tense, aspect and mood. The verbs were always used naturally in the translations, independently of the source language.

# 4 Discussion and future research directions

The reported translator's qualitative feedback indicates that the HTs specifically dedicated to the MT evaluation might have different properties than HTs generated for other purposes, similarly to differences between other types of texts (HTs and original texts, PEs and HTs). These differences may be reflected by different types and amounts of introduced translation shifts.

The reported observations open a number of questions and directions for future work. Having been written by an author who is mainly involved in MT evaluation, it is possible that some important points from TS have been missed in this paper. Nevertheless, the main goal of this work is to give an account of a potential common ground of translation procedures and MT, as well as to initialise further research on the topic, both from the MT evaluation point of view as well as from the aspect of TS.

## 4.1 Systematic analysis of translation shifts

First of all, it would be interesting to see the results of a systematic quantitative analysis, such as extracting statistics of different shifts in different HTs. The potential of automatic differentiation between HTs could be investigated, too.

Furthermore, several parameters should be taken into account in the future. One factor is the language pair (and translation direction), because each language pair involves distinct sets of mandatory and optional shifts. Another important factor which can have influence on the amount of performed/avoided translation divergences is translators' background, including his/her attitude towards MT. Last but not least, the primary goal of the intended MT evaluation has to be clear and well defined. For the evaluation tasks described here, where the goals of the evaluation were to estimate the MT system's ability to generate accurate and well-formed text and/or to estimate the progress during development of an MT system, HTs with a reduced number of translation shifts are definitely more convenient. On the other hand, if a high quality of MT output is desired, evaluating on natural HTs with a rich lexical variety and a number of translation shifts is a better option. And if the aim of the evaluation is to explore the remaining gap between MT and HT, the used HTs should definitely be completely natural, containing a number of shifts, having a large lexical variety, and should originate from demanding genres and domains. Ideally, these HTs should be free from any influence of MT. An objective and informative analysis in this direction was carried out on literary texts (Toral and Way, 2018).

### 4.2 Bringing together translation procedures and MT

In the process of translating, translators transform one linguistic system which is given (in the source language) to another which they partially can adapt to their preferences (in the target language). This transformation can be performed using different translation procedures, ranging from direct word-to-word mapping to complex adaptations. Broadly speaking, translators can choose one of the two methods, namely literal (direct) translation (staying as faithful as possible to the source) and oblique (complex) translation (adapt the source language text to the target language) (Vinay and Darbelnet, 1958). This has also been referred to as literal in contrast to natural translation (Newmark, 1988), or, for literary texts translated into English, domesticating the text (bringing the text to the reader in the target language), in contrast to foreignizing the text (bringing the reader to the text similar to the source language) (Venuti, 2001).

The question of which kind of translating procedure is better has been the focus of a discussion for a very long time. Vinay and Darbelnet (1958) claim that the literalness should be preserved as much as possible and the oblique translation methods should only be used with good reason and within strictly defined limits. A similar position is presented by Newmark (1988), stating that the only valid argument against an acceptable literal translation is if it seems unnatural or clumsy in the target language. Venuti (2001) argues that "foreignising" (literal translation) is appropriate for literary translation in order to maximally preserve the original linguistic effect, whereas "domesticating" should be implemented in technical translation in order to ensure immediate intelligibility.

With the emergence of MT technologies, the (positive and negative aspects of) literality might be revisited including the additional MT point of view. Several general strategies for approaching MT from the perspectives of TS were proposed by Čulo (2014), although connecting translation procedures and MT has not been mentioned. A

step in this direction is described in (Jones and Irvine, 2013), where the authors investigate potentials and limits of statistical MT to perform literal vs. oblique translation. Exploring the new state-of-the-art MT approach, namely neural machine translation (NMT), in this sense would be a very interesting line of research, especially taking into account the general ability of NMT systems to produce fluent translations. It can be supposed that some of the free/flexible/oblique translations would be easier for an (N)MT system to generate than some others. A systematic analysis of translation shifts, possibly including different types of text (for example scientific and literary) and more than one NMT system, would certainly bring interesting insights.

Another line of future work is adding the MT evaluation aspect into the debate about literal vs. oblique translation. While this discussion may appear rather philosophical at first sight, it is connected with some important practical aspects, such as the previously mentioned final goal of the intended MT evaluation (obtaining an overall numeric score, ranking two or more MT outputs, analysis of grammatical errors, analysis of lexical and/or stylistic errors, comparing MT with HT, etc.).

Furthermore, MT evaluation can be interpreted as the purpose of the translated text in the framework of Skopos theory (Reiss and Vermeer, 1984). Skopos theory is another translation perspective which is no longer limited by conventional source-text orientated views. It focusses on a purpose of a translated text, and this purpose then determines translation strategies and procedures. In order for the translator to be able to interpret the purpose and apply appropriate strategies for this purpose, a translation brief provided by the client is deemed necessary (Nord, 2006). This brief should contain information about the intended function of the target text, the target text recipient, the time and place of text reception, the medium over which the text will be transmitted, and the motive for the production or reception of the text. For translations intended for MT evaluation, such brief would have MT evaluation as purpose, MT researchers and developers as recipients, assessment and development of MT system(s) as the motive for the production/reception of the text.

## 5 Conclusions

This work reports a qualitative feedback from the author, a translator with an extensive experience in MT evaluation who has tended to perform fewer translation shifts than usual when working on a task related to MT evaluation. The divergences which were thoroughly avoided are related to keeping the similarity on the sentence level, since state-of-the-art MT systems still cannot go beyond this level. Other lexical and structural divergences were diminished due to the awareness of the translation purpose.

In spite of this experience, the author is not convinced that introducing such guidelines (for translation shifts and/or broader ones) on a more general level would be beneficial for MT research. One reason are the previously mentioned claims and hype about MT reaching human parity. Another reason is the objectively rapid development and improvement of MT systems. If more literal/less natural translations would be provided and used for MT on a large scale, some of these data sets could be repeatedly used for a longer period of time (for example, the English-German test set from WMT 2014 is still widely used for assessing new MT systems in 2019). In this way, the overall progress of MT would be measured using too literal and not fully natural texts, which does not seem appropriate.

On the other hand, a number of MT systems is still being developed under sub-optimal conditions (such as low-resourced languages, low computational resources, etc.). For such systems, guidelines on reducing translation shifts would help to better identify main problems and directions for further development. One possibility would be to specify the goal of each particular evaluation as purpose in a translation brief, for example "finding most prominent errors in MT hypotheses", "estimating post-editing effort", "measuring the progress of an MT system over time", etc.

The presented observations and suggestions are certainly influenced by the perspective of the author whose experience is closely related to MT evaluation. Still, these findings will hopefully initialise future research on the topic and bring translation procedures and MT together. This line of research could generally bring the fields of MT and TS closer, and initialise more collaborations between translators and MT researchers.

## Acknowledgments

This research was supported by the ADAPT Centre for Digital Content Technology at Dublin City University, funded under the Science Foundation Ireland Research Centres Programme (Grant 13/RC/2106) and co-funded under the European Regional Development Fund.
Special thanks to Federico Gaspari for his great support and invaluable advices.

## References

Ahrenberg, Lars. 2006. Codified close translation as a standard for MT. In *Proceedings of the 10th Annual Conference of the European Association for Machine Translation (EAMT 2005)*, pages 218–229, Budapest, Hungary, May.

Ahrenberg, Lars. 2017. Comparing machine translation and human translation: A case study. In *Proceedings of the Workshop Human-Informed Translation and Interpreting Technology*, pages 21–28, Varna, Bulgaria, September.

Albrecht, Joshua S. and Rebecca Hwa. 2008. Regression for machine translation evaluation at the sentence level. *Machine Translation*, 22(1-2):1–27, March.

Avramidis, Eleftherios, Aljoscha Burchardt, Sabine Hunsicker, Maja Popović, Cindy Tscherwinka, David Vilar Torres, and Hans Uszkoreit. 2014. The taraXÜ Corpus of Human-Annotated Machine Translations. In *Proceedings of the 9th International Conference on Language Resources and Evaluation (LREC 2014)*, pages 2679–2682, Reykjavik, Iceland, May.

Baroni, Marco and Silvia Bernardini. 2006. A new approach to the study of translationese: Machine-learning the difference between original and translated text. *Literary and Linguistic Computing*, 21(3):259–274, September.

Bojar, Ondřej, Rajen Chatterjee, Christian Federmann, Yvette Graham, Barry Haddow, Shujian Huang, Matthias Huck, Philipp Koehn, Qun Liu, Varvara Logacheva, Christof Monz, Matteo Negri, Matt Post, Raphael Rubino, Lucia Specia, and Marco Turchi. 2017. Findings of the 2017 conference on machine translation (wmt17). In *Proceedings of the Second Conference on Machine Translation, Volume 2: Shared Task Papers*, pages 169–214, Copenhagen, Denmark, September.

Bojar, Ondej, Christian Federmann, Mark Fishel, Yvette Graham, Barry Haddow, Matthias Huck, Philipp Koehn, and Christof Monz. 2018. Findings of the 2018 conference on machine translation (wmt18). In *Proceedings of the Third Conference on Machine Translation, Volume 2: Shared Task Papers*, pages 272–307, Belgium, Brussels, October. Association for Computational Linguistics.

Catford, John Cunnison. 1965. *A Linguistic Theory of Translation: An Essay in Applied Linguistics*. Oxford University Press, Oxford, UK.

Čulo, Oliver and Jean Nitzke. 2016. Patterns of terminological variation in post-editing and of cognate use in machine translation in contrast to human translation. In *Proceedings of the 19th Annual Conference of the European Association for Machine Translation (EAMT 2016)*, pages 106–114, Riga, Latvia.

Čulo, Oliver. 2014. Approaching machine translation from translation studies – a perspective on commonalities, potentials, differences. In *Proceedings of the 17th Annual Conference of the European Association for Machine Translation (EAMT 2014)*, pages 199–206, Dubrovnik, Croatia, June.

Curys, Lea. 2006. Building a resource for studying translation shifts. In *Proceedings of the 5th International Conference on Language Resources and Evaluation (LREC 2006)*, pages 1240–1245, Genoa, Italy, May.

Daems, Joke, Orphée De Clercq, and Lieve Macken. 2017. Translationese and post-editese : how comparable is comparable quality? *Linguistica Antverpiensia New Series – Themes in Translation Studie*, 16:89–103.

Farrell, Michael. 2018. Machine translation markers in post-edited machine translation output. In *Proceedings of the 40th Conference Translating and the Computer*, pages 50–59, London, UK, November.

Fomicheva, Marina, Núria Bel, and Iria da Cunha. 2015. Neutralizing the effect of translation shifts on automatic machine translation evaluation. *Computational linguistics and Intelligent Text Processing*, pages 596–607.

Hassan, Hany, Anthony Aue, Chang Chen, Vishal Chowdhary, Jonathan Clark, Christian Federmann, Xuedong Huang, Marcin Junczys-Dowmunt, Will Lewis, Mu Li, Shujie Liu, Tie-Yan Liu, Renqian Luo, Arul Menezes, Tao Qin, Frank Seide, Xu Tan, Fei Tian, Lijun Wu, Shuangzhi Wu, Yingce Xia, Dongdong Zhang, Zhirui Zhang, , and Ming Zhou. 2018. Achieving human parity on automatic chinese to english news translation. In *arXiv*.

Jones, Ruth and Ann Irvine. 2013. The (Un)faithful Machine Translator. In *Proceedings of the 7th Workshop on Language Technology for Cultural Heritage, Social Sciences, and Humanities*, pages 96–101, Sofia, Bulgaria, August.

Lohar, Pintu, Maja Popovi'c, and Andy Way. 2019. Building English-to-Serbian Machine Translation System for IMDb Movie Reviews. In *Proceedings of the 7th Workshop on Balto-Slavic Natural Language Processing (BSNLP 2019)*, Florence, Italy, August.

Newmark, Peter. 1988. *A Textbook of Translation*. Prentice Hall, New York.

Nord, Christiane. 2006. Translating as a purposeful activity: A prospective approach. *TEFLIN*, 17(2):131–143.

Popović, Maja and Mihael Arčan. 2016. PE2rr Corpus: Manual Error Annotation of Automatically Pre-annotated MT Post-edits. In *Proceedings of the 10th International Conference on Language Resources and Evaluation (LREC 2016)*, Portoro, Slovenia, may.

Popović, Maja, Mihael Arcan, and Filip Klubička. 2016a. Language Related Issues for Machine Translation between Closely Related South Slavic Languages. In *Proceedings of the 3rd Workshop on NLP for Similar Languages, Varieties and Dialects (VarDial3)*, pages 43–52, Osaka, Japan, December.

Popović, Maja, Mihael Arçan, and Arle Lommel. 2016b. Potential and limits of using post-edits as reference translations for MT evaluation. In *Proceedings of the 19th Annual Conference of the European Association for Machine Translation (EAMT 2016)*, pages 218–229, Riga, Latvia, June.

Rabinovich, Ella and Shuly Wintner. 2015. Unsupervised identification of translationese. *Transactions of the Association for Computational Linguistics*, 3:419–432, December.

Reiss, Katharina and Hans Vermeer. 1984. *Towards a General Theory of Translational Action; Skopos Theory Explained (Grundlegung einer allgemeinen Translationstheorie)*. Routledge, London.

Toral, Antonio and Andy Way. 2018. What level of quality can neural machine translation attain on literary text? In *Translation Quality Assessment. Machine Translation: Technologies and Applications*, pages 263–287. Springer.

Toral, Antonio, Sheila Castilho, Ke Hu, and Andy Way. 2018. Attaining the Unattainable? Reassessing Claims of Human Parity in Neural Machine Translation. In *Proceedings of the 3rd Conference on Machine Translation (WMT 2018)*, pages 113–123, Belgium, Brussels, October. Association for Computational Linguistics.

van Leuven-Zwart, Kitty M. 1989. Translation and original: similarities and dissimilarities, i. *Target*, 1(2):151–181.

van Leuven-Zwart, Kitty M. 1990. Translation and original: similarities and dissimilarities, ii. *Target*, 1(2):69–95.

Venuti, Lawrence. 2001. Strategies of translation. In Baker, M., editor, *Routledge Encyclopedia of Translation Studies*, pages 240–244. Routledge, London & New York.

Vinay, Jean-Paul and Jean Darbelnet. 1958. *Comparative Stylistics of French and English: A Methodology for Translation*. John Benjamins.

Wintner, Shuly. 2016. Translationese: Between human and machine translation. In *Proceedings of the 26th International Conference on Computational Linguistics (COLING 2016): Tutorial Abstracts*, pages 18–19, Osaka, Japan, December.

# Comparative Analysis of Errors in MT Output and Computer-assisted Translation: Effect of the Human Factor


**Irina Ovchinnikova**

Sechenov First Moscow State Medical
University, Moscow, Russia /
Trubetskaya str., 8, building 2,
119992 Moscow, Russia

Lichi Translations LTD /
P.O. Box 18,
Be'er Ya'akov, 70300 Israel
`Ira.ovchi@gmail.com`

**Daria Morozova**

HEC Paris /
1 rue de la Libération,
78351 Jouy-en-Josas, France
`daria.morozova@hec.edu`


## Abstract


The paper presents a comparative analysis of errors in outputs of MT and Computer-assisted Translation (CAT) platforms in translation from Hebrew into Russian. A MT system, shared translation memory (TM), and dictionaries are available on CAT platforms. The platforms allow for editing and improving any MT output as well as performing manual translation. Evaluation of the efficiency of the platforms in comparison with the MT systems shows advantages of the CAT platforms in the translation industry. The comparison reveals the impact of the human factor on the CAT output providing developers with the feedback from translation industry. The research was conducted on documents translated from Hebrew into Russian (approximately 35,000 words, 3118 segments) on Smartcat. Errors in MT output for Russian as a target language show almost equal shares of fluency and accuracy errors in PBSTM and prevalence of the accuracy errors in NMT. Errors on the Smartcat platform reveal difficulties in mastering semantic and stylistic coherence of the whole document. In general, however, the translation is accurate and readable. The influence of English as lingua franca appears in peculiar orthographic and punctuation errors. The errors in translation on Smartcat performed by professional translators uncover insufficiency of CAT tools for the language pair as well as peculiar problems in applying CAT tools while translating from Hebrew into Russian.


## 1 Introduction

The objective of the study is to analyze the peculiar errors in translation from Hebrew into Russian on a CAT platform as compared to the errors in the MT output and reveal their sources to provide developers with the translators' feedback. The comparison is efficient from the practical point of view since a target text, being translated by a MT system or human translator, must deliver the source message and has to be relevant to the target culture. In the translation industry, revised MT outputs compete with human translations, including those performed on CAT platforms. Therefore, awareness of the peculiar errors in translation on the platforms will provide basis for improving Hebrew-Russian MT and for choosing the way to translate the particular project applying MT or hiring a human translator who has access to a CAT platform.

The research was conducted on the material of translation projects on Smartcat.[1] In the paper, we discuss Hebrew-Russian translation of a tourist guide (9 files in Smartcat; 35,000[2] word forms approximately; 3118 segments; on average, 10 word forms in a segment) by a team of professional translators. The errors in the MT



[1] Smartcat Platform Inc. 2019 https://www.smartcat.ai/

[2] It is hard to determine the exact number of word forms because the author amended the text in Hebrew owing to the necessity to provide the accurate data and information. Nevertheless, the number of segments was constant.

output are considered as a baseline for analysis of errors on Smartcat.

To the best of our knowledge, translation from Hebrew into Russian on a CAT platform was not analyzed in the aspect of the errors type as compared to the MT output. Meanwhile, the comparison allows for developers and users to revise tools on the platforms. Translators will get the insight into specific advantages of MT systems depending on the language pair. Being aware of the advantages, translators can improve the quality of target texts combining MT and human translation.

All tools of computer-assisted translation in one place (CAT platforms) provide translators with an opportunity to quickly deliver a readable and accurate output. The platforms support the cycle of translation projects: selecting translators, teamwork, project management, delivery of the final product, and payment transfer. A CAT platform includes a MT system, access to shared TM, dictionaries, thesauruses and other necessary resources. Collaborators have the opportunity to discuss options, comment on the source text, and share information required to understand the content. Nevertheless, translators and revisers cannot avoid errors while using all of the advantages.

Classification of translators' errors varies according to domains. In the industry, the classification is very simple and pragmatically oriented. In academia, the errors are classified with respect to the target text functioning in the target culture, mental mechanisms of bilingualism and code switching. Since a human bilingual translator operates the platform, the output reveals particular errors. Thus, we take into consideration the classification of translation errors in both domains (See: Hansen, 2009: 316).

## 2 Related Work: Classification of Typical Errors in MT Output

On Smartcat, a translator can use different MT systems evaluating and editing their output. Thus, we consider the errors distribution for phrase-based statistical and neural MT systems (PBSMT and NMT, respectively).

Distribution of the errors in MT outputs is usually described in the aspect of quality difference between statistical and neural MT systems (Bentivogli, et al., 2016). Human and automatic quality evaluations of outputs of MT systems show different results; however, NMT quality substantially surpasses that of PBSMT (Shterionov et al., 2018).

Researchers differentiate between errors in fluency and accuracy of translation. Fluency errors reduce the readability of the target text, while accuracy errors distort its content. According to the data from different evaluation systems and different languages, fluency errors are more prevalent than accuracy errors (Aranberri et al., 2016). The most typical fluency errors are grammatical errors (close to 80%: Aranberri et al., 2016: 1880). They include morphological, word order and syntax errors. In general, NMT systems outperform PBSMT in fluency (Bentivogli et al., 2016).

The target language affects the kind of morphological information learned by the NMT system. Words of the source text are better represented in a morphologically poorer target language, while a morphologically rich language (e.g., Hebrew and Russian) needs character-based representation of less frequent words in the NMT to enhance the quality of translation (Belinkov et al., 2017). Bilingual post-editors handle the errors in the MT output.

### 2.1 Errors in Hebrew in MT Output

Hebrew as a source or target language of MT has undeservingly received very sparse researchers' attention. As a morphologically rich language, Hebrew features grammatical affixes, endings and cliticization. The inflections and addition of the subordinate elements to the main word evokes difficulties in processing morphology that were overcome in SMT thanks to pre-processing techniques based on morphological analysis and disambiguation (Singh and Habash, 2012).

In general, NMT outperform PBSMT in Hebrew-Arabic / Arabic-Hebrew translation (Belinkov and Glass, 2016). For better results, Hebrew needs a character-based encoding / decoding model that improves identification of word structure for less frequent words, while words that are more frequent are possible to be identified in the word-based model (Belinkov et al., 2017; Richardson et al., 2016). Nowadays, the most suitable solution for MT translation from Modern Hebrew is Google's Multilingual NMT that involves English as an interlanguage (Johnson et al., 2017). In translation from Hebrew (Modern and Archaic) into English, the omissions and additions occur due to high degree of compression in Hebrew (Cheesman and Roos, 2017: 11).

## 2.2 Errors in Russian in MT Output

Errors in Hebrew-Russian MT output have not been described or explained in publications. In the translation industry, translators often prefer to apply a Hebrew-English-Russian MT, as in the case of Google's Multilingual NMT. Due to this practice, we need to consider errors in English-Russian MT output. According to human evaluation, NMT English-Russian output received marks "Near native or Native" for 75% segments, whilst PBSMT got the same marks for 60% of segments in the output (Castilho et al., 2017b: 121). The most frequent errors are morphological (42% for PBSMT, 38% for NMT), wrong word order occurs in 12% and 9% of the segments for PBSMT and NMT, respectively (Castilho et al., 2017b: 124).

The distribution of the accuracy errors varies in different domains and genres (Castilho et al., 2017a). The category of accuracy errors includes additions, omissions, mistranslations, and terminology (Burchardt et al., 2017). The class of terminology errors contains wrong choice in terminology, while mistranslations concern general lexicon (Lommel, 2014). In English-Russian output, omissions occur in 12% of segments, equally for NMT and PBSMT; almost the same frequency describes the additions (11% equally for the both) (Castilho et al., 2017b: 124). Meanwhile, mistranslations cover 23% in PBSMT and 30% in NMT (Castilho et al., 2017b: 125). In Russian-English output, PBSMT also outperforms NMT in accuracy of lexical choice (Toral and Sánchez-Cartagena 2017). In translations into Russian as a language with rich morphology, NMT systems lead to less accurate output as compared to the best of PBSMT; the PBSMT contained fewer mistranslations (Castilho et al., 2017b: 125).

## 2.3 Classification of Errors

In the MT output evaluation, the category of fluency errors includes grammatical (morphological, word order, syntax), orthographic and punctuation errors. The category of accuracy errors contains omissions, additions, mistranslations, and wrong terminology choice. The classification does not account for discourse and pragmatic errors because to detect and prevent these errors, additional tools are needed (Khadivi et al., 2017). A reviser of the MT output evaluates semantic correlation between two segments (the source and the target) and adequacy of the target segment in the aspect of the target language norms and usage.

In general, the target text delivers its message and performs the adequate function in the target culture thanks to the accuracy of its discourse and pragmatic features, and their correspondence to those of the source text. For different target languages, peculiar MT systems were developed to translate English texts of various domains (Specia et al., 2017). Since every source text is semantically coherent and has contiguity, pragmatic purposes, and discourse peculiarities, application of a relevant MT system affects the corresponding quality of the MT output. Meanwhile, the peculiar MT systems do not exist for Hebrew-Russian or Hebrew-English-Russian. Therefore, every Hebrew-Russian MT output needs post-editing in the aspect of its discourse and pragmatic peculiarities.

The discourse and pragmatic characteristics describe the whole document, while the object of the MT output evaluation is a text segment. Thus, the evaluation of the MT output does not consider discourse-pragmatic errors. Eliminating these errors, the evaluation of MT output considers the segment of the target text but skips the evaluation of the correspondence between the source and target messages. Rules for software localization envisage consideration of the discourse and pragmatic issues in the MT output (Specia et al., 2017: 61). The CAT platforms acquire tools for localization of the target text. Therefore, in the evaluation of Smartcat output, we take into consideration all types of errors described in (Hansen 2009: 316). We apply the data of the errors distribution in the MT output as the baseline to consider whether a human translator offers a better option than a raw or even post-edited output of MT systems. Errors and mistakes in translation on Smartcat disclose the value of the human factor as a contributor to the quality of the final product.

## 3 Results: Description of Errors in Translation on Smartcat

### 3.1 Working on Smartcat

CAT platforms transform the translators' environment into computer-mediated communication (CMC) with colleagues and customers. In CMC and in the translation industry, English functions as lingua franca. CMC restricts the feedback to comments in a chat window on the platform. Facilitating decoding and encoding, working on a CAT platform exposes a translator / editor / reviser to the effect of text formatting in the working window with segments of the source text. Under the effect, even a competent translator experiences interference of different languages in CMC. Smartcat provides tools for monitoring task performance, navigating in the document, tracking revisions of target segments, and quality assurance. The CAT platform enhances the efficacy of the translator's work, on the one hand; on the other hand, it makes possible the mixed influence of the human factor on the final product: a post-editor revises the output enhancing the target text, although it is an opportunity to miss errors. Translators and post-editors rarely use a particular post editor's tool or environment to identify the errors (Blagodarna 2018: 16). In addition, they often neglect the MT and shared TM in the process of translation (Zaretskaya, Pastor, Seghiri 2015).

## 3.2 Distribution of the Errors: Comparison between MT and Smatrcat

We analyze the completed translation of a tourist guide that was accepted by the customer as the first draft of the book to be edited by a professional writer. Three professional revisers performed the manual error evaluation. An expert, the professional linguist,[3] annotated the errors. Such expert evaluation of the final product appears to be a common practice in the industry. In the revised Hebrew-Russian Smartcat translation of the tourist guide, 11 segments with various errors include approximately 1080 word forms (3% of the word forms of the source text). The distribution of the errors reflects particular characteristics of the translation and target text revision on Smartcat (See Table 1).

| Type | Discourse – pragmatic | Orthographic | Punctuation | Terminology / lexical choice | Grammatical | Omission / Addition |
|------|------|------|------|------|------|------|
| % | 40 | 18 | 18 | 14 | 9 | 1 |

Table 1. Errors distribution in the Hebrew-Russian translation on Smartcat (percentage to all errors in the draft).

The distribution differs from that in the MT output for Russian.

1)      The most typical of the Smartcat translation failures are the discourse-pragmatic errors. We are not able to compare our data with the volume of the discourse errors in the MT output due to the difference in the errors classification between the industry and academia. Some of the discourse-pragmatic errors are considered as mistranslations in the MT output.

2)      In Smartcat, omissions, additions and wrong lexical choice account for 15% of all errors, while in the MT output the accuracy errors occur in 46% of segments for PBSMT and 53% for NMT.[4]

3)      Style-shifting usually manifests in a wrong choice of a word from the synset. The errors are represented on Smartcat as a 10% share included in the category of discourse-pragmatic errors. In the MT output, the style-shifting is probably identified as mistranslations. Therefore, the difference in the distributions of accuracy errors between Smartcat and MT could appear less essential.

4)      Smartcat output is almost error-free from grammatical errors. Nevertheless, errors in orthography and punctuation diminish the fluency of the target text.

## 4 Discussion of the Errors in Hebrew-Russian Translation on Smartcat

### 4.1 Reasons for Errors of Different Types

Even after revisions, **the discourse-pragmatic errors** (unnecessary style-shifting and provocative intertextual associations) occur regularly. The stylistic errors (included in the category of discourse-pragmatic errors) reflect the well-known peculiarities in Hebrew-Russian translation caused by the rich network of synonyms in the Russian vocabulary in comparison with the Hebrew lexicon, and usage of the distinctive syntactic constructions in Russian texts according to the particular style. For example, in the following sentence, official and high literary styles are mixed: *Шахматная держава, национальная и международная, прославившаяся достижениями как в юношеской, таки и во взрослой категориях* (literal translation: *Chess empire, national and international, famous for achievements in both youth and adult categories*). Besides that, the meaning of the lexeme *держава* (*empire*) semantically contradicts the attribute *международная* (*international*). However, the content of the sentence is most seriously damaged by the association generated by *Chess empire*: the phrase associates with *Ostap Bender*, a popular

---

[3] The expert is Professor, PhD in Russian Linguistics from Saint-Petersburg State University.

[4] See the data in 2.2.

adventurer from Russian satirical novels. The association adds an ironic estimation to the city described as *Chess empire*. The irony ruins the pragmatic purpose of the city guide translation.

The percent of **the orthographic and punctuation errors** is surprisingly high as Smartcat presupposes automatic spelling and grammar checking to prevent the errors. In table 2, we provide examples of the orthographic errors (marked by bold).

| Description of error | % | Example |
|---|---|---|
| Skipping spaces between words | 27 | в **концешестидесятых** годов |
| Overuse of capitalisation | 59 | Война за **Независимость** Израиля |
| Wrong spelling and misprint | 11 | На территории центра действуют городская консерватория "Акадма", балетная школа и студия танца, местные ансамбли исполнителей и городские оркестры, а **так же** великолепный **музеей** искусств, известный по всей стране и за рубежом. |
| Erratum in compound | 3 | Ультра-**ортодоксальный** |

Table 2. Description of the orthographic errors in the target text

The **orthographic errors** reveal interference with the English language norms and gaps in technological competence and fluency in the target language. The effect of text formating in the working field of Smartcat appears because of the use of signs preserving the formatting of the source text. The signs mask the space between words, so what is displayed on the work screen is not what will be transferred into the final output in the target text.

The misuse of capitalization shows the effect of the English language norm on the Russian output. In Hebrew, capitalization is not in use. In Russian, the norms usually prescribe to capitalize the first word in compound names of organizations and events. The translator made mistakes under the influence of English as lingua franca.

The two reasons – display of the translated text and the influence of English as lingua franca – explain 86% of the orthographic errors on Smartcat. Another 11% of orthographic errors are caused by gaps in the translator's target language competence.

Similar reasons cause the **punctuation errors**. Under the influence of the English language, translators overused commas (,) after complements in the beginning of the sentence and often use a colon (:) instead of an em dash (–). Due to the signs of text formatting on the platform, translators miss marks in compound sentences. Almost 30% of the errors show insufficient competence in Russian punctuation norms.

**Terminology and lexical errors** in Smartcat are similar to those in MT; they reveal misunderstanding of terminology and wrong lexical choices. For example, instead of *блуждающие пески* (*wondering sand*) the translator used *зыбучие пески* (*quicksand*). The most typical of the lexical choice errors concerns wrong selection within the synset ignoring collocations and semantic restrictions. MT systems outperform human translators in the lexical choice associated with peculiar semantic restriction. For example, to refer to people or other entities in Russian, speakers need to choose between two different words; *имя* (*name*) is appropriate only for people, while objects are referred to by their *название* (*name*). NMT systems are able to process the semantic difference offering the relevant Russian word in Hebrew-English-Russian translation.

The **grammatical errors** are akin to those in Russian colloquial speech. Translators and a post-editor recognized the specific errors similar to those in the MT output, but they sometimes failed to identify word forms and idioms that belong to official style, which is irrelevant for the tourist guide. The most typical of the grammatical errors belong to the morphological class when a wrong inflection generates wrong syntactic dependencies in long clauses. In addition, adverbial participles regularly occur in impersonal sentences that is prohibited in Russian: *Проведя* (Adv. Participle-past-perf.) *время в парке, рекомендуется* (Verb-pres.-imper.-impersonal) *продолжить прогулку в южном направлении по прекрасной прогулочной дороге* (literal translation: *After spending time in the park, it is recommended to continue walking in the south direction along the beautiful walking road*).

Translating into Russian, professional translators attempt to shorten target segments and sometimes this leads to omissions (Kunilovskaya, Morgoun, Pariy 2018). Meanwhile, omissions and additions in the MT output from Hebrew appear due to a concise character of the language (Cheesman, Roos 2017: 11). The omission, as well as the addition, can be useful for semantic coherence of the whole document as means to avoid repetition in contact segments and establish cohesion for distant segments. Thus, an omission of information in the process of Hebrew-Russian translation represents an error in accuracy in the segment, but can be purposeful in the whole text perspective. Nevertheless, in the human-revised Hebrew-Russian translation on Smartcat, some of the omissions and additions lead to the distortion of information in the target segment: *Исследователи приводят два возможных вариантов жителей крепости, руины которой находятся на холме* (literal translation: *The researchers raised two possible options of the inhabitants of the fortress whose remains were found on the hill*). In the source segment in Hebrew, the author mentioned two different theories explaining the origin of the fortress inhabitants.

### 4.2 The Human Factor as the Ground for Errors on Smartcat

In summary, orthographic and punctuation errors reveal insufficient command of the CAT tools and gaps in the target language competence of translators. On the one hand, it is necessary to train skills to master CAT beforehand; on the other hand, due to the errors, CAT platform developers can foresee particular problems of implementing text-formatting instruments in the platform. The orthographic and punctuation errors uncover interlanguage interference and impact of English in Hebrew-Russian translation as English strongly affects CMC (Jiménez-Crespo 2010). The discourse-pragmatic errors are caused by neglecting the target language usage, the target cultural context and the purpose of the text (the message itself). Alongside with lexical errors, they break the contiguity of the target text and its semantic coherence.

Compared to the errors in the MT outputs, the translation errors on the CAT platform disclose a skillful mastery of the target language grammar and more accurate lexical choice. However, the MT provides post-editors with the translation that is almost free of orthographic errors. Smartcat improves the technological environment for translators and overcomes disadvantages of MT thanks to the opportunity to use different tools according to the particular source segment.

### 4.3 Errors Associated with Design of CAT Platform

The source text segmentation and working window formatting on the CAT platform provoke difficulties in expressing the coherence and the anaphora resolution in distant semantically coherent segments. The problems are similar to those that occur in the MT output. Incorrect use of pronouns can be recognized in the process of post-editing the target text.

Peculiar errors reveal the problems associated with the source text segmentation into sentences. This can trigger a translator to preserve the sentence boundaries and use a complicated Russian compound sentence leading to punctuation errors.

## 5 Conclusion

Our study of the set of errors in Hebrew-Russian translation on the CAT platform found that CAT platforms provide users with good translation quality. The quality is better than the MT output for this pair of languages. The negative impact of the human factor is associated with the mismatch of the capabilities of the CAT tools and the degree of their use by translators. Our analysis found that the particular errors are caused by the effect of English as lingua franca in the translation industry and CMC. These errors diminish the fluency, while the discourse-pragmatic errors decrease the accuracy of the target text. In this aspect, the translation on the Smartcat is similar to the NMT output for Russian in that the fluency of the target text is better than the accuracy. The discourse-pragmatic errors are not recognised in the MT output evaluation because the contiguity of the whole text does not appear as an object of the MT quality evaluation. By combining human competence and computer tools, translation on the CAT platforms enables acceptable translation quality to be quickly generated.

The comparison of errors in MT and on the CAT platform for the Hebrew-Russian language pair provides a basis for training MT systems to achieve the acceptable quality. The distribution of the errors in translation on Smartcat shows the direction for translator and post-editor training. These results are also of importance to developers of CAT platforms as enhancement of user interfaces considering the human factor-triggered errors might contribute to greater accuracy and efficiency of translations.

## References

Aranberri, Nora, Eleftherios Avramidis, Aljoscha Burchardt, Ondřej Klejch, Martin Popel, and Maja Popovic. 2016. Tools and Guidelines for Principled Machine Translation Development. *Proceedings of the 10th Conference on Language Resources and Evaluation (LREC).* Portorož, Slovenia 1877–1882.

Belinkov, Yonatan, Nadir Durrani, Fahim Dalvi, Hassan Sajjad, and James Glass. 2017. What do neural machine translation models learn about morphology? *Proceedings of the 55th Annual Meeting of the Association for Computational Linguistics (ACL).* Vancouver, Canada 861–872.

Belinkov, Yonatan, and James Glass. 2016. Large-scale machine translation between Arabic and Hebrew: Available corpora and initial results. *Proceedings of the Workshop on Semitic Machine Translation*, Austin, Texas, USA 7–12.

Bentivogli, Luisa, Arianna Bisazza, Mario Cettolo and Marcello Federico. 2016. Neural versus phrase-based machine translation quality: a case study. *Proceedings of the 2016 Conference on Empirical Methods in Natural Language Processing*, Austin, Texas, USA 257–267.

Blagodarna, Olena. 2018. Insights into post-editors' profiles and post-editing practices. *Revista Tradumàtica. Tecnologies de la Traducció*, 16: 35–51.

Burchardt, Aljoscha, Vivien Macketanz, Jon Dehdari, Georg Heigold, Jan-Thorsten Peter, and Philip Williams. 2017. A linguistic evaluation of rule-based, phrase-based, and neural MT engines. *The Prague Bulletin of Mathematical Linguistics*, 108(1), 159–170.

Castilho, Sheila, Joss Moorkens, Federico Gaspari, Iacer Calixto, John Tinsley, and Andy Way. 2017a. Is neural machine translation the new state of the art?. *The Prague Bulletin of Mathematical Linguistics*, 108(1), 109–120.

Castilho, Sheila, Joss Moorkens, Federico Gaspari, Rico Sennrich, Vilelmini Sosoni, Panayota Georgakopoulou, Pintu Lohar, Andy Way, Antonio Barone, and Maria Gialama, M. 2017b. A comparative quality evaluation of PBSMT and NMT using professional translators. *Proceedings of Machine Translation Summit XVI, vol. 1: Research Track.* Nagoya, Japan 116–132.

Cheesman, Tom, and Avraham Roos. 2017. Version Variation Visualization (VVV): Case Studies on the Hebrew Haggadah in English. *Journal of Data Mining and Digital Humanities, July, 5, 2017, Special Issue on Computer-Aided Processing of Intertextuality in Ancient Languages.* 1–12.

Hansen, Gyde. 2009. A classification of errors in translation and revision. *CIUTI-Forum 2008: Enhancing Translation Quality: Ways, Means, Methods.* Peter Lang, Bern, Switzerland. 313–326.

Jiménez-Crespo, Miguel A. 2010. Localization and writing for a new medium: a review of digital style guides. *Tradumàtica: traducció i tecnologies de la informació i la comunicació*, 8, 1–9.

Johnson, Melvin, Mike Schuster, Quoc V. Le, Maxim Krikun, Yonghui Wu, Zhifeng Chen, Nikhil Thorat, Fernanda Viégas, Martin Wattenberg, Greg Corrado, Macduff Hughes, and Jeffrey Deanet. 2017. Google's multilingual neural machine translation system: Enabling zero-shot translation. *Transactions of the Association for Computational Linguistics*, vol. 5, 339–351.

Khadivi, Shahram, Patrick Wilken, Leonard Dahlmann, and Evgeny Matusov. 2017. Neural and Statistical Methods for Leveraging Meta-information in Machine Translation. *Proceedings of Machine Translation Summit XVI, vol. 1: Research Track.* Nagoya, Japan 41–54.

Kunilovskaya, Maria, Natalia Morgoun, and Alexey Pariy. 2018. Learner vs. professional translations into Russian: Lexical profiles. *Translation & Interpreting*, 10(1), 33–52

Lommel, Arle R., Aljoscha Burchardt, and Hans Uszkoreit. 2014. Multidimensional Quality Metrics (MQM): A Framework for Declaring and Describing Translation Quality Metrics. *Revista tradumàtica: traducció i tecnologies de la informació i la comunicació*, 12, 455–463.

Richardson, John, Taku Kudo, Hideto Kazawa, and Sadao Kurohashi. 2016. A generalized dependency tree language model for SMT. *Information and Media Technologies*, 11, 213–235.

Shterionov, Dimitar, Riccardo Superbo, Pat Nagle, Laura Casanellas, Tony O'Dowd, and Andy Way. 2018. Human versus automatic quality evaluation of NMT and PBSMT. *Machine Translation*, 32(3), 217–235.

Singh, Nimesh, and Nadir Habash. 2012. Hebrew morphological preprocessing for statistical machine translation. *Proceedings of The European Association for Machine Translation (EAMT12)*, Trento, Italy 43–50.

Specia, Lucia, Kim Harris, Frederic Blain, Vivien Macketanz, Aljoscha Burchardt, Inguna Skadina, Matteo Negri, and Marko Turchi. 2017. Translation Quality and Productivity: A Study on Rich Morphology Languages. *Proceedings of Machine Translation Summit XVI, vol. 1: Research Track.* Nagoya, Japan 55-71.

Toral, Antonio, and Victor M. Sánchez-Cartagena. 2017. A multifaceted evaluation of neural versus phrase-based machine translation for 9 language directions. *Proceedings of the 15th Conference of the European Chapter of the Association for Computational Linguistics, vol. 1: Long Papers*, Valencia, Spain 1063–1073.

# A Comparative Study of English-Chinese Translations of Court Texts by Machine and Human Translators and the Word2Vec Based Similarity Measure's Ability To Gauge Human Evaluation Biases


**Ming Qian**
Pathfinders Translation,
Interpretation & Research
513 Elan Hall Rd
Cary, NC 27519, USA

qianmi@pathfinders-transinterp.com

**Jessie Liu**
California Court Certified Interpreter
15421 Hoover Ln
Fontana, CA 92336, USA

jessiel@middlebury.edu

**Chaofeng (Joseph) Li**
California Court Certified Interpreter
1300 E Main Street. #209G
Alhambra, CA 91801, USA

jl.interpreting@gmail.com

**Liming Pals**
ATA Certified Translator
Ivy Tower International LLC
3114 Whitetail Ln, Ames, IA 50014
Limingpals@gmail.com



## Abstract

In this comparative study, a jury instruction scenario was used to test the translating capabilities of multiple machine translation tools and a human translator with extensive court experience. Three certified translators/interpreters subjectively evaluated the target texts generated using adequacy and fluency as the evaluation metrics. This subjective evaluation found that the machine generated results had much poorer adequacy and fluency compared with results produced by their human counterpart. Human translators can use strategic omission and explicitation strategies such as addition, paraphrasing, substitution, and repetition to remove ambiguity, and achieve a natural flow in the target language. We also investigate instances where human evaluators have major disagreements and found that human experts could have very biased views. On the other hand, a word2vec based algorithm, if given a good reference translation, can serve as a robust and reliable similarity reference to quantify human evalutors' biases beacuse it was trained on a large corpus using neural network models. Even though the machine generated versions had better fluency performance compared to their adequacy performance, the human translator's fluency performance was still far superior. The lack of understanding by machine translators led to inaccurate and improper word/phrase selections, which led to bad fluency.


## 1 Objective

The purpose of this study is to evaluate the quality of machine translation by comparing the target texts generated by multiple machine translation tools with texts translated by an expert human translator/interpreter.

Three expert human translators/interpreters evaluated the target texts. We also evaluate the word2vec as an algorithm tool to measure the similarity between machine generated sentences and human generated sentences. In addition, we analyzed various quality problems of the machine translation results, their severity levels, and possible causes.

## 2 Methods

We used a video clip of a judge giving a jury instruction (Pastor 2011) as the test script.

A certified court interpreter with many years of experience interpreted what the judge said in

English into Chinese in real-time. In addition, the same interpreter got the chance to take as much time as she wanted to translate the same content from English to Chinese.

Three machine translation tools (Google Translator, Microsoft-Bing Translator, and Mr. Translation by Tencent) were used to translate the same content from English to Chinese.

Two certified court interpreters and an ATA-certified translator were asked to evaluate the five versions of targeted text generated (three generated by machines, and two generated by a human expert). They were asked to fill out a questionnaire with a 5-level Likert Scale regarding adequacy and fluency (relying on an intuitive understanding of these notions by the evaluators).

Human experts also discussed the various quality issues of machine translated results, their severity levels, and possible causes.

## 3 Translation and interpretation Results

Due to the limitation on the number of pages allowed, we list five versions of targeted text generated by machines and humans for ten text segments on the following website:

https://sites.google.com/Pathfinders-transinterp.com/mainsite/machine-translation-summit-tables?authuser=0

This is the raw data for the analyses below.

## 4 Results of Quality Evaluation

### 4.1 Questionnaires on Translation Adequacy and Fluency

Two California court certified interpreters and one ATA (American Translator Association) certified translator evaluated the adequacy and fluency of the results (Koehn 2017). Adequacy answers the question of whether the translation output conveys the same meaning as the input. Is part of the message lost, added, or distorted? Fluency answers the question on whether the translation output can be considered fluent Chinese or not? This involves both grammatical correctness and idiomatic word choices. Evaluators relied on an intuitive understanding of these notions to make judgments and were asked to provide reasons for sentences on which evaluators had major opinion differences.

The Likert Scale was used for the questionnaires. Evaluators were offered a choice of five pre-coded responses with the neutral point being neither agree nor disagree.

People are represented by counsel Mr Wolcott and Miss Brazil. All the jurors and all the alternates are present.

人们由律师 Wolcott 先生和巴西小姐代理。所有陪审员和所有候补人员都在场。

|          | Strongly Disagree | Disagree | Neutral | Agree | Strongly Agree |
| --- | --- | --- | --- | --- | --- |
| accurate | ○ | ○ | ○ | ○ | ○ |
| fluent   | ○ | ○ | ○ | ○ | ○ |

Figure 1: Likert scale evaluation questionnaires are used to evaluate adequacy and fluency of the target texts.

### 4.2 Questionnaire Results

The results based on feedback from the three evaluators are listed in Table 1. Annotations S1-S10 represent text segments 1 to 10. Check marks ($\sqrt{}$) represent the votes given by the interpreters and translators. For example, in the "Strongly Agree" cell, $\sqrt{}\sqrt{}\sqrt{}$ (S1) means that all three evaluators chose to "Strongly Agree" that the translation using the specific translation version has good adequacy or fluency.

The evaluation results showed that compared with the human translator/interpreter, the machine generated versions were of poorer quality (in terms of both adequacy and fluency). In addition, the adequacy in these cases was on average worse than the fluency.

### 4.3 Adequacy Analyses

For text segment 2, the word "exhibits" was translated as "展览" (the items in an exhibition) by the google translator, while a better Chinese word would be "证物" (forensic evidence).

For text segment 3, all three machine generated versions translated the word "feverishly" as "狂热", while the human translator chose to forgo direct translation and intentionally left out the word. This is because the jury in this case did not really exhibit fanatic enthusiasm.

For text segment 5, all machine generated versions seemed to have a hard time figuring out who the bailiff (court room policeman) was. Google version chose to leave the word in its English form, The Microsoft-Bing version used the transliteration approach (translating the sound of pronunciation), and Mr. Translator generated the Chinese word "联谊会", which means "friendship association", which is obviously a mistranslation.

For text segment 7, the Chinese texts produced by all machine translation tools said that "可能会有一点不同" (there might be some variability), but no explanation was given. The human translator, in this case, mentioned that the (reading) time might be a little different. Therefore, a reason was given to explain the variability.

For text segment 8, the human translator chose to omit "Page 1 is always the best page", since it was just a small quip by the judge that was not elaborated on. Leaving this phrase in could potentially confuse readers, and for this reason the human translator chose to omit it.

For text segment 10, Google Translator translated the phrase "master set" as "主人套装". Here "主人" means master relative to slave. Obviously, this is not the right word. Microsoft-Bing and Mr. Translator translated the phrase as "主集" which is a good translation. The human translator provided an even better solution "公用文件" (a document set shared by the group).

source language because it is apparent from either the context or the situation. For example, in sentence 7, all machine generated versions used the literal translation "会有一点不同(变化)" (there could be varieties). The human translator added the implicit reason "时间或长或短" (the reading time could a bit longer or shorter).

## 4.4 Human Adequacy Evaluations and word2vec Similarity Results

In this section, we select instances of adequacy evaluation in which three evaluators had very different opinions. We asked the evaluators to provide the reasons for their choices.

In addition, we compare the machine generated version with the human translation version which

| Evaluation Categories | Likert Scale Choices | Google Translator | Microsoft-Bing Translator | Mr. Translator by Tencent | Human Interpretation (real-time) | Human Translation |
|---|---|---|---|---|---|---|
| Adequacy | Strongly Disagree | vv(s1) vv(s2) vv(s3) vvv(s4) vvv(s5) vv(s6) v(s7) vvv(s8) vv(s10) | vvv(s1) v(s2) v(s3) v(s4) vvv(s5) v(s8) v(s10) | v(s1) vv(s2) v(s3) v(s4) vv(s5) v(s7) v(s8) | vv(s10) | v(s8) v(s10) |
| | Disagree | v(s1) v(s2) v(s3) v(s6) v(s7) v(s9) v(s10) | vv(s3) vv(s4) v(s6) vv(s7) vv(s8) v(s9) vv(s10) | vv(s1) vv(s3) vv(s4) v(s5) v(s6) v(s8) vvv(s9) v(s10) | v(s1) v(s3) v(s5) vv(s6) vvv(s7) v(s9) v(s10) | |
| | Neutral | vv(s9) | vv(s2) | v(s2) v(s7) vv(s6) | v(s3) vv(s4) v(s5) v(s9) | v(s8) |
| | Agree | v(s7) | vv(s6) v(s7) vv(s9) | v(s7) v(s8) vv(s10) | v(s1) vvv(s2) v(s4) v(s5) v(s6) vvv(s8) v(s9) | v(s1) v(s3) v(s4) v(s5) v(s6) v(s7) v(s9) v(s10) |
| | Strongly Agree | | | | v(s1) v(s3) | vv(s1) vv(s2) vv(s3) vv(s4) vv(s5) vv(s6) vv(s7) v(s8) vv(s9) v(s10) |
| Fluency | Strongly Disagree | v(s3) v(s5) v(s6) v(s8) v(s9) v(s10) | v(s2) v(s3) v(s6) v(s8) v(s9) v(s10) | v(s1) v(s2) vv(s5) v(s6) v(s8) v(s9) | v(s10) | |
| | Disagree | vv(s1) v(s2) v(s3) v(s4) v(s5) v(s6) vv(s7) v(s8) v(s9) v(s10) | vv(s1) v(s3) v(s4) vv(s5) v(s6) vv(s7) v(s8) vv(s9) v(s10) | v(s1) v(s3) v(s6) vvv(s7) v(s8) v(s9) | v(s2) v(s5) v(s6) v(s10) | |
| | Neutral | v(s2) vv(s4) v(s5) v(s8) v(s10) | v(s2) v(s4) v(s5) v(s10) | v(s2) v(s3) v(s4) v(s6) v(s8) v(s9) v(s10) | vv(s4) v(s5) v(s6) v(s7) | v(s10) |
| | Agree | v(s2) v(s3) v(s6) v(s9) | v(s3) v(s4) v(s6) v(s7) v(s8) | vv(s4) v(s5) vv(s10) | v(s1) v(s2) v(s3) v(s4) v(s6) v(s7) v(s8) v(s9) | v(s4) v(s8) v(s9) |
| | Strongly Agree | v(s1) v(s7) | v(s1) v(s2) | v(s1) v(s2) v(s3) | v(s1) v(s2) vv(s3) v(s5) v(s7) vv(s8) vv(s9) v(s10) | vvv(s1) vvv(s2) vvv(s3) vv(s4) vvv(s5) vvv(s6) vvv(s7) vv(s8) vv(s9) vv(s10) |

Table 1: Evaluation Results on Adequacy and Fluency of the Ten Text Segments.

As described in the ATA's (ATA BOD 2019) position paper on machine learning, machines understand neither the source nor the target text. The problems we found in the examples show that the adequacy suffered significantly due to the lack of understanding of context.

On the other hand, the human translator applied the tactics of strategic omission to reduce distraction. For example, the human translator chose to omit the phrase "The first page is always the best" in Sentence 8 because it was a distractor deviating from the main message.

The tactic of explicitation (Vinay et al., 1958/1995 and Gumul, 2006) was used by the human translator as well. This tactic made explicit in the target language what remains implicit in the

has the best adequacy. The comparison is done using word2vec2. Word2vec is a two-layer neural net that processes text (Artificial Intelligence Wiki). Its input is a text corpus and its output is a set of vectors: feature vectors for words in that corpus. The objective of Word2vec is to group the vectors of similar words together in a vector space. Therefore it can be used to detect the similarity of two sentences. The Chinese word2vec model used can be found on the website below: https://pan.baidu.com/s/1TZ8GII0CEX32ydjsfMc0zw, and the 64-dimension model was trained using the news, Baidu Encyclopedia, and Chinese novels. The python code used to calculate the word2vec similarity between two sentences is listed in table

2. The similarity score is between 0 and 1 and a higher score indicates higher similarity.

```
import gensim
import jieba
import numpy as np
from scipy.linalg import norm

model_file    =    'word2vec/news_12g_baidu-
baike_20g_novel_90g_embedding_64.bin'

model       =       gensim.models.KeyedVec-
tors.load_word2vec_format(model_file,      bi-
nary=True)

def vector_similarity(s1, s2):
    def sentence_vector(s):
        words = jieba.lcut(s)
        v = np.zeros(64)
        for word in words:
            v += model[word]
        v /= len(words)
        return v

    v1, v2 = sentence_vector(s1), sentence_vec-
tor(s2)
    print(v1, v2)
    return  np.dot(v1,  v2)  /  (norm(v1)  *
norm(v2))

strings0 = [
    '随后我们会做简短的休息',
    '我们会做简短的休息'
  ]

print("Sentence 0 Vector Similarity Results Be-
low:");
print(vector_similarity(strings0[0], strings0[1]));
```

Table 2: Python code to calculate word2vec based sentence similarity.

Table 3 shows an example in which the three evaluators exhibit disagreement. Evaluator 1 believed that the Google version is literal and accurate, while evaluator 2 and 3 observed some mistranslation and grammar/syntax errors. We found that some evaluators can have very biased view. For example, evaluator 2 believed that "才能阅读完" (finish reading in 28 minutes and 14 seconds) is very different from "需要28分14秒才能阅读" (needs 28 minutes and 14 seconds to read). Realistically, those two expressions are not that different from each other.

Since word2vec measures cannot be performed on empty spaces and punctuation, we measured the clause similarities between the google result and the result generated by the human translator (as the reference). Two clauses had similarity scores of around 0.88 and 0.78, while one clause "这会有所不同" (that vary a little bit can) had a very low similarity score (0.1058) compared to the human version "时间或长或短" (the reading time could be longer or shorter). This is in line with the comment by evaluator 3. The major difference is that the human version mentioned "时间" (time), while the Google version did not specify what varies. If we add the time ("时间") to the Google generated clause and change it to "时间会有所不同", then the word2vec based similarity changes from 0.1058 to 0.6617. That shows that the word2vec provides a very reliable similarity measure, and a good indicator of human bias. In this case, only the evaluator 3's opinion was supported by the word2vec results.

| |
|---|
| Original English: It should take about 28 minutes and 14 seconds for me to read these instructions to you.  That's going to vary a little bit but it'll take just about a half an hour for me to read the instructions to you. |
| Google translator result: 我需要大约28分14秒才能阅读这些说明 (word2vec similarity calculated against human generated translation = 0.8806)。这会有所不同 (word2vec similarity calculated against human 0generated translation = 0.1058)，但我需要大约半小时的时间 (word2vec similarity calculated against human generated translation = 0.7865) 才能阅读说明书。 |
| Evaluator 1 -> Agree: The translation is accurate and literal, but without taking into consideration the English conversation style and properly converting that to the target language, an accurate translation doesn't necessarily convey a message accurately.<br>Evaluator 2 -> Disagree: Here "to read" is translated to "才能阅读", which is a literal translation, but in Chinese, a more accurate translation should be "才能阅读完", meaning ""to finish reading".<br>Evaluator 3 ->Strongly Disagree: 1. Missing "to you". 2. Literal translation of "vary a little bit" which can cause confusion. |

Table 3: Google translator result for sentence No.7, evaluators' Likert scale evaluation and comments, and word2vec similarity measures.

Table 4 shows another example in which the three evaluators disagreed. Evaluators 1 and 2 believed that the translation is not adequate because it should be a polite request instead of a conditional statement. On the other hand, Evaluator 3 believed that the adequacy is acceptable. Using the word2vec measure, we measured the clause similarity between the Tencent result and the result generated by the human translator "请大家翻到指示文件的第一页" (as the reference), and the similarity score is 0.5166. If we change the Tencent result based on what Evaluators 1 and 2 suggested, the new similarity score is 0.6507. This shows that Evaluators 1 and 2 had a valid point, but while the improvement is significant, it is limited. Again, the word2vec based similarity measure

| | |
|---|---|
| Original English: So if you would turn to page 1 which is always the best page. Page 1 of the instructions. Post-introductory series. | |
| Tencent Mr Translator: 因此，如果你想翻到第一页(0.5166)，这始终是最好的一页。说明第1页：审判后介绍性系列(0.6646)。 | |
| Evaluator 1 -> Strongly Disagree: The translation is too literal to keep the intended meaning intact. "If you would turn to page 1" in the sentence isn't a conditional statement, although grammatically incorrect, it's a polite way to give a command, to tell the jurors to do something, and such command shall be reflected in the translation, instead of a conditional statement. | |
| Evaluator 2 -> Disagree "so if you would turn to page 1" is translated to "如果你想翻到第一页", which means "if you want to" But the original meaning is basically a polite way of requesting jury member to "please turn to page 1". A more accurate translation is "请翻到" | |
| Evaluator 3 -> Agree: The overall quality is OK. However, there are a few places that can be improved. Literal translation is an issue. | |

Table 4: Tencent Mr. translator result for text segment No.8, evaluators' Likert scale evaluation and comments, and word2vec similarity measures.

These examples showed that a word2vec based algorithm, if given a good reference translation, can serve as a robust and reliable similarity reference to quantify human evaluators' biases because it was trained on a large corpus using neural network models.

| Human Evaluator's opinion | Word2Vec similarity measure given a good reference translation | Human evaluator's bias |
|---|---|---|
| Table 3 example: | Similarity score changes from | The evaluator's opinion is confirmed |
| "这会有所不同" (that vary a little bit can) is not accurate given the context | 0.1058 to 0.6617 after adding the word "time" ("时间") | by the Word2Vec result (the similarity score changed by more than 0.5) |
| Table 4 example: The sentence "if you would turn to page 1" should be translated as a request instead of a conditional statement. | Similarity score changes from 0.5166 to 0.6507 after the sentence was translated as a request | The evaluator's opinion has some merits. But the improvement is as significant based on the Word2Vec result (the similarity score only changed by less than 0.15)) |

Table 5: Word2vec based similarity measures serve as a robust and reliable similarity reference to quantify human evaluators' biases.

### 4.5 Fluency Analyses

The subjective evaluation results (Table 1) show that the fluency performances of machine translators were not as bad compared to their adequacy performances. Nevertheless, their fluency performances were still inferior to the human translator's.

The machine translated results for Sentences 6, 8, and 9 by all three machine translators were categorized as the worst by human evaluators, since because majority of evaluators answered "strongly disagree" or "disagree" in regards to these sentences being fluent and adequate translations.

For Sentence 6, the human translator chose to omit the phrase "As I'm going to be telling you in just a few moments". This is an intelligent move because obviously the judge is telling them right at that moment, not a few moments later. Also, for the sentence "It was provided to each of you", the human translator used "刚才就给你们提供过的" to represent the past tense while all three machine translators failed to reflect the past tense. This is important because unlike English, the form of a Chinese verb never changes, regardless of whether it is present, past, or future tense. The past tense has to be represented using a timing word such as "刚才".

For Sentence 8, by leaving out the phrase "Page 1 is always the best page", the human translator avoided confusing the readers, and made the sentence as a whole flow much better. In addition, all machine translators used "做完那以后" (after I am done）, which is not a conventional Chinese expression. "读完以后" (After finishing the reading) is a better Chinese expression in this case.

For Sentence 9, the human translator used "你们可能需要休息一下了" while all three machine translators used "你们可能需要它". In Chinese, "它"(with the meaning "it") is usually not used in this context. "休息一下" (with the meaning "take a break") better matches Chinese convention.

Again, our observation is that machine translators lack understanding of the source and target texts, and the lack of understanding context and background led to inaccurate and improper word/phrase selection, which led to unnatural flow (bad fluency).

## 5    Conclusion

In this comparative study, we used a jury instruction scenario to test multiple machine translation tools and a human translator with extensive court experience. Three certified translators/interpreters evaluated the target texts generated using adequacy and fluency as the evaluation metrics.

We found that machine generated results had much worse adequacy performance compared with their human counterparts. Since machine translation tools understand neither the source nor the target text, unlike the human translator, they cannot minimize the misunderstanding across language and culture. Human translators can use strategic omission and explicitation strategies such as addition, paraphrasing, substitution, and repetition to remove ambiguity.

We also evaluate the word2vec as a tool to evaluate the similarity between machine generated results and human generated results. Word2vec trained neural network models on a large corpus to map words onto a vector space. Therefore it can be used to detect the similarity of two sentences. We use multiple examples to show that the word2vec serves as a robust and reliable similarity reference to quantify human evalutors' biases.

Even though the machine generated versions had better fluency performance relative to their adequacy performance, the human translator's fluency performance was still far superior. The lack of understanding by machine translators led to inaccurate and improper word/phrase selections, which led to unnatural flow (bad fluency).

## References


The ATA Board of Directors (BOD). 2019. *ATA Position Paper on Machine Translation: A Clear Approach to a Complex Topic*, https://www.ata-net.org/chronicle-online/extra/ata-position-paper-on-machine-translation/

Artificial Intelligence Wiki, *A Beginner's Guide to Word2Vec and Neural Word Embeddings*, https://skymind.ai/wiki/word2vec.

Gumul, Ewa, 2006. Explicitation in Simultaneous Interpreting: A Strategy or A By-product of Language Mediation. *Across Languages and Cultures* 7 (2), pp. 171-190.

Pastor, Michael (Judge), Conrad Murray Trial: Judge Instructions to Jury. 2011. https://www.youtube.com/watch?v=GRf9bZkE-mE

Philipp Koehn and Rebecca Knowles. 2017. Six Challenges for Neural Machine Translation. *In Workshop on Neural Machine Translation. Vancouver, BC. ArXiv*: 1706.03872. 171-190.

Vinay, J-P. and Darbelnet, J., 1958/1995. Comparative Stylistics of French and English: A Methodology for Translation, Amsterdam/Philadelphia: John Benjamins.

# Translating Terminologies: A Comparative Examination of NMT and PBSMT Systems


**Long-Huei Chen**
The University of Tokyo
Tokyo, Japan
`longhuei@g.ecc.u-tokyo.ac.jp`

**Kyo Kageura**
The University of Tokyo
Tokyo, Japan
`kyo@p.u-tokyo.ac.jp`



## Abstract

Terminology translation is a critical aspect in translation quality assurance, as it requires exact forms not typically expected of conventional translation. Recent studies have examined the quality of machine translation, but little work has focused specifically on the translation of terms. We present a comparative evaluation of the success of NMT and PBSMT systems in term translation. We selected eight language pairs among English, French, German, Finnish, and Romanian, taking into account their diverse language families and resource abundance. Based on the evaluation of Exact Match (EM) and recall scores, we concluded that NMT, in general, performs better with context, but PBSMT outperforms when translating without context, and found that significant differences often arise from language nature.


## 1   Introduction

Term translation is an important facet of translation quality assurance. Since terminologies are essential for communication among domain experts, term forms need to be consistent and context-independent to maintain the integrity of the underlying conceptual system during knowledge exchange (Sager, 1990). As such, term banks (collections of cross-lingual, cross-domain terminologies) ensure correct term usage across languages in the translation pipeline of humans.

The rise of machine learning in recent years has, for better or for worse, changed the landscape of translation forever. The typical evaluation of machine translation, due to a requirement of fast, automatic metrics during the training phase, typically involves the comparison with a set of human translation in what is calculated as the BLEU or the NIST scores of the translation (Papineni et al., 2002; Doddington, 2002). These approaches run counter to widely accepted frameworks of translation quality assurance (Görög, 2014; Peter et al., 2016) as the measures do not single out aspects of translation that humans traditionally attach importance.

Machine translation in general does not produce the exactness in forms required in term translation. Unlike translation of a text, where target text similar in meanings are equivalent as long as they fulfill the required functions, translated term forms must adhere to term banks (Kageura and Marshman, 2019). Machine translation also has implications in terminology building during the human translation process, as it can provide an automatic way to generate and validate the terminology resource that is available to translators (House, 2014; Chiocchetti and Lusicky, 2017; Yamada and Onishi, 2019). This is why we are also interested in learning how well the machine translation systems perform in term translation without context (Matis, 2010).

Here we present a comparative evaluation in the effectiveness of machine translation for terminology transfer across multiple languages. We investigate language pairs of varying training resource abundance on different machine translation architecture to understand the underlying factors of the effectiveness of terminology translation. We test systems with bidirectional translations and validate the terminology equivalence by referring to an established term bank.

## 2   Related Work

**The Special Case for Terminology Translation**

Traditional translators often approach terminology translation within the lenses of semasiological assumptions and treat terminology as a type of lexical elements (Achkasov, 2014). Nevertheless, when we take on an onomasiological point of view and understand that terms (Adamska-Salaciak, 2010; Lyding et al., 2006) are essentially definitions of concepts, then the degrees of equivalence are expected to be higher.

A key aspect of terminology translation is that the formation of a term in some language/domain is not solely at the discretion of the translator, but has structural, pragmatic, functional, and stylistic aspects that need to be taken into account (Achkasov, 2014). This produces a need for translation of terminologies that takes into account the domain terminology that is in existence (Kageura, 2012; Leitchik and Shelov, 2007)

**Terminology in Translation Quality Assurance**

Accuracy of terminologies in translated work is an essential element in translation quality assessment (Arango-Keeth and Koby, 2003; Görög, 2014; Peter et al., 2016). According to the standards establishing the essentiality of special treatments of terminology translation (ISO, 2010), policies relating to the adaptation of terminologies in translation work is necessitated and needs to be widely implemented. Substantial efforts have been expended in the past to evaluate the state of terminology translation in both phrase-based statistical machine translation (PBSMT) and more recently neural machine translation (NMT).

Yin et al. (2013) investigated consistency of terminology translation by cross-referencing patent documents in English and Chinese. Vintar (2018) evaluated both PBSMT and NMT between English and Slovene, a relatively lower-resource language pair. She concluded that thought Google's NMT serves a large amount of user-generated content at a large scale, the accuracy of its terminology translation within text leaves something to be desired.

**Empirical Evaluation of NMT/SMT with Textual Corpora**

Several studies examined the effectiveness of neural machine translation and statistical machine translation when applied to general text. Wu et al. in their original paper describing Google's NMT system (2016) observed increased performance compared to their previous public PBSMT system. Shterionov et al. (2017) conducted a comprehensive study on text translation and found NMT improved performances in multiple metrics as evaluated by humans. Dowling et al. (2018) tested both NMT and SMT systems on a lower-resourced language that is Irish and found that a domain-specific SMT system in some cases outperform NMT.

Muzaffar and Behera (2018), on the other hand, examined translation results in English-Urdu, a relatively resource-poor language pair, and concluded that NMT brings forward better comprehensibility and grammaticality. Castilho et al. (2017) recruited professional translators and found that as a tool for translators, NMT results do not reduce post-editing time compared to PBSMT. Work on specific genre includes (Toral and Way, 2018), which examine NMT vs. PBSMT performances on literary work, and found that NMT significantly increased the readability of the text for human readers. Kinoshita et al. (2017) examined the use of NMT and SMT in the translation of patent documents and concluded that NMT is superior in terms of human evaluations.

## 3   Machine Translation Models

### 3.1   Neural Machine Translation (NMT)

#### 3.1.1   The Encoder-decoder Architecture

The basic structure of the modern neural machine translation system involves the encoding of a series of source text tokens, which can be words or sub-word unit encoding, into a hidden state representation (Cho et al., 2014).

$$z = \mathrm{ENCODE}\,(w^s)$$

$$w^t|w^s \sim \mathrm{DECODE}(z)$$

where $z$ is the learned hidden state, $w$ refers to the distributional representation of words, with the suffix $s$ or $t$ referring to source or target origin. In the simplest sequence-to-sequence architecture, the encoder hidden state came is learned from the long short-term memory (LSTM) unit applied on the source sentence words (Sutskever et al., 2014).

The encoder hidden state is then passed along to the decoder, which is then passed along to the decoder for output. The decoder generates the target sentence token-by-token while continuous updating its internal state. In addition, neural attention mechanisms encourage compositional decoding by taking into account the context in the decoder. At each step in the decoding, an attentional score is calculated from the decoding hidden state along with the encoding sentence tokens.

### 3.1.2 Zero-shot Translation

As Google's Neural Machine Translation system takes input from any training pairs across all languages (Johnson et al., 2017), cross-lingual transfer learning was made possible with the addition of a language-specific token designating the output languages. The same shared parameters are applied to allow for translation into any target languages. As a result, even when parallel data are lacking across specific language pairs, resulting in the so-called zero-shot translation, which is impossible in previous systems. This allows the highly-effective use and wide coverage of Google's systems, even in cases where parallel corporal resources are lacking for specific language pairs.

### 3.2 Phrase-Based Statistical Machine Translation (PBSMT)

Statistical machine translation models statistically enumerating and maximizing the adequacy and fluency of the target translation by maximizing the probability across all possible assignments, usually with the expectation-maximization (EM) algorithm. Phrase-based statistical machine translation (PBSMT) extends this approach to account for the fact that phrases often form the smallest unit of translation, and allows for phrase-level alignments to suggest the most likable translation.

## 4 Approach

We conduct our experiment by pairing a term bank, which are sources of cross-lingual translations of specialized terms, with a set of technical documents in which the translators are expected to adhere to the term source. We extract sentence pairs from the documents by searching for a context where the term appears in accordance with the term bank.

### 4.1 Data Source

The **Inter-Active Terminology for Europe (IATE)** (Johnson and Macphail, 2000) is the official term bank sanctioned by the European Union (EU). It is the go-to source with approximately 1.4 million multilingual entries of terminologies containing the cross-lingual translation of terms

| Source | Target | Sentence Pairs |
|---|---|---|
| English | French | 58362 |
| French | English | 53470 |
| English | German | 38879 |
| German | English | 38879 |
| English | Finnish | 30994 |
| Finnish | English | 17486 |
| English | Romanian | 7676 |
| Romanian | English | 5151 |

**Table 1:** Size of the source-term sentence pairs, where only the source sentence is validated to contain the source term while the target term may or may not contain the target term.

| Source/Target | Sentence Pairs |
|---|---|
| English-French | 21057 |
| English-German | 14070 |
| English-Finnish | 17486 |
| English-Romanian | 2685 |

**Table 2:** Size of the human-validated sentence pairs, where the sentence pair is validated such that both source/target sentences contain the source/target term translation.

for translators working with the official European Union languages. The **European Parliament Proceedings (EuroParl) parallel corpus** is extracted from the proceedings of the European Parliament and includes versions in 24 European languages (Koehn, 2005). Size of the parallel corpora differs across language pairs, ranging from 400,000 to around 2.2 million sentence pairs.

Since IATE is the official EU-wide terminology as maintained and consulted by the translators under EU's employment, the combination of the two reflects the typical translation procedure when a commonly-agreed term source is provided for translators.

### 4.2 Language Pairs and Data Size

We choose to investigate four language pairs of the EuroParl parallel corpus, namely English-French (en-fr), English-German (en-de), English-Finnish (en-fi) and English-Romanian (en-ro). The languages are chosen by taking into account language families and data sizes.

1. **Source-term sentence pairs** are extracted from the corpora, and the source sentence is guaranteed to contain the source term, but the human-translated target sentence may or may not contain the target term. (Table 1)

2. **Human-validated term sentence pairs** are

those where both the source and the target sentences contain the source/target term from the terminology. They can be regarded as cases that the context of the sentences is guaranteed to reflect the definition of the terminology (Table 2)

We consider the second dataset as an equivalent operation when the human-translator chose the exact term translation as it appears in the term bank. This replaces the needs for human terminologists manually annotating the dataset, as the term bank has already been validated.

### 4.3 Google Cloud Translation APIs

The Google Cloud Translation API provides a programmatic interface for translating sentences across the supported languages using state-of-the-art translation models. The APIs include two models, the "nmt" model which is their new NMT model, and a "base" model, which as stated is a PBSMT model. We query the APIs to apply the model as needed.

### 4.4 Evaluation: Exact Match (EM) and Recall Scores

We compare term occurrence in results coming from target text produced from Google's Translation APIs and those from the official, human-translated target text. We presume that in cases where the term bank entry is present in the human-translated or machine-translated sentences, the term use in these cases are validated and considered correct usage.

Rather than using traditional measures of translation quality, in this work, we are mainly concerned with the success of different systems in their adequate reproduction of the relevant terminologies in the target text. Specifically:

1. **Exact Match (EM)** scores is defined as the exact occurrence of the ground truth target terms in the translated target sentence.

2. **Recall** is defined as the fraction of known target term words that occur in the target text.

For our evaluation, we do not make a distinction between the infections of terms. We chose this strict interpretation of exact match as we want to see how well these machine translation systems can fare in creating terminology resources for translators without context, in which case the exact form (including inflections) must be properly transferred across language barriers. The same scheme is also applied for with context translation

We recognize that, since both MT systems and human translation do not include an annotation as to the exact location of the term translation in the sentence, we are unable to verify the precision of the term translation or the F1 score. Also, we argue that since terms, unlike most multi-worded expressions, are technical in nature and have specific forms, it is less likely to occur by random in the target sentence and not as a translation, justifying our automated approach to evaluation.

## 5 Experiments

### 5.1 Adherence to Term Banks: Human v. NMT

In the first experiment, we apply translation systems to the source-term sentence pairs as detailed in §4.2. We compare performances of the system with the human translated sentences on how much the term bank target term is correctly translated in the target sentence. Results are given in Figure 1.

Cases in which the NMT scores are higher than that of human translations should *not* be interpreted as NMT performing better, but that the NMT systems adhere more to the term bank in a rote way. Humans may make the call on whether the particular term entry is applicable, or choose to use pronouns to avoid repetition of terms, and our evaluation may exclude the term variation deemed acceptable by humans.

- Despite varying human performances, NMT surpasses human scores for some language pairs but performs worse than human in others. This reflects the discongruity in a single end-to-end language model in its treatment of language pairs (§3.1.2).

- We observe that languages where parallel corpora resources are plentiful achieve lower NMT scores compared to the human scores. This suggests more parallel training data may shift the model's focus to language modeling and fluency rather than simple phrase-level correspondence, and indirectly hurt performance (§3.1).

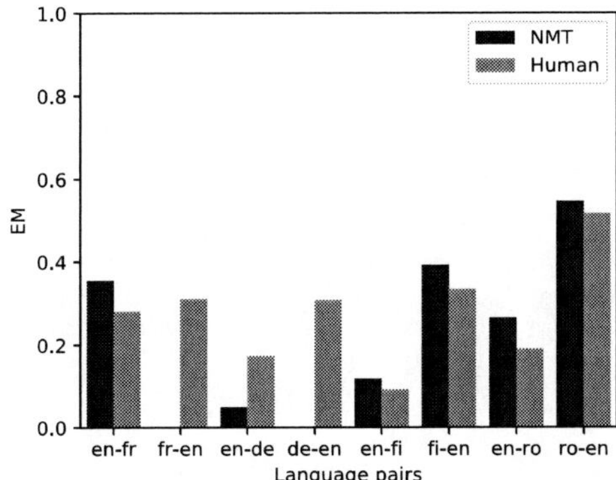

**(a)** EM scores

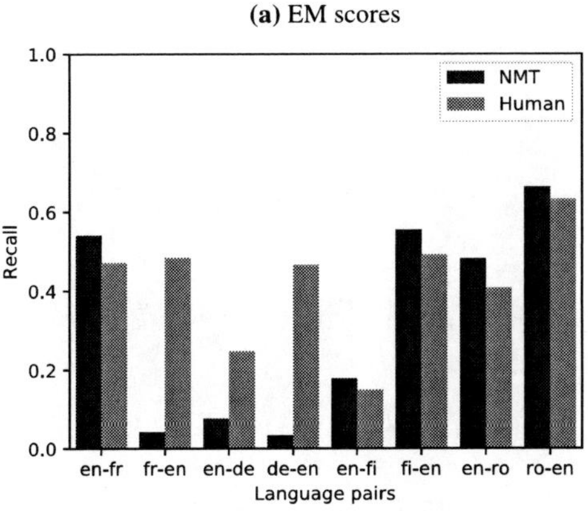

**(b)** Recall scores

**Figure 1:** Comparing human performances with NMT, using datasets where only the source sentence with context is validated to contain the source term. We test the recall and EM scores with regards to the term bank translation and the target sentence.

## 5.2 Translating Term with and without Context: NMT v. PBSMT

In these experiments, we apply the human-validated sentence pairs to the MT systems; this set includes both source/target terms in their source/target sentences, so the terms are human-validated to reflect the context.

For resulting scores in Figure 2a and 2c, we translate the terms along with the context sentences and observe how well the translated sentences adhere to the term bank translations. In Figure 2b and 2d, we see results when we translate the terms only *without the context* in which the term occur.

- Two obvious outliers are cases when translating English to German or Finnish. German and Finnish both have a significant amount of compound words, which has proven to be difficult to translate or rather for language processing in general (Eckman, 1981; Selmer and Lauring, 2015), and the system is expected to translate phrases (in English) to compounds.

- In general, Google's SMT systems outperform NMT when we translate term with context; but NMT performs slightly better in many cases across languages when we translate term without context. This reflects a fundamental difference in the translation mechanisms: in that the NMT end-to-end model pushes the model to translate the sentences holistically, whereas PBSMT systems can handle terms as phrasal units (§3.2).

- Differences in performance among languages are less prominent when we translate without context. This suggests the increased performances among some languages are a result of the language modeling available to the translation system (§3.1.1).

We also conducted a brief analysis of some of the errors we see with regards to term length (number of words) across languages but did not observe significant differences in scores.

## 5.3 Qualitative Analysis

We do a brief glance at the errors and observe human translation and NMT/SMT among language pairs and directionality.

- For cases where the target language is not English, we observe that NMT are more guilty of paraphrasing not allowed in term translation, like translating "réguler le marché" instead of the correct "réglementer le marché." For English as the target language translation, NMT and SMT both suffer from minor differences that do not affect meaning, suggesting that the English language models are of higher quality.

- English-to-Finnish translation is an outlier in that NMT outperforms SMT when translating *with* or *without* context. We conclude that NMT is better at handling compound words such as "lisäsuojatodistuksen", which is translated from the English multi-word term "supplementary protection certificate."

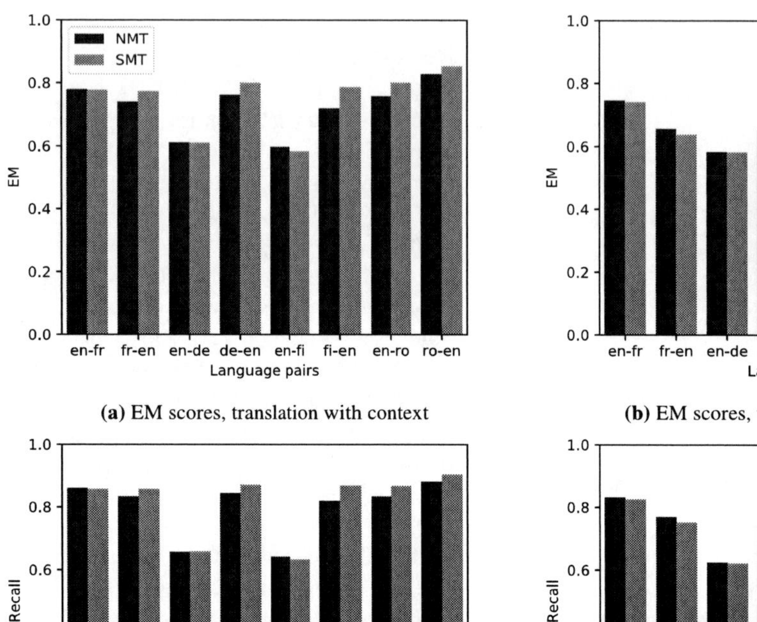

**(a)** EM scores, translation with context

**(b)** EM scores, translation without context

**(c)** Recall scores, translation without context

**(d)** Recall scores, translation without context

**Figure 2:** For the set of sentence pairs where both source and target sentences are validated to contain the source/target term entries as defined in the term bank, we compare scores for NMT v. SMT systems, applying translation either with context or only the source term itself as input.

- For English-Romanian, a lower-resource language pair, we see that NMT is slightly worse-off with or without context. An example of the errors made is translating "self-determination" as "auto-determinarea popoarelor" instead of "autodeterminare a popoarelor", which is a minor language error unrelated to meaning. We surmise this reflects the zero-shot approach (§3.1.2) in Google's NMT deemphasizes the nuances of translating resource-poor language pairs.

## 6 Conclusion

We reach conclusions on NMT/SMT systems compared with human translations that have implications in addition to term validation in translation assurances. Our experiments on translating terms without context show that such MT systems can be useful for the term resource construction process, and can assist translation companies in their work on consolidating terminologies for translators' referencing purposes.

In the future, we plan to better validate the document-level consistency of terminologies, another key aspect in quality assurance of translation. Specifically, due to the nature of the data applied in this study, we are unable to validate if the terms are *consistently* translated into a single form throughout the whole document. Also, due to our use of publicly-facing commercial MT APIs for our translation models, we have limited insight (based on published work and general knowledge of models) to the inner workings of the systems, and are unable to completely grasp the nature of the training data used by Google in development. This is a trade-off we had to face (as training our own models would be less similar to real-world usage and the model cannot be as extensive due to difficulty in acquiring data), but future work can be based on a balance of both approaches.

## Acknowledgement

This work was partially supported by JSPS KAK-ENHI Grant Number 19H05660.

## References

Achkasov, Andrei V. 2014. What translators do to terminology: Prescriptions vs. performance. *Journal of Siberian Federal University. Humanities & Social Sciences*, 2:210–221.

Adamska-Salaciak, A. 2010. Examining equivalence. *International Journal of Lexicography*, 23:387–409.

Arango-Keeth, Fanny and Geoffrey S Koby. 2003. Translator training evaluation and the needs of industry quality assessment. In Baer, Brian James and Geoffrey S. Koby, editors, *Beyond the Ivory Tower: Rethinking Translation Pedagogy*, pages 117–134.

Chiocchetti, Elena and Vesna Lusicky. 2017. Quality assurance in multilingual legal terminological databases. *The Journal of Specialised Translation*, 27:164–188.

Cho, Kyunghyun, Bart van Merrienboer, Caglar Gulcehre, Dzmitry Bahdanau, Fethi Bougares, Holger Schwenk, and Yoshua Bengio. 2014. Learning phrase representations using rnn encoder–decoder for statistical machine translation. In *Proceedings of the 2014 Conference on Empirical Methods in Natural Language Processing*, pages 1724–1734.

Doddington, George. 2002. Automatic evaluation of machine translation quality using n-gram co-occurrence statistics. In *Proceedings of the second international conference on Human Language Technology Research*, pages 138–145. Morgan Kaufmann Publishers Inc.

Eckman, Fred R. 1981. On predicting phonological difficulty in second language acquisition. *Studies in Second Language Acquisition*, 4(1):18–30.

Görög, Attila. 2014. Quantifying and benchmarking quality: the taus dynamic quality framework. *Tradumàtica*, (12):0443–454.

House, Juliane. 2014. Translation quality assessment: Past and present. In *Translation: A multidisciplinary approach*, pages 241–264. Springer.

2010. Iso 29383:2010: Terminology policies – development and implementation. Standard, International Organization for Standardization, Geneva, CH.

Johnson, Ian and Alastair Macphail. 2000. IATE–Inter-Agency Terminology Exchange: Development of a single central terminology database for the institutions and agencies of the european union. In *Proceedings of the Workshop on Terminology resources and computation, LREC 2000 Conference*.

Johnson, Melvin, Mike Schuster, Quoc V Le, Maxim Krikun, Yonghui Wu, Zhifeng Chen, Nikhil Thorat, Fernanda Viégas, Martin Wattenberg, Greg Corrado, et al. 2017. Google's multilingual neural machine translation system: Enabling zero-shot translation. *Transactions of the Association for Computational Linguistics*, 5:339–351.

Kageura, Kyo and Elizabeth Marshman. 2019. Translator training evaluation and the needs of industry quality assessment. In O'Hagan, Minako, editor, *The Routledge Handbook of Translation and Technology*, pages 236–331.

Kageura, Kyo. 2012. *The quantitative analysis of the dynamics and structure of terminologies*, volume 15. John Benjamins Publishing.

Koehn, Philipp. 2005. Europarl: A parallel corpus for statistical machine translation. In *MT summit*, volume 5, pages 79–86.

Leitchik, Vladimir M and Serguey D Shelov. 2007. Commensurability of scientific theories and indeterminacy of terminological concepts. *Indeterminacy in terminology and LSP: Studies in honour of Heribert Picht/Ed. by BE Antia. Amsterdam: John Benjamin's Publishing House*, pages 93–106.

Lyding, Verena, Elena Chiocchetti, Gilles Sérasset, and Francis Brunet-Manquat. 2006. The lexalp information system: Term bank and corpus for multilingual legal terminology consolidated. In *Proceedings of the workshop on multilingual language resources and interoperability*, pages 25–31. Association for Computational Linguistics.

Matis, Nancy. 2010. Terminology management during translation projects: Professional testimony. *Lingua-Culture*, 1:107–116.

Papineni, Kishore, Salim Roukos, Todd Ward, and Wei-Jing Zhu. 2002. BLEU: a method for automatic evaluation of machine translation. In *Proceedings of the 40th annual meeting on association for computational linguistics*, pages 311–318. Association for Computational Linguistics.

Peter, Jan-Thorsten, Tamer Alkhouli, Hermann Ney, Matthias Huck, Fabienne Braune, Alexander Fraser, Aleš Tamchyna, Ondřej Bojar, Barry Haddow, Rico Sennrich, et al. 2016. The qt21/himl combined machine translation system. In *Proceedings of the First Conference on Machine Translation: Volume 2, Shared Task Papers*, volume 2, pages 344–355.

Sager, Juan C. 1990. *Practical course in terminology processing*. John Benjamins Publishing.

Selmer, Jan and Jakob Lauring. 2015. Host country language ability and expatriate adjustment: The moderating effect of language difficulty. *The International Journal of Human Resource Management*, 26(3):401–420.

Sutskever, Ilya, Oriol Vinyals, and Quoc V Le. 2014.
Sequence to sequence learning with neural networks.
In *Advances in Neural Information Processing Systems*, pages 3104–3112.

Toral, Antonio and Andy Way. 2018. What level of
quality can neural machine translation attain on literary text? In *Translation Quality Assessment*, pages
263–287. Springer.

Yamada, Marasu and Nanami Onishi. 2019. Can students still work as a post-editor? In *Proceedings
of 25th Annual Meeting of the Japanese Association of Natural Language Processing*, pages 738–
741. Japanese Association of Natural Language Processing.

# NEC TM DATA PROJECT


**Alexandre Helle**
Pangeanic / B.I. Europe
PangeaMT Technologies Division
Valencia, Spain
a.helle@pangeanic.com

**Manuel Herranz**
Pangeanic / B.I. Europe
PangeaMT Technologies Division
Valencia, Spain
m.herranz@pangeanic.com



## Abstract

The objective of project NEC TM Data[1] is to organise unexploited national bilingual assets that can be used as open data and general data for machine learning, in order to lower translation costs at a national level and across member states. It runs a study on the expenditure at the national level on translation contracts, as well as at the regional and municipal levels. The software will help member states centralise these language assets with the *NEC TM* database, following industry best practices.

*NEC TM* is based on the ElasticSearch[2] (Gormley, 2015) *ActivaTM* server which is a centralised translation memory (TM) server independent of any computer-assisted translation (CAT) tool for efficient data sharing, TM matching, TM retrieval, and domain categorisation of resources. In short, ActivaTM separates the need of every CAT tool to have its own TM server. It is possible to store bilingual assets and later retrieve them through any CAT tool using the API calls to *NEC TM* Translators can translate and access each other's work simultaneously from different CAT tools.

*ActivaTM* is the basis for the *NEC TM* (fork-out) for the scope of this project. It has been selected as a CEF (Connecting Europe Facility) project by the European Commission as the database of choice to provide unified translation memory


services to EU public administrations and collect and build bilingual big data from public translation contracts.

Each European country will be able to install their own *NEC TM* and new translation contracts from translation companies will benefit from fuzzy matching analysis and will be able to work online and connect to each national *NEC TM* server.

Translation data will be categorised in *NEC TM*, and a connection provided to eTranslation and ELRC.

The consortium for the project is composed by Pangeanic, Tilde, Ciklopea and Secretary of State for Digital Progress (SEAD) of Spain.

The NEC TM Data project consortium advocates for the facilitation of a single digital market. It will act as a meeting point for European data gathering efforts and the collection of national digital big data. By building a data bridge between public administrations and translation vendors, NEC TM Data project will promote the free flow of data between Public Administrations and translation professionals.

## References


Gormley, Clinton, and Zachary Tong. 2015. Elasticsearch: The definitive guide: A distributed real-time search and analytics engine. *O'Reilly Media, Inc.*




[1] Action No. 2017-EU-IA-0149 shall run from 01/09/2018 until 28/02/2020
[2] https://www.elastic.co/es/products/elasticsearch

# APE-QUEST: an MT Quality Gate

**Joachim Van den Bogaert, Heidi Depraetere, Sara Szoc, Tom Vanallemeersch,
Koen Van Winckel, Frederic Everaert**
CrossLang
Kerkstraat 106
9050 Gentbrugge, Belgium
{first.lastname}@crosslang.com

**Lucia Specia, Julia Ive**
University of Sheffield
{initial.lastname}@sheffield.ac.uk

**Maxim Khalilov, Christine Maroti, Eduardo Farah*, Artur Ventura**
Unbabel
Rua Visconde de Santarém, 67B
1000-286 Lisboa, Portugal
{firstname}@unbabel.com, *{first.lastname}@unbabel.com

## Abstract

The APE-QUEST project (2018–2020) sets up a quality gate and crowdsourcing workflow for the eTranslation system of EC's Connecting Europe Facility to improve translation quality in specific domains. It packages these services as a translation portal for machine-to-machine and machine-to-human scenarios.

## 1 Objectives

The APE-QUEST project (Automated Post-editing and Quality Estimation) is funded by the EC's CEF Telecom programme (Connecting Europe Facility, project 2017-EU-IA-0151) and runs from October 2018 until September 2020. The project provides a quality gate and crowdsourcing workflow for the eTranslation machine translation (MT) system. The latter system is developed by the Directorate-General for Translation, supports all 24 official EU languages, and is provided by the CEF Automated Translation building block[1] of the Directorate-General for Communications Networks, Content and Technology (DG CNECT) as a service to Digital Service Infrastructures (DSIs) of the EC and to public administrations of Member States. The APE-QUEST consortium consists of two companies, CrossLang (project coordinator) and Unbabel, and the University of Sheffield.

APE-QUEST provides a quality gate by injecting quality estimation (QE) and automated post-editing (APE) into the translation workflow. QE and APE may be applied to the output of eTranslation or to crowdsourced translation. The main objectives of this injection are (1) to improve MT quality with additional linguistic services and (2) to create data aggregation opportunities by making translations and post-edits "locally owned", in the sense that the data is generated and curated at the end user's site, thus following the similar main principle of the EC's ELRC action.[2]

The APE-QUEST project focuses on integration of mature technologies: systems for MT, QE and APE, and an evironment for secure and reliable exchange of data, i.e. the EC's eDelivery building block. The tests in the project involve four languages, i.e. English, Portuguese, French

---



[1] https://ec.europa.eu/cefdigital

[2] http://lr-coordination.eu (European Language Resources Coordination)

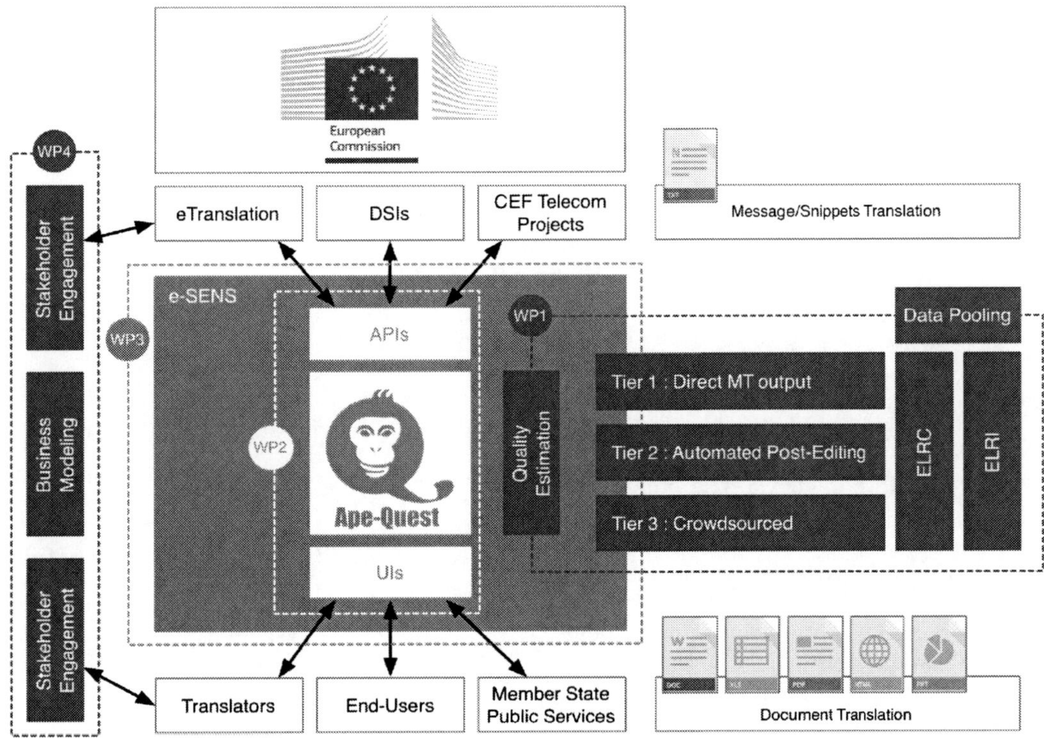



*Figure 1 Architecture of APE-QUEST*

and Dutch, and several domains, such as e-procurement and online dispute resolution.

## 2 Architecture

The workflow consists of three tiers: (1) MT output with acceptable quality flows directly to the end user or connected system, (2) moderate-quality MT is enhanced through APE, and (3) low-quality MT is sent to a workflow for manual PE (crowdsourcing), after which QE and APE can be applied optionally, as an additional quality assurance step.

The input to the workflow consists of text snippets (messages) or full text documents originating from the project's stakeholders, such as DSIs, public services in Member States, and organisations involved in CEF Telecom projects that make use of eTranslation. The input is provided through an API or a user interface (UI) and is segmented into sentences to allow for complex routing. For example, if only one low-quality sentence is detected, only one tier 3 request is issued, while the rest of the sentences is routed to tiers 1 and 2.

The injection of a PE workflow allows for collecting user data for system improvement. These data will be made available to re-train and adapt the eTranslation system, and to re-train the QE and APE systems. The data will also be made available to ELRC, thus extending the latter's resources with postedited data, and to the ELRI project,[3] which collects, prepares and shares language resources.

APE-QUEST's reference implementation will be compliant with the eTranslation system and the eDelivery building block (developed in the framework of the EC's e-SENS[4] project), will contain a portal-style front end, and will be packaged in an easily deployable form for DSIs and public administrations of Member States. The workflow will be backward-compatible for systems that use the current eTranslation interface.

## Acknowledgement

APE-QUEST is funded by the EC's CEF Telecom programme (project 2017-EU-IA-0151).

---

[3] http://www.elri-project.eu (European Language Resource Infrastructure)

[4] https://www.esens.eu

# PRINCIPLE: Providing Resources in Irish, Norwegian, Croatian and Icelandic for the Purposes of Language Engineering


**Andy Way & Federico Gaspari**
ADAPT Centre
School of Computing
Dublin City University
Dublin 9, Ireland
`{Firstname.Lastname}@adaptcentre.ie`


## Abstract


PRINCIPLE is a new 2-year project starting in September 2019 funded by the European Commission under the Connecting Europe Facility (CEF) programme. Parallel data for Croatian, Icelandic, Irish and Norwegian are in relatively short supply, so that the quality of the eTranslation machine translation (MT) engines is less than would be the case if larger parallel corpora were available. PRINCIPLE will gather parallel data for these languages and English, evaluate the quality of the gathered resources via MT, and deliver corpora deemed to be of high quality to eTranslation for improved MT engine training.


## 1 Languages, Activities and Partners

The PRINCIPLE project focuses on the identification, collection and processing of language resources (LRs) for four under-resourced European languages: Croatian, Icelandic, Irish, and Norwegian (covering both varieties: Bokmål and Nynorsk).

It focuses on providing data to improve translation quality in two Digital Service Infrastructures (DSIs)[1] – eJustice and eProcurement – via domain-specific MT engines, over a 2-year period (September 2019 to August 2021).

The main activities in PRINCIPLE are:

(i)    use-case analysis, data requirements and data preparation,

(ii)    identification and collection of LRs,

(iii)    development, evaluation and deployment of MT systems,

(iv)    exploitation and sustainability, and

(v)    dissemination.

The project is coordinated by the ADAPT Centre at Dublin City University (Ireland), and the partners are Iconic Translation Machines (Dublin, Ireland), the University of Zagreb (Croatia), the National Library of Norway in Oslo, and the University of Iceland in Rejkyavik.

## 2 Data Collection and Verification

PRINCIPLE will provide high-quality curated data via ELRC-SHARE,[2] a repository for documenting, storing, browsing and accessing LRs collected through the European Language Resource Coordination[3] network to feed the CEF eTranslation engines. MT engines will be offered to the 'early adopter' public administration partners in the four countries to validate the LRs collected based on the specific use-cases determined by public bodies within each country.

While public administrations are already able to upload their data sets directly to ELRC-SHARE, for low-resource languages such as those of focus in the project, this has been relatively unsuccessful to date. In PRINCIPLE, partners will

---



[1] https://ec.europa.eu/digital-single-market/en/news/connecting-europe-facility-cef-digital-service-infrastructures
[2] https://elrc-share.eu/
[3] http://lr-coordination.eu/

avail of their local contacts in each (relatively small) country to try to persuade key stakeholders of the benefit of releasing corpora in their possession, negotiating in each case the most permissive terms possible for distribution and further reuse.

However, rather than just acting as data collectors, and passing data blindly to ELRC-SHARE, the ADAPT MT team at DCU, Iconic and the University of Zagreb all have ample experience of building MT engines, including for the low-resource language pairs of the project. Dowling et al. (2018) compare statistical MT and neural MT performance for English-Irish; Klubička et al. (2017) built Croatian-English neural MT systems with superior quality to Google Translate;[4] and Gupta et al. (2019) addresses the issue of robustness in real commercial neural MT systems.

Accordingly, PRINCIPLE will build in-house baseline MT engines for each language pair and domain, add incremental amounts of data gathered, retrain the MT engines, and only submit data to eTranslation if improvements in MT quality are clearly visible via both automatic metrics and human evaluation.

Once the utility of the datasets has been verified in this way by the project partners, parallel data in 50K sentence-pair batches will be uploaded to ELRC-SHARE for use by the eTranslation engines which will be important to break down language barriers via MT capability to provide multilingual access to all DSIs by European and national public administrations for the languages covered under this project.

As well as these clear benefits to eTranslation, public administrations which have agreed to partner with the project will be able to use the in-house MT engines developed by the PRINCIPLE technical partners for the duration of the project.

## 3    Relationship with other CEF Projects

The experience of evaluating commercial MT systems for deployment in public administrations in the iADAATPA project[5] (cf. Castilho et al., 2019) will greatly benefit PRINCIPLE.

PRINCIPLE intends to promote awareness and use of National Relay Stations (NRSs), which are designed to effectively collect, process and share language resources that can be used for MT training under the European Language Resource Infrastructure (ELRI) project (Etchegoyen et al., 2018).[6] NRSs have already been made available and promoted by ELRI in Ireland, France, Portugal and Spain. PRINCIPLE will encourage the extension of new NRSs to Croatia, Iceland and Norway for their respective languages.

## Acknowledgements

PRINCIPLE is generously co-financed by the European Union Connecting Europe Facility under Action 2018-EU-IA-0050 with the specific grant agreement INEA/CEF/ICT/A2018/1761837.

## References

Castilho, Sheila, Natalia Resende, Federico Gaspari, Andy Way, Tony O'Dowd, Marek Mazur, Manuel Herranz, Alex Helle, Gema Ramirez-Sanchez, Victor Sanchez-Cartagena, Marcis Pinnis, and Valters Sics. 2019. Large-scale Machine Translation Evaluation of the iADAATPA Project. In *Proceedings of MT Summit XVII*, Dublin, Ireland.

Dowling, Meghan, Teresa Lynn, Alberto Poncelas and Andy Way. 2018. SMT versus NMT: Preliminary comparisons for Irish. In *Proceedings of the AMTA 2018 Workshop on Technologies for MT of Low Resource Languages (LoResMT 2018)*, Boston, MA., pp.12—20.

Etchegoyhen, Thierry, Borja Anza Porras, Andoni Azpeitia, Eva Martínez Garcia, Paulo Vale, José Luis Fonseca, Teresa Lynn, Jane Dunne, Federico Gaspari, Andy Way, Victoria Arranz, Khalid Choukri, Vladimir Popescu, Pedro Neiva, Rui Neto, Maite Melero, David Perez Fernandez, Antonio Branco, Ruben Branco and Luis Gomes. 2018. ELRI - European Language Resources Infrastructure. In *Proceedings of The 21st Annual Conference of the European Association for Machine Translation (EAMT 2018)*, Alicante, Spain, p.351.

Gupta, Rohit , Patrik Lambert, Raj Patel and John Tinsley. 2019. Improving Robustness in Real-World Neural Machine Translation Engines. In *Proceedings of MT Summit XVII*, Dublin, Ireland.

Klubička, Filip, Antonio Toral and Victor Sánchez-Cartagena. 2017. Fine-grained human evaluation of neural versus phrase-based machine translation. *The Prague Bulletin of Mathematical Linguistics* **108** (1): 121—132.

---

[4] http://translate.google.com
[5] http://iadaatpa.com/

[6] http://www.elri-project.eu/

# iADAATPA Project: Pangeanic use cases


**Mercedes García-Martínez, Amando Estela,
Laurent Bié, Alexander Helle, Manuel Herranz**

m.garcia/a.estela/l.bie/a.helle/m.herranz@pangeanic.com



## Abstract

The iADAATPA[1] project coded as N°
2016-EU-IA-0132 that ended in February
2019 is made for building of customized,
domain-specific engines for public administrations from EU Member States. The
consortium of the project decided to use
neural machine translation at the beginning
of the project. This represented a challenge
for all involved, and the positive aspect is
that all public administrations engaged in
the iADAATPA project were able to try,
test and use state-of-the-art neural technology with a high level of satisfaction.

One of the main challenges faced by all
partners was data availability. Although
all public administrations had some data
available, it was clearly insufficient for
high-level customization. In some cases,
we had merely a few hundred words or several tens of thousand words. Each domain
(field) has its own unique word distribution
and neural machine translation systems are
known to suffer a decrease in performance
when data is out-of-domain.

Pangeanic is a language service provider
(LSP) specialised in natural language processing and machine translation. It provides solutions to cognitive companies,
institutions, translation professionals, and
corporations. The problem faced by
the iADAATPA project at Pangeanic was
twofold:


1. Availability of training data in some
   language combinations.
2. How to successfully train a translation model on multi-domain data.

**Language pairs and domains**
Pangeanic's use cases are for 2 Span-
ish public administrations: (1) Generalitat
Valenciana (regional administration)
translating from Spanish into and out of
English, French, Catalan/Valencian, Ger-
man, Italian, Russian and (2) SEGITTUR[2]
(tourism administration) translating from
Spanish into and out of English, French,
German, Italian, Portuguese.

**Data acquisition** For translation from
Spanish to Russian there was no available
in-domain data. Therefore, 2 translators
were contracted as part of the project to
create 30,000 segments of in-domain data,
translating public administrations websites. They also cleaned United Nations
material and post-edited general-domain
data that was previously filtered as in-
domain following the "invitation model"
(Hoang and Sima'an, 2014). For the
other language pairs, the input material
was 30,000 post-edited segments. The
main part of the training corpora (approximately 75%) was part of Pangeanic's own
repository harvested through web crawling and also OpenSubtitles (Tiedemann,
2012). The rest of the corpus was automatically validated synthetic material using general data from Leipzig (Goldhahn
et al., 2012).



[1] http://iadaatpa.com/

[2] https://www.segittur.es/es/inicio/index.html

**Engine customization** The data was cleaned using the Bicleaner tool (Sánchez-Cartagena et al., 2018). The data was lowercased and extra embeddings were added in order to keep the case information. The tokenization used was the one provided by OpenNMT[3] and words were divided in subwords according to the BPE (Sennrich et al., 2016) approach. The models were trained with multi-domain data and we improved performance following a domain-mixing approach (Britz et al., 2017). The domain information was prepended with special tokens for each target sequence. The domain prediction was based only on the source as the extra token was added at target-side and there was no need for a-priori domain information. This approach allowed the model to improve the quality for each domain.

**Acknowledgements** The work reported in this paper was conducted during the iADAATPA project, which was funded by INEA through grant N° 2016-EU-IA-0132 as part of the EU's CEF Telecom Programme.

## References

Britz, Denny, Quoc Le, and Reid Pryzant. 2017. Effective domain mixing for neural machine translation. In *Proceedings of the Second Conference on Machine Translation*, pages 118–126. Association for Computational Linguistics.

Goldhahn, Dirk, Thomas Eckart, and Uwe Quasthoff. 2012. Building large monolingual dictionaries at the leipzig corpora collection: From 100 to 200 languages. In *Proceedings of the Eighth International Conference on Language Resources and Evaluation (LREC12)*, pages 759–765.

Hoang, Cuong and Khalil Sima'an. 2014. Latent domain translation models in mix-of-domains haystack. In *Proceedings of COLING 2014, the 25th International Conference on Computational Linguistics: Technical Papers*, pages 1928–1939. Dublin City University and Association for Computational Linguistics.

Sánchez-Cartagena, Víctor M., Marta Bañón, Sergio Ortiz-Rojas, and Gema Ramírez-Sánchez. 2018. Prompsit's submission to wmt 2018 parallel corpus filtering shared task. In *Proceedings of the Third Conference on Machine Translation, Volume 2: Shared Task Papers*, pages 95–103, Brussels, Belgium, October. Association for Computational Linguistics.

Sennrich, Rico, Barry Haddow, and Alexandra Birch. 2016. Neural machine translation of rare words with subword units. In *Proceedings of the 54th Annual Meeting of the Association for Computational Linguistics (Volume 1: Long Papers)*, pages 1715–1725, Berlin, Germany, August. Association for Computational Linguistics.

Tiedemann, Jörg. 2012. Parallel data, tools and interfaces in OPUS. In *Proceedings of the Eighth International Conference on Language Resources and Evaluation (LREC-2012)*, pages 2214–2218, Istanbul, Turkey, May. European Languages Resources Association (ELRA).

---

[3] http://opennmt.net/

# MICE


**Joachim Van den Bogaert,
Heidi Depraetere, Tom Vanallemeersch,
Frederic Everaert, Koen Van Winckel**
CrossLang
Kerkstraat 106
9050 Gentbrugge
Belgium
{first.lastname}@crosslang.com

**Artūrs Vasiļevskis, Valters Sics**
Tilde IT
Naugarduko g. 100
LT-03160 Vilnius
Latvia
{first.lastname}@tilde.lt

**Katri Tammsaar, Ingmar Vali,
Tambet Artma, Piret Saartee,
Laura Katariina Teder**
RIK
Lubja 4
19081, Tallinn
Estonia
{first.lastname}@rik.ee

**Johan Haelterman, David Bienfait**
Bureau for Standardisation
Rue Joseph II 40 PO box 6
1000, Brussels
Belgium
{first.lastname}@nbn.be



## Abstract

The MICE project (2018 – 2020) will deliver a middleware layer for improving the output quality of the eTranslation system of the European Commission's Connecting Europe Facility, through additional services, such as domain adaptation and named-entity recognition. It will also deliver a user portal, allowing for human post-editing.


## 1 Objectives

The MICE project (Middleware for Customised eTranslation), which is funded by the CEF Telecom programme (Connecting Europe Facility) and runs from October 2018 to September 2020, delivers a middleware layer for the improvement of the eTranslation machine translation (MT) system. The latter is developed by the Directorate-General for Translation (DGT), supports all 24 official EU languages, and is provided by the CEF Automated Translation building block of the Directorate-General for Communications Networks, Content and Technology (DG CNECT), as a service to digital service infrastructures (DSIs) of the European Commission (EC) and to public administrations of Member States. The project consortium of MICE consists of two companies, CrossLang (coordinator) and Tilde, and two public organisations, NBN (Bureau for Standardisation, Belgium) and RIK (Centre of Registers and Information Systems, Estonia).

The middleware layer consists of the following services:

- domain adaptation;
- terminology resolution;
- named-entity recognition;
- document filtering;
- normalisation.

MICE will also provide a human and automated post-editing (PE) environment for CEF eTranslation output. This will help users to dynamically improve the MT output and aggregate data for further system improvement.

The tests in the project involve four languages, i.e. English, Dutch, French and Estonian, and two domains, i.e. standards and e-Business/e-Land[1] register information, in two countries (Belgium and Estonia). Domain-specific neural MT systems will be made available by the project consortium.

---



[1] e-Land registers are electronic land registries that register the ownership of land and property.

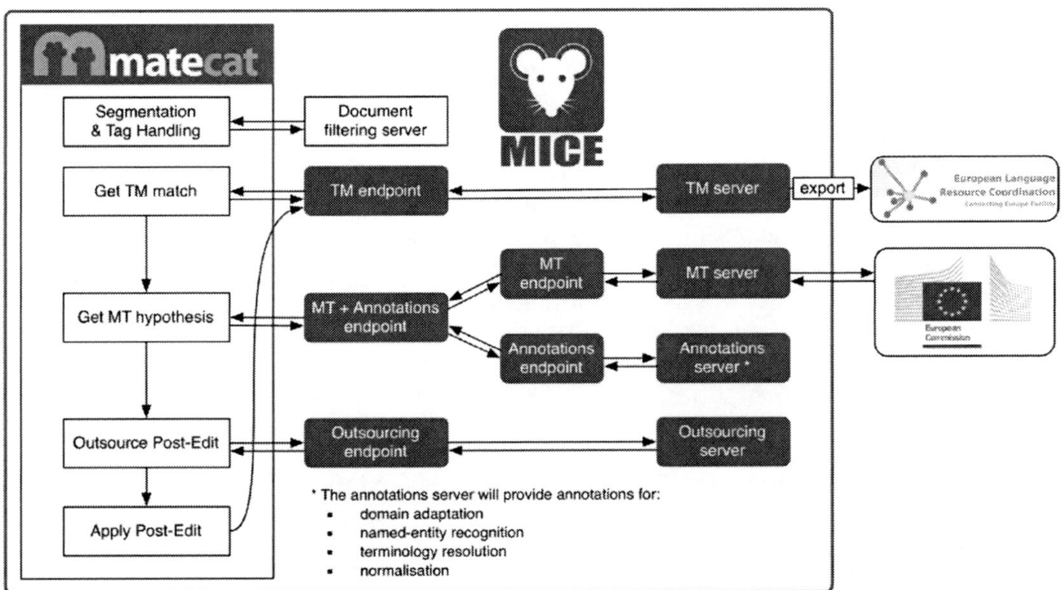



*Figure 1: MICE architecture*

## 2 Architecture

MICE will expose its middleware layer for customisation through APIs and a user portal, in order to increase its impact and usability. Tasks will be performed in real-time or offline, depending on user preference. The input consists of text snippets (messages in plain text of maximally 5,000 characters) or full-text documents (Microsoft Office, open document formats, etc.). The security level will be compliant with the Electronic Simple European Networked Services (e-SENS).

The MICE project will create a reference implementation for the automated translation of standards and e-Business/e-Land register information in Belgium and Estonia, and be extensible to allow for future add-ons of MT-related services, such as automated domain detection or combination of MT systems.

The architecture (outlined in Figure 1) will incorporate the open source MateCat[2] computer aided translation (CAT) tool to provide user portal functionality (user interface and configuration management).

Existing integrations for translation memory (TM) leveraging, MT and post-editing outsourcing will be abstracted into service endpoints that can be connected to external services. For example:

- The TM endpoint will allow for connecting MateCat to any TM server. Exports can be added to the European Language Resource Coordination repository.

- The MT + annotations endpoint will allow for connectivity with the CEF eTranslation service (or any other third-party MT service) while integrating advanced features, such as named-entity recognition.

- The outsourcing endpoint will allow for dispatching post-editing jobs to third-party providers.

While developing the MICE solution, existing interfaces will be upgraded to allow for advanced MT/TM features:

- The existing MT interface will be extended to encode annotations information, instructing MT engines to apply a distinct treatment to named entities, detected terms, etc.

- The TM interface will be adapted to allow for the storage of post-editing triplets. Currently, most TMs only store the source and target sentence. By storing also the MT hypothesis, instead of overwriting it with the human translation, MICE will contribute to the development of corpora for the training of quality estimation and automated post-editing systems.

## Acknowledgement


MICE is funded by the European Commission 's CEF Telecom programme (project 2017-EU-IA-0169).


---

[2] See https://github.com/matecat/MateCat

# ParaCrawl: Web-scale parallel corpora for the languages of the EU


**M. Esplà-Gomis, M.L. Forcada**
Dept. Lleng. i Sist. Inform.
Universitat d'Alacant
E-03690 St. Vicent del Raspeig
Spain
{mlf,mespla}@dlsi.ua.es

**G. Ramírez-Sánchez**
Prompsit Language Engineering
Av. Universitat, s/n
E-03202 Elx
Spain
gema@prompsit.com

**H. Hoang**
School of Computing
University of Edinburgh
Edinburgh HE8 4AB
UK
Hieu.Hoang@ed.ac.uk



## Abstract

We describe two projects funded by the Connecting Europe Facility, *Provision of Web-Scale Parallel Corpora for Official European Languages* (2016-EU-IA-0114, completed) and *Broader Web-Scale Provision of Parallel Corpora for European Languages* (2017-EU-IA-0178, ongoing), which aim at harvesting parallel corpora from the Internet for languages used in the European Union. In addition to parallel corpora, the project releases successive versions of the free/open-source web crawling software used.


## 1 Introduction

Two projects are described in this abstract: *Provision of Web-Scale Parallel Corpora for Official European Languages* (Action 2016-EU-IA-0114, September 2017–March 2019, completed) or **Paracrawl**, and *Broader Web-Scale Provision of Parallel Corpora for European Languages* (Action 2017-EU-IA-0178, September 2018–September 2020, ongoing), or **Paracrawl-2**. Both are funded by the Connecting Europe Facility and have the same objective: to harvest parallel data from the Internet for languages used in the European Union. Namely, the first action focuses on parallel data between English and the other 23 official languages of the European Union, while the second one includes new pairs of languages, such as the pairs consisting of Spanish and the three regional languages recognized by Spain (Catalan, Basque, and Galician) or the two Norwegian languages (Bokml and Nynorsk). In addition to parallel corpora (see section 2, the project periodically releases versions of



the free/open-source web-crawling software used, Bitextor (see section 3).

### 1.1 The consortium

Five partners are involved in these projects; two academic partners and three companies: The University of Edinburgh (coordinator), Edinburgh (UK); Universitat d'Alacant, Alacant (Spain); Prompsit Language Engineering S.L., Elx (Spain); TAUS B.V, Amsterdam (the Netherlands); Omniscien Technologies (trading) B.V., Zoetermeer (the Netherlands, only *Paracrawl2*).

## 2 Corpora built

Table 1 summarizes the most recent release, version 4, of parallel data between English and the remaining 23 languages of the European Union.

ParaCrawl corpora are publicly available under the Creative Commons CC0 license and can be found at the ParaCrawl website[1] and the ELRC-share repository. [2]

Random samples of 2,000 sentences for each language combination were validated by language experts for version 3 of the corpora allowing to tackle some of the most prominent issues before the release of version 4. Also, an extrinsic evaluation through MT was performed for some language pairs. It consistently confirms the positive impact of adding ParaCrawl corpora to baseline systems.[3]

## 3 Free/open-source crawling pipeline

One of the outputs of these projects is the free/open-source pipeline implemented to build the corpora in Table 1. The last version of this pipeline has been

---

[1] https://paracrawl.eu/releases.html
[2] https://elrc-share.eu/
[3] Adding Paracrawl 4 corpora to the WMT 2018 baseline improved the BLEU score in 11 out of 12 language pairs tested, https://paracrawl.eu/releases.html.

| language paired with English | number of segment pairs | number of English tokens |
|---|---|---|
| Bulgarian | 1,039,885 | 21,109,546 |
| Croatian | 1,002,053 | 19,904,218 |
| Czech | 2,981,949 | 48,918,151 |
| Danish | 2,414,895 | 48,240,290 |
| Dutch | 5,659,268 | 108,197,376 |
| Estonian | 853,422 | 16,537,397 |
| French | 31,374,161 | 664,924,148 |
| Finnish | 2,156,069 | 41,564,859 |
| German | 16,264,450 | 307,786,150 |
| Greek | 1,985,233 | 38,322,532 |
| Hungarian | 1,901,342 | 30,835,267 |
| Irish | 357,399 | 8,241,515 |
| Italian | 12,162,239 | 260,361,435 |
| Latvian | 553,060 | 10,996,032 |
| Lithuanian | 844,643 | 15,087,805 |
| Maltese | 195,510 | 4,100,912 |
| Polish | 3,503,276 | 65,618,419 |
| Portuguese | 8,141,940 | 156,125,200 |
| Romanian | 1,952,043 | 39,882,223 |
| Slovak | 1,591,831 | 26,711,854 |
| Slovenian | 660,161 | 14,489,659 |
| Spanish | 21,987,267 | 476,409,854 |
| Swedish | 3,476,729 | 70,088,534 |

**Table 1:** Statistics for the Paracrawl corpus, version 4

released as version 7 of the parallel-data-crawling tool Bitextor.[4] This pipeline covers all the stages from crawling data from websites on the Internet to delivering a clean parallel corpus. Namely, the stages included in this process are: (1) downloading HTML documents from the Internet; (2) preprocessing, normalizing and augmenting information from these documents; (3) aligning documents that are parallel; (4) aligning the segments in each of the document pairs identified; (5) filtering noisy data, deduplicating and formatting the output.

From the beginning of Paracrawl actions, several tools and modules have been contributed by the partners of the consortium and integrated in Bitextor. After a partial re-implementation of the pipeline control module (workflow manager), the tool is now highly configurable, allowing to run the pipeline using alternative components for the different stages of processing. Bitextor 7 was designed for high scalability in order to tackle the challenges of dealing with large amounts of data coming from thousands, or hundreds of thousands, of websites crawled from the Internet. It is built to work with distributed clusters such as SLURM and PBS Pro and cloud computing, with specific support for Azure.

It is also worth to mention Bicleaner,[5] a tool to filter parallel data that has been integrated in the Bitextor pipeline. This tool, which ranked among the best systems in the shared task on parallel corpora cleaning at WMT 2018 (Sánchez-Cartagena et al., 2018), is especially useful when dealing with noisy corpora such as those obtained through massive crawling from the Internet.

All the modules released as part of Bitextor 7 can be used within the pipeline or independently, to create new pipelines for specific purposes.

## 4 Future work

Paracrawl2 action is ongoing; some of the most relevant objectives for the next months of project are: adding Icelandic, Norwegian (Bokmål and Nynorsk), Basque, Catalan/Valencian, and Galician to the languages already covered languages; covering formats different to HTML (PDF, DOCX, ODT, etc.);including domain identification to support the extraction of relevant data from ParaCrawl corpora; processing the Internet Archive[6] to gather new parallel data; improving Bitextor by improving document and segment alignment and corpus cleaning; improving data exploitation by repairing rather than simply discarding and by segmenting too long sentences into clauses; delivering randomised, anonymised, partially omitted and mixed data sets to extend their usage; formalising human and automatic evaluation for quality testing.

In addition to the work covered in the ongoing action, four of the partners of the Paracrawl2 consortium have recently been awarded a new Connecting Europe Facility action, *Continued Web-Scale Provision of Parallel Corpora for European Languages* (Action 2018-EU-IA-0063, *Paracrawl-3*), which will extend the results of the previous projects.

## References


Sánchez-Cartagena, Víctor M., Marta Bañón, Sergio Ortiz-Rojas, and Gema Ramírez-Sánchez. 2018. Prompsit's submission to the WMT 2018 parallel corpus filtering shared task. In *Proceedings of the Third Conference on Machine Translation, Volume 2: Shared Task Papers*, pages 968–975, Brussels, Belgium, October. Association for Computational Linguistics.


[4] https://github.com/bitextor/bitextor

[5] https://github.com/bitextor/bicleaner
[6] https://archive.org/

# Pivot Machine Translation in INTERACT Project


**Chao-Hong Liu, Andy Way**
ADAPT Centre
Dublin City University, Ireland
chaohong.liu@adaptcentre.ie
andy.way@adaptcentre.ie

**Catarina Silva and André Martins**
Unbabel
Lisbon, Portugal
catarina@unbabel.com
andre.martins@unbabel.com



## Abstract

The INTERnAtional network on Crisis Translation (INTERACT) project under EU Marie Skłodowska-Curie Actions (MSCA) Research and Innovation Staff Exchange (RISE) Programme aimed at researching translation in crisis scenarios. In this extended abstract, we present the work on Pivot Machine Translation under the INTERACT project.


## 1  Introduction

The EU INTERACT project is a staff exchange project which brings together researchers from different disciplines to collaborate on the issues arise in delivering translation in crisis scenarios. The project is led by Dr. Sharon O'Brien at Dublin City University and the consortium also includes University College London, Unbabel, Microsoft, Translators without Borders, Cochrane, University of Auckland, Arizona State University. The project starts from April 2017 for 36 months.

There are many issues addressed in different work packages in the project, e.g. involving civil translator and ethics. In this extended abstract, we describe the work on automatic translation, which includes building and adapting machine translation (MT) systems for health-related contents in scenario language translation pairs.

As a target scenario to bring translation for crisis situations, we focused on building MT systems for translation of health-related contents where parallel corpora for a language pair are very small or do not even exist.

There are several approaches to build MT systems under this circumstance. For example, in Wu and Wang (2007), a small parallel corpus is used to interpolate translation probabilities of a target translation pair in statistical machine translation (SMT). Utiyama and Isahara (2007) also compared two different SMT strategies, phrase-translation and sentence-translation. pivot machine translation (Pivot MT) is the sentence-translation strategy which builds two cascading MT systems (A-to-B and B-to-C) to realize translation from A to C, with the assumption that the parallel corpora (A—B and B—C) are much larger than direct A—C parallel corpus. The zero-shot neural MT (NMT) approach is another method to build MT systems without any direct parallel corpus (Johnson, Schuster, Le, et al.) However, experiments on the UN Parallel Corpus showed that pivoting with sentence-translation strategy is still the best practice under this circumstance.

We took three major steps to improve MT quality for health-related contents. First, manually collected and edited parallel corpora for Arabic—English and Greek—English are curated. These are small corpora at the scale of two thousand sentence pairs, and each of them are separated into development and test sets for the training of the MT systems.

Second, we used data selection methods (term frequency–inverse document frequency, cross-entropy difference and feature decay algorithm) to select data from a large parallel corpus and used the selected subset to train the resulting MT




(Grant No. 734211; the EU INTERACT project). The ADAPT Centre for Digital Content Technology is funded under the SFI Research Centres Programme (Grant No. 13/RC/2106) and is co-funded under the European Regional Development Fund.

systems. The results show that it also improved performance of NMT systems, in terms of BLEU, although the gain is smaller compared to that of SMT (Silva, Liu, Poncelas, and Way, 2018).

Third, we adapted the MT models using the curated development sets to improve the performance of in-domain (health-related contents) translation. We also compared pivot MT systems using UN Parallel Corpus 1.0 and participated in the China Workshop on Machine Translation (CWMT) shared task on pivot MT (Liu, Silva, Wang, and Way, 2018). Our pivot MT system took the first place in terms of METEOR and translation edit rate (TER) in the shared task.

In this project, we have reviewed, identified and built MT systems where only small parallel corpora are available in the scenario language translation pairs. We also manually curated Arabic—English and Greek—English parallel corpora of health-related contents in crisis situations, as development and test sets for MT system training. The performance is improved in terms of BLEU using the strategies described above and is now being evaluated by professional linguists for detailed assessment.

## References


Catarina Cruz Silva, Chao-Hong Liu, Alberto Poncelas and Andy Way, "Extracting In-domain Training Corpora for Neural Machine Translation Using Data Selection Methods," pp. 224–231, The Third Conference on Machine Translation (WMT18).

Chao-Hong Liu, Catarina Cruz Silva, Longyue Wang, and Andy Way, "Pivot Machine Translation Using Chinese as Pivot Language," The 14th China Workshop on Machine Translation (CWMT 2018). In: Chen J., Zhang J. (eds) Machine Translation. CWMT 2018. Communications in Computer and Information Science, vol 954. Springer, Singapore.

Johnson, M., Schuster, M., Le, Q.V., Krikun, M., Wu, Y., Chen, Z., Thorat, N., Viégas, F., Wattenberg, M., Corrado, G., Hughes, M., Dean, J.: Google's multilingual neural machine translation system: Enabling zero-shot translation. Transactions of the Association for Computational Linguistics 5, 339–351 (2017)

Utiyama, M., Isahara, H.: A comparison of pivot methods for phrase-based statistical machinetranslation. In: Proceedings of Human Language Technologies, The Conference of the NorthAmerican Chapter of the Association for Computational Linguistics (NAACL 2007). pp.484–491. Rochester, USA (2007)

Wu, H., Wang, H.: Pivot language approach for phrase-based statistical machine translation.Machine Translation21(3), 165–181 (2007)

# Global Under-Resourced Media Translation (GoURMET)

Alexandra Birch,[1] Barry Haddow,[1] Ivan Titov,[1] Antonio Valerio Miceli Barone,[1] Rachel Bawden,[1]
Felipe Sánchez-Martínez,[2] Mikel L. Forcada,[2] Miquel Esplà-Gomis,[2] Víctor M. Sánchez-Cartagena,[2]
Juan Antonio Pérez-Ortiz,[2] Wilker Aziz,[3] Andrew Secker,[4] Peggy van der Kreeft[5]

[1]University of Edinburgh (GBR), [2]Universitat d'Alacant (ESP)
[3]Universiteit van Amsterdam (NDL), [4]BBC (GBR), [5]Deutsche Welle (DEU)

## Abstract

We present the EU H2020 GoURMET project (2019-2021) which aims to tackle the challenge of low-resource machine translation for our media partners. This will help them to both monitor news in a wider range of languages, and also more efficiently produce content especially for languages from Africa and India.

## Overview

Machine translation (MT) is an increasingly important technology for supporting communication in a globalised world. Over the last few years neural machine translation methods have led to significant improvements in translation quality. However, they rely on large parallel corpora for training and are not able to deliver usable translations for the vast majority of language pairs in the world. The aim of GoURMET is to significantly improve the robustness and applicability of neural machine translation for low-resource language pairs and domains. The project is co-ordinated by the University of Edinburgh, and the other partners are: the Universitat d'Alacant, the Universiteit van Amsterdam, the British Broadcasting Corporation, and Deutsche Welle. So far we have delivered 8 translation models to our user partners (BBC and DW) for evaluation. These models cover the language pairs of English to and from Turkish, Gujarathi, Swahili and Bulgarian.

## Objectives

1. Advancing low-resource deep learning for natural language applications;

2. High-quality machine translation for low-resource and diverse language pairs and domains;

3. Development of tools for media analysts and journalists;

4. Sustainable, maintainable platform and services;

5. Dissemination and communication of project results to stakeholders.

## Use Cases

1. Global content creation – managing content creation in several languages efficiently by providing machine translations for correction by humans;

2. Media monitoring for low-resource language pairs – tools to address the challenge of monitoring media in strategically important languages;

3. International business news analysis – reliably translating and analysing news in the highly specialised financial domain.

## Impact

The outputs of the project will be field-tested at partners BBC and DW, and the platform will be further validated through innovation intensives such as the workshops centred around our user group and BBC NewsHacks.

## Contact

```
info@gourmet-project.eu
www.gourmet-project.eu
```

**Acknowledgement** This project has received funding from the European Union's Horizon 2020 research and innovation programme under grant agreement No. 825299.

# Neural machine translation system for the Kazakh language


**Ualsher Tukeyev**
Al-Farabi Kazakh National University
71 Al-Farabi ave., Almaty, 050040,
Kazakhstan
ualsher.tukeyev@gmail.com

**Zhandos Zhumanov**
Al-Farabi Kazakh National University
71 Al-Farabi ave., Almaty, 050040,
Kazakhstan
z.zhake@gmail.com



## [1] Abstract

"Development and research of the Kazakh language neural machine translation system" is a 3-year-long project funded by the Science Committee of Ministry of Education and Science of the Republic of Kazakhstan. The project is being executed by the team of the Laboratory of Intelligent Information Systems at the Research Institute of Mathematics and Mechanics of al-Farabi Kazakh National University. Duration of the project: January 2018 – December 2020.


## 1 The purpose of the project

The purpose of the project is to create neural machine translation technology for the Kazakh language aiming at a high quality of machine translation, specifically adapted to the features of the Kazakh language.

Since 2013 the direction of machine translation based on recurrent neural networks, that is, neural machine translation, is intensively developing, and is actively explored for popular world languages. Practical applications of neural machine translation, in particular, in Google Translate, show impressive results. At the same time, neural machine translation research for the Kazakh language as a low resource language is a topical task. This project aims to fill that gap.

## 2 Project objectives

One problem that affects the quality of neural machine translation for Kazakh is the fact that parallel corpora with large volumes of data are not developed for the Kazakh language. Currently we have a small parallel corpus of approximately 140 000 Kazakh–English sentences, and a Kazakh–Russian corpus of a similar size. To solve this problem, in the project we will leverage on existing corpora of related languages.

The objectives of the project are investigation of:

- the basic version of the neural machine translation of the Kazakh language, using standard technology of NMT to Kazakh;
- the morphological segmentation for the Kazakh language NMT;
- the development of syntactic corpora for NMT of Kazakh;
- the development of models and algorithms for solving the problem of unknown words for the neural machine translation of the Kazakh language;
- the evaluation of the quality of the neural machine translation of the Kazakh language.

Our team had worked on a project titled "Development of free/open-source machine translation system for Kazakh–English and Kazakh–Russian (and vice versa) on the base of Apertium platform." in 2015–2017. Language resources created in the previous project are used in the current one [1, 2, 3].

Investigation of the basic version of the neural machine translation of the Kazakh language is based on the use of recurrent neural networks using the "encoder–semantic representation–decoder" model [4]. Along with that we will explore transformer architecture as well.

---

## 3 Expected results of the project

Project results will include technology (models, algorithms and software) of neural machine translation, adapted to the features of the Kazakh language. The system of neural machine translation of the Kazakh language will be developed as a free/open-source system.

## 4 Current results and future plans

The first part of the project is focused on Kazakh–English language pair. The second part will be focused on Kazakh–Russian language pair. At the end of the first year, the following results were achieved: the technology of hybrid automaton-neural machine translation of the Kazakh language based on the complete system of Kazakh language endings [5]; the preprocessor of morphological segmentation in Kazakh–English neural machine translation system; the postprocessor of morphological desegmentation in Kazakh–English neural machine translation system. Because of agglutinative nature words in Kazakh are formed by adding affixes. Different forms of the same word could be used in text and treated as different words if segmentation is not applied. The fact that the rules for adding affixes are very strict allows for creation of a complete system of Kazakh language endings, which simplifies segmentation and helps reducing vocabulary.

Current work is directed at gathering more parallel corpora by crawling multilingual web-sites with various tools, experimenting with different neural machine translation architectures, translation of unknown (out of vocabulary) words and integrating all of techniques that prove to be effective into one neural translation system. Our team consists from 7 members, described project have

45 million tenge (100 000 euro) on three year (2018–2020) funded by Kazakh government.

## References


[1] Tukeyev U.A., Rakhimova D.R., Zhumanov Zh.M., Kartbayev A.Zh. Single state transducer model for Kazakh and Russian morphology // KazNU BULLETIN, Mathematics, Mechanics, Computer Science Series. – Алматы, «Қазақ университеті». – 2016. – №2 (89). – P. 110-117.

[2] Rakhimova D. R., Tukeyev U.A., Zhumanov Zh.M. Methodology of the automated enrichment of machine translation system dictionaries for Kazakh–Russian and Kazakh–English language pair // Proceedings of 4th International conference on Turkic languages ("TurkLang–2016"). – Bishkek, Kyrgyzstan, 2016. – C. 81-85.

[3] Zhumanov Zh., Madiyeva A., Rakhimova D. New Kazakh Parallel Text Corpora with On-line Access. Lecture Notes in Computer Science. – 2017. – 10449. – pp. 501-508.

[4] Tomas Mikolov, Wen-tau Yih, and Geoffrey Zweig. Linguistic Regularities in Continuous Space Word Representations. The Association for Computational Linguistics. In HLTNAACL, p. 746–751(2013).

[5] Tukeyev U., Sundetova A., Abduali B., Akhmadiyeva Zh., Zhanbussunov N. Inferring of the morphological chunk transfer rules on the base of complete set of Kazakh endings // LNAI 9876, Computational Collective Intelligence, Part 2, Springer, 2016, pp. 563-574

# Leveraging Rule-Based Machine Translation Knowledge for Under-Resourced Neural Machine Translation Models

Daniel Torregrosa and
Nivranshu Pasricha and
Bharathi Raja Chakravarthi and
Maraim Masoud and Mihael Arcan
Insight Centre for Data Analytics
Data Science Institute
National University of Ireland Galway
`name.surname@insight-centre.org`

Juan Alonso and Noe Casas
United Language Group
`name.surname@ulgroup.com`

## Abstract

Rule-based machine translation is a machine translation paradigm where linguistic knowledge is encoded by an expert in the form of rules that translate from source to target language. While this approach grants total control over the output of the system, the cost of formalising the needed linguistic knowledge is much higher than training a corpus-based system, where a machine learning approach is used to automatically learn to translate from examples. In this paper, we describe different approaches to leverage the information contained in rule-based machine translation systems to improve a corpus-based one, namely, a neural machine translation model, with a focus on a low-resource scenario. Our results suggest that adding morphological information to the source language is as effective as using subword units in this particular setting.

## 1  Introduction

In rule-based machine translation (RBMT), a linguist formalises linguistic knowledge into lexicons and grammar rules. This knowledge is used by the system to analyse sentences in the source language and translate them. While this approach does not require any training corpora and grants control over the translations created by the system, the process of encoding linguistic knowledge requires great amounts of expert time. Notable examples of RBMT systems are the original, rule-based Systran (Toma, 1977), Lucy LT (Alonso and Thurmair, 2003) and Apertium (Forcada et al., 2011).

Instead, corpus-based machine translation systems learn to translate from examples, usually in the form of sentence-level aligned corpora. On the one hand, this approach is generally more computationally expensive and offers limited control over the generated translations. Furthermore, it is not feasible for language pairs that have little to no available parallel resources. On the other hand, it boasts a much higher coverage of the targeted language pair, depending on the availability of parallel corpora. Examples of corpus-based machine translation paradigms are statistical phrase-based translation (Koehn et al., 2003) and neural machine translation (NMT) models (Bahdanau et al., 2015).

In this work, we focused on leveraging RBMT knowledge for improving the performance of NMT systems in an under-resourced scenario. Namely, we used information contained in Lucy LT, an RBMT system where the linguistic knowledge is formalised by human linguists as computational grammars, monolingual and bilingual lexicons. Monolingual lexicons are collections of lexical entries; each lexical entry is a set of feature-value pairs containing morphological, syntactic and semantic information. Bilingual lexicon entries include source-target lexical correspondences and, optionally, contextual conditions and actions. Grammars are collections of transformations to annotated trees. The Lucy LT system divides the translation process into three sequential phases: analysis, transfer, and generation. During the analysis phase, the source sentence is tokenised and morphologically analysed by means of a lexicon that identifies each surface form and all its plausible morphological readings. Next, the Lucy LT chart parser together with a analysis grammar consisting of augmented syntactic rules extracts the underlying syntax tree structure and annotates it. The transfer and generation grammars are then applied in succession on that tree, which undergoes multiple annotations and transformations that add information about the equivalences in the target language and adapt the original source language structures to the appropriate ones in the target language. Finally, the terminal nodes of the generation tree are assembled into the translated sentence. We focused on the analysis phase, with special interest for two of the features used: the morphological category (CAT) and the inflection class (CL) or classes of the lexical entries.

In order to test this approach, we focused on English-Spanish (both generic and medical domain), English-Basque, English-Irish and English-Simplified Chinese in an under-resourced scenario, using corpora with around one million parallel entries. Results suggested that adding morphological information to the source language is as effective as using subword units in this particular setting.

## 2 Related work

Sennrich and Haddow (2016) demonstrated the inclusion of various linguistic knowledge, such as morphological features, part of speech (POS) tags and syntactic dependency labels, as input features for the English-German and English-Romanian NMT systems. Baniata et al. (2018) proposed a multitask-based NMT system with POS information for translation between English, modern standard Arabic and Arabic dialects, i.e. Levantine Arabic and Maghrebi Arabic. The work demonstrated that the POS information for the low resourced Arabic dialects was beneficial for the translation quality, specifically if pre-trained FastText models were injected during the NMT training step. Niehues and Cho (2017) jointly trained several English-German natural language processing tasks in one system with shared encoder and one attention model and decoder per task. By integrating additional linguistic resources via multitask learning, the performance of each individual task was improved. Bastings et al. (2017) showed that incorporating syntactic structure such as dependency tree using graph convolutional encoders was beneficial for neural machine translation. Their work focused on exploiting structural information on the source side by adding a second encoder. The goal of their work was to provide the encoder with access to rich syntactic information without placing rigid constraints on the interaction between syntax and the translation task

Etchegoyhen et al. (2018) studied NMT, RBMT, and phrase-based statistical machine translation approaches for Basque-Spanish. The authors focus on different subword unit representations, i.e. linguistically-motivated or frequency-based word

segmentation method. Shi et al. (2016) investigated whether an encoder-decoder translation system learns syntactic information on the source side as a side affect of training the neural models. Several syntactic labels of the source sentence were created and logistic regression models using the learned sentence encoding vectors or learned word by word hidden vectors were used to predict these syntactic labels. Aharoni and Goldberg (2017) presented a method to incorporate syntactic information of the target language in an NMT system, showing improved word reordering compared to their baseline system. Eriguchi et al. (2016) proposed an NMT model leveraging syntactic information to improve the accuracy for English→Japanese translation. The phrase structure of the source sentence was recursively encoded in a bottom-up fashion to first produce a vector representation of the sentence, then decode it while aligning the input phrases and words with the output. Bastings et al. (2017) relied on graph-convolutional networks primarily developed for modelling graph-structured data. These networks used predicted syntactic dependency trees of source sentences to produce representations of words that are sensitive to their syntactic neighbourhoods. Nadejde et al. (2017) introduced CCG supertags within the target word sequence as syntactic information, processed by the decoder of their NMT system. Their evaluation showed translation quality improvements for the German→English and Romanian→English translation directions. Similarly, their approach outperformed multi-tasking approach for the same language pairs. García-Martınez et al. (2016) trained their NMT model to simultaneously generate the lemma and its corresponding factors, i.e. POS, gender, and number, demonstrating that factored architecture increases the vocabulary coverage while decreasing the number of unknown words. Ataman and Federico (2018) described the addition of a recurrent neural network to generate compositional representations of the input words, obtaining better results than systems using byte-pair encoding when translating from morphologically rich languages to English. Banerjee and Bhattacharyya (2018) compared two different approaches for subword units when translating from English to Hindi and Bengali, byte pair encoding and morpheme-based segmentation, showing that the latter approach improves the translations, and further improvements can be achieved by combining both.

```
("snake" NST ALO "snake" CL (P-S S-01) KN CNT ON CO SX (N) TYN (ANI))
("snake" VST ALO "snak" ARGS ((($SUBJ N1 (TYN CNC LOC C-POT)) ($ADV DIR))
    CL (G-ING I-E P-ED PA-ED PR-ES1) ON CO PLC (NF))
```

**Figure 1:** The word *snake* as a noun (NST) and a verb (VST) in Lucy LT dictionaries. Each entry is composed of a canonical form, the category (POS), and a list of key-value features, such as the inflection class (CL), the vocalic onset (ON), etc.

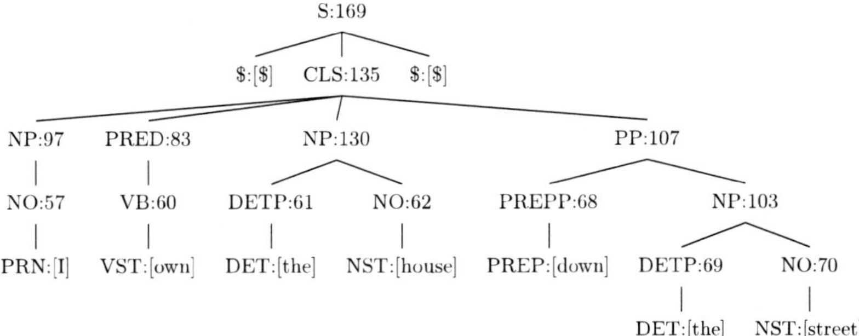

**Figure 2:** Example of the parse tree for the English sentence *I own the house down the street.*

## 3 Methodology

In this section, we describe the methodology to leverage rule-based machine translation (RBMT) information in neural machine translation (NMT).

### 3.1 Information acquisition from RBMT

Lucy LT monolingual lexicons are language-pair independent (i.e. the same English knowledge is used for all translation pairs including English as a source or target language) and mainly encode morphological and contextual information. Each entry has a word or multi-word expression (MWE) along with several features, such as the part of speech (POS) and morphological features. The bilingual lexicons mainly encode word-to-word or MWE-to-MWE translations and describe which target language word should replace each source language word. Still, the direct usage of the lexicon entries as a source of information presented a challenge, as there is no means to determine ambiguous surface words. For example, in English, most nouns will also be classified as verbs, as they share the same surface form; e.g. the word *snake* can be both a noun and a verb (Figure 1). For addressing this problem, we took two different approaches: using **ambiguity classes** that describe all the possible analysis for a given surface word; and using **external information** (in the form of a monolingual POS tagger) to disambiguate. For the former approach, we used a unique tag for each possible CAT and CL values concatenation; e.g. the categories NST and VST and all the inflection classes (CL) for *snake* (Figure 1). For the latter, we used the Stanford POS tagger (Toutanova et al., 2003), that uses the Penn Treebank (Marcus et al., 1994) tag

set for English, and the AnCora (Civit and Martí, 2004) tag set for Spanish, and the IXA pipeline POS tagger (Agerri et al., 2014) with the Universal Dependencies POS tag set (Nivre et al., 2018) for Basque. All POS tag sets were mapped to the tag set used by Lucy LT. If the tagger provided POS tag was equivalent to one or more Lucy LT tags, then the non matching Lucy LT tags were removed. Otherwise, we kept the set of tags; e.g. if the POS tag emits noun as the most likely tag, then only NST and the concatenation of all the inflection classes for the corresponding entry would be used as additional information. As a comparison, we also evaluated NMT models trained with Stanford or IXA POS tags as additional information.

### 3.2 Leveraging Syntactic Tree Information

In addition to the direct use of the linguistic knowledge in lexicon entries, the grammars (monolingual and bilingual lexicons) were indirectly used by exploring the results of each internal intermediate stage of the translation process, which Lucy LT expresses as annotated trees. For example, the sentence parsed in Figure 2,

*I own the house down the street*

is encoded as

⦅*I own* ⦅*the house*⦆ ⦅*down* ⦅*the street*⦆⦆⦆.[1]

We use this representation as source text when training the NMT models, as sequence-to-sequence deep neural network models do not generally accept hierarchical information. We also used an additional feature: the linguistic phrase the word belongs to. This information is present in the grandparent of

---

[1] To avoid collisions with parenthesis in the text, we used the left (⦅, U+2985) and right (⦆, U+2986) white parenthesis.

| | | Source (English) | | Target | | |
|---|---|---|---|---|---|---|
| | | # of Subwords | # of Uniq. Subwords | # of Subwords | # of Uniq. Subwords | # of Lines |
| English– | train | 17,919,926 | 33,212 | 18,408,749 | 33,076 | 1,000,000 |
| –Spanish | validation | 180,290 | 15,714 | 185,662 | 18,804 | 10,000 |
| (generic) | evaluation | 178,841 | 15,031 | 181,188 | 18,810 | 10,000 |
| English– | train | 14,440,740 | 27,112 | 15,872,405 | 29,290 | 1,036,058 |
| –Spanish | validation | 186,685 | 11,599 | 204,174 | 14,306 | 10,000 |
| (EMEA) | evaluation | 219,752 | 9,412 | 242,137 | 10,979 | 10,000 |
| English– | train | 11,760,808 | 30,946 | 10,309,229 | 32,369 | 1,357,475 |
| –Basque | validation | 85,919 | 9,150 | 76,532 | 13,593 | 10,000 |
| | evaluation | 85,163 | 9,283 | 75,309 | 13,546 | 10,000 |
| English– | train | 15,234,432 | 31,834 | 16,983,046 | 32,183 | 1,090,418 |
| –Irish | validation | 135,986 | 12,648 | 152,224 | 16,113 | 10,000 |
| | evaluation | 140,696 | 11,613 | 152,064 | 16,174 | 10,000 |
| English– | train | 27,878,268 | 31,471 | 25,199,106 | 41,458 | 995,000 |
| –Simplified | validation | 138,640 | 12,451 | 126,191 | 14,490 | 5,000 |
| Chinese | evaluation | 129,440 | 12,175 | 119,577 | 14,431 | 4,500 |

**Table 1:** Statistics on the used training, validation and evaluation datasets.

each node; e.g. in Figure 2 the noun *house* appears in a noun phrase (NP).

## 4 Experimental Setting

In this section, we describe the resources we used to train and evaluate the systems, along with the neural machine translation framework used.

### 4.1 Training and Evaluation Datasets

In this work, we focused on NMT for under-resourced scenarios. On the one hand, we consider languages, such as Basque or Irish, which do not have a significant amount of parallel data necessary to train a neural model. On the other hand, an under-resourced scenario can be a specific domain, e.g. medical, where a significant amount of data exists, but does not cover the targeted domain. The Table 1 shows the statistics on the used datasets.

For Basque and Irish, we used the available corpora stored on the OPUS webpage.[2] We used OpenSubtitles2018 (Lison and Tiedemann, 2016),[3] Gnome and KDE4 datasets (Tiedemann, 2012). Additionally, the English-Irish parallel corpus is augmented with second level education textbooks (*Cuimhne na dTéacsleabhar*) in the domain of economics and geography (Arcan et al., 2016).

In addition to that, we also focused on well resourced languages (Spanish and Simplified Chinese), but limited the training datasets to around one million aligned sentences. To ensure a broad lexical and domain coverage of our NMT system, we merged the existing English-Spanish parallel corpora from the OPUS web page into one parallel data set and randomly extracted the sentences. In addition to the previous corpora, we added Europarl (Koehn, 2005), DGT (Steinberger et al., 2014), MultiUN corpus (Eisele and Chen, 2010), EMEA and OpenOffice (Tiedemann, 2009). To evaluate the targeted under-resourced scenario within medical domain, we exclusively used the EMEA corpus. For Simplified Chinese, we used a parallel corpus provided by the industry partner, which was collected from bilingual English-Simplified Chinese news portals.

The corpora were tokenised using the OpenNMT toolkit, with the exception of Simplified Chinese, that was tokenized using Jieba,[4] and lowercased.

### 4.2 NMT framework

We used OpenNMT (Klein et al., 2017), a generic deep learning framework mainly specialised in sequence-to-sequence models covering a variety of tasks such as machine translation, summarisation, speech processing and question answering as NMT framework. Due to computational complexity, the vocabulary in NMT models had to be limited. In order to overcome this limitation, we used byte pair encoding (BPE) to generate subword units (Sennrich et al., 2016). BPE is a form of data compression that iteratively replaces the most frequent pair of bytes in a sequence with a single, unused byte. We also added the different morphological and syntactic information as word features.

We used the following default neural network training parameters: two hidden layers, 500 hidden

[2] opus.nlpl.eu
[3] www.opensubtitles.org

[4] github.com/fxsjy/jieba

LSTM (long short term memory) units per layer, input feeding enabled, 13 epochs, batch size of 64, 0.3 dropout probability, dynamic learning rate decay, 500 dimension embeddings, maximum vocabulary size of 50,000 subwords, maximum of 32,000 unique BPE merge operations, unlimited different values for the word features and between 11 and 23 dimension embeddings for word features.[5]

### 4.3 Evaluation

In order to evaluate the performance of the different systems, we used BLEU (Papineni et al., 2002), an automatic evaluation that boasts high correlation with human judgements, and translation error rate (TER) (Snover et al., 2006), a metric that represents the cost of editing the output of the MT systems to match the reference. Additionally, we used bootstrap resampling (Koehn, 2004) with a sample size of 1,000 and 1,000 iterations, and reported statistical significance with $p < 0.05$. We also presented a box-and-whisker plot with the first, second and third quartiles as a box, and the first ($<0.025$) and last ($\geq 0.975$) 40-quantiles as whiskers, corresponding to $p < 0.05$. In addition, we compared the performance of our NMT systems with the NMT-based Google Translate,[6] and the translations performed using Lucy LT RBMT; for the latter, only English-Spanish and English-Basque models are available.

## 5 Results

In this section we describe the quantitative and qualitative evaluation of the different models: the NMT baseline (Baseline), baseline enhanced with ambiguous CAT and CL (CAT-CL), baseline with disambiguated CAT and CL (CAT-CL D), baseline with external POS tags (POS), baseline with indirect CAT, CL and syntactic information (CAT-CL L), the hierarchical model (Tree), Lucy LT (RBMT) and Google Translate (Google).

### 5.1 Quantitative results

The quantitative results of the evaluation are presented in Figure 3. All the models tested significantly outperformed the RBMT system Lucy LT both when using BLEU and TER as evaluation metrics. Even when trained with only around a million sentences, the NMT baseline model for English-Basque and English-Irish performed better than Google Translate with generic domain corpora, and were not statistically significantly different for English→Simplified Chinese. Unsurprisingly, the in-domain medical domain English-Spanish models outperformed Google Translate. Conversely, Google Translate was significantly better than the NMT baselines only for the English-Spanish generic domain, excluding English→Spanish TER. While some of the feature-enriched models obtained slightly better results in terms of BLEU and TER compared to the baseline, no model obtains scores that are statistically significantly different than the baseline subword model. We also observed that the kind of information we added to the system in the form of CAT and CL features can also be learned by NMT models based on subword units, that may split the root from the rest of the word. In case of the tree model, the results were consistently lower than the rest. Finally, we learned that the system could not cope with this complex representation with the amount of data available.

### 5.2 Qualitative results

Table 2 analyses a sentence translated using all different models from Spanish to English. The analysis showed that, even when RBMT makes some grammatical mistakes, the sentence still conveyed the correct message. Nevertheless, it was the only hypothesis with a BLEU of 0, as it shared no four-gram with the reference, and was the hypothesis with the highest TER. The baseline model hypothesis was tied for the best TER score and the second best BLEU score, but it failed to convey the proper message, as it lacked translation for *easing of price increases*.

## 6 Conclusions and future work

In this work we explored the use of rule-based machine translation (RBMT) knowledge to improve the performance of neural machine translation (NMT) models in an under-resourced scenario, showing that adding morphological information to the source language is as effective as using subword units in this particular setting. We also found that RBMT translations were often adequate but both BLEU and TER poorly reflected this, often scoring worse than incorrect NMT-generated translations.

One of the paths of our future work will further focus on the extraction of RBMT knowledge and the inclusion of transfer rules to improve the performance of the NMT model. A second improvement

---

[5]The size of the embedding for word features depend on the number of unique values for the feature.
[6]translate.google.com retrieved March 2019.

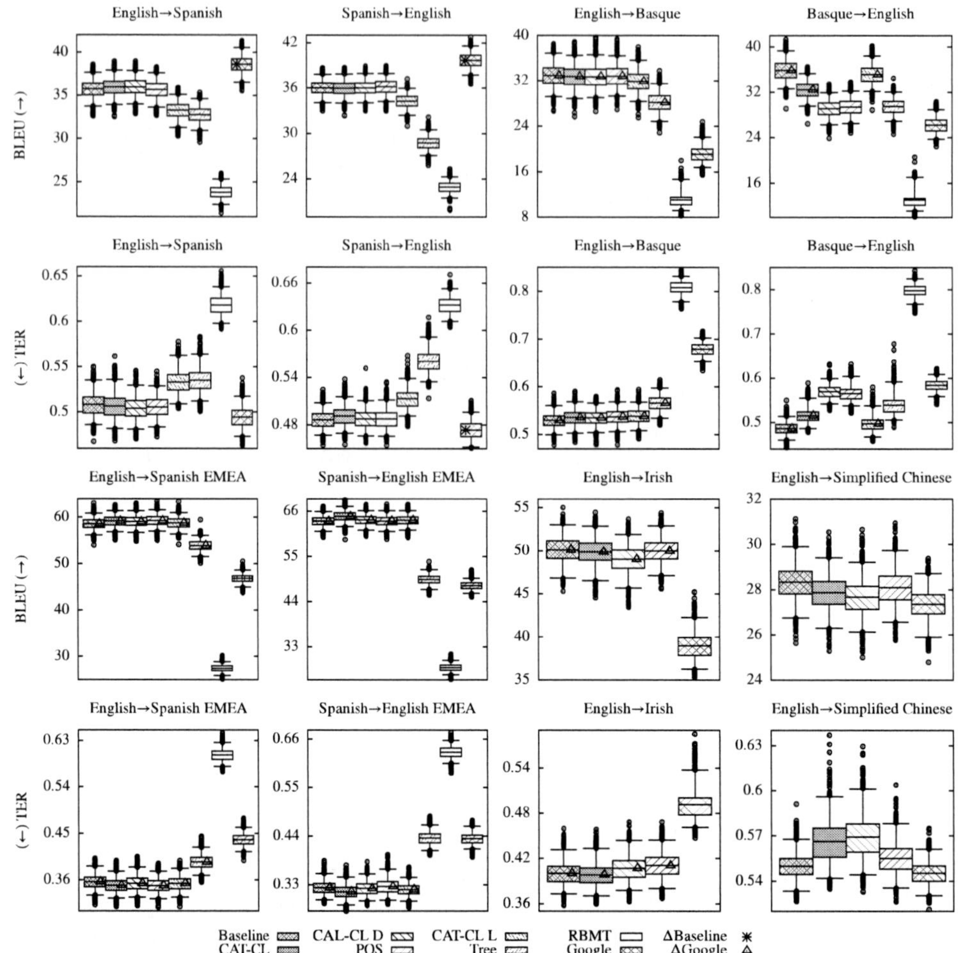

**Figure 3:** Results for the evaluation for English-Spanish, both for generic and medical (EMEA) domains, English-Basque, English→Irish and English→Simplified Chinese. No RMBT models are available for Irish and Simplified Chinese in Lucy LT. Models marked with ∗ are significantly better than the NMT baseline, and models marked with △ are significantly better than Google Translate. All models are statistically significantly better than RBMT.

| Source | Pese a que los incrementos de los precios fueron menores en el segundo semestre de 2008 , los precios siguen siendo muy elevados . | BLEU | TER |
|---|---|---|---|
| Reference | Despite an easing of price increases in the second half of 2008, prices remain at very high levels. | | |
| Baseline | Despite the increases in prices in the second half of 2008, prices remain very high. | 47.48 | 0.35 |
| CAT-CL | *Although* price increases were **minor** in the second half of 2008, prices remain very high. | 47.48 | 0.35 |
| CAT-CL D | *Although* increases in prices were lower in the second half of 2008, prices remain high. | 44.50 | 0.45 |
| POS | *Despite the fact that* price increases were lower in the second half of 2008, prices remain very high. | 48.25 | 0.35 |
| CAT-CL L | *Although* price increases were lower in the second half of 2008, prices remain very high. | 47.48 | 0.35 |
| Tree | *Although* **prices of** prices were lower in the second half of 2008 prices remain very high. | 45.51 | 0.40 |
| RBMT | *Even though* the increases of the prices **were smaller** in the second *semester* of 2008, the prices **keep being** *sky-high*. | 0.00 | 0.70 |
| Google | *Although* the price increases *were lower* in the second half of 2008, prices *are still* very high. | 41.81 | 0.40 |

**Table 2:** Qualitative analysis of a sentence translated by all models for Spanish to English translation. Fragments in bold face are translation mistakes, and fragments in italics are translation alternatives that, while being penalised by TER and BLEU, can be considered correct.

path would be using multiple encoders. This approach has been used to improve the performance NMT (Zoph and Knight, 2016), but, in our scenario, one of the inputs would be the output of the RBMT system. As previously mentioned, corpus-based machine translation gives limited control over the output to the user, specially when dealing with homographs and terminology; instead, RBMT gives total control. Combining the source sentence with the RBMT output that contains the user-selected translations might lead to improvements in domain-specific or low resource scenarios.

Finally, we also plan to leverage information contained in other freely available RBMT systems, such as Apertium. While Apertium is a shallow-transfer system, meaning that there is less syntactic information, features similar to the ones used in this work are available in Apertium.

## Acknowledgments

This publication has emanated from research supported in part by a research grant from Science Foundation Ireland (SFI) under Grant Number SFI/12/RC/2289, co-funded by the European Regional Development Fund, and the Enterprise Ireland (EI) Innovation Partnership Programme under grant agreement No IP20180729, NURS – Neural Machine Translation for Under-Resourced Scenarios.

## References

Agerri, Rodrigo, Josu Bermudez, and German Rigau. 2014. IXA pipeline: Efficient and Ready to Use Multilingual NLP tools. In Calzolari, Nicoletta, Khalid Choukri, Thierry Declerck, Hrafn Loftsson, Bente Maegaard, Joseph Mariani, Asuncion Moreno, Jan Odijk, and Stelios Piperidis, editors, *Proceedings of the Ninth International Conference on Language Resources and Evaluation (LREC'14)*, Reykjavik, Iceland, may. European Language Resources Association (ELRA).

Aharoni, Roee and Yoav Goldberg. 2017. Towards String-To-Tree Neural Machine Translation. In *Proceedings of the 55th Annual Meeting of the Association for Computational Linguistics*, volume 2: Short Papers, pages 132–140, Vancouver, Canada, July. Association for Computational Linguistics.

Alonso, Juan A and Gregor Thurmair. 2003. The Comprendium Translator system. In *Proceedings of the Ninth Machine Translation Summit*.

Arcan, Mihael, Caoilfhionn Lane, Eoin Ó Droighneáin, and Paul Buitelaar. 2016. Iris: English-irish machine translation system. In *Proceedings of the Ninth International Conference on Language Resources and Evaluation (LREC 2016)*, Portorož, Slovenia.

Ataman, Duygu and Marcello Federico. 2018. Compositional Representation of Morphologically-Rich Input for Neural Machine Translation. *Proceedings of the 56th Annual Meeting of the Association for Computational Linguistics*, pages 305–311.

Bahdanau, Dzmitry, Kyunghyun Cho, and Yoshua Bengio. 2015. Neural Machine Translation by Jointly Learning to Align and Translate. *Proceedings of the Third International Conference on Learning Representations*.

Banerjee, Tamali and Pushpak Bhattacharyya. 2018. Meaningless yet meaningful: Morphology grounded subword-level NMT. In *Proceedings of the Second Workshop on Subword/Character LEvel Models*, pages 55–60, New Orleans, June. Association for Computational Linguistics.

Baniata, Laith H., Seyoung Park, and Seong-Bae Park. 2018. A Multitask-Based Neural Machine Translation Model with Part-of-Speech Tags Integration for Arabic Dialects. *Applied Sciences*, 8(12).

Bastings, Joost, Ivan Titov, Wilker Aziz, Diego Marcheggiani, and Khalil Simaan. 2017. Graph Convolutional encoders for syntax-aware neural machine translation. In *Proceedings of the 2017 Conference on Empirical Methods in Natural Language Processing*, pages 1957–1967, Copenhagen, Denmark, September. Association for Computational Linguistics.

Civit, Montserrat and Ma Antònia Martí. 2004. Building cast3lb: A spanish treebank. *Research on Language and Computation*, 2(4):549–574.

Eisele, Andreas and Yu Chen. 2010. MultiUN: A Multilingual Corpus from United Nation Documents. In Tapias, Daniel, Mike Rosner, Stelios Piperidis, Jan Odjik, Joseph Mariani, Bente Maegaard, Khalid Choukri, and Nicoletta Calzolari (Conference Chair), editors, *Proceedings of the Seventh conference on International Language Resources and Evaluation*, pages 2868–2872. European Language Resources Association (ELRA), 5.

Eriguchi, Akiko, Kazuma Hashimoto, and Yoshimasa Tsuruoka. 2016. Tree-to-Sequence Attentional Neural Machine Translation. In *Proceedings of the 54th Annual Meeting of the Association for Computational Linguistics*, volume 1: Long Papers, pages 823–833. Association for Computational Linguistics.

Etchegoyhen, Thierry, Eva Martínez Garcia, Andoni Azpeitia, Gorka Labaka, Iñaki Alegria, Itziar Cortes Etxabe, Amaia Jauregi Carrera, Igor Ellakuria Santos, Maite Martin, and Eusebi Calonge. 2018. Neural Machine Translation of Basque.

Forcada, Mikel L, Mireia Ginestí-Rosell, Jacob Nordfalk, Jim O'Regan, Sergio Ortiz-Rojas, Juan Antonio Pérez-Ortiz, Felipe Sánchez-Martínez, Gema Ramírez-Sánchez, and Francis M Tyers. 2011. Apertium: a free/open-source platform for rule-based machine translation. *Machine translation*, 25(2):127–144.

Garcia-Martınez, Mercedes, Loıc Barrault, and Fethi Bougares. 2016. Factored Neural Machine Translation Architectures. In *International Workshop on Spoken Language Translation (IWSLT'16)*, Seattle, US.

Klein, Guillaume, Yoon Kim, Yuntian Deng, Jean Senellart, and Alexander M. Rush. 2017. OpenNMT: Open-Source Toolkit for Neural Machine Translation. *Proceedings of the 55th Annual Meeting of the Association for Computational Linguistics*, System Demonstrations:67–72.

Koehn, Philipp, Franz Josef Och, and Daniel Marcu. 2003. Statistical phrase-based translation. In *Proceedings of the 2003 Conference of the North American Chapter of the Association for Computational*

*Linguistics on Human Language Technology*, volume 1, pages 48–54. Association for Computational Linguistics.

Koehn, Philipp. 2004. Statistical significance tests for machine translation evaluation. In *Proceedings of the 2004 conference on empirical methods in natural language processing*.

Koehn, Philipp. 2005. Europarl: A Parallel Corpus for Statistical Machine Translation. In *Conference Proceedings: the tenth Machine Translation Summit*. AAMT.

Lison, Pierre and Jörg Tiedemann. 2016. OpenSubtitles2016: Extracting Large Parallel Corpora from Movie and TV Subtitles. In *Proceedings of the Tenth International Conference on Language Resources and Evaluation (LREC 2016)*, Paris, France, may. European Language Resources Association (ELRA).

Marcus, Mitchell, Grace Kim, Mary Ann Marcinkiewicz, Robert MacIntyre, Ann Bies, Mark Ferguson, Karen Katz, and Britta Schasberger. 1994. The Penn Treebank: Annotating Predicate Argument Structure. In *Proceedings of the Workshop on Human Language Technology*, HLT '94, pages 114–119, Stroudsburg, PA, USA. Association for Computational Linguistics.

Nadejde, Maria, Siva Reddy, Rico Sennrich, Tomasz Dwojak, Marcin Junczys-Dowmunt, Philipp Koehn, and Alexandra Birch. 2017. Predicting target language ccg supertags improves neural machine translation. In *Proceedings of the Second Conference on Machine Translation*, pages 68–79, Copenhagen, Denmark, September. Association for Computational Linguistics.

Niehues, Jan and Eunah Cho. 2017. Exploiting Linguistic Resources for Neural Machine Translation Using Multi-task Learning. In *Proceedings of the Second Conference on Machine Translation*, pages 80–89, Copenhagen, Denmark, September. Association for Computational Linguistics.

Nivre, Joakim, Mitchell Abrams, Željko Agić, Lars Ahrenberg, Lene Antonsen, Katya Aplonova, Maria Jesus Aranzabe, Gashaw Arutie, Masayuki Asahara, Luma Ateyah, Mohammed Attia, Aitziber Atutxa, Liesbeth Augustinus, Elena Badmaeva, Miguel Ballesteros, Esha Banerjee, Sebastian Bank, Verginica Barbu Mititelu, Victoria Basmov, John Bauer, Sandra Bellato, Kepa Bengoetxea, Yevgeni Berzak, Irshad Ahmad Bhat, Riyaz Ahmad Bhat, Erica Biagetti, Eckhard Bick, Rogier Blokland, Victoria Bobicev, Carl Börstell, Cristina Bosco, Gosse Bouma, Sam Bowman, Adriane Boyd, Aljoscha Burchardt, Marie Candito, Bernard Caron, Gauthier Caron, Gülşen Cebiroğlu Eryiğit, Flavio Massimiliano Cecchini, Giuseppe G. A. Celano, Slavomír Čéplö, Savas Cetin, Fabricio Chalub, Jinho Choi, Yongseok Cho, Jayeol Chun, Silvie Cinková, Aurélie Collomb, Çağrı Çöltekin, Miriam Connor, Marine Courtin, Elizabeth Davidson, Marie-Catherine de Marneffe, Valeria de Paiva, Arantza Diaz de Ilarraza, Carly Dickerson, Peter Dirix, Kaja Dobrovoljc, Timothy Dozat, Kira Droganova, Puneet Dwivedi, Marhaba Eli, Ali Elkahky, Binyam Ephrem, Tomaž Erjavec, Aline Etienne, Richárd Farkas, Hector Fernandez Alcalde, Jennifer Foster, Cláudia Freitas, Katarína Gajdošová, Daniel Galbraith, Marcos Garcia, Moa Gärdenfors, Sebastian Garza, Kim Gerdes, Filip Ginter, Iakes Goenaga, Koldo Gojenola, Memduh Gökırmak, Yoav Goldberg, Xavier Gómez Guinovart, Berta Gonzáles Saavedra, Matias Grioni, Normunds Grūzītis, Bruno Guillaume, Céline Guillot-Barbance, Nizar Habash, Jan Hajič, Jan Hajič jr., Linh Hà Mỹ, Na-Rae Han, Kim Harris, Dag Haug, Barbora Hladká, Jaroslava Hlaváčová, Florinel Hociung, Petter Hohle, Jena Hwang, Radu Ion, Elena Irimia, Ọlájídé Ishola, Tomáš Jelínek, Anders Johannsen, Fredrik Jørgensen, Hüner Kaşıkara, Sylvain Kahane, Hiroshi Kanayama, Jenna Kanerva, Boris Katz, Tolga Kayadelen, Jessica Kenney, Václava Kettnerová, Jesse Kirchner, Kamil Kopacewicz, Natalia Kotsyba, Simon Krek, Sookyoung Kwak, Veronika Laippala, Lorenzo Lambertino, Lucia Lam, Tatiana Lando, Septina Dian Larasati, Alexei Lavrentiev, John Lee, Phương Lê Hồng, Alessandro Lenci, Saran Lertpradit, Herman Leung, Cheuk Ying Li, Josie Li, Keying Li, KyungTae Lim, Nikola Ljubešić, Olga Loginova, Olga Lyashevskaya, Teresa Lynn, Vivien Macketanz, Aibek Makazhanov, Michael Mandl, Christopher Manning, Ruli Manurung, Cătălina Mărănduc, David Mareček, Katrin Marheinecke, Héctor Martínez Alonso, André Martins, Jan Mašek, Yuji Matsumoto, Ryan McDonald, Gustavo Mendonça, Niko Miekka, Margarita Misirpashayeva, Anna Missilä, Cătălin Mititelu, Yusuke Miyao, Simonetta Montemagni, Amir More, Laura Moreno Romero, Keiko Sophie Mori, Shinsuke Mori, Bjartur Mortensen, Bohdan Moskalevskyi, Kadri Muischnek, Yugo Murawaki, Kaili Müürisep, Pinkey Nainwani, Juan Ignacio Navarro Horñiacek, Anna Nedoluzhko, Gunta Nešpore-Bērzkalne, Lương Nguyễn Thị, Huyền Nguyễn Thị Minh, Vitaly Nikolaev, Rattima Nitisaroj, Hanna Nurmi, Stina Ojala, Adédayọ̀ Olúòkun, Mai Omura, Petya Osenova, Robert Östling, Lilja Øvrelid, Niko Partanen, Elena Pascual, Marco Passarotti, Agnieszka Patejuk, Guilherme Paulino-Passos, Siyao Peng, Cenel-Augusto Perez, Guy Perrier, Slav Petrov, Jussi Piitulainen, Emily Pitler, Barbara Plank, Thierry Poibeau, Martin Popel, Lauma Pretkalniņa, Sophie Prévost, Prokopis Prokopidis, Adam Przepiórkowski, Tiina Puolakainen, Sampo Pyysalo, Andriela Rääbis, Alexandre Rademaker, Loganathan Ramasamy, Taraka Rama, Carlos Ramisch, Vinit Ravishankar, Livy Real, Siva Reddy, Georg Rehm, Michael Rießler, Larissa Rinaldi, Laura Rituma, Luisa Rocha, Mykhailo Romanenko, Rudolf Rosa, Davide Rovati, Valentin Roșca, Olga Rudina, Jack Rueter, Shoval Sadde, Benoît Sagot, Shadi Saleh, Tanja Samardžić, Stephanie Samson, Manuela Sanguinetti, Baiba Saulīte, Yanin Sawanakunanon, Nathan Schneider, Sebastian Schuster, Djamé Seddah, Wolfgang

Seeker, Mojgan Seraji, Mo Shen, Atsuko Shimada, Muh Shohibussirri, Dmitry Sichinava, Natalia Silveira, Maria Simi, Radu Simionescu, Katalin Simkó, Mária Šimková, Kiril Simov, Aaron Smith, Isabela Soares-Bastos, Carolyn Spadine, Antonio Stella, Milan Straka, Jana Strnadová, Alane Suhr, Umut Sulubacak, Zsolt Szántó, Dima Taji, Yuta Takahashi, Takaaki Tanaka, Isabelle Tellier, Trond Trosterud, Anna Trukhina, Reut Tsarfaty, Francis Tyers, Sumire Uematsu, Zdeňka Urešová, Larraitz Uria, Hans Uszkoreit, Sowmya Vajjala, Daniel van Niekerk, Gertjan van Noord, Viktor Varga, Eric Villemonte de la Clergerie, Veronika Vincze, Lars Wallin, Jing Xian Wang, Jonathan North Washington, Seyi Williams, Mats Wirén, Tsegay Woldemariam, Tak-sum Wong, Chunxiao Yan, Marat M. Yavrumyan, Zhuoran Yu, Zdeněk Žabokrtský, Amir Zeldes, Daniel Zeman, Manying Zhang, and Hanzhi Zhu. 2018. Universal Dependencies 2.3. LINDAT/CLARIN digital library at the Institute of Formal and Applied Linguistics (ÚFAL), Faculty of Mathematics and Physics, Charles University.

Papineni, Kishore, Salim Roukos, Todd Ward, and Wei-Jing Zhu. 2002. BLEU: a method for automatic evaluation of machine translation. In *Proceedings of the 40th annual meeting on association for computational linguistics*, pages 311–318. Association for Computational Linguistics.

Sennrich, Rico and Barry Haddow. 2016. Linguistic Input Features Improve Neural Machine Translation. In *Proceedings of the First Conference on Machine Translation*, volume 1: Research Papers, pages 83–91. Association for Computational Linguistics.

Sennrich, Rico, Barry Haddow, and Alexandra Birch. 2016. Neural Machine Translation of Rare Words with Subword Units. *Proceedings of the 54th Annual Meeting of the Association for Computational Linguistics*, abs/1508.07909.

Shi, Xing, Inkit Padhi, and Kevin Knight. 2016. Does String-Based Neural MT Learn Source Syntax? In *Proceedings of the 2016 Conference on Empirical Methods in Natural Language Processing*, pages 1526–1534, Austin, Texas, November. Association for Computational Linguistics.

Snover, Matthew, Bonnie Dorr, Richard Schwartz, Linnea Micciulla, and John Makhoul. 2006. A study of translation edit rate with targeted human annotation. In *Proceedings of association for machine translation in the Americas*, volume 200.

Steinberger, Ralf, Mohamed Ebrahim, Alexandros Poulis, Manuel Carrasco-Benitez, Patrick Schlüter, Marek Przybyszewski, and Signe Gilbro. 2014. An overview of the european union's highly multilingual parallel corpora. *Language Resources and Evaluation*, 48(4):679–707.

Tiedemann, Jorg. 2009. News from OPUS – A Collection of Multilingual Parallel Corpora with Tools and Interfaces. In *Advances in Natural Language Processing*, volume 5, pages 237–248. Borovets, Bulgaria.

Tiedemann, Jörg. 2012. Parallel data, tools and interfaces in opus. In Calzolari, Nicoletta, Khalid Choukri, Thierry Declerck, Mehmet Uğur Doğan, Bente Maegaard, Joseph Mariani, Jan Odijk, and Stelios Piperidis, editors, *Proceedings of the Eight International Conference on Language Resources and Evaluation*, Istanbul, Turkey, may.

Toma, Peter. 1977. Systran as a multilingual machine translation system. In *Proceedings of the Third European Congress on Information Systems and Networks, Overcoming the language barrier*, pages 569–581.

Toutanova, Kristina, Dan Klein, Christopher D Manning, and Yoram Singer. 2003. Feature-rich part-of-speech tagging with a cyclic dependency network. In *Proceedings of the 2003 Conference of the North American Chapter of the Association for Computational Linguistics on Human Language Technology*, volume 1, pages 173–180. Association for Computational Linguistics.

Zoph, Barret and Kevin Knight. 2016. Multi-Source Neural Translation. In *Proceedings of the 2016 Conference of the North American Chapter of the Association for Computational Linguistics: Human Language Technologies*, pages 30–34, San Diego, California, June. Association for Computational Linguistics.

# Bootstrapping a Natural Language Interface to a Cyber Security Event Collection System using a Hybrid Translation Approach

**Johann Roturier*, Brian Schlatter**, and David Silva***
* Symantec Research Labs, Dublin, Ireland
** Symantec, Culver City, CA
{johann_roturier,brian_schlatter,david_silva}@symantec.com

## Abstract

This paper presents a system that can be used to generate Elasticsearch (database) query strings for English-speaking cyber-threat hunters, security analysts or responders (agents) using a natural language interface. This system relies on a hybrid translation approach combining translation memory, information extraction and text classification techniques. The resulting queries may be used to (i) speed up the on-boarding of agents that are not (too) familiar with a specific, flexible database schema and (ii) collect question-to-query mappings with a view to train future models using a more robust framework (e.g. NMT). The system presented in this paper supports multiple data sources, including an industry-standard knowledge base and collections of existing queries provided by individual or corporate threat hunters. It allows users to ask questions about specific cybersecurity event or incident details and generates Elasticsearch query strings that can be executed against a database containing security event data. This paper presents the key components of the backend system and highlights some of the user interface design choices that were made to maximize user adoption.

## 1   Introduction

Studying the translation of natural language into SQL queries has a very long history. Earlier



work focused on specific databases thus requiring further customization to generalize to each new database (Warren and Pereira, 1982) (Giordani and Moschitti, 2012) (Tamas and Salomie, 2016) (Wang et al., 2017). More recent work has explored the use of deep neural networks (Zhong et al., 2017) especially for Wiki-based information retrieval (Yu et al., 2018). Related areas have also been studied, such as natural language interfaces to Web APIs  (Su et al., 2017), (Su et al., 2018), and dialogue-based query generation (Gur et al., 2018). However, little attention has been devoted to document-oriented databases with flexible schemas (e.g. Elasticsearch) that are often used as Security Information and Event Management (SIEM) systems. Such databases are commonly used in the context of cyber-threat hunting (or discovery) as shown for instance by the availability of the HELK stack (Rodriguez, 2019). When hunting for advanced threats, domain experts typically have to craft complex queries (Kindlund, 2018). Very often, however, little training data is available apart from API/schema descriptions and raw events so using a fully data-driven approach is often not practical. Using interactive learning in a dialogue-based scenario may alleviate this issue (Filar et al., 2017) (Filar and Seymour, 2019), but it is not clear that advanced users will have the patience to answer a long series of questions (e.g. *which user do you mean?*, *what devices are you talking about?*) that are often required to fill slots.

In the present paper, we therefore present an alternative approach to tackle the problem of bootstrapping a natural language-based system for threat hunting or security incident investigation. This hybrid approach is based on multiple techniques, including semantic search techniques (Mangold, 2007), whereby the Source Language user input (English) is analyzed using a number of components (mostly based on rules) in order to extract entities and phrases or infer text categories that are then mapped into the Target Language's fields and terms before an actual Elasticsearch query string can be generated (ElasticsearchB.V., 2019). Using a combination of text classification and slot filling has indeed been shown to provide very competitive natural language to SQL baseline systems (Finegan-Dollak et al., 2018). Even though some of these rules have to be manually created, their precision is well suited to this task, especially as far the generation step is concerned to ensure that users are provided with valid queries. The rest of the paper is organized as follows: Section 2 describes the various data sources used to create some of the linguistic components of our backend system (either manually or automatically). Section 3 presents the actual system components with some examples. The two final sections provide some discussion of the design choices that were made to create the user interface and outline some directions for future work.

## 2  Data sources

In this section the main data sources used to bootstrap our system are described. The data sources include:

- An API schema file from which field descriptions, values and value mappings can be extracted for the *Event* object of an actual endpoint detection and response (EDR) system. This file required custom parsing in order to extract enumerated (and potentially mapped) values from free-text descriptions.[1]

- Raw event data from an actual EDR system that is used in production (about 1000 samples). These samples were used to automatically create linguistically-oriented entity recognition rules.

- 49 manually curated pairs of queries and descriptions pertaining to the underlying EDR system. This set was extracted by parsing a PDF file containing threat discovery guidance.[2]

- The enterprise matrix from MITRE's cyberthreat intelligence (CTI) dataset, which is an industry-standard knowledge base providing some information for each of the 223 techniques defined in the ATT&CK model (Mitre, 2019). A file in STIX format is parsed in order to extract relevant information.[3]

- 285 manually curated pairs of queries and descriptions originating from the Sigma project (Roth and Patzke, 2019). This set was extracted by parsing YAML files.

- 230 manually curated pairs of queries and descriptions originating from the Lolbas project (LOLBAS, 2019). This set was extracted by parsing YAML files.

- A subset of the annotations from 39 Advanced Persistent Threat (APT) reports (containing 6,819 sentences) with attribute labels from the Malware Attribute Enumeration and Characterization (MAEC) vocabulary (Lim et al., 2017).[4]

### 2.1  The API Schema dataset

In order to define the domain covered by our system, we rely primarily on an API schema file based on the OpenAPI specification (OpenAPI, 2019). This file, which is available in JSON format, contains a full-fledged description of multiple methods and objects pertaining to an actual endpoint detection and response (EDR) system. Some of these methods are very narrow in scope (e.g. how to contain an endpoint) and can be covered by simple OpenC2 commands (OASIS, 2019). Others, however, can be much more complex (e.g. querying a database system to find specific security events based on several search criteria). Examples of fields pertaining to the *Event* object include (i) an integer representing a port number, (ii) a specific type ID, whose integer value maps to a textual description (e.g. *8000* for a session event), (iii) a host name string for the client computer, (iv) a MITRE tactic string corresponding to one of the 11 tactics defined by the MITRE's ATT&CK model (Mitre, 2019), or (v) an overloaded integer value mapping to multiple descriptions depending on the value of another field. The overall number of fields for the

---

[1] https://help.symantec.com/bucket/
SymantecEDR_4.0/lists_of_all_symantec_
edr_event_schemas
[2] https://support.symantec.com/us/en/
article.doc11273.html

[3] https://oasis-open.github.io/cti-
documentation/stix/intro
[4] https://github.com/MAECProject/schemas/
blob/master/vocabs.json

*Event* object is very large (more than 500) but the actual number of fields will vary depending on the type of event (e.g. a file reputation request event or a session event). Such events tend to include a few dozens fields so the goal of this system is to cover those that appear the most frequently in the data (raw events).

## 2.2 The threat discovery guide dataset

While the previous section focused on specific fields and associated values, threat hunters often need to craft more advanced queries whose textual mappings do not include specific field values or descriptions. For instance, a question such as *show me the outbound traffic occurring on non-standard ports* has to be matched with:

```
type_id:8007 AND
-target_ip:["192.168.0.0/16" OR
"10.0.0.0/8" OR "172.16.0.0/12"
OR "127.0.0.0/8"] AND
-target_port:[80 OR 443].
```

In this example, the phrase *non-standard port* cannot be found in the API Schema but obviously a domain expert is able to associate it with all ports apart from *80* and *443* in the context of HTTP traffic. The same applies to the phrase *outbound traffic*.

Since the number of descriptions/queries pairs is quite small in this dataset (less than 50), these complex mappings cannot be learnt using a data-driven approach. However, we can try and detect some of these phrases in the user input and either (i) apply a translation memory technique to retrieve partial (or fuzzy) matches or (ii) offer suggestions via the user interface. These two approaches will be described in sections 3.1 and 4 respectively.

## 2.3 The MITRE CTI dataset

The MITRE cyber-threat intelligence (CTI) dataset provides some textual information for each of the 223 techniques defined in the ATT&CK model. We leverage this dataset in two ways: First, we use the technique names to detect their mentions as entities in user input (as described in Section 3.2). Second, we use additional information in order to train a multi-class text categorizer. This information includes a brief description of the techniques as well as guidance on how to detect and mitigate against such attacks. Some examples of malware or attack group using this technique may also be provided. All of this information can be parsed and

split into sentences. The initial data set, referred to as *mitre-6.5k*, is quite small (6500 sentences) and not very balanced as most techniques (140/223) (classes) contain less than 23 sentences. In order to deal with this data shortage issue, we can supplement the training data with sentences extracted from external references (e.g. web pages, PDF documents) cited in the MITRE pages. This strategy allows us to increase the size of the training data to about 60K sentences (referred to as *mitre-60k*). This text classifier will be presented in Section 3.5.

## 2.4 The Sigma and Lolbas datasets

While the previous two datasets are directly associated with the EDR system of interest, other datasets could be relevant to users of that system. For instance, the Sigma project contains a number of detection rules that may be used to query security information and event management system logs. Some experienced cyber-security professionals may actually be more familiar with these rules (and their default fields) than the schema presented in section 2.1. Similarly, the Lolbas project makes a number of detection rules available to identify anomalous or suspicious usage of legitimate system or administration tools. Such rules are associated with a description and/or a title whose words could appear in user input. These rules from these datasets are therefore parsed by our system and made available to users via interactive suggestions and partial matching. One of the challenges with these datasets is that the queries or commands they expose are not fully compatible with our target Elasticsearch index. For instance, the following Lolbas command includes a *Command* field that must be mapped to a *process.cmd_line* field:

```
Command: rundll32.exe
shdocvw.dll,OpenURL
"C:\test\calc.url"
```

This example also includes a test parameter `"C:\test\calc.url"` that would have to be replaced with a proper value in a successful query. In order to deal with this problem, this test parameter can be easily filtered out by parsing the command in order to generate the following query:

```
process.cmd_line:["rundll32.exe"
AND "shdocvw.dll,OpenURL"]
```

Interestingly, both of these data sources also include references to MITRE technique IDs in their rules. This is useful for two reasons. First, when the query includes fields that cannot easily be mapped (e.g. *Event ID 13: RegistryEvent (Value Set)* generated by Sysmon (Russinovich and Garnier, 2019)), the MITRE technique ID may be suggested to the user who would then be able to filter out the results interactively. Second, we can use 420 labelled sentences from these datasets (referred to *test-set*) to evaluate our system's text classification component trained on the actual MITRE data.

## 3 System Overview

Our system is implemented on top of a Spacy pipeline (Honnibal and Montani, 2017) using a number of default and custom components. Specifically, we rely on Spacy's default tokenizer, tagger, named entity recognizer and dependency parser for English.[5] We also designed a number of custom components to address some of the issues described in the previous section. These six components, which are shown in Figure 1, are described in the next sections.

### 3.1 Index-based Phrase Matcher

This component relies on the descriptions/queries pairs described in the previous section. The descriptions are first lemmatized, lower-cased and split into n-grams (with a minimum length of 3). These n-grams are then stored as the keys of an inverted index in order to point to relevant queries (and associated metadata, such as description, source, etc.). When user input is submitted, this index is used to find an exact match or partial match, by computing a similarity score (between 0 an 1) using the n-gram overlap technique for text reuse described by Clough et al. (2002). When an exact match is found, the other steps from the pipeline may be skipped.

### 3.2 Named Entity Recognition

When a partial match or no match is found, the user input is processed by the modules performing named entity recognition. Default entity types such as *ORG* or *GPE* are considered as they proved relevant on the sample of raw events. For instance, some fields contain country or organization names when the event has been enriched with a domain's WHOIS information or when it includes file-based

digital certificate information. The *PERSON* entity also proved relevant for fields containing user names such as email addresses or host names. In other cases, however, custom entity types have to be defined. Since we wanted to automate this process as much as possible, we performed some analysis on the raw event samples to find some fields whose values contained specific word shapes or word lemmas. For instance, we found that device names followed a specific pattern that could be learnt from specific word shapes. Since device naming will vary from one organization to the next, using this approach provides a lot of flexibility. This approach also allows to support variants or synonyms, for instance to handle adversary groups that tend to be named in multiple ways in the industry. Finally, when ambiguity is present (i.e. when a value occurred across multiple fields, such as "suspicious") or when the pattern seems too complex to learn automatically, we rely on the rules-based phrase matcher which is presented next.

### 3.3 Rules-based Phrase Matcher

Since this component requires the creation of manual rules to annotate specific token sequences from the input text, it is reserved to a small set of significant fields that may rely on ambiguous values. For instance, the *operation* field can refer to a creation event that may take a different value depending on the context (e.g. deleting a registry key value or deleting a file). Using a high-precision rule to match such token sequences is well suited to tackle this problem. Besides, it allows us to quickly add variants (e.g. synonyms) to extend the rule's coverage. In order to speed up the identification of variants for specific verbs and nouns, we rely on the annotations from the MalwareTextDB dataset (Lim et al., 2017) for those annotations whose MAEC attribute label overlaps with some of the Event field descriptions (e.g. "delete file"). This strategy allows to recover a number of variants, such as "delete", "clean", "wipe", "remove", or "destroy" for "delete file", or "connect", "communicate", "establish", "initiate" for "send network packet".

### 3.4 Entity Relation Extractor

This component relies on additional manually created rules that cannot easily be expressed using the formalism of the rules-based phrase matcher. This module makes use of dependency parsing in-

---

[5] In our experiments, we used their *small* model trained on OntoNotes5.

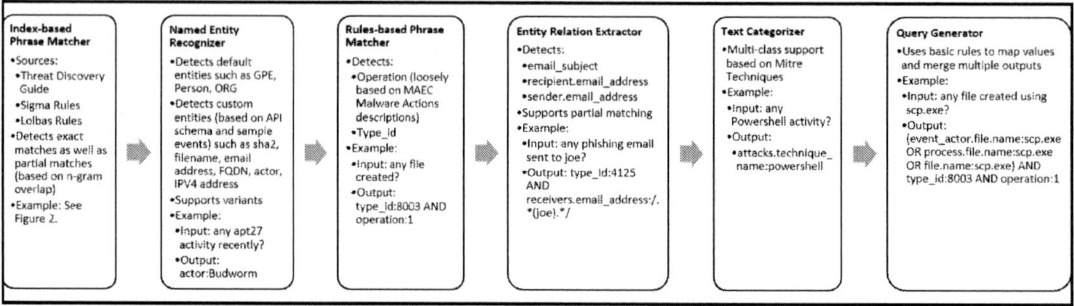



**Figure 1:** Custom components included in the pipeline

formation to target specific event types. Specifically, email-related events (including phishing and spear-phishing) tend to involve a number of entities (i.e. sender, recipients(s)) and properties (e.g. subject, attachment, message status) that can be very challenging to handle even when substantial training data is available. For instance, Su et al. (2017) report 57% accuracy for generating valid *GET-Messages* API calls using Microsoft's email search API when these calls contain 1 to 4 parameters. One of the rules used by our component navigates the parse tree of the user input and looks for subtrees starting with prepositions such as *to* (for the email recipient), *from* or *by* (for the sender), *about* (for the subject), and *with* (for the attachment). The content of the subtree is then analyzed to determine whether they contain specific entities (such as email addresses, person names or filenames). When such entities are found, they can be associated with the actual field names.

### 3.5 Text Classification

When no entities or matches are found in the user input, we rely on a fall-back component. This component is completely different from the previous ones as it does not rely on rules. Instead, we train a multi-class (223) categorization model (a stacked ensemble of a bag-of-words model and a convolutional neural network model) using the MITRE technique training data sets described in Section 2. Even if the performance of this bootstrapped model is poor (16% on *test-set* when trained on *mitre-6.5k* and 24% accuracy when trained on *mitre-60k*) it allows for the initial labelling of user input with a MITRE technique ID (i.e. when the class probability is greater than 0.5) even when the actual MITRE technique name is not explicitly present. The performance of the model is expected to improve as usage data is col-

lected.

### 3.6 Query Generator

Once all of the analysis components have been executed on the user input, their output is combined in order to generate an Elasticsearch query string following the syntactic constraints of this mini language. Some field/value combinations are much easier to handle than others (e.g. actor:actor_name). In some cases, however, a mapping is required to restore the expected value. When multiple values are present for a given field, these values are joined together with an *OR* operator in a list. All fields/terms pairs are currently joined with the *AND* operator, unless field ambiguity must be handled (e.g. an *IP address* entity may refer to multiple fields so the various options must be present in the query). Finally, we have introduced some basic support for regular expression patterns when specific entities are found instead of others. As mentioned in Section 3.4 a person name may be used to search for specific email events. Since an email address is expected for this field, the query will not return the expected results unless the person name (e.g. `John`) is turned into a pattern such as `/John.*/`).

## 4 User Interface

When designing the user interface, four main requirements were taken into account:

1. The interface should be familiar to users who may have been relying on *conversion* systems to convert their queries from one SIEM system to another. Tools such as *Uncoder*[6] or *Sigma UI*[7] allow users to write, save and convert queries in a number of formats, but do not

[6]`https://uncoder.io/`
[7]`https://github.com/socprime/SigmaUI`

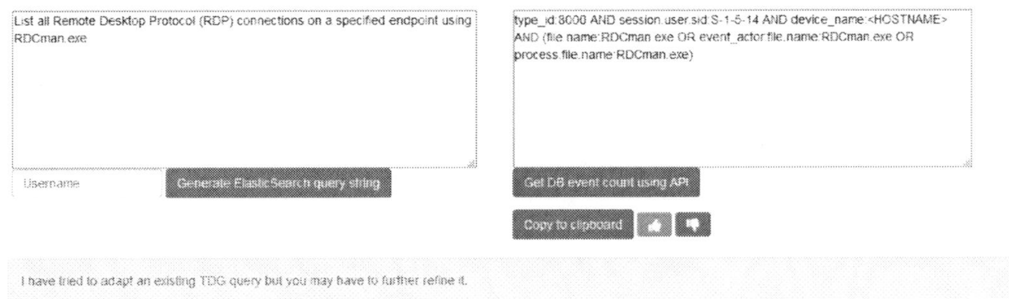



**Figure 2:** Web-based standalone user interface

allow users to use natural language to generate a new query. Using a 2-column format where (source) user input and (target) generated query are displayed side by side in the middle of the screen is a well-known layout for (machine) translation or conversion applications. Using this layout prevents usability issues that are typically associated with chat widgets as they only use a fraction of the screen.

2. The interface should be as intuitive as possible, so the number of UI elements should be limited to the following functions: (i) generating a query after entering some text (e.g. question), (ii) executing the query against the DB (possibly via an API call, (iii) copying the query to the clipboard, (iv) indicating whether the query was useful (or not), and (v) giving the user a chance to access the source of a leveraged rule via a hyperlink.

3. To minimize user frustration due to misinterpretation, question suggestions should be made available as a drop-down selection once the user has typed at least one word. These suggestions are based on those question/query pairs described in Section 2 that have not been rated negatively by users.

4. The interface should be able to be deployed as a standalone application or as a widget within an existing Web application (e.g. a Kibana instance).[8] In the latter scenario, a bookmarklet can be made available to users and some contextual application can be leveraged to influence the query generation step. For instance,

when a user name or incident ID is detected on the page of the host application, this information can be passed to the query generator component to (i) skip queries that may have been rated as poor by a given user or (ii) disambiguate some entities.

These four main requirements led to the creation of a simple interface whose standalone version is shown in Figure 2. Since this interface can be easily integrated within existing applications, it allows for a seamless collection of question/query/rating triplets that we plan to make use of in the future as explained in the next section.

## 5 Future work

One of the next steps is to make the system available to real users and study how they would benefit from using such system. Once the system is deployed, we would also like to investigate the feasibility of using an NMT framework to leverage the user feedback. Specifically, we would like to further improve training data generation and create robust sequence to sequence models so that both novice and expert users can perform their work in a proficient manner. Also, we would like to support additional input languages, including the possibility to generate natural language descriptions of queries entered by expert users. Additional future work also includes a better handling of specific query conditions (e.g. NOT) that are not currently covered by our rules, thus requiring additional user input.

---

[8] https://www.elastic.co/products/kibana

## References

Clough, Paul, Robert Gaizauskas, Scott S. L. Piao, and Yorick Wilks. 2002. Meter: Measuring text reuse. In *Proceedings of the 40th Annual Meeting on Association for Computational Linguistics*, ACL '02, pages 152–159, Stroudsburg, PA, USA. Association for Computational Linguistics.

ElasticsearchB.V. 2019. The elasticsearch query string mini-language. `https://www.elastic.co/guide/en/elasticsearch/reference/current/query-dsl-query-string-query.html`.

Filar, Bobby and Rich Seymour. 2019. Going deep with artemis 3.0. `https://www.endgame.com/blog/technical-blog/going-deep-artemis-30`. Last accessed: 2019-04-15.

Filar, Bobby, Richard Seymour, and Matthew Park. 2017. Ask me anything: A conversational interface to augment information security workers. *CoRR*, abs/1707.05768.

Finegan-Dollak, Catherine, Jonathan K. Kummerfeld, Li Zhang, Karthik Ramanathan, Sesh Sadasivam, Rui Zhang, and Dragomir Radev. 2018. Improving text-to-sql evaluation methodology. In *Proceedings of the 56th Annual Meeting of the Association for Computational Linguistics (Volume 1: Long Papers)*, pages 351–360, Melbourne, Australia, July. Association for Computational Linguistics.

Giordani, Alessandra and Alessandro Moschitti. 2012. Translating questions to SQL queries with generative parsers discriminatively reranked. In *Proceedings of COLING 2012: Posters*, pages 401–410, Mumbai, India, December. The COLING 2012 Organizing Committee.

Gur, Izzeddin, Semih Yavuz, Yu Su, and Xifeng Yan. 2018. Dialsql: Dialogue based structured query generation. In *Proceedings of the 56th Annual Meeting of the Association for Computational Linguistics (Volume 1: Long Papers)*, pages 1339–1349, Melbourne, Australia, July. Association for Computational Linguistics.

Honnibal, Matthew and Ines Montani. 2017. spacy 2: Natural language understanding with bloom embeddings, convolutional neural networks and incremental parsing. `https://github.com/explosion/spaCy`.

Kindlund, Darien. 2018. Using natural language searches for fast incident response. `https://insightengines.com/blog/using-natural-language-searches-fast-incident-response/`. Last accessed: 2019-04-15.

Lim, Swee Kiat, Aldrian Obaja Muis, Wei Lu, and Chen Hui Ong. 2017. Malwaretextdb: A database for annotated malware articles. In *Proceedings of the 55th Annual Meeting of the Association for Computational Linguistics (Volume 1: Long Papers)*, pages 1557–1567, Vancouver, Canada, July. Association for Computational Linguistics.

LOLBAS. 2019. Living off the land binaries and scripts. `https://github.com/LOLBAS-Project/LOLBAS`.

Mangold, Christoph. 2007. A survey and classification of semantic search approaches. *Int. J. Metadata Semant. Ontologies*, 2(1):23–34, September.

Mitre. 2019. Cyber threat intelligence repository expressed in stix 2.0. `https://github.com/mitre/cti`.

OASIS. 2019. The open command and control (openc2) language specification. `http://docs.oasis-open.org/openc2/oc2ls/v1.0/oc2ls-v1.0.html`.

OpenAPI. 2019. The openapi specification. `https://github.com/OAI/OpenAPI-Specification`.

Rodriguez, Roberto. 2019. The hunting elk. `https://github.com/Cyb3rWard0g/HELK`.

Roth, Florian and Thomas Patzke. 2019. Sigma: Generic signature format for siem systems. `https://github.com/Neo23x0/sigma`.

Russinovich, Mark and Thomas Garnier. 2019. Sysmon v9.0. `https://docs.microsoft.com/en-us/sysinternals/downloads/sysmon`.

Su, Yu, Ahmed Hassan Awadallah, Madian Khabsa, Patrick Pantel, Michael Gamon, and Mark Encarnacion. 2017. Building natural language interfaces to web apis. In *Proceedings of the 2017 ACM on Conference on Information and Knowledge Management*, CIKM '17, pages 177–186, New York, NY, USA. ACM.

Su, Yu, Ahmed Hassan Awadallah, Miaosen Wang, and Ryen W. White. 2018. Natural language interfaces with fine-grained user interaction: A case study on web apis. In *The 41st International ACM SIGIR Conference on Research & Development in Information Retrieval*, SIGIR '18, pages 855–864, New York, NY, USA. ACM.

Tamas, Ionut and Ioan Salomie. 2016. Artemis - an extensible natural language framework for data querying and manipulation. In *IEEE 12th International Conference on Intelligent Computer Communication and Processing, ICCP 2016, Cluj-Napoca, Romania, September 8-10, 2016*, pages 85–91.

Wang, Chenglong, Alvin Cheung, and Rastislav Bodik. 2017. Synthesizing highly expressive sql queries from input-output examples. *SIGPLAN Not.*, 52(6):452–466, June.

Warren, David H.D. and Fernando C.N. Pereira. 1982. An efficient easily adaptable system for interpreting natural language queries. *Computational Linguistics*, 8(3-4):110–122.

Yu, Tao, Rui Zhang, Kai Yang, Michihiro Yasunaga, Dongxu Wang, Zifan Li, James Ma, Irene Li, Qingning Yao, Shanelle Roman, Zilin Zhang, and Dragomir R. Radev. 2018. Spider: A large-scale human-labeled dataset for complex and cross-domain semantic parsing and text-to-sql task. *CoRR*, abs/1809.08887.

Zhong, Victor, Caiming Xiong, and Richard Socher. 2017. Seq2sql: Generating structured queries from natural language using reinforcement learning. *CoRR*, abs/1709.00103.

# Improving Robustness in Real-World Neural Machine Translation Engines


**Rohit Gupta, Patrik Lambert, Raj Nath Patel and John Tinsley**[*]
Iconic Translation Machines Ltd.
Invent Building, DCU Campus, Glasnevin,
Dublin 9, Ireland.
`rohit,patrik,raj,john@iconictranslation.com`



## Abstract

As a commercial provider of machine translation, we are constantly training engines for a variety of uses, languages, and content types. In each case, there can be many variables, such as the amount of training data available, and the quality requirements of the end user. These variables can have an impact on the robustness of Neural MT engines. On the whole, Neural MT cures many ills of other MT paradigms, but at the same time it has introduced a new set of challenges to address. In this paper, we describe some of the specific issues with practical NMT and the approaches we take to improve model robustness in real world scenarios.


## 1 Introduction

As a commercial provider of bespoke machine translation (MT) solutions for enterprise users, we train engines all day, every day for a variety of different languages, and content types, with different quantities and quality of training data. On a case by case basis, there are a lot of variables to contend with.

The breakthrough of Neural MT (NMT) over the past number of years, and the step change in quality it can produce, means that it is a no-brainer to adopt and make an integral part of our technology stack. However, there are still some practical gaps that need to be addressed in the core technology, in order to make it broadly production ready and flexible. These are either specific issues or topics that were already resolved in Statistical MT and have been reintroduced, or new types of issues unique to neural models.

This can include, but is not limited to, the need for a more rigorous data cleaning step, a lack of robustness around handling terminology and various types of mistranslations, and the ability to adapt to different domains.

Sometimes we can handle these issues elegantly in the models, but certain variables such as the volume of training data available in each case, make it a little less predictable. In some cases, we have to find more practical workarounds in our data preparation, and pre- and post-processing steps, in order to get engines production ready.

In this paper, after giving an overview of our NMT pipeline, we will focus on how we address the following issues in order to better prepare NMT engines for real-world deployment: 1) data cleaning, 2) over-generation, 3) improving robustness when translating entities, and 4) domain adaptation.

### 1.1 Our Pipeline

Our NMT pipeline is composed of several components, which are described in the following sections. Training data is first processed through a corpus preparation pipeline. This pipeline includes data cleaning and filtering scripts (see Section 2), as well as a processing pipeline. At test time, this processing pipeline is applied to the source text. Do-not-translate words are replaced by placeholders and replaced back in the translation (Section 3.2.1). This technique can also be used to force the translation of specific terminology. Before training, the tokens are split into sub-words to limit the vocabulary size (see Section 3). The model is dynamically adapted to the source sentence if a similar segment is found in the training corpus (Section 4). After translation, a post-processing module deletes over-generation patterns based on the source sentence (Section 2.2).

## 2 Training Data cleaning

Garbage in, garbage out. This is more relevant than ever for NMT which has been shown to be more sensitive to noisy data. In the following, we describe some steps we take to prepare different corpora prior to training.

### 2.1 Description

The data cleaning pipelines includes the following steps:

- **Character and encoding cleaning:** cleans encoding issues, cleans and normalizes incorrect characters.

- **Punctuation and digit filtering:** the following sentence pairs are filtered: (i) if in one of the sides, less than half of the characters are digits or letters; and (2) if in one of the sides, the sentences is only composed of digits and spaces. The intuition behind these steps is that sentence pairs formed mostly by punctuation or digit are not very useful for training and thus can be discarded.

- **Copy filtering:** sentence pairs in which the target side is a copy of the source side are filtered out. It has been observed that copied sentences are very harmful for NMT (Khayrallah and Koehn, 2018).

- **Duplicate removal:** in this step, repeated sentence pairs are removed.

- **Length-based filter:** sentence pairs in which one of the sides has less characters than a threshold are filtered out, as well as sentence pairs in which the length ratio is less than a threshold. Specifically, the average ratio of source and target sentence length in the training corpus is first calculated, as well as its standard deviation. The sentence pairs whose ratio differ more than 6 standard deviations from the average are discarded.

- **Language-based filter:** sentence pairs whose respective language are not the correct one are discarded. The language identification is performed in two stages. First,

the main script of the sentence is identified. Based on this information, the set of possible languages is determined. If the correct language is not part of the set of possible languages, the sentence is discarded. Otherwise, the language identification is performed within the set of possible languages. To limit the number of false negatives, we split the sentence in two and consider that the language is incorrect only if both halves have been classified as the same incorrect language.

- **Do-not-translate word replacement:** words and phrases detected as do-not-translated entities are replaced by a placeholder if they appear in both sides of the sentence pair.

- **Processing pipeline:** each side of the training corpus is processed independently with processors pertinents for the task at hand, including tokenization and truecasing.

- **training/development/test sets splitting:** the splitting strategy ensures the same distribution of sentences with do-not-translate entities as well as of each length range in the development and test data. It also keeps 5% of development set sentences overlapping with the training set, which is helpful for training.

| | sentence pairs | English words |
|---|---|---|
| Train (Iconic) | 202,249 | 1,868,403 |
| Train (Moses) | 205,434 | 1,884,124 |
| Dev (Iconic) | 2000 | 22,502 |
| Dev (random) | 2000 | 19,501 |
| Test | 2100 | 24,571 |

**Table 1:** Statistics of KDE4 data for the training, development and test corpora processed by Iconic pipeline and Moses tools.

### 2.2 Experiments

We evaluated the impact of our data cleaning pipeline on the KDE4 German-English data, obtained from the OPUS corpus[1]. We compared the training with data processed by our pipeline and with data processed by Moses tools (tokenization, length-based filter and true-casing). We used the same length parameters for the length-based filter

---

[1] http://opus.nlpl.eu/

| Corpus Preparation | BLEU | 1-TER | OVER | REP | UNDER | DROP |
|---|---|---|---|---|---|---|
| Moses tools | 31.4 ±0.3 | 47.2 ±0.3 | 29.3 ±2.3 | 5.1 ±0.5 | 8.0 ±1.0 | 9.5 ±0.8 |
| Iconic | 33.7 ±0.4 | 50.2 ±0.1 | 29.3 ±5.8 | 3.3 ±0.3 | 8.3 ±0.6 | 8.7 ±0.3 |
| Iconic+DNT | 32.5 ±0.2 | 48.5 ±0.3 | 26.0 ±6.0 | 2.9 ±0.1 | 6.7 ±1.2 | 8.8 ±0.5 |
| Iconic + rep-del | 33.7 ±0.3 | 50.2 ±0.1 | 17.3 ±2.1 | 3.1 ±0.2 | 8.3 ±0.6 | 8.7 ±0.2 |
| Iconic+DNT+rep-del | 32.4 ±0.2 | 48.4 ±0.3 | 13.3 ±3.1 | 2.7 ±0.1 | 6.7 ±1.2 | 8.8 ±0.5 |

**Table 2:** Evaluation scores for training on data processed by Moses tools, our pipeline without (Iconic) and with (Iconic+DNT) replacement of do-not-translate phrases by placeholders.

(175 words) and the same true-casing models. The statistics of the data are shown in Table 1. In the case of the Moses pipeline, the development set was selected at random. The test set was the same, but processed according to each pipeline.

We trained small transformer models with the Fairseq tool (Ott et al., 2018), with the same parameters as those indicated in the fairseq github site for IWSLT'14 German to English. We averaged the 5 checkpoints around the best model. We repeated the training 3 times and report the average and standard deviation of the 3 runs.

Results are reported in Table 2. Training with our pipeline improves BLEU (Papineni et al., 2002) and TER (Snover et al., 2006) scores respectively by 2.3 and 3.0 points. The difference is larger than standard deviation error bars, thus it is statistically significant according to this criterion. This suggests that efforts to better clean the data and to choose the validation set carefully are beneficial in terms of automated quality metrics.

NMT models are not perfect at controlling the output length and sometimes drop or duplicate content. To evaluate this category of errors, the rest of metrics measure over-generation (repetitions) and under-generation (source text not covered). OVER simply counts repetitions in the output, while UNDER counts under-generation based on the ratio of number of source and output words. REP and DROP count respectively the number of repetitions and under-generation in the output based on the alignment with the source (Malaviya et al., 2018). Interestingly, the REP score is significantly lower with our pipeline. The DROP score average is also lower although the difference lies within the standard deviation. This suggests that the engine is more robust to under- and over-generation with our pipeline.

Replacing do-not-translate phrases (DNTs) by placeholders (see section 3.2.1) yields slightly worse BLEU and TER scores. However, the OVER, REP and UNDER scores are improved.

Thus using DNTs may improve robustness. The worsening of BLEU and TER may be due to the fact that we used only one type of placeholder to replace entities which appear in different contexts (for example, URLs and numbers). Using different types would improve the modelling of each one.

Our pipeline includes a module to detect duplicated content in the translation and to delete it. The detection is based on the source sentence. That is, if the source text contains a repetition, it is not incorrect to have it in the translation. To decide whether a repetition should be deleted or not, we adopted a conservative criterion favoring precision rather than recall. We delete repeated words if they are aligned with the same source word. The alignment may be given by the attention weights or by an external alignment.

Table 2 also shows the impact of using our source-based repetition deletion module ("rep-del"). This module drops the average number of repetitions (OVER) of the Iconic system from 29.3 to 17.3 and the REP score from 3.3 to 3.1. Applied to the system with DNTs, OVER drops from 26.0 to 13.3 and the REP score from 2.9 to 2.7. Thus this module is effective at removing repetitions, with no significant impact on BLEU and TER.

## 3 Tokenization & Subword Encodings

Whereas Statistical was fairly predictable in terms of how it would perform on certain inputs - for good or for bad - neural models can react in a peculiar manner on unseen input. This can manifest itself more with things like named entities and, often, these are of critical importance in real-world scenarios where they may refer to drug names, email address, defendent namess, etc., so the MT needs to be robust and predictable.

### 3.1 Preparation

After cleaning we tokenize and normalize our data. We also apply subword encodings. They are particularly helpful to limit the vocab size for an NMT system. Subwords also help in tackling out-of-vocabulary (OOV) problem in NMT. It helps in improving the coverage by splitting words. Therefore, the system can translate different forms of a word even if it was not seen during training.

## 3.2 Issues with Tokenization

Too much tokenization can also cause issues. We often come across words and phrases which should be left untouched during translation. They are in general entities and they can represent file numbers, file paths, formatting tags, commands, product names, email address, URLs, terms etc. In Neural MT, this process of copying is also learned during translation  (Knowles and Koehn, 2018). However, if we do not pay attention to such entities it gets difficult to recover then successfully as some parts of the entities may get modified during translation.

Therefore, we focus on learning the translation part and normalize the other data where we require untouched copy as a part of pre-processing and post-processing.

### 3.2.1 Do Not Translate Terms

We define do-not-translate terms (DNTs) as terms which are exact copy from the source. They are neither translated nor transliterated. The languages where the source and target have different scripts and do not share characters, it is easier to determine such terms. For example, when translating from Chinese to English it is easy to spot English text in the Chinese sentence and such words are almost always exact copy from the source. The languages who share alphabets e.g. if both languages belong to Latin, in such language pairs, we need much context to determine.

We determine following expressions as DNT terms:

- Email addresses, URLs

- Numbers with two or more digits (without comma and dot)

- Any combination of number (at least two digits) and English characters

- File names and paths with valid extensions

- XML Tags

- English characters when the source is Non-Latin and target is English

### 3.2.2 How DNTs are helpful?

We detect DNTs in the source and replace them with a placeholder token during translation. For example, the following segment from the MultiUN dataset can be converted to have two DNTs (DNTID1 and DNTID2).

- "For more information about the project and all **19** targets, visit **www.post2015consensus.com**"

- "For more information about the project and all **DNTID1** targets, visit **DNTID2**"

Here DNTID1 is 19 and DNTID2 is www.post2015consensus.com. The system learns to copy DNTID1 and DNTID2 placeholders instead of actual numbers and URLs. We issue multiple DNTs (here ID1 and ID2) so as to have position information when there are more than one DNTs in a sentence.

### 3.2.3 Issues with Subwords

Subword translation is an approach used in NMT to tackle out-of-vocabulary (OOV) problem using byte-pair encoding (BPE) or other similar segmentation techniques. It is now defacto to use subwords in NMT as with the better vocab coverage it enables the NMT models with excellent copying capability. The copying behaviour is required when the named entities need to be copied from the source text to the target translation. Although subword NMT works quite well at copying, it sometimes fails to copy the complete sequence of subwords in the translated text and results in spelling errors.

### 3.2.4 Spelling Errors in Subword NMT

In general, NMT models perform quite poorly on rare words, (Luong and Manning, 2015; Sennrich et al., 2016; Arthur et al., 2016) due to the fixed vocabulary of NMT models. The most common categories of rare words are named entities and nouns. These entities often pass through the NMT system unchanged. For example, the word "*Gonzalez*" is broken into "*G@@ on@@ z@@ al@@ e@@ z*" by BPE and passes through the NMT system unchanged. However, when it fails, the model can drop or wrongly translate subwords which results in perceived misspellings.

**Subword Dropped**  In this case when a subword (which is part of a named entity) is not copied in the translated text. For example, the word *Stephen* is split into "Ste@@ p@@ hen" and say in the translation process NMT system failed to copy subword "p@@", then the resulting translation would be *Stehen*.

**Subword Translated**    In this case one or more subwords, which were meant to be copied, are actually translated. For example, in our German-English NMT system, the named entity *littlebits* is translated as *littlement*. It was due to the fact that applying byte pair encoding, the word *littlebits* is split into "li@@ tt@@ leb@@ it@@ s" where the subwords @@*it s* are translated as "*ment*".

## 3.3  Tackling Subword Issues

We suggest that the above mentioned issues causing spelling errors in named entities are mainly because of over splitting. In BPE, the algorithm checks each subword in the given vocab and if not found, it will recursively split the segment into smaller units (by reversing byte-pair encoding merge operations) until all units are either invocabulary, or cannot be split further (often character level splits). For named entities, it is quite common to have unseen subwords resulting into character level splits. We propose two methods to resolve byte-pair encoding issues.

**No More Split**    In this method, we restrict the encoding algorithm from splitting unseen subwords into characters. The intuition behind is that copying single unseen token would be easier than copying a sequence of characters.

**Protect Unseen Words**    After applying the encoding, this method counts the unseen subwords (not in-vocabulary) and if the count is more than a threshold value it keeps the original word. The logic is to use UNK-token translation transferring these entities in the target text. However, this method is highly dependent on accuracy of alignment and UNK-translation.

|       | #segments | #words  |
|-------|-----------|---------|
| train | 160239    | 3998597 |
| dev   | 7283      | 181021  |
| test  | 6750      | 153697  |

**Table 3:** Data distribution after cleaning and applying tokenizer (source side)

### 3.3.1  Experiments & Results

Our sample results here are based on the publicly available IWSLT dataset [2]. The distribution of train, dev, and test datasets is detailed in Table 3. We randomly select a development set from the training data. The test set is created by combining dev (2010, 11), and test (2010, 11, 12) sets of earlier IWSLT shared tasks.

We use a shared vocabulary BPE Model (Sennrich et al., 2016) for subword segmentation, with a code of 32000 merge operations. We use convolutional (Gehring et al., 2017) encoder-decoder (15x15) architecture with the size of hidden units and word embedding of 512. For the training of model parameters, we use NAG (Qu and Li, 2017) with cross entropy as a loss function. We start with a learning rate of 0.25 and reduce it by a factor of 10 if there is no change in the validation perplexity for a fixed number of epochs. BLEU (Papineni et al., 2002) and TER (Snover et al., 2006) scores are computed with tokenized lower-cased output and references using the "evaluater" binary from Moses.

|                      | BLEU  | 1-TER |
|----------------------|-------|-------|
| baseline             | 30.75 | 50.71 |
| no more split*       | 30.74 | 49.82 |
| protect unseen,K=1   | 29.44 | 47.78 |
| protect unseen,K=2   | 30.15 | 48.78 |
| protect unseen,K=3   | 30.35 | 49.55 |
| protect unseen,K=4   | 30.78 | 50.11 |

**Table 4:** Evaluation scores. K: threshold for the unk-count

The evaluation scores are detailed in Table 4. The quality scores have not improved using the proposed methods, but in manual evaluation, it was found that the model trained with "no more split" setting preserves better the named entities. This is depicted with an example in Table 5. The model with "protect unseen" with threshold value of 4 is slightly better than baseline, but in manual evaluation, we have seen that it is not better at translating the named entities compared to the baseline.

## 4  Domain Adaptation

As shown by Koehn and Knowles (2017), NMT is even more sensitive to the domain than phrase-based SMT. Translation quality drops abruptly when the source text is in a different domain to

[2]https://wit3.fbk.eu/archive/2014-01/texts/de/en/de-en.tgz

| input | die idee hinter **littlebits** ist , dass es eine wachsende bibliothek ist . (de) |
|---|---|
| reference | *the idea behind **littlebits** is that its a growing library . (en)* |
| baseline | die idee hinter **li@@ tt@@ leb@@ it@@ s** ist , dass es eine wachsen@@ de bibliothe@@ k ist .(de) <br> *the idea behind **littlement** is that its a growing library . (en)* |
| no more split | die idee hinter **li@@ tt@@ leb@@ its** ist , dass es eine wachsende bibliothek ist .(de) <br> *the idea behind **littlebits** is that its a growing library . (en)* |

**Table 5:** Comparison of translation on a sentence from test corpus

the training data. A standard technique to adapt a generic model to a specific domain is to continue the training with a small amount of in-domain parallel data. This technique, referred to as fine-tuning, is very effective.

Our translation models are dynamically adapted to the source text context at each sentence, using fine-tuning but without knowing the source domain in advance. This adaptation is performed with a method similar to that proposed by Farajian et al. (2017). If a segment similar to the source sentence is found in the training corpus, the model is fine-tuned with the corresponding sentence pair for a few epochs. To this end, the training corpus is indexed into a translation memory. At test time, the translation memory is queried with the source sentence by information retrieval tools[3]. The number of epochs and the learning rate of the fine tuning with the retrieved sentence pair depends on the similarity between its source side and the source sentence. If they are not similar, fine tuning the model with the retrieved sentence may worsen the translation. The more they are similar, the more fine tuning can be beneficial and thus the higher the learning rate and number of epochs. This technique has thus more impact when the source text is very close to the training data.

We ran our pipeline with dynamic domain adaptation on the KDE4 German–English task (see Tables 1 and 2). The results are shown in Table 6

|  | BLEU | 1-TER |
|---|---|---|
| without adaptation | 33.5 | 50.2 |
| with adaptation | 34.1 | 50.7 |

**Table 6:** Evaluation scores for dynamic domain adaptation.

The impact of dynamic adaptation on this corpus is positive according to automated metrics, but modest. This is because for most sentences in the test set, there is no sentence in the translation mem-

ory being similar enough to fine-tune the model on it (see Farajian et al. (2017) for more details). Table 7 shows an adaptation example. After fine-tuning on the corpus sentence pair "Größe des Verlaufs@@ speichers :"–"clipboard history size :" (same as the source with a semicolon at the end), the model does not omit the word "Clipboard" any more.

| input | Größe des Verlaufsspeichers |
|---|---|
| reference | Clipboard history size |
| baseline | History size |
| adapted | Clipboard history size |
| TM source | Größe des Verlaufsspeichers : |
| TM target | clipboard history size : |

**Table 7:** Example of dynamic adaptation.

## 5  What does all of this mean in practice?

In real-world MT scenarios, it is often the finer details around the edges that can be of most importance. For example, in legal use cases like e-discovery, it is critical to get entities like names and addresses correct, because the resulting output is not being read by people, but rather being input into search tools where these entities will likely be search terms.

In other cases, such as MT for post-editing, where an end user will be working with the output, we may need the flexibility to act on specific feedback in order to address issues or concerns with the output.

The issues described above can manifest themselves in general, untrained engines, and the techniques we apply require an understanding of what is happening in the model, and the ability to be able to affect change. Then, finally, building upon strong baseline models to produce the most effective output for an particular use case.

When looking at automated metrics, the impact of these techniques may not be very apparent, further emphasizing the need to human assessments prior to deploying an engine in production, particularly in certain scenarios.

---

[3]Concretely we use Lucene (McCandless et al., 2010), a very efficient open-source information retrieval library.

# References


Arthur, Philip, Graham Neubig, and Satoshi Nakamura. 2016. Incorporating discrete translation lexicons into neural machine translation. *arXiv preprint arXiv:1606.02006*.

Farajian, M. Amin, Marco Turchi, Matteo Negri, and Marcello Federico. 2017. Multi-domain neural machine translation through unsupervised adaptation. In *Proceedings of the Second Conference on Machine Translation*, pages 127–137, Copenhagen, Denmark, September. Association for Computational Linguistics.

Gehring, Jonas, Michael Auli, David Grangier, Denis Yarats, and Yann N Dauphin. 2017. Convolutional sequence to sequence learning. In *Proceedings of the 34th International Conference on Machine Learning-Volume 70*, pages 1243–1252. JMLR. org.

Khayrallah, Huda and Philipp Koehn. 2018. On the impact of various types of noise on neural machine translation. In *Proceedings of the 2nd Workshop on Neural Machine Translation and Generation*, pages 74–83, Melbourne, Australia, July. Association for Computational Linguistics.

Knowles, Rebecca and Philipp Koehn. 2018. Context and copying in neural machine translation. In *Proceedings of the 2018 Conference on Empirical Methods in Natural Language Processing*, pages 3034–3041.

Koehn, Philipp and Rebecca Knowles. 2017. Six challenges for neural machine translation. In *Proceedings of the First Workshop on Neural Machine Translation*, pages 28–39, Vancouver, August. Association for Computational Linguistics.

Luong, Minh-Thang and Christopher D Manning. 2015. Stanford neural machine translation systems for spoken language domains. In *Proceedings of the International Workshop on Spoken Language Translation*, pages 76–79.

Malaviya, Chaitanya, Pedro Ferreira, and André F. T. Martins. 2018. Sparse and constrained attention for neural machine translation. In *Proceedings of the 56th Annual Meeting of the Association for Computational Linguistics (Volume 2: Short Papers)*, pages 370–376, Melbourne, Australia, July. Association for Computational Linguistics.

McCandless, Michael, Erik Hatcher, and Otis Gospodnetic. 2010. *Lucene in Action, Second Edition: Covers Apache Lucene 3.0*. Manning Publications Co., Greenwich, CT, USA.

Ott, Myle, Sergey Edunov, David Grangier, and Michael Auli. 2018. Scaling neural machine translation. In *Proceedings of the Third Conference on Machine Translation: Research Papers*, pages 1–9, Belgium, Brussels, October. Association for Computational Linguistics.

Papineni, Kishore, Salim Roukos, Todd Ward, and Wei-Jing Zhu. 2002. BLEU: A Method for Automatic Evaluation of Machine Translation. In *Proceedings of the 40th annual meeting on association for computational linguistics*, pages 311–318. Association for Computational Linguistics.

Qu, Guannan and Na Li. 2017. Accelerated distributed nesterov gradient descent. *arXiv preprint arXiv:1705.07176*.

Sennrich, Rico, Barry Haddow, and Alexandra Birch. 2016. Neural machine translation of rare words with subword units. In *Proceedings of the 54th Annual Meeting of the As-sociation for Computational Linguistics*, volume 1, page 1715–1725, Association for Computational Linguistics, Berlin, Germany,.

Snover, Matthew, Bonnie Dorr, Richard Schwartz, Linnea Micciulla, and John Makhoul. 2006. A Study of Translation Edit Rate with Targeted Human Annotation. In *Proceedings of association for machine translation in the Americas*, pages 223–231.

# Surveying the potential of using speech technologies for post-editing purposes in the context of international organizations: What do professional translators think?


Jeevanthi Liyanapathirana

World Trade Organization
Rue de Laussane 154
Geneva, Switzerland

jeevanthi.liyana@wto.org

Pierrette Bouillon

Fac. de traduction et d'interprétation
University of Geneva, 1211
Geneva, Switzerland

pierrette.bouillon@unige.ch

Bartolomé Mesa-Lao

Universitat Oberta de Catalunya
Av. Tibidabo, 39-43
08035 Barcelona, Spain

bmesa@uoc.edu



### [1] Abstract

The present study has surveyed professional translators working in six international organizations in order to know more about their views and attitudes with regard to new translation workflows involving two different types of technologies, i.e. machine translation and speech recognition. The main aim of this survey was to identify how feasible it is to implement new post-editing workflows in an international organization using speech as an input method to edit inaccurate machine translation outputs. Overall, the results suggest that the surveyed translators do not hold a negative view on the use of ASR as part of their translation workflow, which provides a promising first step towards investigating the integration of speech based post-editing to translation workflows for productivity and ergonomic gains.


## 1    Introduction

Automatic speech recognition (ASR) software has quietly created a niche for itself in many situations of our daily lives (Joscelyne, 2018). It can be found at the other end of customer-support hotlines, it is built into operating systems and it is offered as an alternative text-input method for smartphones. On another front, given the significant improvements in Machine Translation (MT) quality and the increasing demand for translations, post-editing of MT has become a popular practice in the translation industry, since it has been shown to allow for larger volumes of translations to be produced saving time and costs. Workflows in the translation industry have experienced a significant transformation and it is in this new context that speech technology is likely to contribute to further innovation. With post-editing services becoming common practice among language service providers and speech recognition gaining momentum, it seems reasonable to start exploring interplays between both fields to create new business solutions and workflows (Mesa-Lao, 2014b). Most traditional international organizations with translation needs (see section 3.2) have already added a machine translation component as one of the resources offered to their human translators. However, not much has been said yet when it comes to the attitude of such professional translators using machine translation and, more specifically, using speech technology to edit machine translation outputs in the context of a large scale international organization.

In this study, we conducted qualitative research on the usage of speech and post-editing in a selected set of large scale international organizations. To our knowledge, this is the first study conducted on using post-editing and speech together in large scale international organizations. The paper is structured as follows: section 2 mentions related work for this study, followed by our method in section 3. Section 4 describes the results, leading to the discussion and conclusions in section 5.

---

## 2   Related work

The use of speech as an input method to interact with computers and generate text is as old as the idea of computers themselves. In the context of machine-aided human translation and human-aided machine translation, different scenarios have been investigated where human translators are brought into the loop interacting with a computer through a variety of input modalities to improve the efficiency and accuracy of the translation process.

In the context of translation, dictaphones were a popular tool in the context of large international organisations in the 1960s and 1970s and professional translators often collaborated with transcriptionists to dictate their translations. In the 1990s and 2000s, computational researchers began to explore ASR for translation purposes. Such developments focused mainly on reducing ASR word error rates by combining ASR and MT (Vidal et al., 2006). More recently, further efforts have been made by Translation Studies scholars in order to assess the performance of translation students and professionals when using commercial ASR systems (Dragsted et al., 2011; Zapata, 2012); to assess and analyze professional translators' needs and opinions about ASR (Ciobanu, 2014, 2016, and 2018), and to explore ASR in mobile and multimodal environments (Zapata, 2016a,b). More recently, the potential of using ASR for post-editing purposes has also been investigated (García-Martínez et al., 2014; Mesa-Lao, 2014a,b; Torres-Hostench et al., 2017, and Zapata et al., 2017). For example, it was shown in previous pilot experiments that post-editing with the aid of a speech recognition system was the fastest method for translation (Zapata et al., 2017), that voice input is more interesting than the keyboard alone for post-editing (García-Martínez et al., 2014) and that 12 out of 15 translators would welcome the integration of voice as one of the possible input modes for performing PE tasks (Mesa-Lao, 2014a,b).

ASR systems have the potential to improve the productivity and comfort of performing computer-based tasks for a wide variety of users, allowing them to enter both text and commands into the computer using just their voice. However, further studies need to be conducted in order to build up new knowledge about the way in which state-of-the-art ASR software can be applied to one of the most common tasks translators face nowadays, i.e. post-editing of MT outputs.

The present study has two related objectives:

a) To understand the current situation of technology usage (specifically speech technologies) in selected international organizations with substantial translation needs.
b) To analyze the potential of introducing speech technologies to post-edit MT within such organizations.

As a first step towards these two objectives, the following section describes our pilot survey in detail, our participants' profile and our methodology.

## 3   Method

In order to answer our research questions, we used two steps. As a first step, we investigated the current usage of translation technology solutions in a selected set of organizations. As a second step, we selected a set of professional translators from those organizations to gain further insights about their perceptions on using speech and other tools as part of their translation workflow.

### 3.1   Overview

As part of this research, two main questionnaires were designed and deployed as a survey. The first survey was distributed to a total of six organizations and contained six questions about current translation technology usage. This survey was filled up by technology managers in the respective organizations. The second survey consisted of 15 questions targeting professional translators working in the selected international organizations. Both surveys were carried out in March 2019.

### 3.2   Participants profile

This study involved five large scale international organizations based in Geneva and one large scale international organization based in Luxembourg.

17 participants were selected from these six organizations using snowball sampling. The selected group included 11 females and 6 males, belonging to different age groups (3 translators between ages 20-35, 8 between 36-50, and 6 older than 50). All 17 participants are professional translators within these organizations, with multiple years of translation experience (7 translators with +20 years experience, 2 with 16-20 years, 3 with 11-15 years, 1 with 6-10 years, and 4 translators between 0-5 years experience). Their language combinations involved translating to/from English, French, Russian, and Spanish. The sample included translators working with different post-editing scenarios, i.e. post-editing via typing, translation from scratch using speech, translation from scratch using a keyboard, translation from scratch using a dictaphone, and post-editing via speech (Figure 1).

16 out of the 17 translators were familiar with standard computer-aided translation software (i.e. SDL Trados) and 14 out of the 17 translators claimed to be familiar with different categories of speech technologies which will be described in detail in the analysis section. In addition, 6 translators declared to use speech input methods in their day to day life (e.g. to dictate messages in a smartphone or to issue commands to Google Home, Amazon Alexa, etc.).

### 3.3 Procedure

In the first questionnaire, the managerial staff of each organization received a short questionnaire via email where they had to answer 6 simple questions on their current translation workflows. The second questionnaire was distributed internally by each international organization to their professional translators and contained 15 questions covering the following topics:

1. General information about their profile: including age, translation experience (years), employment status, and exposure to CAT tools.
2. Current translation workflow (translating from scratch, post-editing by typing,

post-editing by speech, and use of dictaphones).
3. Information about their usage of ASR as compared to other input methods (e.g. typing), and their likes and dislikes about it.
4. Their attitude towards different methods of translation, including speech based post-editing.

The first questionnaire consisted of open-ended questions. The second questionnaire was a mix of different types of questions: multiple choice questions, preference ranking questions, and dichotomous questions. These questionnaires can be found in the appendices (A and B).

### 3.4 Data collection and analysis

Regarding questionnaires' data, responses to quantitative items were entered into a spreadsheet, where mean responses were calculated. For binary or numeric results, the results were plotted in graphs to have a clearer overview. Open-ended questions and comments were analysed separately.

## 4 Survey Results

### 4.1 Distribution of translation technology among translators

As explained in section 3.3, the translators provided information on the translation technologies they involve in their translation processes. Figure 1 displays the results. The translators could select different technologies at the same time, since they could be competent in multiple translation workflows.

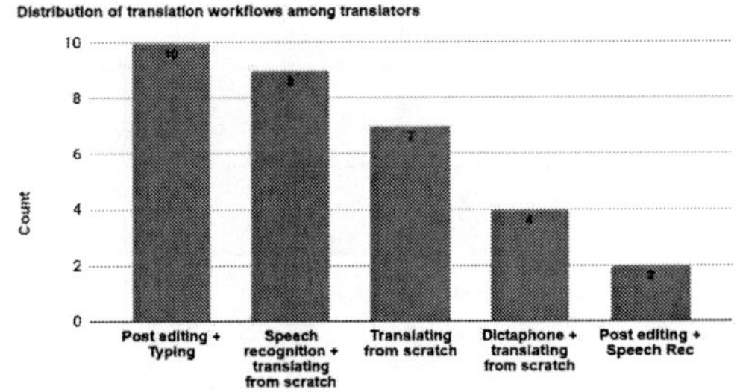


Figure 1. Translation technology usage among translators

10 out of 17 translators use typing to post-edit, 9 out of 17 already use speech recognition for translating (from scratch), and 4 out of 17 translators use a dictaphone for translation. Thus, the selected set of translators can be considered as representative of the variety of techniques used in international organizations. Also, these data show that usage of speech for the purpose of translating is not uncommon in the selected environments (at least 9 out of 17 translators are already competent in workflows involving ASR).

## 4.2 Usage of speech-based input methods

In order to determine why participants would decide to use ASR in the future to post-edit MT, we asked them to rate the importance of eight different reasons, on a scale from 1 to 8, being 8 the lowest in importance. The scale was 1 to 8 since there are eight reasons to be ranked by the translators - see Appendix B. The top reason for deciding to use ASR was that using speech was considered to be faster by the surveyed translators, followed by speech helping them with ergonomy. The mean value of the translator input score was neither negative nor positive with regard to the notion of speech technologies being accurate, providing a mean value of 4.0 (Table 1).

| Reason | Mean |
| --- | --- |
| Using speech is less tiring for me | 3.9 |
| Using speech is faster for me | 2.4 |
| Using speech is easier for me | 3.7 |
| Speech is a cool technology | 6 |
| Not many other alternatives for me | 7.1 |
| Personal preference | 5 |
| Speech technologies are accurate | 4 |
| Speech helps me with ergonomy | 2.6 |

Table 1. Ranking of reasons for using speech-based inputs in translation, rated on a scale from 1 (highest) to 8 (lowest).

## 4.3 Usage of non-speech input methods

Participants were also asked about their reasons for choosing non-speech input methods (i.e. keyboard and mouse). They rated the importance of six reasons on a scale from 1 (the most important) to 6 (the least important). The scale was 1 to 6 since there are six reasons to be ranked by the translators - see Appendix B. Table 2 describes the reasons why translators would not use speech input.

| Reason | Mean |
| --- | --- |
| Not using speech is easier. | 3.7 |
| Speech requires a lot of training | 4 |
| Speech is frustrating | 3.4 |
| Speech is not faster | 3.7 |
| To rest my voice after speaking | 3.5 |
| Speech is trendy but not efficient | 2.7 |

Table 2. Ranking of reasons for choosing non-speech input methods, rated on a scale from 1 (highest) to 6 (lowest).

The results were not very conclusive, but the main reason for their negative perception on speech technologies was their concern about its efficiency, which confirms the "neutral" attitude towards accuracy of speech recognition in Table 1.

The surveyed translators also provided open ended comments about negative views on using speech recognition. It was interesting to see how the biggest negative point of using speech recognition would be the noise factor (11 people out of 17 think speech recognition will disturb colleagues when working in an open space). This issue illustrates that using speech technologies in an organization would involuntarily depend on logistics factors. 9 out of 17 thought that using speech recognition can be tiring as well.

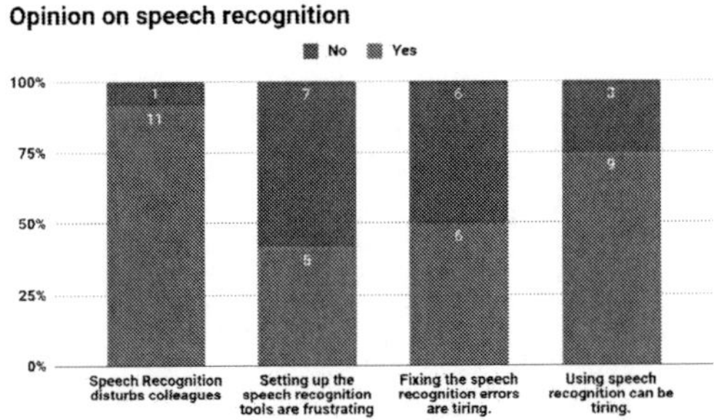


Figure 2. Translator views on using speech recognition for translation purposes.

### 4.4 Preferred choice of input method by translators based on requirement

The sampled translators were asked whether they would choose speech input or typing when considering the six reasons mentioned in the Figure 3 below.

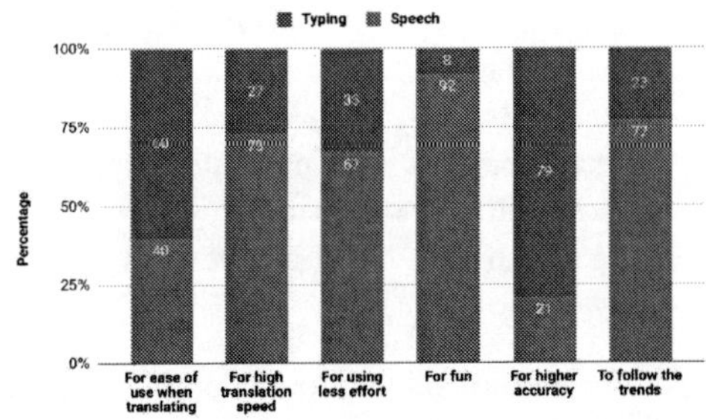


Figure 3. Choice of input method by the percentage of translators (speech/typing). Data labels illustrate percentages.

As can be seen from the results in Figure 3, a higher number of translators are open to the idea of using speech as a faster (73%) and less tiring (67%) input method when compared to typing. However, while the majority of the translators think that using speech as an input method is faster (73%), 79% do not believe that it is more accurate than typing, which agrees with our findings in Table 1 and 2.

### 4.5 Openness to different workflows

Since one of the main objectives of this study was to identify the potential of introducing speech input for post-editing purposes, translators were also asked about their openness to different workflows during translation. Figure 4 displays the results of our survey. 8 out of 17

translators were open to the idea of speech-based post-editing for translation and only 2 out of 17 assumed that mixing speech and post-editing together would be confusing.

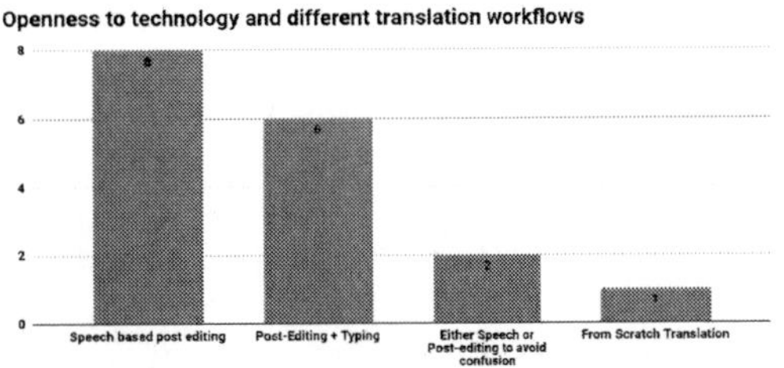


Figure 4. Translators' openness to different translation workflows.

As a second step, we further analyzed the translator's opinions in Figure 4, this time considering their current translation approaches as well. We analyzed the current translation workflow of each translator against the following three new workflows: 1) speech-based post-editing, 2) typing based post-editing, and 3) using either speech or typing post-editing but not together. Translators were divided into two categories based on their current skills: using dictaphone/any type of speech recognition tool and using typing for translation purposes. Figure 5 shows the translators' breakdown of openness to different workflows based on their translation workflow experience.

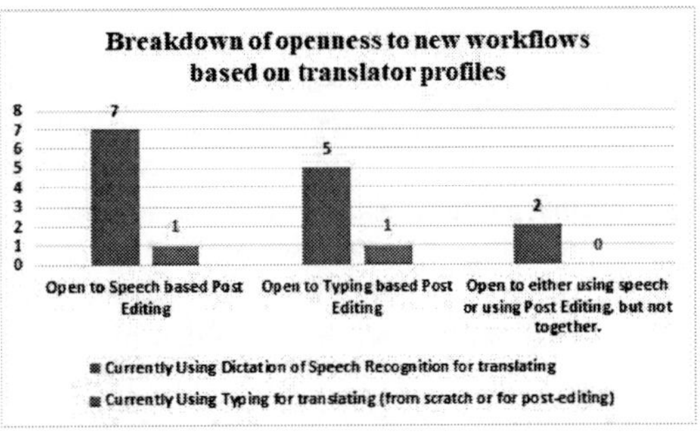


Figure 5. Breakdown of openness to new workflows based on translator profiles.

As expected, 7 out of 8 translators willing to use speech-based post-editing were already using either dictaphones or speech recognition tools, which explains their positive attitude towards using speech along with MT post-editing.

## 4.6 Translator input on their choice of preferred method

As part of the second questionnaire, translators were asked to elaborate on when they would use translating from scratch, when they would prefer to post-edit via keyboard and when they would be interested in using speech as input to their translation workflow (results are displayed in Appendix D, E, and F). The main factor of choosing post-editing instead of typing from scratch was the availability of high quality machine translation or translation memory suggestions (11 out of 17 translators). Translators also mentioned that they would post-edit if "the translation does not require creativity" (2 translators), when "the translation has to be more accurate than fluent" (1 translator), and when "the translation has to be done quickly" (1 translator). Translators also mentioned that they would choose speech technologies to translate when "the text to be translated is long" (6 translators) and "when speech recognition quality is good with less errors" (4 translators). This feedback emphasizes the necessity of having not only high quality speech recognition, but also better machine translation/translation memory output, if we want to invite more translators to the idea of speech-based post-editing.

## 5    Discussion and Conclusion

Many other questions regarding the effective use of ASR in translation could be surveyed, but this preliminary study shows that our sample of professional translators do not hold a negative view on the use of ASR as part of their translation workflow. In general, our findings suggest that professional translators working in the context of an international organization can benefit from the integration of ASR as one of the possible input methods when translating from scratch or when editing text for post-editing purposes.

The main findings of this study are:

1. Speech as an input method (i.e. ASR or dictaphones) is mainly used by translators to translate from scratch, rather than to post-edit MT output.
2. The majority of the surveyed translators believed that speech is faster than typing and less tiresome (more ergonomic). However, they are still in doubt regarding the accuracy level of available speech recognition toolkits.
3. Along with the necessity of high-quality ASR software solutions, this survey exposed multiple other factors which make translators more inclined towards the use of speech-based post-editing. These factors include working with high-quality machine translation or translation memory suggestions, larger amounts of texts for translation, and the possibility to use private or protected workstations for translation purposes using ASR. Provided that these requirements are met, the majority of translators were open to try speech-based post-editing as a new translation workflow.

These observations thus provide a promising first step for us to continue towards a more ambitious study, where we will conduct quantitative research evaluating the productivity gains derived from speech-based post-editing. We also plan to investigate how currently available CAT tools with integrated speech support (e.g. Matecat, memoQ, and SDL Trados) can be used for this purpose.

We thus conclude this first survey on translators' perceptions on using ASR in large scale international organizations with positive results.

### Acknowledgement

We would like to thank our anonymous participants from different international organizations for their valuable time and involvement in this preliminary survey.

## References

Ciobanu, D. (2014). Of Dragons and Speech Recognition Wizards and Apprentices. *Revista Tradumàtica*, 12: 524–538.

Ciobanu, D. (2016). Automatic Speech Recognition in the Professional Translation Process. *Translation Spaces*, 5(1): 124–144.

Ciobanu, D. (2018). Automatic Speech Recognition in the professional translation process. In Ehrensberger-Dow, M., Englund Dimitrova, B. (Eds). *Exploring the Situational Interface of Translation and Cognition* (123–143). John Benjamins Publishing Company.

Dragsted, B., Mees, I. M., and Hansen, I. G. (2011). Speaking your translation: students' first encounter with speech recognition technology. *Translation & Interpreting*, 3(1): 10–43.

García-Martínez, M., Singla, K., Tammewar, A., Mesa-Lao, B., Thakur, A., Anusuya, M. A., Bangalore, S., Carl, M. (2014). SEECAT: ASR & Eye-tracking Enabled Computer-Assisted Translation. In *Proceedings of the 17th Annual Conference of the European Association for Machine Translation*, pages 81–88, Dubrovnik, Croatia

Joscelyne, A. (2018). Translators in the Algorithmic Age. Briefing based on the TAUS Industry Leaders Forum, Amsterdam, Netherlands.

Matecat. (2019). *Advanced options – Matecat.* [online] Available at: https://www.matecat.com/ phrase-based-vs-neural-mt-webinar-questions/adva nced-options/ [Accessed 17 Apr. 2019].

Mesa-Lao, B. (2014a). Post-editing through Speech Recognition: A Feasibility Study with Post-editor Trainees. Abstract from 2014 *CRITT - Conference: Translation in Transition: Between Cognition, Computing and Technology* - Copenhagen Business School, Frederiksberg, Denmark.

Mesa-Lao, B. (2014b). Speech-Enabled Computer-Aided Translation: A Satisfaction Survey with Post-Editor Trainees. In *Workshop on Humans and Computer-assisted Translation*, pages 99-103, Gothenburg, Sweden.

SDL. (2018). *Increase your translation speed in 2018 with voice recognition software.* [online] Available at: https://www.sdltrados.com/video/increase-your-translation-speed-in-2018-with-voice-recognition-software/128377/ [Accessed 17 Apr. 2019].

Torres-Hostench, O., Moorkens, J., O'Brien, S., and Vreeke, J. (2017). Testing interaction with a Mobile MT post-editing app. Translation & Interpreting, 9(2):138-150.

Vidal, E., Casacuberta, F., Rodríguez, L., Civera, J., Martínez-Hinarejos. C.D. (2006). *Computer-Assisted Translation Using Speech Recognition. IEEE Transactions on Audio, Speech, and Language Processing*, 14(3): 941-951.

Zapata, J. (2016a). Translating On the Go? Investigating the Potential of Multimodal Mobile Devices for Interactive Translation Dictation. *Revista Tradumàtica*, 14: 66–74.

Zapata, J. (2016b). Translators in the Loop: Observing and Analyzing the Translator Experience with Multimodal Interfaces for Interactive Translation Dictation Environment Design. PhD thesis. University of Ottawa.

Zapata, J., Castilho, Sh., and Moorkens, J. (2017). Translation dictation vs. post-editing with cloud-based voice recognition: a pilot experiment. In *Proceedings of MT Summit XVI 2*, Nagoya, 123–136.

## Appendices

### Appendix A. First questionnaire

**1) What type of CAT tools do you use in your organization? Please name them.**

**2) Do the employees of your organization use dictaphone to translate? If yes, please mention what the resources and toolkits are.**

**3) Do the employees of your organization use speech recognition toolkits to translate? If yes, please mention what the resources and toolkits are.**

**4) Do the employees of your organization use machine translation suggestions during translation? If yes, please mention what the resources and toolkits are.**

**5) Do the employees of your organization use machine translation suggestions to post-edit by typing? If yes, please explain.**

**6) Do the employees of your organization use speech recognition techniques to post-edit machine translation suggestions? If yes, please explain.**

**Appendix B. Second questionnaire**

<u>Questions</u>

**1) What is your age range?**

    a) 20-35       b) 35-50       c) 50 or more

**2) What type of translation experience do you have?**

    a) I work in an academic organization

    b) I work in an international organization

    c) I have experience in both
       (academic/international organizations)

**3) How long have you worked in the translation industry (experience can be academic or industrial)?**

    a) 0-5 years   b) 6-10 years   c) 11-15 years

    d) 16-20 years   e) 20+ years

**4) Which are your language pairs during translation? e.g. English-French, etc.**

**5) Which of these statements is applicable to you? Multiple statements can be applicable, since you might be using different techniques for different requirements.**

    a) I use translation suggestions (MT/TM) for my translation purposes and I type to work on them.

    b) I use a dictaphone for translating from scratch.

    c) I use speech recognition toolkits (e.g. Dragon) to speak out my translations from scratch (and then correct them if necessary).

    d) I use speech recognition toolkits (e.g. Dragon) to post-edit translation suggestions (MT/TM).

    e) I prefer to type and translate from scratch.

**6) Do you use any computer-assisted translation tools (e.g. SDL Trados)? If so, which ones?**

**7) Have you used any speech recognition toolkit for other purposes, e.g. SIRI. Please explain briefly.**

**8) Following are some of the major reasons <u>for using speech-based input methods</u> (according to** previous research). Could you please rank them according to the importance?**

*1 would be the most important, and 8 would be the least important.*

| Reason | Rank |
|---|---|
| Using speech is less tiring for me. | |
| Using speech is faster for me. | |
| Using speech is easier for me. | |
| Speech is a cool technology. | |
| There are not many other alternatives for me. | |
| Using speech is a personal preference. | |
| Speech technologies are accurate. | |
| Speech helps me with ergonomy. | |

**9) Following are some of the reasons for not using speech-based input methods. Could you please rank them according to the importance?**

*1 would be the most important, 6 would be the least important*

| Reason | Rank |
|---|---|
| Not using speech is much easier for me. | |
| Speech requires a lot of setup and training | |
| I get frustrated using speech. | |
| Using speech is not faster (at least for me). | |
| I don't use speech to rest my voice. | |
| Using speech is just trendy, but not efficient. | |

**10) Which technique would you use (speech recognition or typing ) during the translation? Please use "yes" and "no" in each column.**

| Feature | Typing | Speech |
|---|---|---|
| For ease of use when translating | | |
| For high translation speed | | |
| For using less effort | | |
| For fun | | |
| For higher accuracy | | |
| To follow trends | | |

**11) Please type "yes" or "no" next to each of these statements according to your own personal views.**

| Feature | no/yes |
|---|---|
| Speech recognition disturbs colleagues | |
| Setting up speech recognition is frustrating | |
| Fixing speech recognition errors is tiring | |
| Using speech recognition can be tiring. | |

**12) Could you please mention reasons or situations you came across when you preferred post-editing translation suggestions rather than typing from scratch?**

**13) Could you please mention reasons or situations you came across when you preferred translating from scratch rather than post-editing machine translation suggestions?**

**14) As part of our research, we are investigating whether we can use speech technology for post-editing. In this hypothetical scenario, the users will get a machine translation suggestion or a translation memory suggestion for a given input. We would like to see if translators can use speech commands to post-edit the translation suggestion (the suggestions can come from translation memories or machine translation).**

**Could you please type "yes" next to the statement that is most applicable to you?**

a) Yes, I am open to the idea of speech-based post-editing.

b) Yes, I would like to use speech for translation, but without having to work on translation suggestions coming from translation memories or machine translation. This setup would be confusing.

c) Speech is not an option for me. I still enjoy translating from scratch via keyboard without having to work on machine translation outputs.

d) Speech is not an option for me. I still enjoy translating from scratch via keyboard and I am happy to use machine translation outputs as a starting point.

**15) Please mention situations where you would like to use speech technologies as a translation support (*e.g. I would use it for long paragraphs, I would use it for short sentences, etc.*).**

**Appendix C. Tool Usage in organizations**

| Category | Details |
|---|---|
| **CAT tools used** | Eluna, SDL Trados and Multitrans, DtSearch, MultiTerm, Groupshare, Euramis, memoQ, SmartLing. |
| **MT tools** | WipoTranslate, DeepL, eTranslate |
| **Usage of dictaphone** | 2 organizations out of 5. One out of those two uses the dictaphone very rarely. |
| **Speech recognition usage (e.g. Dragon)** | 4 organizations out of 5 use speech recognition. |
| **Machine translation usage** | 4 organizations out of 5 use machine translation. |
| **Post-editing using typing** | 4 organizations out of 5 use post-editing using typing. |
| **Post-editing using speech** | Only one translator of one organization could be found using post-editing using speech. |

**Appendix D. When would you choose post-editing machine translation instead of typing from scratch?**

| Reason | Frequency |
|---|---|
| When MT/TM quality is good | 11/17 |
| When accuracy is more important than fluency | 1/17 |
| When translation does not need creativity | 2/17 |
| To translate quickly | 1/17 |

**Appendix E. When would you choose typing from scratch instead of post-editing machine translation?**

| Reason | Frequency |
|---|---|
| When MT/TM quality is not good | 13/17 |
| When fluency is more important than accuracy | 1/17 |
| When text is short | 2/17 |
| When creativity is necessary | 1/17 |

**Appendix F: When would you choose speech technologies to translate?**

| Reason | Frequency |
|---|---|
| To translate long texts (paragraphs, articles) | 6/17 |
| I would use it anytime if the speech recognition quality is good | 4/17 |
| I would only use it to dictate long texts where post-editing is too much effort | 1/17 |
| To translate quickly | 1/17 |

# Automatic Translation for Software with Safe Velocity


**Dag Schmidtke**
Microsoft E+D Global, Ireland
dags@microsoft.com

**Declan Groves**
Microsoft E+D Global, Ireland
dgroves@microsoft.com



## Abstract

We report on a model for machine translation (MT) of software, without review, for the Microsoft Office product range. We have deployed an automated localisation workflow, known as Automated Translation (AT) for software, which identifies resource strings as suitable and safe for MT without post-editing. The model makes use of string profiling, user impact assessment, MT quality estimation, and customer feedback mechanisms. This allows us to introduce automatic translation at a safe velocity, with a minimal risk to customer satisfaction. Quality constraints limit the volume of MT in relation to human translation, with published low-quality MT limited to not exceed 10% of total word count. The AT for software model has been deployed into production for most of the Office product range, for 37 languages. It allows us to MT and publish without review over 20% of the word count for some languages and products. To date, we have processed more than 1 million words with this model, and so far have not seen any measurable negative impact on customer satisfaction.


## 1   Introduction

The use of machine translation (MT) for localisation in Microsoft started in the late 1990s. We have two main use-cases: post-editing, and raw-MT publishing (publishing MT directly without review).

Initially raw-MT publishing, in combination with use of translation memories (a process referred to internally as 'recycling'), was limited to help content for technical audiences, but over the past five years it has become the dominant localisation model for both technical and end-user support documentation for Office. We now consider it proven for all support content types. Our content localisation workflow makes extensive use of customer listening and feedback systems, and recycling, to profile and balance the use of MT versus human translation optimally, while minimising impact on customer satisfaction (Schmidtke, 2016). More than 75% of all translation volume for Office content is now routed through a recycling and MT workflow (a process which we refer to internally as 'AT' or 'Automatic Translation'), for up to 36 languages.

For software localisation, the translation of strings in the product UI, we have been using post-editing since 2012. The introduction of raw-MT into the software localisation process has however proven to be more complex than it was for content. The risks are greater, both with respect to potentially causing functional bugs in the product, and with respect to low quality translations negatively impacting the customer experience. This could, in the worst-case, lead to the loss of customers (Poor, 2018).

In this paper we describe the system we developed to introduce raw MT publishing into the software localisation process for Office. The overall goal is to find the right balance between cost efficiency and quality of localisation, i.e. to maximise the amount of MT, while minimising negative impact on the user experience and customer satisfaction.

## 2 The Microsoft Office Software Localisation System

Microsoft Office spans a number of products ranging from Office 365 Subscription, with Word, Excel, PowerPoint, Outlook, etc., to server products like SharePoint, the Skype/Teams family, and a variety of other apps. There are about 50 separate products and services, released across a number of platforms, including Win32/64, Mac/IOS, web and Android. Office 365 Subscription ships monthly, some products have more frequent releases.

The Office international team is responsible for localising the Office products into over 100 languages and maintaining a continuous release cadence on par with the English language product. To accomplish this, we rely on an internal tools solution called Office Resource Fabric (ORF), which includes resource management (a resource here being any piece of text that is to be localised), localisation workflow, translation editor, and product build capabilities. The system supports large-scale continuous flow translation with validation functionality. ORF is an Azure-hosted solution which supports direct extranet connectivity for translators worldwide.

We use a proprietary recycling component, which supports traditional TM as well as contextual match capabilities. Contextual matches make use of metadata relating to resource, project and product information. This recycling component handles intricacies of different file formats, internal mark-up and placeholders, and it is also the integration point for MT. We have dedicated pre- and post-processing for software resources, and configurable support for calling Microsoft's Custom Translator[1] domain-tuned neural MT models, trained on TM data specific to Office.

We deal with large volumes on a continual basis, on average approx. 2 million fully paid for words are translated across all languages per month. Total word counts processed and recycled are substantially higher; about 2 million resources are processed per month. The typical human translation turnaround time is 48 hours.

## 3 AT for Software Model - Safe Velocity

The principal challenge in integrating a raw-MT workflow into the Office software localisation system is how we maintain **safe velocity**, that is how we apply MT optimally with minimal negative impact on customer experience and satisfaction (CSAT).

As we strive to increase the volume of MT, some machine translated strings will invariably be of lower quality. Additionally, for all the strings we translate, some will be more important and visible to the users than others and therefore will have a higher negative business impact if mistranslated. As we increase the use of MT, we need to minimise the intersection between low quality MT and high business impact strings, as this poses the greatest risk for negative CSAT impact (Figure 1).

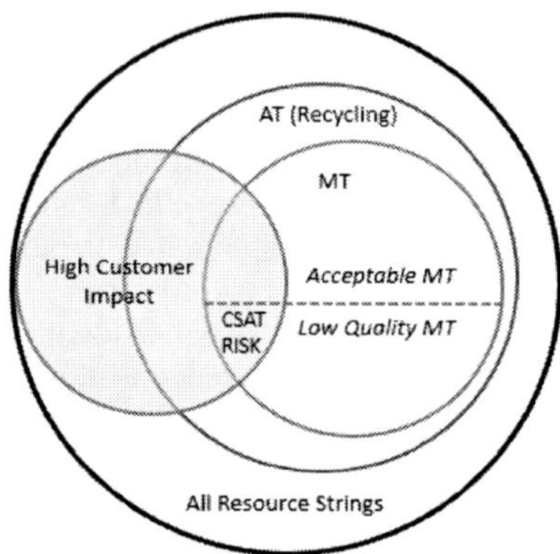


*Figure 1: Safe velocity model for AT for software*

The safe velocity approach we have adopted breaks down into three components: **Confidence in Translation Quality**: configuring the model to maximise the use of high quality TMs and apply MT to strings that are likely to translate well; **Business Impact**: how visible and impactful the string would be to the user, and therefore an indication of the impact of a poorly localised string; and **Listening and Response**: our ability to reliably and quickly detect, gather and respond to user feedback in relation to the customer experience of the localised product.

We applied lessons from our previous MT work to create a configurable model drawing on the strengths of Microsoft and Office localisation and product development. These include well-written source text; a good localisation infrastructure; large high-quality TM databases and state of the art customisable neural MT; and finally, good business intelligence, listening and customer feedback mechanisms. This has allowed us to manage the primary challenges with using MT, namely the significant and unpredictable variability of MT

---

[1] https://www.microsoft.com/en-us/translator/

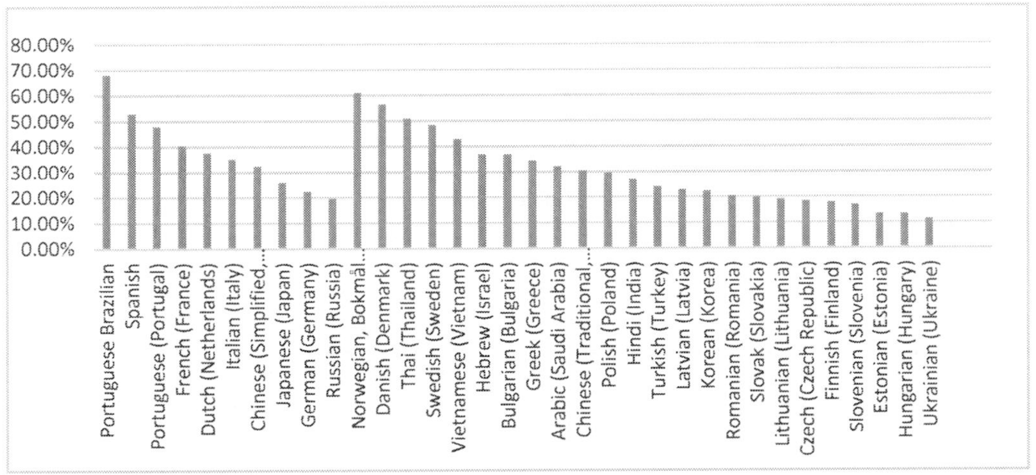

*Figure 2: The % of acceptable MT (<=0.3 TER) based on post-editing for Office software strings, 2015-2018*

quality, both between languages, and between different strings within the same language.

### 3.1 Confidence in Quality

For content localisation, lower MT quality in a specific language can be offset against increased reliance on recycling at an article level (Schmidtke, 2016). We cannot however directly balance recycling and MT within a single software resource string.

The translation unit for software is a resource string, and most of these are short (less than 5 words in length). However, we can use string length to inform raw-MT application.

While most resource strings are short, most word count volume is concentrated in longer strings. For example, restricting raw-MT application to resource strings 10 words or longer leaves about 60% of word count in scope for raw-MT while short strings, which are more prevalent in ribbons, menus and dialogs (i.e. more visible), remain human translated. Also, in line with other work on the use of MT in commercial settings, we have found that MT quality declines for very short strings (Levin et al., 2017). We have good data on MT quality by language, as we have large volumes of post-edited Office software strings and can calculate average TER scores per language (Snover et al., 2006). We have found that these scores correlate well with human judgements of MT acceptability, so we use TER as our primary automated MT eval metric. Our historical TER data when analysing post-edit triples (triples comprise the source, MT and post-edited resource) is shown in Figure 2.

This data allows us to assess the impact MT will have on perceived language quality by our customers. For some languages, like Brazilian-Portuguese, the quality of MT is quite high, whereas for others, the quality is more challenging. We therefore need to tailor our MT model on a per-language basis.

Our main focus for quality management to date has been to build and deploy custom neural models with Microsoft Custom Translator, which have given us a notable lift in translation quality over SMT, and also to deploy Quality Estimation, as further described in section 4 below.

### 3.2 Business Impact

For content articles, we have used page view statistics to identify where human translation should be prioritised. For software, resource usage statistics would be very valuable, but unfortunately this data is only available to a limited extent. We have, however, used resource loading statistics to confirm our intuition that shorter strings do get loaded, and therefore seen, more often. This is another reason why managing raw-MT scope by string length is helpful.

In addition, we use specific filters (known as AT exclusion rules) to remove known identifiable high business impact (HBI) strings from MT scope. These are strings where a low-quality translation would have a significant negative user impact, such as strings pertaining to important legal and licensing information. We also exclude marketing strings such as 'What's New' that typically require transcreation, adaptation, or more idiomatic rather than literal translation. We can filter out individual strings, specific resource files or larger projects with high proportions of HBI strings.

### 3.3 Customer Feedback

The risk introduced by shipping low quality MT can be mitigated by paying careful attention to customer feedback. Users ultimately provide the most important measure of localisation quality and success of the localisation effort. If we can detect and respond to customer feedback quickly, we can minimise the negative impact of a bad translation.

We use two primary feedback mechanisms to measure the impact of MT and user perceptions of linguistic quality in general. The first is a Microsoft-specific language quality metric called Net Language Quality Score (NLQS), similar to Net Promotor Score (NPS), which allows us to track overall language quality satisfaction. The second is customer verbatim feedback, that is the ability of customers to report on specific issues, through different mechanisms such as 'Send a Smile'[2].

An ideal scenario for customer feedback is if we could get feedback early enough, and of sufficient volume, so that we can reliably measure the actual user impact of MT and also address any issues before reaching a large audience. If users also provide suggestions for improvement, validated by a user community, we come close to a self-regulating system. Preferably users should also be able to comment and suggest improvements to translations directly in the product user interface.

We have considered how we might be able to expand Office customer feedback mechanisms in this direction. This is however a hard challenge, especially given the broad range of products and platforms in Office, and we have only made limited progress in this area thus far.

## 4 Quality Estimation for MT

With the challenges of limited customer feedback mechanisms and the variable nature of MT quality, we need a reliable and automated way of ensuring that the MT that we do publish directly into the product does not fall below an agreed acceptable translation quality level. TER allows us to monitor MT quality after the fact for post-edited strings, but this information is not available to the model at runtime. Sentence-level quality estimation (QE), therefore, presents itself as an interesting solution.

QE has a long history in MT research (Ueffing and Ney, 2007, Specia et al., 2009, 2010, 2015; Callison-Burch et al., 2012; Luong et al., 2014;). More recently, there have been encouraging examples of successful use of QE in commercial scenarios (e.g. Martin et al, 2017, Astudillo et al., 2018). We began investigating QE in 2016, specifically for the AT for software use-case. For our particular scenario we are less interested in the discrete quality of the MT string but more so in the ability to use QE as a binary decision mechanism to determine whether an MT string is 'good enough' to be published without human review. In this way QE can act as a filter to help us manage the volume of acceptable vs low quality MT we choose to allow through the system by calibrating based on the precision of the model.

Despite recent advances in neural-based approaches to QE (Patel and M, 2016; Kim et al., 2017; Martins et al., 2017; Jhaveri et al., 2018), our QE implementation was based initially on the QuEst++ framework (Specia et al., 2015) which we have significantly augmented, including extending the feature set and developing a sophisticated pre-processing, training and deployment pipeline. Our automated pipeline includes data extraction, normalisation, feature extraction, data sampling, model training, tuning and publishing the model as a service in Azure. The choice of a feature-based approach provides us with the ability to efficiently scale to support many languages and to provide an efficient QE service that has negligible impact on our overall workflow efficiency.

For training our QE models, we used large volumes of historical post-edited MT. When selecting our training data, we ensure a balanced distribution of MT quality ranges (based on TER scores) in order to avoid overfitting, resulting in training sets of approx. 75k samples per language. We used cross-validation for parameter tuning and evaluated on a held-out test set of between 20-30K strings (depending on language). This held out test set contains a distribution of TER scores that reflect what we are likely to see in production for the language, thus giving us the most accurate prediction of the performance of the deployed models.

Our initial proof of concept work demonstrated that the QE models we built were able to predict TER scores, and hence which strings would have

---

[2] https://www.microsoft.com/en-us/microsoft-365/blog/2012/08/03/got-feedback-send-a-smile-or-a-frown/

acceptable MT, with a precision that exceeded the average TER acceptance rate in post-editing, for at least 5 languages. Based on these findings we continued scaling to more languages. QE also gives us substantially greater confidence in avoiding very low-quality MT strings (TER $>0.7$). A snapshot of area under the curve (AUC) and root mean square error (RMSE) results for 10 QE languages is provided in Table 1.

| Language | AUC | RMSE |
|---|---|---|
| Portuguese Brazilian | 0.6763 | 0.3031 |
| Spanish | 0.6659 | 0.2935 |
| Japanese | 0.7065 | 0.2774 |
| French | 0.6976 | 0.2825 |
| Dutch | 0.6984 | 0.2974 |
| German | 0.7116 | 0.2729 |
| Italian | 0.6931 | 0.3122 |
| Chinese (Simplified) | 0.7008 | 0.2997 |

*Table 1: AUC and RMSE scores for QE models, when TER of 0.3 is set as the decision boundary of acceptable vs unacceptable MT*

### 4.1 QE Model Calibration for Safe Velocity

We use QE within our AT for software workflow by choosing a QE pass threshold on a per-language basis, based on a balanced approach between the model's precision and throughput (the volume of words the QE model will pass) as calculated over the held-out evaluation set. Our goal, in line with our safe velocity approach, is to maximise the overall volume of raw MT that we publish, therefore we take into account a model 'error tolerance' when selecting the optimal QE threshold. We choose a value that will maximise the volume of acceptable MT the model will pass while also passing a certain percentage of low quality MT. This error tolerance is chosen by considering what percentage of translation errors we typically see with our human/post-edited translations based on historical linguistic reviews. Based on this analysis we have set 10%, on average, to be the volume of words of low-quality MT that we are comfortable with releasing, on a per language basis.

## 5 The AT for Software String Lifecycle

The AT for software workflow brings all the elements of our model together.

### 5.1 Translation Workflow

All new or updated strings first go through recycling and custom domain MT. A QE score is generated based on the QE model deployed and configured for the specific language and product.

Next, at the AT decision point, rules determine if the string translation fits the criteria to be published as AT:

1. Context match recycling
2. Long 100% match and no AT exclusion
3. Long 99% match and no AT exclusion
4. QE Pass & over length threshold & no AT exclusion

For long 100% and long 99% matches[3], recycled strings with a word count of 10 words or longer do not need a review for correctness in context. AT Exclusion is as described in Section 3.2. QE Pass means that the QE score is over the threshold calibrated as per Section 4.1. If the string passes the rule checks, it will be set to AT, and by-pass post-editing. It is still subject to validation, including placeholder and markup checks, and geopolitical sensitive string checks. See Figure 3 for a high-level overview of the workflow.

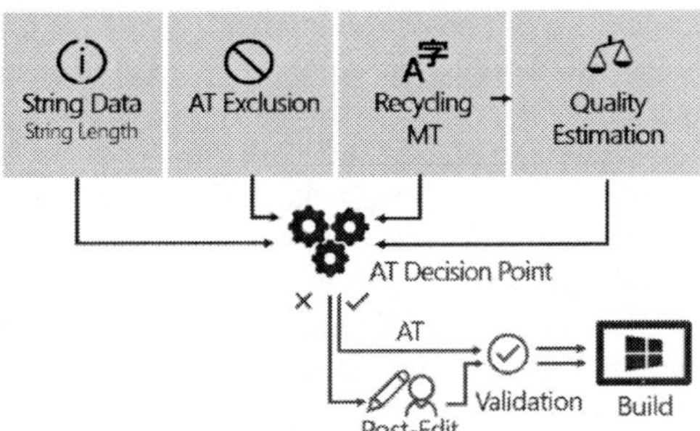


*Figure 3. ORF AT for Software decision point workflow*

### 5.2 User Validation and Feedback Channels

Office builds go through several stages of user validation. First are daily 'dogfood' builds, for Microsoft-internal staff. A second stage consists of insiders, users that are signed up to see new builds early. If builds pass insider stages, they progress to general release. For the main Office 365 product, this takes about a month. Feedback channels are open through these rings of validation, and any issues, functional or linguistic, can be reported.

Once the build is fully deployed to the general public, we monitor feedback channels via our

---

[3] 100% matches constitute perfect TM matches; 99% are matches that differ only in punctuation or capitalisation.

internal feedback classification system (Bentley and Batra, 2016), which also tracks feedback for international releases. In addition, we organise regular surveys to gather targeted linguistic quality feedback.

Through these mechanisms, we can detect and react to user reports on linguistic quality issues. However, such feedback remains rare in relation to the overall volume of customer feedback.

## 6 Results: AT for Software in Production

We enabled the AT for software workflow in May 2018, and we have now enabled 90% of the Office product line. Our workflow is highly configurable; we started out with conservative settings, to validate the model and feedback channels. The QE models have proven to be reliable, even as we have moved from statistical to neural MT. This is likely down to the general nature of our software strings which remain similar over time and that the output of our neural MT systems, although offering significant improvements for a number of languages (Hassan et al., 2018), are not so different from SMT as to impact the ability for QE to provide accurate predictions of translation quality.

We use word count volumes as a key measure of success in terms of business value. The translation volume in scope for MT in our system, when allowing for recycling, and taking length-based and AT exclusion into account, is in the order of 30-40% of total translation word count.

The volume of MT we ship without post-editing is regulated by QE. It varies between 10% and 30%, depending on the language. Table 2 shows data for selected languages from May 2019. In this table we show recycling, exclusion, MT volume (QE Pass), and QE fail, which is the portion not passed by QE, e.g. when the QE score does reach the calibrated threshold. The volume of MT varies between 27% for Brazilian and 9% for Russian. This reflects the variation in MT quality in line with our historical data as shown in Figure 1, and the calibration chosen for QE, to ensure low quality MT is kept to at, or, below 10%.

So far, we have received very few negative linguistic feedback comments related to the MT effort, and our overall customer satisfaction metrics have not been negatively impacted.

The total MT wordcount for May 2019 was over 250,000 words, across 37 languages enabled for AT for software, and so far we have machine translated and shipped over 1 million words with this model.

| Language | Recy-cling | AT Ex-clusion | Length ex-clusion | MT (QE pass) | QE fail |
|---|---|---|---|---|---|
| Portuguese Brazilian | 26% | 20% | 24% | 27% | 3% |
| Indonesian | 28% | 21% | 24% | 23% | 4% |
| Spanish | 28% | 21% | 24% | 20% | 7% |
| French | 24% | 21% | 27% | 18% | 10% |
| Ukrainian | 29% | 19% | 24% | 18% | 10% |
| Japanese | 26% | 22% | 25% | 15% | 12% |
| Chinese (Simplified) | 26% | 22% | 25% | 14% | 13% |
| German | 28% | 20% | 26% | 14% | 12% |
| Dutch | 27% | 22% | 25% | 14% | 12% |
| Russian | 27% | 22% | 26% | 9% | 16% |

*Table 2: Translation numbers for May 2019.*

## 7 Future Work

In terms of future work, we are planning to improve the QE component by moving to neural QE. Preliminary investigations have shown that neural QE models can lead to average AUC improvements of between 10-20%, relative depending on language. As the overall model matures and is proven in production, we plan to increase the MT scope, by adjusting length thresholds and also reviewing the percentage of low-quality MT allowed. We also hope to revisit and grow customer listening and feedback by leveraging advanced crowd engagement solutions. As Microsoft Custom Translator continues to improve, we expect to further increase raw-MT volumes.

Challenges remain in specific areas of translation, such as terminology and branding, but there has been some promising work recently in this area (Chatterjee et al., 2017; Hasler et al., 2018). We plan to investigate improved term translation solutions, including contextual disambiguation. Additionally, we are partnering with ADAPT[4] in relation to understanding MT impact on software usability via telemetry (Guerberof 2018).

### Acknowledgements

The AT for software model was developed by the Office GSX (Global Service Experience) team in the Microsoft European Development Centre, from 2017 to 2018. The following people were involved; Siobhan Ashton, Antonio Benítez Lopez, Brian Comerford, Gemma Devine, Vincent Gadani, Craig Jeffares, Sankar Kumar Indraganti, Anton Masalovich, David Moran, Glen Poor and Simone Van Bruggen, in addition to the authors.

---

[4] https://www.adaptcentre.ie

# References

Michael Bentley, and Soumya Batra. 2016. Giving Voice to Office Customers: Best Practices in How Office Handles Verbatim Text Feedback. In 2016 IEEE International Conference on Big Data (Big Data), pp. 3826-3832. IEEE, 2016.

Chris Callison-Burch, Philipp Koehn, Christof Monz, Matt Post, Radu Soricut, and Lucia Specia. 2012. Findings of the 2012 workshop on Statistical Machine Translation. In Proc. WMT 2012.

Rajen Chatterjee, Matteo Negri, Marco Turchi, Marcello Federico, Lucia Specia, and Frederic Blain. 2017. Guiding neural machine translation decoding with external knowledge. In Proceedings of the Second Conference on Machine Translation, Volume 1: Research Papers, pages 157–168, Copenhagen, Denmark. Association for Computational Linguistics.

Ana Guerberof, 2018, Correlations between localisation quality and usability on machine and human translated user interface strings: a study using eye-tracking and telemetry, poster presented at the 12th annual Irish Human Computer Interaction conference 2018, Limerick, Ireland.

Eva Hasler, Adrià De Gispert, Gonzalo Iglesias, and Bill Byrne. 2018. Neural Machine Translation Decoding with Terminology Constraints. 2018. In Proceedings of the 2018 Conference of the North American Chapter of the Association for Computational Linguistics: Human Language Technologies, Volume 2 (Short Papers), pages 506-512. New Orleans.

Hany Hassan, Anthony Aue, Chang Chen, Vishal Chowdhary, Jonathan Clark, Christian Federmann, Xuedong Huang, Marcin Junczys-Dowmunt, Will Lewis, Mu Li, Shujie Liu, Tie-Yan Liu, Renqian Luo, Arul Menezes, Tao Qin, Frank Seide, Xu Tan, Fei Tian, Lijun Wu, Shuangzhi Wu, Yingce Xia, Dongdong Zhang, Xhirui Zhang, and Ming Zhou. 2018. Achieving Human Parity on Automatic Chinese to English News Translation. *Computing Research Repository*, arXiv:1803.05567.

Nisarg Jhaveri, Manish Gupta, and Vasudeva Varman. 2018. Translation quality estimation for indian languages. In Proceedings of the 21st International Conference of the European Association for Machine Translation (EAMT), pages 159-168. Alicante, Spain.

Hyun Kim, Jong-Hyeok Lee, and Seung-Hoon Na. 2017. Predictor-estimator using multilevel task learning with stack propagation for neural quality estimation. In Proceedings of the Second Conference on Machine Translation (WMT), pages 562–568, September.

Pavel Levin, Nishikant Dhanuka, and Maxmim Khalilov. 2017. Machine Translation at Booking.com: Journey and Lessons Learned. In Proceedings of the 20th International Conference of the European Association for Machine Translation (EAMT), pages 80–85. Prague, Czech Republic.

Ngoc-Quang Luong, Laurent Besacier, and Benjamin Lecouteux. 2014. LIG system for word level QE task at WMT14. pages 335–341. Baltimore, USA.

André F.T. Martins, Marcin Junczys-Dowmunt, Fabio N. Kepler, Ramn Astudillo, Chris Hokamp, and Roman Grundkiewicz. 2017. Pushing the limits of translation quality estimation. Transactions of the Association for Computational Linguistics, 5:205–218.

Raj Nath Patel and Sasikumar M. 2016. Translation quality estimation using recurrent neural network. In Proceedings of the First Conference on Machine Translation (WMT), pages 819–824. Berlin, Germany.

Mirko Plitt, and F, Masselot. 2010. A Productivity Test of Statistical Machine Translation Post-Editing in a Typical Localisation Context. The Prague Bulletin of Mathematical Linguistics, 93:7–16.

Glen Poor. 2018. Use more Machine Translation and Keep Your Customers Happy. Commercial Keynote at AMTA 2018, Boston

Dag Schmidtke. 2016. Large scale Machine Translation publishing, with acceptable quality, for Microsoft Support content. Paper presented at AMTA 2016 Workshop on Interacting with Machine Translation (MT 2016). Austin.

Dag Schmidtke. 2018. MT Tresholding: Achieving a defined quality bar with a mix of human and machine translation. Paper presented at AMTA 2016 Users Track, Austin.

Matthew Snover, Bonnie Dorr, Richard Schwartz, Linea Micciulla, and John Makhoul. 2006. A study of translation edit rate with targeted human annotation. In Proceedings of AMTA, pages 223– 231, Boston, MA. Association for Machine Translation in the Americas.

Lucia Specia, Marco Turchi, Nicola Cancedda, Marc Dymetman and Nello Cristianini 2009. Estimatingthe Sentence-Level Quality of Machine Translation Systems. In Proceedings of the 13th Annual Conference of the EAMT, pages 28-35. Barcelona, May 2009

Lucia Specia, Dhwaj Raj, and Marco Turchi. 2010. Machine translation evaluation versus quality estimation. Machine Translation, 24(1):39–50.

Lucia Specia, Gustavo Paetzold, and Carolina Scarton. 2015. Multi-level Translation Quality Prediction with QuEst++. In Proc. ACL, pages 115–120. Beijing, China.

Nicola Ueffing and Hermann Ney. 2007. Word-Level Confidence Estimation for Machine Translation. Computational Linguistics, 33(1):9–40.

# Application of Post-Edited Machine Translation in Fashion eCommerce


**Kasia Kosmaczewska**
TranslateMedia
11 Carteret Street
SW1H 9DJ London, UK
<name>@translatemedia.com

**Matt Train**
TranslateMedia
11 Carteret Street
SW1H 9DJ London, UK
<name>@translatemedia.com



## Abstract

Machine translation (MT) and post-edited machine translation (PEMT) have traditionally been explored primarily in the context of legal and medical content types, where MT results are often easier to predict due to the heavily standardised language structure and unambiguous nature of terminology used. Each content type and domain presents its unique challenges to both MT systems and linguists performing the post-editing tasks. This paper describes how PEMT can be applied in the fashion eCommerce domain, taking a popular British fashion brand – Topshop – as an example. This paper aims to explore different aspects of delivering PEMT to a fashion eCommerce client, the most prominent being linguists' involvement in machine translation-related activities, including their key role in transitioning from human translation to statistical machine translation (SMT), and then from SMT to neural machine translation (NMT). The implications of switching from full human translation to PEMT for the end client and overall learnings made by the language service provider (LSP) during these transitions will be also discussed.


## 1 Introduction

With machine translation technology going through a period of intense development, the focus of the industry often shifts away from the human actors without which this technology would not have emerged in the first place.

Taking Topshop as an example, this paper aims to analyse the role of humans involved in the PEMT cycle, namely:

- the client who orders post-editing jobs;
- linguists who handle the post-editing;
- account managers and project managers who oversee the process on the LSP's side.

This is an attempt to describe the impact that the emergence of machine translation technology and related services such as PEMT has had on human actors in the localisation chain.

While machine translation has undisputedly allowed for more automation and increased time-efficiencies in a number of localisation scenarios, it is of utmost importance to evaluate how it has impacted the way fashion eCommerce clients, linguists and LSPs work, in order to be able to continue leveraging this technology adequately in the future.

## 2 Specific challenges of translating for fashion eCommerce

Providing translations for any domain has its own specific challenges that need to be effectively addressed.

Fashion eCommerce is of growing importance to the global economy as fashion retailers have been quick in grasping the opportunity to grow their businesses internationally, increasingly via online channels.

In 2012, overseas sales accounted for over 13% of total UK online sales. It is predicted that online sales from outside the UK will rise dramatically from circa £4bn generated in 2012 to an estimated

£28bn by 2020, accounting for around 40% of total online sales revenue.[1]

When going global, fashion retailers often opt for localising their content, and this decision is supported by research by Common Sense Advisory showing that consumers prefer to buy in their own language (Sargent, 2014). One of the most prominent challenges that linguists and LSPs are presented with when working for fashion eCommerce clients is correctly and accurately predicting what would appeal to the target audience in the target market in terms of the tone of voice, vocabulary and the general feel of the target language copy, in a way that satisfies the brand managers in each target location.

Meeting these specific challenges can often mean the difference between the client making its international trading programme a success or a failure. If the target consumer identifies with the way that they are being addressed by a foreign fashion retailer in their native language, then they will be more likely to purchase goods produced by this retailer. On the other hand, if the consumer finds the style and tone of communication in their target language inadequate, it can damage the brand's image in the target market and result in the brand becoming unsuccessful in that location.

When transitioning the service provided to Topshop from full human translation to PEMT, it was of paramount importance not to lose that focus and for the switch between services not to have any detrimental effect on the tone of voice of the localised content.

## 3 Client profile

Topshop is a global fashion retailer with over 500 shops in 58 countries and, at the time of writing, a considerable eCommerce presence. Topshop has been continuously proactive in communicating with its global consumers using highly targeted, localised content since taking its eCommerce website international in 2011.

Given the international nature of the business, the brand has extensive localisation needs. To address these needs, the LSP has worked with Topshop since 2011, providing translations of brand messages, features, articles, blog posts and product descriptions. The high quality of the translations is of significant importance given that vast majority of these serve to communicate directly with consumers and therefore shape the brand perception in their minds.

### 3.1 Topshop product descriptions

Topshop's largest requirement in terms of volume is localisation of product descriptions published on the transactional eCommerce website www.topshop.com. With dozens of new products being added to Topshop's website on a daily basis and hundreds of others regularly requiring updates with new specifications, prompt turnaround times have been an important aspect of the localisation cycle for the client.

Apart from needing to put products online as soon as possible, Topshop had a particular yet not unique concern that publishing products on different language websites at different times would disappoint customers. If products become available on the UK website first, customers from other countries are likely to enquire why the same goods are not available on the local version of the site or order goods to be shipped from the UK to their country, which creates operational issues for the retailer and puts a strain on its customer service teams.

To respond to that urgency, since the beginning of the collaboration, Topshop has been using a custom-built integration between their eCommerce platform and the LSP's translation management system to send all products requiring translation automatically, without the client having to manually flag any new items for translation or press a button to make new and updated product descriptions available to the LSP for translation.

Each product description contains between 20 and 100 words and each one of them follows the same structure – it begins with a product name, which is no more than 100 characters long, followed by a long description. The long description comprises of a specification of the product, including washing or handling instructions and garment material composition.

Each batch of product descriptions, containing between 40 and 100 items on average, is turned around and sent back to the client's system within 24 hours so that it can be promptly published on international sites. At the time of writing, this amounts to 1,332 words on average per day, including weekends.

---

[1] https://www.statista.com/statistics/284559/e-commerce-sales-of-retailers-in-the-united-kingdom-by-foreign-and-domestic/

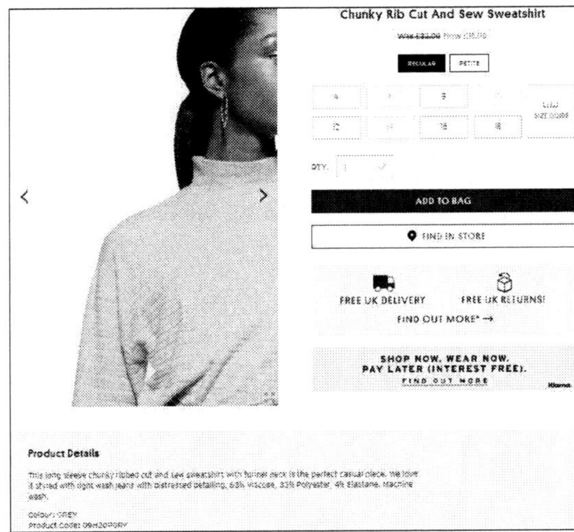

Figure 1. An example of a Topshop product description in English[2]

## 4   Switch from full human translation to post-edited machine translation

Five years after Topshop started collaborating with the LSP, it became apparent that the translation memories had grown to over 2m words and the translation memory savings slowly started to plateau.

Due to the nature of the content – well-structured, often repetitive product descriptions – and the language combination in question (English into German), switching the service provided from human translation to post-edited machine translation seemed the optimal way forward to further improve turnaround times, keep the current quality and consistency of the translations and also allow for cost efficiencies on the client's side.

In 2016, the LSP decided to appoint an external machine translation provider to support Topshop's needs. That provider built a custom statistical MT engine based on Moses using publicly available generic data as a baseline and supplementing it with Topshop's translation memory and term bases. The translation memory used to train the first iteration of the model contained approximately 204,641 translation units.[3]

It was important for the LSP to maintain the positive working relationship with linguists who had been working on Topshop translations over the years. Therefore, the LSP made sure the linguists played a key part in transitioning to PEMT

by involving them in planning, testing, and regular group video conferences to discuss the project.

In the human translation workflow, there were two linguists involved – one translator and one reviser. The LSP wanted to retain the same number of linguists in the PEMT workflow, with the change that the first linguist would act as a post-editor while the second continued as a reviser. This workflow was chosen in order to ensure high quality and consistency of the target language copy, especially in the period when post-editors were still learning how to perform post-editing tasks and finding the right balance between under- and over-editing. Another reason for keeping two linguists in the process was to continue providing a regular stream of jobs for all the linguists who have been involved with Topshop rather than reducing the number of jobs available to each linguist. This was a way for the LSP to show their recognition of the efforts that the linguists have invested in working with Topshop over the years.

In the initial stages of working with statistical MT engine, the LSP had a core team of four post-editors and one reviser working on the post-editing jobs.

Prior to the change, the LSP's internal Topshop team, comprising of an account manager and two project managers, was trained on machine translation technology so that they were able to better assist linguists with any questions and feedback that could arise in relation to post-editing after the go-live date.

### 4.1   Post-editing with statistical machine translation

During the first phase of implementing PEMT on Topshop product descriptions, which lasted approximately 2 years, the crucial part of the transition was training all involved linguists on how to perform post-editing, including becoming sensitive to the type of errors specific to machine translation systems (Daems, Vandepitte, Hartsuiker and Macken, 2017) and how to address them effectively.

This meant a significant change in the way linguists were used to work for this client (Doherty, 2016). It also meant that they needed to acquire a new set of skills since post-editing presented them with different challenges in comparison to standard translation.

---

[2] https://www.topshop.com/en/tsuk/product/clothing-427/hoodies-sweats-6864676/chunky-rib-cut-and-sew-sweatshirt-8274864

[3] Since the paper is being written retrospectively and the LSP did not record the exact number of translation units when the initial training was done, the data provided is an approximation.

Since the post-editing effort is directly related to the quality of the machine translation output (Germann, Koehn, 2014), the SMT engine in question was re-trained on a monthly basis with corrections made by linguists during the post-editing stage in order to make sure the quality was improving over time.

The post-editing distance was measured by the external MT provider using the Levenshtein algorithm. Levenshtein distance calculates the minimum number of character edits that are necessary to transform one string into another string (Levenshtein, 1966).[4]

Apart from re-training the statistical engine, in order to reduce the post-editing effort, post-editing rules were also used to automate repetitive post-edits. To create and implement these rules, regular qualitative feedback was provided by the post-editors, who were asked to report on recurring issues that were not resolved by the monthly re-training of the engine.

Throughout the collaboration, Topshop has specified a number of brand rules and requirements that govern the target language copy in German, in the form of a German language style guide. An example of this specific requirement is using proper case in the line name in the German translation, even though it is often fully capitalised in the source. A real-life example of a segment pair demonstrating this requirement can be found below:

Source: **MATERNITY** Premium White Mom Shorts
Target: **Weiße Premium Mom **Umstandsshorts**

This output was achieved through post-editing rules when the LSP was using statistical machine translation.

### 4.2 Post-editing with neural machine translation

In early 2018, due to the increasing reliability of neural machine translation systems (Srivastava, Shukla, Tiwari, 2018) as well as the increased quality that they are able to return when compared to SMT systems (Volkart, Bouillon, Girletti, 2018), the LSP decided to retire the SMT solution in favour of an NMT system.

The LSP selected an external provider that offers a scalable adaptive neural MT solution. In this provider's approach, the MT output is produced using baseline models trained on generic data but is also adapted in real time to any similar content stored not only in the existing client-specific translation memory but also any similar translation memories. This approach eliminates the need to train one custom engine for each client or domain, which is very appealing to the LSP in terms of scalability.

This means that MT models are much more agile and flexible – the MT output is adapted to each client's specific style, tone of voice and terminology on the fly. Corrections made by post-editors are sent back to the model upon completion of each job, which eliminates the need for any manual re-training of the model.

At that point in time, the Topshop translation memory contained 282,332 translation units.

The decision to switch from SMT to NMT was made following a period of trials and assessments aiming at verifying whether NMT was going to be a sustainable solution to handle eCommerce fashion content effectively. Comparing results produced by SMT and NMT systems for the same source text is a common evaluation method (Calixto et al., 2017; Castilho et al., 2017). The LSP asked two Topshop post-editors to compare 242 strings translated with the existing SMT engine and the new NMT engine. Each source string was 7 words long on average or 40 characters on average, including spaces. The test set was representative of the live work in terms of content type.

Although each linguist's opinion on individual strings did not always converge, overall both linguists agreed that the new NMT model returned better results than the old SMT model.

In the test, 93 (38%) segments didn't need to be edited when the NMT model was used while only 33 (14%) segments didn't need to be edited when the SMT model was used. These results provided a clear indication for the LSP that NMT was more adequate for the given content type and language combination confirmed that it was time to move onto NMT.

Comparing the output from statistical and neural machine translation engines meant that linguists needed to develop a new set of skills. One of those was sensitivity to machine translation errors which were previously unknown to them, both when they used to provide traditional translation for Topshop and when they did post-editing with SMT engines.

Furthermore, the need for creating post-editing rules significantly decreased when using NMT and the need for monthly engine re-training disappeared completely. As expected, in practice, the

---

<sup>4</sup> http://www.levenshtein.net/

adaptive neural machine translation framework proved considerably more receptive to corrections made by post-editors, learning immediately from the post-edits, leading to an increase in the number of words being post-edited per hour.

This in turn, also meant that linguists did not need to report on recurring translation errors in the machine translation output as frequently as they did when they worked with SMT. This, as well as the quality of the machine translation improving over time, allowed the amount of time linguists spend on handling Topshop jobs to decrease.

Linguists reported a slight drop in the accuracy of terminology when switching to NMT, however this was conveyed as qualitative feedback and not measured in objective terms. The post-editing effort measurements did not converge with linguists' qualitative feedback in this respect.

### 4.3 Measuring effort involved in post-editing

Using similar methods to what is described by Federico, Cattelan and Trombetti (2012), since the very beginning of delivering PEMT to Topshop, the LSP has been recording two indicators of the post-editing effort:

- Post-editing speed – the number of words that the linguist is able to review and edit in an hour;
- Post-editing distance – a percentage value indicating the extent to which the raw machine translation output needed to be edited by the post-editor in order to arrive at the desired quality level.

When working with SMT, the post-editing distance was measured by the MT provider. After the switch to NMT, measuring the post-editing effort, including the implementation of the algorithm to calculate the effort, was passed onto the LSP.

Since the first external MT provider the LSP worked with used the Levenshtein distance, this method has also been followed when the LSP started using NMT. In this way, the LSP aimed to ensure that productivity results from before and after the switch could be correctly compared. This measure is mostly being used to unveil trends rather than meant to be absolutely accurate.

To convert the Levenshtein distance into a percentage value, the LSP uses the following formula:

$$(1 - Lev(a,b) / Max(|a|, |b|)) * 100$$

Data based on these two indicators – post-editing distance and post-editing speed – has been continuously accompanied with qualitative feedback from the linguists. The feedback has been collected in a number of ways, for example as a list of recurring issues in an online spreadsheet, emails, and also during conference calls between the LSP team and linguists. The subjective feedback covers all aspects of post-editing, including the perceived quality of the machine translation output, the perceived effort invested in post-editing as well as any recurring errors and terminology problems.

#### 4.3.1 Post-editing effort with neural machine translation

While the post-editing distance averaged at close to 38%[5] when linguists worked with the SMT framework, after the switch to the NMT framework, the post-editing distanced dropped dramatically with almost immediate effect to 25% on average. 21.15% is currently the lowest average post-editing distance that has been recorded during a one month period.

Occasionally, particularly in jobs with low word count, the post-editing distance drops below 10%, which had never been reached with SMT on Topshop content.

While the number of words post-edited per hour averaged at 787 with SMT, it rose to 1,000 words and above with NMT.

## 5 Overall impact

Topshop was one of the LSP's first fashion eCommerce clients to have content localised using PEMT. Not all aspects of the impact of PEMT on Topshop's product descriptions can be objectively or numerically measured[6]. For instance, whether there has been any emotional change towards working on Topshop on linguists' side or client's satisfaction with the post-edited machine translation in comparison to full human translation. Nevertheless, the impact of PEMT has been observed from three different perspectives – the linguists' perspective, the LSP's internal perspective and the end client's perspective.

---

[5] All values in this section have been obtained using the Levenshtein algorithm.
[6] Although they can be measured in qualitative terms by asking linguists, the client and project managers involved to provide an account of their perceived experience with PEMT.

## 5.1 Linguists

The team of linguists working on Topshop translations from English into German has not changed significantly since the LSP first started to work with the brand.

This means that the team who had been immersed in the brand tone of voice and all unique requirements at the beginning of cooperation and who used that knowledge when doing full human translation was also able to apply the same knowledge to post-editing machine translation. Skeptical towards machine translation at first, German Topshop linguists were determined to continue providing high quality translations to the end client, regardless of the service through which those are delivered.

After the migration from SMT to NMT, the team of linguists working on Topshop shrank from 4 to 3 post-editors and 1 reviser. This was due to one of the post-editors ending her career as a freelancer.

Migrating to PEMT allowed linguists to acquire new skills and knowledge. They were thoroughly trained on how to effectively work with first SMT and then NMT technology; the knowledge and skills gained are easily transferable to other clients that those linguists work with.

Although there are differences in the post-editing speed of individual linguists, overall all linguists involved in the project work faster when post-editing than when translating, meaning they are now able to complete Topshop assignments quicker than they were able to translate then when they first started working for the brand.

Even though some linguists were rather resistant to the idea of PEMT at the start, their dedication to the brand that they had worked on for several years helped them to eventually overcome the initial reservations.

## 5.2 LSP's internal team

Applying PEMT to Topshop's product descriptions was an important opportunity for the LSP to verify whether this service can be relevant to fashion eCommerce content in a real-life scenario. In that sense, the success[7] of the project has led the LSP to offer this service to a number of other fashion eCommerce clients, including some well-known high street clothing brands.

The Topshop example has given project managers and account managers confidence in handling PEMT projects. Similar to linguists, the internal team learnt what to expect from the raw machine translation in the context of fashion eCommerce content and now understand its benefits as well as its limitations.

One of the most prominent learnings on the part of project managers was adequately assisting linguists with the post-editing task through detailed briefings, done in writing and on conference calls. This also included guiding those linguists who were more resistant to idea of post-editing than others as well as finding optimal ways of handling supporting tasks such as gathering linguist feedback.

## 5.3 End client

As a result of switching from full human translation to PEMT, the client has been able to enjoy the same quality of the target language copy at a reduced cost.

Since the quality and consistency of the translations have been maintained, the change in service has had no adverse effect on the brand perception in the target market.

Furthermore, it was an opportunity for Topshop employees responsible for ordering translations to also become familiar with MT technology.

At the time of writing, the Topshop translation memory contained 350,776 translation units and continues to grow.

## 6 Conclusions

This paper aims to demonstrate that PEMT is a viable service option for eCommerce fashion content intended for the German market.

It has transpired that the success of delivering PEMT to Topshop largely depended on ensuring that linguists were well informed and engaged at all stages of the project – that they understood the task well, could rely on project managers to guide them when they had doubts or questions regarding MT, and had a streamlined way of providing feedback. The mutual understanding and good flow of communication have made it possible to efficiently address any issues that arose on the client's or linguists' side in relation to PEMT.

It appears that PEMT can indeed work well for fashion eCommerce content such as product descriptions. Since this service allows for faster turnaround times, while also being available at a lower price point than traditional translation, it opens new localisation opportunities for retailers.

---

[7] Defined by client satisfaction and linguist productivity; the latter being directly related to machine translation quality.

## References

Calixto, Iacer, Daniel Stein, Evgeny Matusov, Sheila Castilho, Andy Way, 2017. *Human Evaluation of Multi-modal Neural Machine Translation: a Case Study on E-commerce Listing Tiles*. Proceedings of the 6th Workshop on Vision and Language. Valencia, Spain, 31-37.

Castilho, Sheila, Joss Moorkens, Federico Gaspari, Rico Sennrich, Vilelmini Sosoni, Yota Georgakopoulou, Pintu Lohar, Andy Way, Antonio Valerio, Barone Miceli Barone, Maria Gialama, 2017. *A Comparative Quality Evaluation of PBSMT and NMT using Professional Translators.* Proceedings of MT Summit XVI, vol.1: Research Track.

Daems, Joke, Sonia Vandepitte, Robert J. Hartsuiker and Lieve Macken. 2017. *Identifying the Machine Translation Error Types with the Greatest Impact on Post-editing Effort*. Frontiers in Psychology.

Doherty, Stephen. 2016. *The Impact of Translation Technologies on the Process and Product of Translation.* International Journal of Communication 10 (2016), University of South New Wales, Australia, 954.

Federico, Marcello, Alessandro Cattelan and Marco Trombetti. 2012. *Measuring User Productivity in Machine Translation Enhanced Computer Assisted Translation.* MateCat Publications, 3.

Germann, Ulrich, and Phillip Koehn. 2014. *The Impact of Machine Translation Quality on Human Post-editing*. Workshop on Humans and Computer-assisted Translation, Gothenburg, Sweden, 38–46.

Levenshtein, Vladimir I. 1965. *Binary codes capable of correcting deletions, insertions, and reversals.* Soviet Physics Doklady 10(8), 707–710.

Sargent, Benjamin B. 2014. *Ten Tricks for Improving Global CX.* Common Sense Advisory, Inc. Cambridge, Massachusetts, United States of America, 1-3.

Srivastava, Siddhant, Anupam Shukla, Ritu Tiwari. 2018. *Machine Translation: From Statistical to Modern Deep-learning Practices*. Computing Research Repository, vol. 1812.04238.

Volkart, Lise, Pierrette Bouillon, Sabrina Girletti. 2018. *Statistical vs. Neural Machine Translation: A Comparison of MTH and DeepL at Swiss Post's Language.* Proceedings of the 40th Conference Translating and the Computer. London, United-Kingdom.

# Morphological Neural Pre- and Post-Processing
# for Slavic Languages


**Giorgio Bernardinello**
STAR Group
Wiesholz 35, CH-8262 Ramsen
Switzerland
`giorgio.bernardinello@star-group.net`



## Abstract

While developing NMT systems for our customers involving Slavic languages, we encountered certain issues that do not affect Latin or Germanic languages. The most striking of these is the morphological complexity inherent in a remarkable number of unique synthetic forms. For each language combination, the aim is always to find the best balance between the size of the vocabulary, the quality of the translation and the performance of the MT model (both training time and translation time). When working with Slavic idioms, the variety of cases and genders makes this challenge even more difficult and engaging. For Slavic source languages, our solution is to add an extra pre-processing step before the actual translation, in which the inflected word is reduced to its components; naturally, in the opposite direction this requires a symmetrical post-processing technique. Tests have proven high-quality results for Slavic languages, either source or target, confirming this as an effective approach.


## 1 Challenge

Slavic languages are characterised by an articulated inflectional structure; i.e. cases (synthetic form) are generally used instead of prepositions (analytic form) to express complements.[1] As an example, the Czech table of a regular adjective inflection is made up of 56

---



[1] Modern Bulgarian and Macedonian are an exception to this rule; noun declension in these languages is actually disappearing.

cells: 7 cases, 4 genders, 2 numbers. Luckily, because many of them are the same, there are "only" 11 unique variants.

These forms are not as frequent in a corpus: some of them may be used ten times less than others, and this can obviously cause the engine to inconsistently translate what appears to be the same word.

As you can see in Table 1, there are many more Czech forms than English ones, and our engine must be able to handle all of them. What makes this task even more difficult is that the customer's training material is often extremely repetitive, with similar forms repeated many times and others just a few.

| To je *pěkná* **kniha**. | This is a *nice* **book**. |
|---|---|
| To jsou *pěkné* **knihy**. | These are *nice* **books**. |
| Viděl jsem tě s *pěknou* **knihou**. | I have seen you with a *nice* **book**. |

Table 1. Sample of Czech inflections of adjectives and substantives.

## 2 Aim

When working with standard tokenization, the initial basic conditions required to achieve good MT translations are quality and the amount of training data. There are two typical scenarios:

- Huge, well-formed corpora that need more extensive technical resources for training (GPU, memory, RAM, etc.)
- Smaller data sets, from which it is often not easy to obtain high-quality results

In both cases, we can improve the process by tweaking the tokenization in a way that allows for intelligent handling of inflections. This can lead to better structuring of the engine's vocabulary, resulting in a win-win situation: instead of filling it with many variants of the same word, it can be made smaller and more efficient without sacrificing quality, or it may contain more terms from different contexts without increasing its size. In simple terms, we could obtain substantial benefits if we could separate stems from affixes.

Another important consideration is that our scenario involves final users with little or no knowledge of one of the languages; in this context, reducing Out Of Vocabulary (OOV) words would be a significant goal.

## 3  A solution between standard tokenization and BPE

With this in mind, we need a tokenizer that works not only on word boundaries, but also in terms of the morphological construction of the token. In this respect, the BPE (Byte-Pair-Encoding) algorithm (Sennrich et al., 2016) may be a valid option, but it is based on the most common sequences of characters and thus it cannot always split words in the way a human would. It is certainly practical in the absence of further grammatical information, but it has already been proven (Ataman et al., 2017) that considering morphological aspects while tokenizing results in higher translation quality.

While observing the inflections in languages such as Czech or Polish, we noticed that the ending may vary depending on the final part of the stem, which means it would be too difficult to manually split the text using a complete list of endings. In addition to this, some of them would be too rare to be learned well by the engine. We therefore supposed that, since a native speaker can implicitly distinguish stems and inflections, a neural model (from now on referred to as a Morpho Model) could be trained to do the same; that is, identify the sequence of letters that can influence the ending and split the word into stem and affix before sending anything to the translation engine. The output tokens from this pre-processing model are the ones that the final translation engine will learn.

This approach differs from pure character-based neural machine translation in that the Morpho Model only needs to parse single complete words rather than translate whole sentences.

Of course, this model is only the core of this pre-processing technology, and can only produce high-quality results as part of a series of steps that guarantee clean input and output data. For example we noticed in the very first phase of tests that irregular forms had to be recognized and handled separately; in fact they represent a relatively small amount of widely used lemmas, with inflections which are hard to be learnt in a general abstract way.

The attempt to find a valid solution that was different from BPE came from the need to have a sort of control over the translation. With the integration of the Morpho Model, as described in the following chapters, we can minimize the risk of unexpected phaenomena, like sub-sets of words considered sequences to be inflected. For our user case it is extremely important to have an output that fulfils the customer's needs regarding not only the general quality of the translation, but also the usage/avoidance of certain forms: therefore we chose to invest resources in a system we can control under almost any aspect.

## 4  Description of the method

In order to successfully implement this process, it is essential to have a map with a sufficient number of examples and a good description of many morphological categories (for example, it would not be enough to know only the gender of a noun, without its case, number, etc.).

The databases we used to create the maps are free online resources. To have an idea of how big the maps are that we used, we can say that our Russian map has more than two million entries, while the Polish one has more than five million. A reduction of the map's size may be possible by comparing words in the training material for the final NMT engine with the contents of the map. Nevertheless, even words which are not contained in the customer's dictionary may help build a more consistent Morpho Model; in fact it should be trained to build up inflections with their letters, regardless of their meaning or occurrences.

Since we are working with Slavic languages as either the source or the target, the Morpho Model is used in both directions; that is to say, from an inflected word to its corresponding morphological information as well as in the opposite direction. To obtain the expected benefits for the engine's vocabulary, we need to train it using a corpus where all inflections have been reduced. However, we also want to be able to parse the engine's output back to a human-readable language, so the reduction needs to be mapped towards a real word.

Although the two directions have the same logic (from opposite perspectives), they may present distinct challenges during the translation process, once the engine has been trained.

### 4.1 Slavic source language

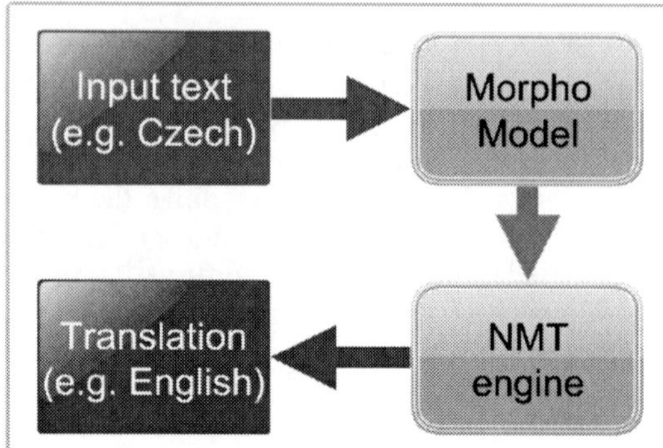


Figure 1. Overview of the process when the Slavic language is the source.

When translating from a Slavic language, the Morpho Model must parse an inflected word into its grammatical information so that the engine has everything it needs to translate properly. Figure 1 shows how the whole workflow should operate; when moving from one step to the next, further text handling may be needed, such as tokenizing or checking the format.

Since the same inflection can be mapped with many definitions (see Table 2), we must ensure that the Morpho Model produces output that can be used by the engine to guarantee a high-quality result; an even more difficult example is that of terms which can belong to two or more different parts of speech, like substantives and verbs or adjectives and verbs. In any case, we should remember that all languages of our experience have ambiguous words which can be understood only with the help of the context and it is one of the NMT engine's tasks to find the correct translation for each of them.

| Inflection | Definition |
| --- | --- |
| *pěkná* | *pěkný* nom. f. s. |
| *pěkná* | *pěkný* voc. f. s. |
| *pěkná* | *pěkný* nom. n. pl. |
| *pěkná* | *pěkný* acc. n. pl. |
| *pěkná* | *pěkný* voc. n. pl. |
| *pěkné* | *pěkný* nom. f. pl. |
| *pěkné* | *pěkný* nom. n. s. |
| *pěkné* | *pěkný* gen. f. s. |
| *pěkné* | *pěkný* dat. f. s. |
| *pěknou* | *pěkný* instr. f. s. |

Table 2. Sample of Czech adjective mapping - Extract.

### 4.2 Slavic target language

When translating into a Slavic language, the Morpho Model is employed from the definition to the inflection. In this case, the engine plays a dominant role. In fact, its translation constitutes the input for the Morpho Model, and it must be extremely reliable in order to correctly build the final word. Consequently, particular care is required when selecting the tokens to be sent to the Morpho Model (it works at word level, so it needs **one** stem and several properties to generate **one** inflected form).

There is a risk of creating incorrect or even artificial words at the end of the process, but our tests show that this risk is minimal.

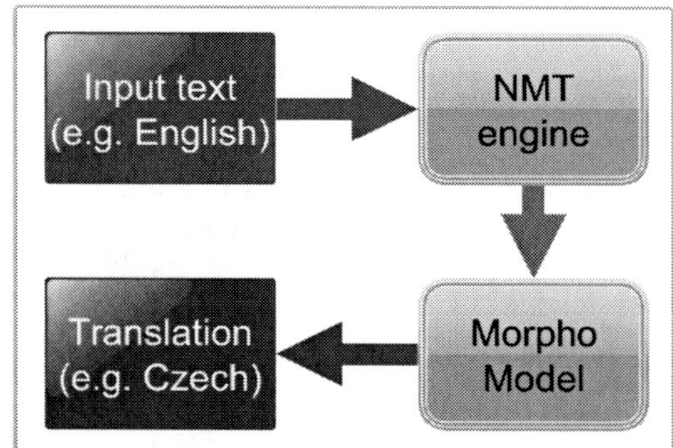


Figure 2. Overview of the process when the Slavic language is target.

### 4.3 Results

Test results[2] involving only the Morpho Model show that when the Slavic language is the source language, the percentage of perfect matches[3] is around 80%. This value is perfectly respectable, considering that the remaining non-perfect matches may fall into one of three categories:

- Alternative definition
- Correct stem with a mistake in the morphological properties
- Mistake in the stem

While the first two cases may cause a degree of confusion and lower the final BLEU evaluation, only the third one actually represents a disturbing factor when used as input for the incoming translation engine.

In any case, we can observe quite astonishing results in the opposite direction (i.e. Slavic as the

---

[2] The test set was made up of 10,000 non-trained words.

[3] We consider a perfect match only when the Morpho Model's output corresponds exactly to the definition of the test inflection (i.e. stem and all grammatical classes)

target language), where the perfect match rate is over 90% for Russian, and even 97% for Polish. The difference up to 100% represents cases in which the user may receive a spurious word that does not really exist, but such an outcome can be avoided or at least strongly reduced with a simple spellchecker, for example.

As regards the evaluation of the whole translation process, results appear not so easy to evaluate. If we take Polish as an example (but the other languages had similar behaviour) we see that pure BLEU values with Morpho Model are in both directions lower than the BPE.[4] Since the number of translations with BLEU below 0.2 was much bigger in the Morpho case than in the BPE, we took a selection of 150 of them and let them be analysed by translators who did not know about our study. We expected to find that recurrent phaenomena showed some kind of inconsistency in one or more steps of our process, but we were told that actually the translation with the Morpho Model often had a better level of comprehensibility. As a final test we let the translators make manual comparisons of BPE and Morpho translations in our web application, with particular focus on the correctness of inflected forms. After this confirmation we decided to use this new technology in production; in fact, we usually proceed only after the approval of a translator or at least a native speaker, especially for such cases when the automatic evaluation doesn't show a significant advantage for a particular case.

## 5   Possible drawbacks

Some reservations have been expressed concerning the time spent on a single translation, as each word has to be handled by the Morpho Model in addition to the time required by the normal NMT engine. In this respect, it is important to note that the Morpho Model is much faster than a conventional engine due to the consistency of material and the low settings required for its training (word vector and RNN far below 100).

Another criticism may be the risk of having less control over the translation, since we are using two neural models instead of one. However, thanks to other pre-/post-processing steps, we can reduce the possibility of unexpected results, as a last resort leaving the source word un-

changed to prevent the model from creating spurious words.

In any case, as a company, we need to consider any MT solution in a practical way: the worst possible output for our average user is an OOV. Thus, reduction of OOVs, coupled with more consistent quality when translating the same lemma, is a major objective. In most cases, a translation containing an OOV is completely incomprehensible, while one containing the correct stem and an incorrect ending is sufficient to justify continuing with the work.

Furthermore, an error rate of 3%, as the one we had for Polish, is probably not far from the human one, especially considering that not everyone among our target users has high linguistic skills.

You might assume that a technique based on morphology requires a deep knowledge of the languages involved. To some extent that is true, in that some linguistic knowledge can be useful (detecting mistakes, faster development, problem solving). However, the grammatical aspects under consideration are not so specialised as to require an expert; at least no more than those involved in conventional training.

## 6   Conclusions

The accuracy of the result is strictly dependent on the quality of the map used to train the Morpho Model. Since a good amount of well-formed linguistic data is required to create the map, it is important to handle this correctly. For example, knowing that the customer generally avoids the use of certain verb forms can lead to a reduction in the size of the map, resulting in a simpler task for both the model and the engine. Moreover, the size of the map is a factor that can influence quality and performance. For customers with a small variety of subjects, the map can be reduced based on the words the engine can translate.

## 7   Further challenges

A potential next step for this logic could be to use it in a scenario where both the source and target languages are Slavic. The result could be a greater reduction in vocabulary; however since Slavic languages are quite a homogeneous family, the difference may not be appreciable compared to conventional training.

Another interesting field of application might be for languages with non-concatenative morphology, such as Arabic, where words are in-

---

[4] de-pl BPE: 0.580, de-pl Morpho: 0.571. pl-de BPE: 0.587, pl-de Morpho: 0.569.

flected with transfixes rather than prefixes or suffixes. The incentive in this case relates not only to the technical challenge, but also to the potential future business opportunities offered by the Middle East and North Africa.

## References

Duygu Ataman, Matteo Negri, Marco Turchi, Marcello Federico. 2017. *Linguistically Motivated Vocabulary Reduction for Neural Machine Translation from Turkish to English*, The Prague Bulletin of Mathematical Linguistics No. 108, 2017:331-342.

Rico Sennrich, Barry Haddow, Alexandra Birch. 2016. *Neural Machine Translation of Rare Words with Subword Units*, Proceedings of the 54th Annual Meeting of the Association for Computational Linguistics, Berlin, Germany, August 7-12:1715-1725.

# Large-scale Machine Translation Evaluation of the iADAATPA Project


Sheila Castilho,* Natália Resende,* Federico Gaspari,* Andy Way*
Tony O'Dowd,† Marek Mazur,† Manuel Herranz,§ Alex Helle,§
Gema Ramírez-Sánchez,‡ Víctor Sánchez-Cartagena,‡ Mārcis Pinnis,** Valters Šics**

*ADAPT Centre, Dublin City University `firstname.lastname@adaptcentre.ie`
†KantanMT `tonyod/marekm@kantanmt.com`
§Pangeanic `m.herranz/a.helle@pangeanic.com`
‡Prompsit `gramirez/vmsanchez@prompsit.com`
** Tilde `marcis.pinnis/valters.sics@tilde.lv`



## Abstract

This paper reports the results of an in-depth evaluation of 34 state-of-the-art domain-adapted machine translation (MT) systems that were built by four leading MT companies as part of the EU-funded iADAATPA project. These systems support a wide variety of languages for several domains. The evaluation combined automatic metrics and human methods, namely assessments of adequacy, fluency, and comparative ranking. The paper also discusses the most effective techniques to build domain-adapted MT systems for the relevant language combinations and domains.


## 1 Introduction

The evaluation reported in this paper was conducted as part of the EU-funded iADAATPA (intelligent, Automatic Domain-Adapted Automated Translation for Public Administrations) project that ended in February 2019.[1] The evaluation was performed by the ADAPT Centre at Dublin City University (DCU) on 34 state-of-the-art domain-adapted machine translation (MT) systems built by four leading MT companies KantanMT, Pangeanic, Prompsit and Tilde. These MT engines supported a wide range of language pairs, including under-resourced ones, for several domains.

The main objective of the project was to lower language barriers with a view to promoting truly multilingual services across EU Member States.

To this end, an innovative platform (MTHub) was developed to offer state-of-the-art domain-adapted MT engines to public administrations (PAs) in addition to the EU's own eTranslation service.[2] In this context, the technical partners of the project built MT engines for the language pairs and in the specific domains that were indicated as priorities by the PAs in the respective countries.

The rest of the paper is structured as follows. The four MT companies involved in this study are presented in Sections 2 (KantanMT), 3 (Pangeanic), 4 (Prompsit), and 5 (Tilde), with a description of the systems that they developed, including the data that they used and how they customized their engines. Section 6 outlines the protocol that was followed for this large-scale automatic and human evaluation. Section 7 reports the key results of the evaluation, and Section 8 concludes with a summary of the most important lessons learned and possibilities for further work in this area.

## 2 KantanMT

KantanMT offers a cloud-based MT platform that enables users to develop and manage customized MT engines. The technologies offered enable users to build MT engines in over 750 language combinations integrated into the user's localisation workflows and web applications.

### 2.1 KantanMT's MT systems

**Language pairs and domains** KantanMT's PA partner was DCU, whose website encompasses more than 120 sub-sites providing informational content for students, lecturers and visitors to the DCU Campus. Due to the amount of content on



[1] http://iadaatpa.com/

[2] https://ec.europa.eu/info/resources-partners/machine-translation-public-administrations-etranslation_en

| Language pair | # segments |
| --- | --- |
| | train |
| English→Bulgarian | 8.3M |
| English→Dutch | 11.8M |
| English→French | 13.6M |
| English→German | 41.2M |
| English→Irish | 1.8M |
| English→Italian | 5.2M |
| English→Polish | 10.7M |
| English→Portuguese | 8.1M |
| English→Romanian | 8.9M |
| English→Spanish | 18.5M |

**Table 1:** Data used to train KantanMT NMT systems

| Language pair | # segments | |
| --- | --- | --- |
| | init | train |
| Spanish→Catalan | 30k | 13.6M |
| Spanish→English | 30k | 14.6M |
| Spanish→French | 30k | 14.6M |
| Spanish→German | 30k | 14.5M |
| Spanish→Italian | 30k | 14.5M |
| Spanish→Portuguese | 30k | 14.6M |
| Spanish→Russian | 30k | 13.8M |

**Table 2:** Data used to train Pangeanic NMT systems

the University's website, a small number of areas were prioritized: News and Events, President Office, School of Applied Languages and Intercultural Studies, and Fiontar – Irish Language Research. The language pairs consisted of English as the source for all the neural MT (NMT) engines into Bulgarian, Dutch, French, German, Irish, Italian, Polish, Portuguese, Romanian, and Spanish.

## 2.2 Data Acquisition

The data used in the customization of KantanMT's engines was selected from publicly available sources, such as the DGT (European Commission's Directorate-General for Translation), EMEA (European Medicines Agency), ECB (European Central Bank) and EuroParl (Koehn, 2005).[3] Table 1 shows the training data for KantanMT's NMT systems.

## 2.3 Engine Customization

All initial NMT engines were developed using the Torch implementation of the OpenNMT framework.[4] The development test reference set, used to generate automated scores and to establish a performance baseline for each engine, consisted of 500 segments chosen at random from the live DCU website. Both recurrent and transformer neural models were trained. The model with the best overall automated scores was then selected as the final release candidate. (For the purposes of engine selection, F-Measure, TER (Snover et al., 2006), BLEU (Papineni et al., 2002), and Perplexity were used as automated scores.)

---

[3]https://www.statmt.org/europarl/
[4]http://www.opennmt.net/

## 3 Pangeanic

Pangeanic (Yuste et al., 2010) is a Language Service Provider (LSP) specialised in Natural Language Processing and MT. It provides solutions to cognitive companies, institutions, translation professionals, and corporations.

### 3.1 Pangeanic's MT systems

**Language pairs and domains** Pangeanic's use-cases were for two Spanish PAs: (1) Generalitat Valenciana (regional administration) translating from Spanish into and out of English, French, Catalan/Valencian, German, Italian, Russian; and (2) Segittur (tourism administration) translating from Spanish into and out of English, French, German, Italian, Portuguese. For this purpose, NMT systems were built.

**Data acquisition** For Spanish→Russian there was no available in-domain data. Therefore, two translators were contracted as part of the project to create 30k segments of in-domain data, translating PAs' websites. They also cleaned UN material and post-edited general-domain data that was previously filtered as in-domain following the "Invitation Model" (Hoang and Sima'an, 2014). For the other language pairs, the input material was also 30k post-edited segments. The main part of the training corpora (approximately 75%) came from Pangeanic's own repository, harvested through web crawling including OpenSubtitles (Tiedemann, 2012). The rest of the corpus was automatically validated synthetic material using general data from Leipzig (Goldhahn et al., 2012). Table 2 shows the size of the in-domain (manual or provided by the PA) and generic training data set.

**Engine customization** The data was cleaned using the Bicleaner tool (Sánchez-Cartagena et al., 2018). Moreover, embeddings for case infor-

| Use-case | Language pair | # segments | |
|---|---|---|---|
| | | init | train |
| Gazette | Spanish→English | 0 | 34.2M |
| Gazette | Spanish→Basque | 820k | 820k |
| R&D | English→Spanish | 0 | 36.3M |
| R&D | Basque→Spanish | 0 | 4.6M |

**Table 3:** Data used to train Prompsit NMT systems

mation and byte pair encoding tokenization were added. The models were trained with multi-domain data and we improved performance following a domain-mixing approach (Britz et al., 2017). The domain information was indicated using special tokens for each target sequence. The domain prediction was based only on the source as the extra token was added at target-side and there was no need for *a priori* domain information. This approach allowed the model to improve the quality for each domain.

## 4 Prompsit

Prompsit is a language technology (LT) provider with a strong focus on tailored MT services involving data curation, training and development of other multilingual applications.

### 4.1 Prompsit's MT systems

**Language pairs and domains** Prompsit partnered with SESIAD, the Spanish State Secretary for Information Society and Digital Agenda, and built eight MT systems for two use-cases: (1) translation of the Spanish Official Gazette from Spanish into Catalan, Galician, Basque and English and (2) translation of R&D content for monitoring purposes from Catalan, Galician, Basque, and English into Spanish. Rule-based MT (RBMT) was used for combinations involving Catalan and Galician (mainly due to the lack of relevant corpora) and NMT was used for the rest.

**Data acquisition** For the RBMT systems, monolingual and bilingual data was crawled from different websites. For the NMT systems, data was compiled by means of web crawling, back- and forward-translation of monolingual corpora, and cross-entropy data selection. Table 3 presents the amount of in-domain parallel segments initially available and finally used to train NMT systems.

**Engine customization** RBMT systems based on Apertium (Forcada et al., 2011) were customized

by extracting candidates for new monolingual and bilingual dictionary entries from a word-aligned parallel corpus generated with ruLearn (Sánchez-Cartagena et al., 2016). For NMT systems, based on OpenNMT, automatic segmentation of long sentences and linguistically informed word segmentation for Basque (Sánchez-Cartagena, 2018) were added to the corpus pre-processing pipeline. Moreover, to ensure translation consistency, carefully designed terminology to restrict translation hypotheses and named entity recognition to control the translation of proper names, places, etc. was added. Finally, mixed fine-tuning (Chu et al., 2017) was applied to some systems to balance the weight of the different sources of training data.

## 5 Tilde

Tilde is an LSP and LT developer offering customized MT system development, as well as a wide range of other cloud-based and stand-alone LT tools and services for terminology management, spelling and grammar checking, speech recognition and synthesis, personalised virtual assistants, and other applications. It provides on-premise and cloud-based LT solutions to public and private organisations as well as LT productivity tools to individual users.

### 5.1 Tilde's MT systems

**Language pairs and domains** The use-cases for Tilde cover political news for English into Bulgarian and Estonian, general news for English into Latvian and legislation (legal acts and legislative news) for English into Lithuanian and Lithuanian into Russian. The Lithuanian language use-cases are intended for the Seimas of the Republic of Lithuania (the Parliament of Lithuania).

**Data acquisition** All NMT systems were trained using a combination of broad domain corpora and synthetic in-domain corpora (i.e. back-translated monolingual corpora). The in-domain corpora were acquired by crawling relevant web domains containing in-domain data as well as by acquiring translation memories from the partner PA. All parallel corpora were normalized, cleaned from noise, and pre-processed using the methodology by Pinnis et al. (2017). The training data statistics for the NMT systems are provided in Table 4.

**Engine customization** At first, initial NMT systems were trained using Nematus (Sennrich et

| Use-case | Lang. pair | # segments | |
|---|---|---|---|
| | | Init | Domain |
| General news | Eng.→Lat. | 15.8M | 11.6M |
| | Lat.→Eng. | 15.8M | 11.1M |
| Political news | Eng.→Est. | 18.9M | 1.7M |
| | Est.→Eng. | 18.9M | 0.7M |
| | Eng.→Bul. | 6.2M | 6.2M |
| | Bul.→Eng. | 6.2M | 6.1M |
| Law | Eng.→Lit. | 10.2M | 0.5M |
| | Lit.→Eng. | 10.2M | 10.1M |
| | Lit.→Rus. | 2.7M | 2.6M |
| | Rus.→Lit. | 2.7M | 2.6M |

**Table 4:** Data used to train Tilde NMT systems

al., 2017) with the multiplicative long short-term memory unit implementation by Pinnis et al. (2017). Then, monolingual in-domain data were back-translated (Poncelas et al., 2018). For systems for which the in-domain data amounted to the same amount as the initial training data, the back-translated synthetic parallel corpora were added to the initial training data and final (domain-specific) systems were trained from scratch. For the remaining systems (English-Estonian and English-Lithuanian), domain adaptation of the initial models was performed using continued training.

## 6  Evaluating iADAATPA's MT Systems

The evaluation of all iADAATPA's MT systems was carried out following current MT assessment practices (see Castilho et al. (2018)) with a combination of automatic evaluation metrics (AEMs) – including BLEU, METEOR (Banerjee and Lavie, 2005), TER and chrF (Popović, 2015) – and human evaluation, consisting of assessing fluency, adequacy and ranking against a baseline. The *Adequacy* rating was based on the statement "The translated sentence conveys the meaning of the original...", which was to be completed with a 3-point Likert scale (1-Poorly, 2-Fairly, 3-Well). The *Fluency* rating was based on the statement "The translated sentence is grammatically...", which was to be completed with a 3-point Likert scale (1-Incomprehensible, 2-Fair, 3-Flawless). The *Ranking* assessment was based on asking the translators to rate the translations from best to worst. Ties were allowed for both "equally well translated" or "equally badly translated".

The baseline MT system selected to be compared against the partners' engines for both au-

tomatic and human evaluation was Google Translate (GNMT).[5] However, for KantanMT's systems, the baseline chosen for the human evaluation was the human reference translations; this choice was made as the systems were not in their final version by the time they were delivered for evaluation, so the partner was keen to know initially how their systems performed against a gold standard in order to subsequently improve them.

### 6.1  Test Sets

The test sets consisted of 500 randomized sentences and were provided by the MT partners. A portion of these data sets was used to compute inter-annotator agreement (IAA, see Section 7.2.1). The partners also provided the reference translations for the source texts, which were translated professionally.

### 6.2  Translators

Each system was evaluated by two professional translators, who did not know whether the translations were from the partner's MT system or the baseline. Guidelines on how to use the evaluation tools and how to assess the translations were provided. IAA was computed on sets of 100 sentences; however, blank data points (skipped evaluations or bugged data points) were removed from the raw data set, which led to a variance in the total number of sentences.

### 6.3  Tool

The tool used to assess fluency, adequacy and ranking was KantanMT's LQR,[6] a cloud-based platform which facilitates the interaction with translators since they are not required to download any software.

## 7  Results

### 7.1  Automatic Evaluation Metrics

Due to space constraints, here we present average scores of the MT engines' AEM results grouped by partner (Engine) against average scores of GNMT (Baseline), pointing out particularly interesting aspects.

KantanMT's MT systems (Fig.1) score higher than GNMT in the majority of the cases, with the exception of the English-Italian system which does not outperform the GNMT system.

---

[5]https://translate.google.com/
[6]https://www.kantanmt.com/overview-kantanlqr.php

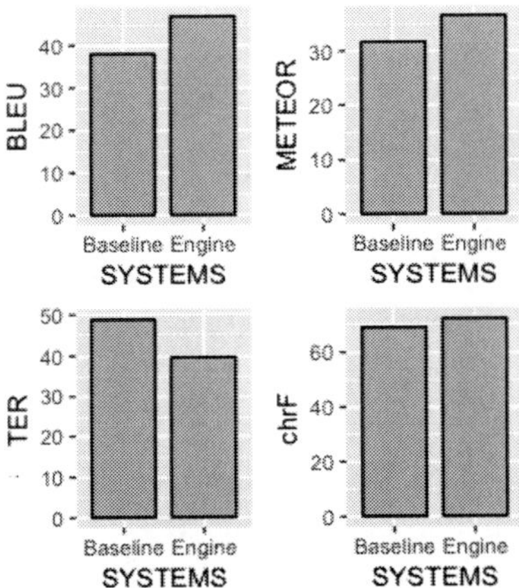

**Figure 1:** Automatic metrics - KantanMT

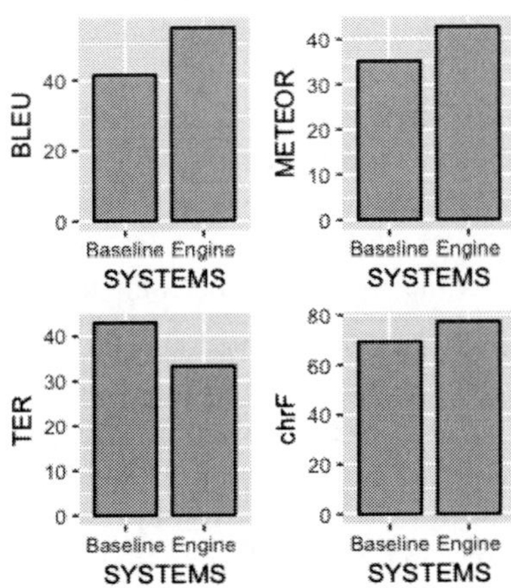

**Figure 2:** Automatic metrics - Pangeanic

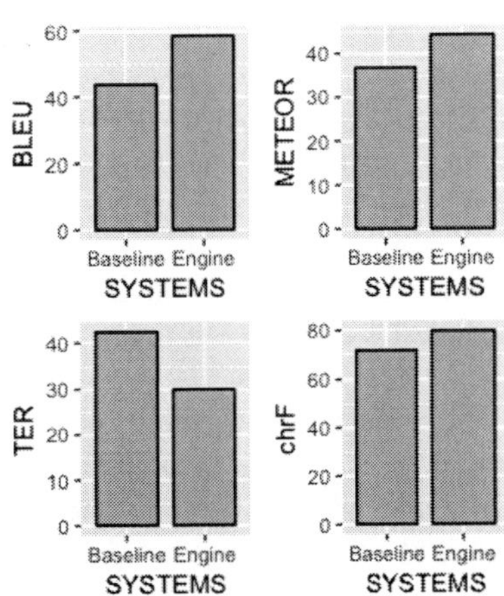

**Figure 3:** Automatic metrics - Prompsit

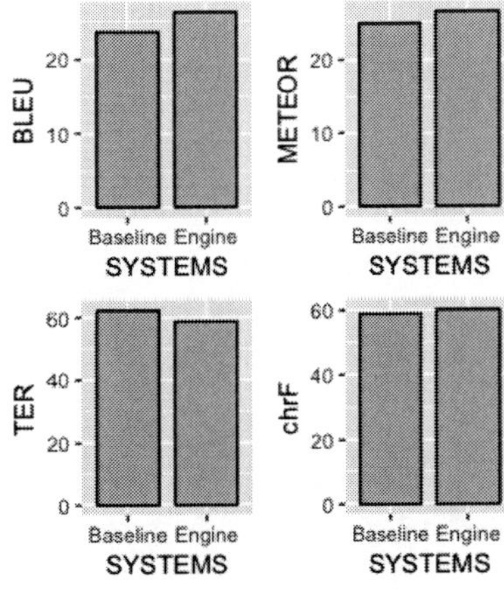

**Figure 4:** Automatic metrics - Tilde

Pangeanic's MT systems (Fig.2) score higher than GNMT in almost all cases. The Spanish-English MT system is the only one that does not outperform the baseline by a statistically significant margin, possibly as a result of the Spanish PA's content being overly generic and thus competing on a general basis against GNMT as opposed to a customized engine.

Prompsit's MT systems (Fig.3) score higher than GNMT for the majority of the cases.

Tilde's MT systems (Fig.4) score higher than GNMT in most cases, with Latvian-English and English-Latvian being the only the engines that do not outperform the baseline (by a statistical significant amount for Latvian↔English).

## 7.2 Human Evaluation

### 7.2.1 Inter-Annotator Agreement

Overall, an average kappa coefficient between 0.21 and 0.40 (moderate) and between 0.40 and 0.60 (fair) was observed for fluency and adequacy for both weighted and non-weighted kappa for all partners' engines and baseline. Poor agreement (k=0.0-0.20) was observed only for non-weighted kappa for fluency ratings of KantanMT's baseline, adequacy ratings of Pangeanic's engines and baseline, and adequacy ratings of Prompsit's engines and baselines.

### 7.2.2 Fluency, Adequacy and Ranking

The results for fluency, adequacy and ranking show that the iADAATPA partners' MT systems systematically outperformed GNMT. These results mean that our partners' systems were considered better than GNMT most of the time and that their output was deemed to be grammatically more fluent and more adequate compared to the source sentences than GNMT's output. The only exception observed is for KantanMT's MT systems (Figure 5), which did not outperform the baseline; however, this was an expected result since the baseline for KantanMT's systems was the human reference translation. In the interest of conciseness, Figures 5, 6, 7 and 8 illustrate the average performance of all partners' MT systems combined (Engine), arranged by company, against the respective baselines.

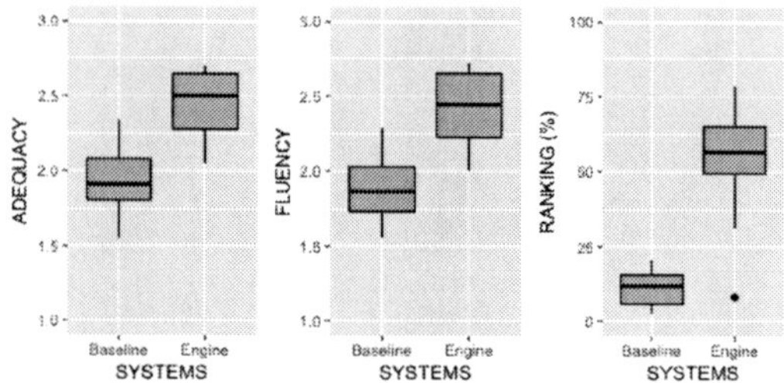

**Figure 8:** Human evaluation - Tilde partner

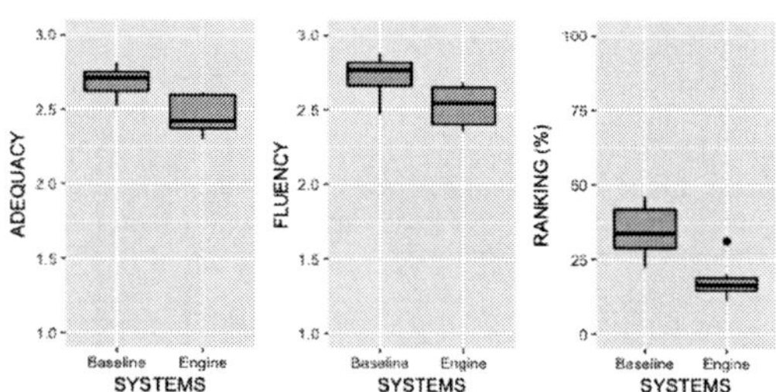

**Figure 5:** Human evaluation - KantanMT partner

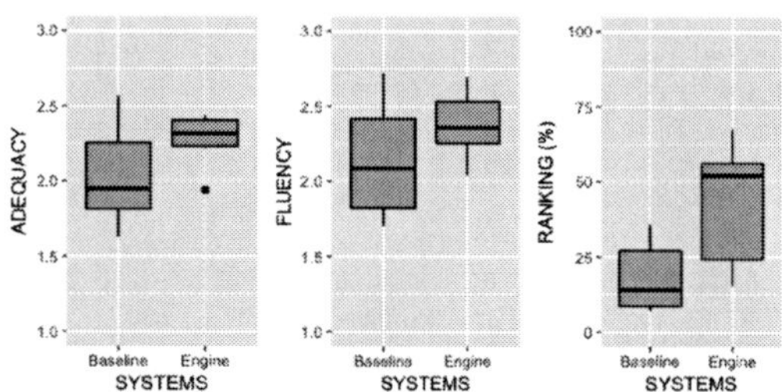

**Figure 6:** Human evaluation - Pangeanic partner

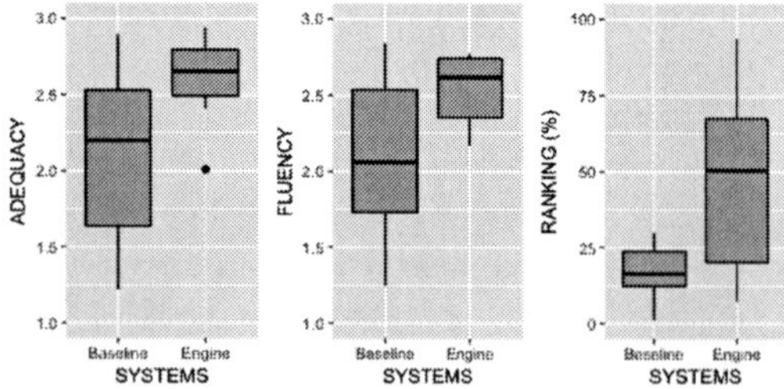

**Figure 7:** Human evaluation - Prompsit partner

## 8 Conclusion

The results of this comprehensive evaluation show that in general the MT systems developed within the iADAATPA project were competitive with the production systems, including for language pairs that lack extensive resources. In particular, the evaluation with the four standard AEMs consistently showed the partners' MT systems to have superior performance compared to the baseline engines. In addition, the human evaluation of fluency and adequacy as well as comparative ranking also yielded very positive results; with the exception of the MT systems developed by KantanMT, which were compared against the human reference baseline, all the other domain-adapted engines prevailed in the human evaluation, with a clear preference over the baseline in the comparative ranking.

The evaluation presented here can be extended in several ways, e.g. including the results for updated versions of the MT systems covered in these experiments; during the iADAATPA project the systems were continuously improved with additional training data and more sophisticated techniques, to optimize their performance vis-à-vis the targeted use-cases indicated by the respective PAs. In addition, we intend to investigate the relationship between the additional development efforts and the improved performance, especially in terms of automatic metrics, as conducting additional human evaluation is unlikely, given that the project is now concluded.

**Acknowledgements** The work reported in this paper was conducted during the iADAATPA project, which was funded by INEA through grant N° 2016-EU-IA-0132 as part of the EU's CEF Telecom Programme. The ADAPT Centre for Digital Content Technology at Dublin City University is funded under the Science Foundation Ireland Research Centres Programme (Grant 13/RC/2106) and is co-funded under the European Regional Development Fund.

## References

Banerjee, Satanjeev and Alon Lavie. 2005. METEOR: An automatic metric for MT evaluation with improved correlation with human judgments. In *Proceedings of the ACL workshop on intrinsic and extrinsic evaluation measures for machine translation and/or summarization*, pages 65–72, Ann Arbor, MI.

Britz, Denny, Quoc Le, and Reid Pryzant. 2017. Effective domain mixing for neural machine translation. In *Proceedings of the Second Conference on Machine Translation*, pages 118–126, Copenhagen, Denmark.

Castilho, Sheila, Stephen Doherty, Federico Gaspari, and Joss Moorkens. 2018. Approaches to human and machine Translation Quality Assessment. In Castilho, Sheila, Joss Moorkens, Federico Gaspari, and Stephen Doherty, editors, *Translation Quality Assessment: From Principles to Practice*, pages 9–38. Springer.

Chu, Chenhui, Raj Dabre, and Sadao Kurohashi. 2017. An empirical comparison of domain adaptation methods for neural machine translation. In *Proceedings of the 55th Annual Meeting of the Association for Computational Linguistics (Volume 2: Short Papers)*, pages 385–391, Vancouver, Canada.

Forcada, Mikel L., Mireia Ginestí-Rosell, Jacob Nordfalk, Jim ORegan, Sergio Ortiz-Rojas, Juan Antonio Pérez-Ortiz, Felipe Sánchez-Martínez, Gema Ramírez-Sánchez, and Francis M. Tyers. 2011. Apertium: a free/open-source platform for rule-based machine translation. *Machine Translation*, 25(2):127–144.

Goldhahn, Dirk, Thomas Eckart, and Uwe Quasthoff. 2012. Building large monolingual dictionaries at the leipzig corpora collection: From 100 to 200 languages. In *Proceedings of the Eighth International Conference on Language Resources and Evaluation (LREC12)*, pages 759–765, Istanbul, Turkey.

Hoang, Cuong and Khalil Sima'an. 2014. Latent domain translation models in mix-of-domains haystack. In *Proceedings of COLING 2014, the 25th International Conference on Computational Linguistics*, pages 1928–1939, Dublin, Ireland.

Koehn, Philipp. 2005. Europarl: a parallel corpus for statistical machine translation. In *MT Summit X, Conference Proceedings: the Tenth Machine Translation Summit*, pages 79–86, Phuket, Thailand.

Papineni, Kishore, Salim Roukos, Todd Ward, and Wei-Jing Zhu. 2002. Bleu: A method for automatic evaluation of machine translation. In *Proceedings of the 40th Annual Meeting on Association for Computational Linguistics*, pages 311–318, Philadelphia, PA.

Pinnis, Mārcis, Rihards Krišlauks, Toms Miks, Daiga Deksne, and Valters Šics. 2017. Tilde's Machine Translation Systems for WMT 2017. In *Proceedings of the Second Conference on Machine Translation, Vol. 2: Shared Task Papers*, pages 374–381, Copenhagen, Denmark.

Poncelas, Alberto, Dimitar Shterionov, Andy Way, Gideon Maillette de Buy Wenniger, and Peyman Passban. 2018. Investigating backtranslation in neural machine translation. In *Proceedings of The 21st Annual Conference of the European Association for Machine Translation*, pages 249–258, Alicante, Spain.

Popović, Maja. 2015. chrF: character n-gram F-score for automatic MT evaluation. In *Proceedings of the Tenth Workshop on Statistical Machine Translation*, pages 392–395, Lisbon, Portugal.

Sánchez-Cartagena, Víctor M., Juan Antonio Pérez-Ortiz, and Felipe Sánchez-Martínez. 2016. Rulearn: an open-source toolkit for the automatic inference of shallow-transfer rules for machine translation. *The Prague Bulletin of Mathematical Linguistics*, 106(1):193–204.

Sánchez-Cartagena, Víctor M., Marta Bañón, Sergio Ortiz-Rojas, and Gema Ramírez-Sánchez. 2018. Prompsit's submission to wmt 2018 parallel corpus filtering shared task. In *Proceedings of the Third Conference on Machine Translation, Vol. 2: Shared Task Papers*, pages 955–962, Brussels, Belgium.

Sánchez-Cartagena, Víctor M. 2018. Prompsits submission to the IWSLT 2018 low resource machine translation task. In *Proceedings of 15th International Workshop on Spoken Language Translation*, pages 95–103, Bruges, Belgium.

Sennrich, Rico, Orhan Firat, Kyunghyun Cho, Alexandra Birch, Barry Haddow, Julian Hitschler, Marcin Junczys-Dowmunt, Samuel Läubli, Antonio Valerio Miceli Barone, Jozef Mokry, and Others. 2017. Nematus: a Toolkit for Neural Machine Translation. In *Proceedings of the Software Demonstrations of the 15th Conference of the EACL*, pages 65–68, Valencia, Spain.

Snover, Matthew, Bonnie Dorr, Richard Schwartz, Linnea Micciulla, and John Makhoul. 2006. A study of translation edit rate with targeted human annotation. In *AMTA 2006: Proceedings of the 7th Conference of the Association for Machine Translation in the Americas*, pages 223–231, Cambridge, MA, USA.

Tiedemann, Jörg. 2012. Parallel data, tools and interfaces in OPUS. In *Proceedings of the Eight International Conference on Language Resources and Evaluation*, pages 2214–2218, Istanbul, Turkey.

Yuste, E., M. Herranz, A. Helle, and H. Suzuki. 2010. Pangeamt - putting open standards to work ... well. In *AMTA 2010: the Ninth conference of the Association for Machine Translation in the Americas*, Denver, CO. 8pp.

# Collecting domain specific data for MT: an evaluation of the ParaCrawl pipeline

Arne Defauw, Tom Vanallemeersch, Sara Szoc, Frederic Everaert, Koen Van Winckel,
Kim Scholte, Joris Brabers, Joachim Van den Bogaert
CrossLang
Kerkstraat 106
9050 Gentbrugge
Belgium
{firstname.lastname}@crosslang.com

## [1] Abstract

This paper investigates the effectiveness of the ParaCrawl pipeline for collecting domain-specific training data for machine translation. We follow the different steps of the pipeline (document alignment, sentence alignment, cleaning) and add a topic-filtering component. Experiments are performed on the legal domain for the English to French and English to Irish language pairs. We evaluate the pipeline at both intrinsic (alignment quality) and extrinsic (MT performance) levels. Our results show that with this pipeline we obtain high-quality alignments and significant improvements in MT quality.

## 1 Introduction

In this paper, we evaluate the performance of the ParaCrawl pipeline[2] to build parallel datasets from multilingual websites related to a specific domain. The pipeline is part of the ParaCrawl[3] project mining millions of parallel sentences from the web and sharing the resulting resources online for free in all official EU languages paired with English. It starts by aligning web pages in multiple languages, applying sentence alignment

for each resulting pair of web pages and a final cleaning step on the resulting sentence pairs.

The aim of this paper is to create in-domain parallel datasets by applying the existing ParaCrawl pipeline and to evaluate the resulting datasets both intrinsically (alignment quality) and extrinsically (extension of a baseline MT system with ParaCrawl results). We describe experiments on websites in the legal domain, which is sufficiently extensive to allow creating a substantial amount of domain-specific parallel data. To improve the quality of the ParaCrawl output, we add an additional topic filtering step after cleaning. We perform experiments for English-French (EN-FR) and the low resource English-Irish (EN-GA) language pairs.

## 2 ParaCrawl pipeline

The ParaCrawl project is co-funded by the Connecting Europe Facility and runs from 2017 to 2019. It incorporates ideas from Buck et al. (2014) and Buck and Koehn (2016a, 2016b).

Given a set of downloaded web pages (such as websites provided by the Common Crawl[4] resource, an open repository of web crawled data), the ParaCrawl pipeline performs document alignment (detection of pairs of translation-equivalent pages for two specified languages) with Malign[5], and aligns the sentences within these pairs of pages using Hunalign[6]. Finally, an additional filtering step is applied, for instance


[2]https://github.com/paracrawl,
https://github.com/bitextor/bitextor
[3]https://paracrawl.eu

[4]http://commoncrawl.org
[5]Now part of https://github.com/bitextor/bitextor
[6]http://mokk.bme.hu/en/resources/hunalign

using Bicleaner[7]. The following sections describe the Malign, Hunalign and Bicleaner tools.

## 2.1 Malign

Considering a set of web pages in two languages[8], Malign matches web pages in the source language with translation-equivalent web pages in the target language, by detecting running text in the latter, segmenting the text and comparing the MT output of the source sentences with the target sentences. To perform this last step, an MT system is required: we trained two X>EN MT systems, one for each language pair[9].

## 2.2 Hunalign

Hunalign detects which sentences or groups of subsequent sentences of a document[10] in source and target language are translation-equivalents of each other. Equivalences may be 1-to-1, but also 1-to-many, many-to-1, many-to-many or null.

Alignment decisions are based on different types of information, such as sentence length and a (optionally provided, but recommended) translation dictionary. To obtain the latter, we ran GIZA++[11] on our baseline training data; from the resulting EN>X and X>EN lexical probabilities files, we generated a bilingual dictionary by multiplying the lexical probability in the EN>X direction with the probability in the X>EN direction. We retained word pairs with a lexical probability >0.1 for EN-FR, and >0.2 for EN-GA (the thresholds were obtained after manual inspection of the dictionary).

In case of alignments involving multiple sentences in one language (1-to-many or many-to-many), Hunalign will concatenate the sentences on one line in the output file. For each aligned segment, a score ranging from 0 to 1 is produced, indicating the quality of the alignment.

## 2.3 Bicleaner

Bicleaner detects noisy sentence pairs in a parallel corpus by estimating the likelihood of a pair of sentences being mutual translations (value near 1) or not (value near 0). Details are described in Sánchez-Cartagena et al. (2018).

Training a classifier with Bicleaner requires a clean parallel corpus (100k sentences is the recommended size) as well as source-target and target-source probabilistic bilingual dictionaries. Pre-trained classifiers for 23 language pairs[12] are already provided, including EN-FR and EN-GA.

## 3 Application to legal-domain data

This section describes the application of the ParaCrawl pipeline on the EN-FR and EN-GA language pairs in the legal domain. First, we describe the creation of the topic classifier and the scraping process. Then, we present and analyze the results of the latter process and of the four steps in the pipeline (document alignment, sentence alignment, cleaning and topic filtering).

## 3.1 Creation of fastText topic classifier

When applying the ParaCrawl pipeline for collecting domain-specific parallel data (rather than any type of bilingual material), it should be taken into account that web pages from domain-specific URLs may also contain text that is not specific to the domain of interest. Therefore, we extend the ParaCrawl pipeline with a topic filtering component. We use fastText[13] to train a model from labeled sentences by making use of sentence embeddings (Bojanowski et al. 2016, Joulin et al. 2016). We run the classifier on the output of Bicleaner and filter out sentences that are not labeled as domain-specific.

As training a fastText classifier requires labeled data, we add labels to the general and domain-specific monolingual corpora, and build a topic model for English (English being the shared source language in our experiments) to infer the topic of sentences. The data are described in Table 1. For the legal domain, we make use of the English half of the EN>FR subset of the JRC-Acquis corpus[14]. The monolingual newstest2008 dataset[15] is used as generic dataset. We retain the first 500k sentences from each corpus, deduplicate both datasets, concatenate the sentences from both datasets, and extract a held-out test set of 100k labeled sentences.

---

[7]https://github.com/bitextor/bicleaner

[8]Malign does not perform language classification, so the language should be specified as part of its input.

[9]Engines were trained using RNN (Recurrent Neural Network) architecture in OpenNMT (Klein et al. 2017) using the baseline training data. See section 5 for more details about the training data.

[10]Documents are split into sentences via a Moses script (see https://github.com/moses-smt).

[11]https://github.com/moses-smt/giza-pp

[12]https://github.com/bitextor/bitextor-data/releases/tag/bicleaner-v1.0

[13]https://fasttext.cc/docs/en/supervised-tutorial.html

[14]http://opus.nlpl.eu/JRC-Acquis.php

[15]http://www.statmt.org/wmt14/training-monolingual-newscrawl/news.2008.en.shuffled.gz

| Domain | Data | #sentences | #retained |
|---|---|---|---|
| Legal | JRC-Acquis | 814,167 | 470,036 |
| Generic | newstest2008 | 12,954,477 | 497,136 |

Table 1: Data for topic modeling

We trained the fastText model for 25 epochs, with a learning rate of 1.0 and the wordNgrams parameter equal to 5. For other parameters we used the default settings. Our model obtains a precision and recall of 99.2% on the test set.

Based on spot-checking of the predictions on sentences from other datasets than the ones the topic model is trained with, it appears that the classifier tends to be very cautious in assigning the label "legal". Therefore, the quality of the subset labeled as legal is very high, whereas many legal sentences are missed by the classifier. This cautiousness is also reflected by the figures for some websites: many sentence pairs resulting from scraping and aligning websites are filtered out based on the topic classifier (see Appendix A). A gold standard would be required to perform a more profound estimation of the topic model's performance. While we did not make use of the possibility provided by fastText to assign probabilities to labels during prediction, such probabilities, in combination with a gold standard, could be used for tuning fastText towards reducing the classifier's undershoot for the label "legal" while keeping its overkill low.

## 3.2 Scraping

We investigated websites in the legal domain (e.g. websites of courts) and spot-checked whether they contain information in both English as well as French and/or Irish, and whether a substantial amount of English content has a translation equivalent in one or more other languages. To make sure the scraping process would be feasible, we also took the structure of the websites into account. As for scraping tools, we use Scrapy[16], allowing to define subparts of websites to be scraped, for instance by specifying rules in a Python script to ensure only URLs with some language code in them are crawled.

A substantial amount of legal-domain content could be scraped for EN>FR, but proved to be much more difficult for the EN>GA language pair. Hence, for this language pair we decided to extend scraping to the other domains as well. While, even then, scraping resulted in a

[16]https://scrapy.org. We note that for the official release of the ParaCrawl corpus Bitextor was used for scraping (https://github.com/bitextor).

significantly smaller amount of parallel data than in the case of EN>FR, the amount of baseline data (see Table 4 in Section 5) is also modest, making the scraped data important in terms of relative size with respect to the baseline.

Table 2 shows the total number of resulting documents and sentences for each language pair. We refer to Appendix A for an overview of statistics for each scraped web-domain individually.

| Pair | #doc. (EN) | #doc. (XX) | #sent. (EN) | #sent. (XX) |
|---|---|---|---|---|
| EN-FR | 46,994 | 49,204 | 1,812,961 | 1,826,992 |
| EN-GA | 19,152 | 4,003 | 1,601,669 | 308,418 |

Table 2: First two columns show the number of resulting documents after scraping for each language pair and each language. Last two columns show the number of extracted sentences from these documents.

## 3.3 Applying the ParaCrawl pipeline

We applied the ParaCrawl pipeline (described in section 2) to the data presented in the previous section. The results are shown in Table 3. The Malign threshold was set to 0.1, and the Bicleaner threshold to 0.7 (the recommended value on the ParaCrawl project website, based on manual inspection). For Hunalign no threshold was set, so cleaning was left to Bicleaner. Again we refer to Appendix A for statistics of each web-domain individually.

Finally, after applying our topic model (see section 3.1) to the resulting corpus we obtain a domain specific corpus. We observe that a lot of sentences are filtered out by our topic model, especially for the EN-FR language pair. Looking at the results on web-domain level, this can partially be explained by the high amount of transcribed speeches scraped from the web domain www.noscommunes.ca, labeled as 'general' by our topic model.

| | #doc. matched (Malign) | #unique aligned sent. (Hunalign) | #unique aligned sent. (Hunalign +Bicleaner) | #sent. after topic filtering (Hunalign +Bicleaner +Topic model) |
|---|---|---|---|---|
| EN-FR | 18,808 | 1,472,511 | 786,515 | 79,838 |
| EN-GA | 1,575 | 167, 928 | 94,278 | 31,696 |

Table 3: Overview of the total number of documents matched with Malign, number of resulting aligned sentences after applying Hunalign (no Hunalign threshold was set),

number of sentences after applying Bicleaner (Bicleaner threshold=0.7), number of Bicleaner-cleaned sentences labeled as 'legal' by our topic model.

## 4 Intrinsic evaluation

We performed an intrinsic evaluation of the aligned sentence pairs resulting from the application of the ParaCrawl pipeline to legal-domain data by comparing the pipeline's output to a gold standard. To create the latter, we manually aligned sentences in a small subset of EN-FR and EN-GA document pairs resulting from Malign. Both automatic and manual alignment start from the same point, i.e. after document alignment and segmentation into sentences. Hence, we are not judging the document alignment component of the pipeline but merely the steps related to sentence alignment. In this section, we describe the evaluation methodology, the data used for creating the gold standard, and evaluation statistics.

### 4.1 Methodology

Sentence alignment involves several types of links. A typical link has a single source and a single target sentence (1-to-1 link), but there are also 1-to-many, many-to-1, many-to-many, and null links (0-to-1 or 1-to-0 links). Evaluating automatic sentence alignment takes place by comparing the output to a manually created gold standard. Manual alignment involves establishing links between one or more subsequent source sentences and one or more subsequent target sentences (Varga et al. 2005), in such a way that the links cannot be divided further into smaller links; Brown et al. (1991) refer to such sets of subsequent sentences as "beads". The automatic sentence alignment is compared to the manual alignment based on the beads that are present in both alignments, or in just one of them. Based on this comparison, precision/recall figures can be calculated, as shown in Section 4.3. Null beads in the automatic or manual alignment are ignored

during evaluation, as we do not want to bias towards this trivial type of link.

### 4.2 Data for Gold Standard

The gold standard was created from 13 resp. 11 document pairs for EN-FR resp. EN-GA obtained after the document alignment step described in Section 2.1.

We observed that the number of 1-to-1 beads in the Gold Standard is high, which indicates that the documents pairs are very parallel. This is not surprising, given the fact that the preceding document alignment step ignores documents that are not sufficiently parallel. We refer to Appendix B for statistics of the Gold standard.

### 4.3 Results

We present precision and recall scores for various thresholds of Hunalign and Bicleaner. Thresholds need to be interpreted as follows: all sentence pairs with a Hunalign probability or Bicleaner score lower than or equal to the corresponding threshold were ignored during evaluation.

To calculate recall, we take the set of gold standard beads, and the set of beads produced by the ParaCrawl sentence alignment steps for a certain threshold of Hunalign and Bicleaner. We divide the total number of shared beads by the total number of beads in the gold standard.

To calculate precision, we take the Paracrawl beads for a certain threshold of Hunalign and Bicleaner. For every bead, we look up whether it is also part of the gold standard. We divide this total number of correct predictions by the total number of predictions by the ParaCrawl pipeline for these thresholds. Precision and recall numbers for EN-FR and EN-GA are shown in Fig. 1 and Fig. 2, respectively. As we are aiming for high-quality alignments, precision is very important. Therefore, we will only consider the two rightmost columns of the matrices, which have a similar precision. These columns make clear that the Bicleaner threshold of 0.7 advised on the ParaCrawl project website is not optimal in case of our datasets: if the threshold is lowered to 0.5, the recall improves substantially.

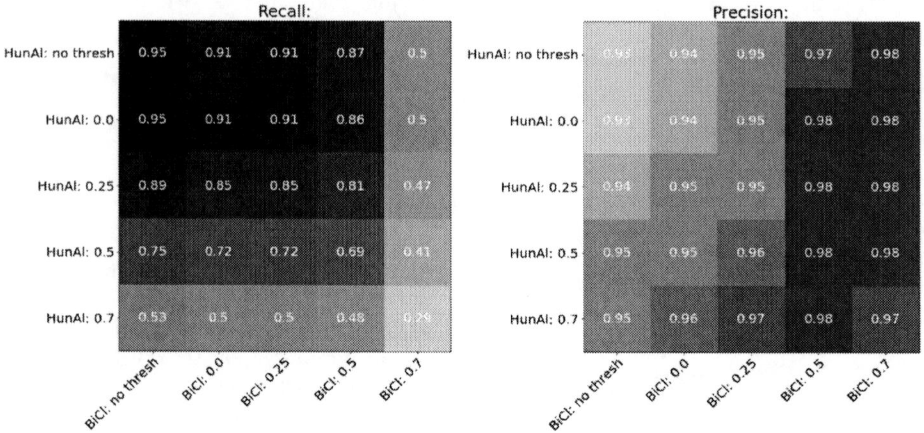

Fig. 1: Recall and precision for various Hunalign and Bicleaner thresholds (EN-FR).

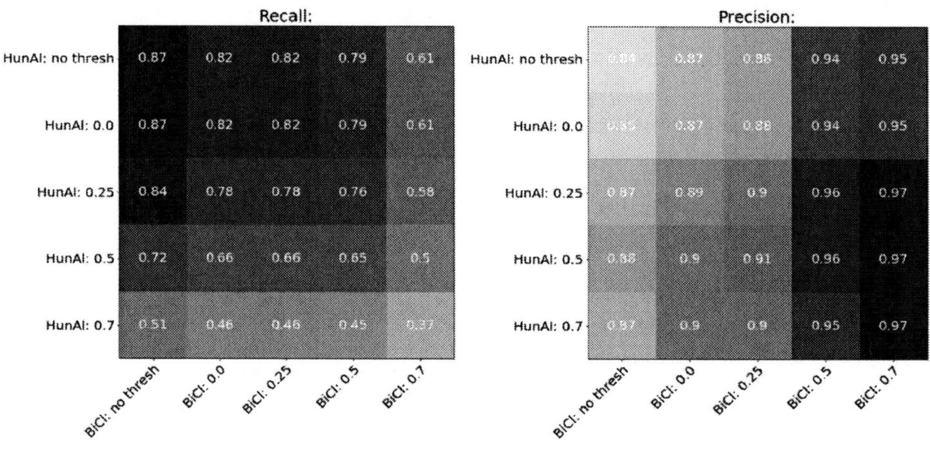

Fig. 2: Recall and precision for various Hunalign and Bicleaner thresholds (EN-GA).

## 5 Extrinsic evaluation

In this section, we describe the extrinsic evaluation of the parallel legal-domain data sets created with the ParaCrawl pipeline. The below sections discuss the baseline data and test sets, the training of our baseline and domain-specific MT systems, and finally the results of the baseline and domain-specific systems.

### 5.1 Baseline and test data

For the baseline training data, we use publicly available corpora. For EN-FR we use the *DGT*, *DCEP*, *EAC* and *ECDC* corpus, while for EN-GA also the *EUbookshop* corpus was used (see appendix C for more details). The resulting total sizes, after deduplication and removal of test sets is given in Table 4. For EN-GA we used all available parallel corpora, with the exception of legal-domain corpora (i.e. Irish legislation[17]) and of less useful corpora like *Ubuntu*.

Two types of test sets were created, in-domain and generic (see Appendix C). The in-domain test-sets were sampled from the JRC-Acquis corpus[18], the EU constitution[19] and the Irish legislation. The test set samples, consisting of unique sentence pairs, were manually verified (e.g. noisy sentences containing special layout codes or exceedingly free translations were removed). The generic test sets were sampled from the baseline data.

[17]https://www.gaois.ie/crp/en/data
[18]http://opus.nlpl.eu/JRC-Acquis.php
[19]http://opus.nlpl.eu/EUconst.php

## 5.2 Training of domain specific MT system

We used the generic data minus the test sets as baseline training data. In case of EN>GA, the in-domain training set has a substantial size compared to the baseline training data: 94k vs. 133k (see Table 4). The weight of the in-domain set being much lower for EN>FR (800k vs. 4M), we decided to reduce the baseline size for EN>FR to a 1M subset in order to obtain a similar weight as for EN>GA.

| Type of data | EN>FR | EN>GA |
|---|---|---|
| Baseline training data | 4,252,861 | 133,104 |
| Baseline test set | 3,000 | 3,000 |
| Baseline sample training data | 1,000,000 | 133,104 (sample=all) |
| + in-domain training data 0.7 | 786,515 | 94,278 |
| Total | 1,786,515 | 227,382 |
| +in-domain training data 0.5 | 1,282,978 | 130,807 |
| Total | 2,282,978 | 263,911 |
| +in-domain training data 0.7, topic filtered | 79,838 | 31,696 |
| Total | 1,079,838 | 164,800 |
| In-domain test | 3,000 | 3,000 |

Table 4: Dataset sizes (#sentence pairs).

We trained EN>FR and EN>GA Neural Machine Translation (NMT) engines with OpenNMT-tensorflow[20] using the Transformer architecture during 20 epochs and default training settings[21]. Preprocessing was done with aggressive tokenization[22], and joint subword (BPE) and vocabulary sizes set to 32k.

We concatenated the baseline training data with the in-domain data and created two domain-specific MT systems for each language pair: one based on the in-domain data produced by Bicleaner, and one on the same data, but after topic filtering (Table 4).

While we applied a threshold of 0.7 for Bicleaner, the intrinsic evaluation described in Section 4 taught us that a threshold of 0.5

[20]https://github.com/OpenNMT/OpenNMT-tf

[21]https://github.com/OpenNMT/OpenNMT-tf/blob/master/opennmt/models/catalog.py

[22]Standard OpenNMT tokenization but only keep sequences of the same character type, see https://github.com/OpenNMT/Tokenizer/blob/master/docs/options.md.

provides a clearly better recall with only a slight loss in precision. Therefore, we also produced in-domain data based on Bicleaner with the lower threshold and trained a third MT-system.

## 5.3 Results

The translation quality of the MT models is measured by calculating BLEU scores on the two test sets. The results are listed in Table 5.

| Type of data | EN>FR generic | EN>FR in-domain | EN>GA generic | EN>GA in-domain |
|---|---|---|---|---|
| Baseline sample training data | 40.0 | 45.7 | 25.0 | 19.7 |
| +In-domain 0.7 | 40.5 | 47.5 | 35.3 | 29.5 |
| +In-domain 0.5 | **41.4** | **53.1** | **37.2** | **32.8** |
| +In-domain 0.7, topic filtered | 40.2 | 47.2 | 30.1 | 24.9 |

Table 5: Evaluation results.

These figures show that adding domain-specific training data consistently leads to improvements for both language pairs, on both generic and in-domain test sets. Nonetheless, the EN>FR systems perform clearly better on the in-domain than on the generic test set, while it is the other way around for EN>GA.

| source | (vii) re-professionalisation of the military and disbanding of para-military groups, |
|---|---|
| reference | vii) reprofessionnalisation de l'armée et démantèlement des groupes paramilitaires; |
| baseline | vii) une reconversion de l'armée et un débarquement de groupes para-militaires, |
| +in-domain 0.7 | vii) la réprofessionnalisation de l'armée et le démantèlement de groupes para-militaires, |
| +in-domain 0.7, topic-filtered | vii) la reprofessionnalisation des militaires et la dissuasion de groupes para-militaires, |

Table 6: EN>FR translations of an example sentence.

When comparing the BLEU scores of the different models, it is also clear that the 0.5-0.7 range of Bicleaner adds many useful information to the parallel data, as there is a substantial increase in BLEU compared to the 0.7-1 range, especially in case of the in-domain test set (EN>FR +5.6, EN>GA +3.3). However, manual inspection of the output given a threshold of 0.5 teaches us that the high BLEU scores are often caused by the fact that a part of the sentence shows a strong n-gram overlap with the reference, while the remainder of the sentence is rather noisy.

As for topic filtering, the evaluation scores indicate it can be a useful step. Even though only 10% of the EN>FR domain-specific data was retained by the topic filter, the improvement in terms of BLEU (+1.5) over the baseline is almost as high as in case of adding the non-filtered data (+1.8), while much less training data is used. In case of EN>GA, the figures are different: adding the unfiltered data leads to an improvement of 9.8, whereas filtered data improves 5.2 BLEU. This difference between EN>FR and EN>GA seems to indicate that the unfiltered data for EN>FR do not add much value to the baseline data in terms of non-domain knowledge, whereas the unfiltered EN>GA data both add value in terms of non-domain and domain knowledge.

## 6   Conclusion

In this paper we applied the ParaCrawl-pipeline to the legal-domain: for two language pairs (EN>FR and EN>GA), we scraped a number of websites, aligned the data on document and sentence level, and added topic classification on top. We performed both intrinsic (using a gold standard) and extrinsic (by comparing a baseline MT system to domain-specific MT systems respectively) evaluations.

For the most resource-poor language pair (EN>GA), we have created a parallel resource that is substantial in size (131k) compared to publicly available data: there are 139k relevant sentence pairs on the Opus website (i.e. excluding corpora like *Ubuntu*) and 325k sentence pairs in the legal-domain. EN>GA MT systems reported on in the literature extract a much more limited amount of sentence pairs from websites or use parallel material that is not publicly available. While the EN>GA MT system Tapadóir (Dowling et al. 2015) also makes use of some websites with multilingual information, they only extracted 10k sentence pairs in total from these websites. The MT system IRIS (Arcan et al. 2016) makes use of a number of resources, among which second level textbooks (373k), which the authors received from a university but are not publicly available.

The intrinsic evaluation results show that we obtain high-quality alignments for EN-FR and EN-GA when comparing to the gold standard. We also tested different Bicleaner thresholds, which showed that 0.5 (when omitting a threshold for Hunalign) leads to a high precision and a sufficiently high recall, although both precision and recall is somewhat lower for EN-GA for all thresholds considered.

The extrinsic evaluation shows that we obtain significant improvements for both EN>FR and EN>GA when adding domain-specific data, which indicates the usefulness of the data produced by the pipeline in an MT context.

The topic filtering proved useful based on the extrinsic evaluation results. Adding only 10% of the EN>FR domain-specific data results in almost the same improvement as the one obtained when adding all data. However, this assumes a strong baseline, as indicated by the figures for EN>GA, which show a much smaller improvement when adding topic-filtered data only.

## Acknowledgement

This work was performed in the framework of the SMART 2015/1091 project ("Tools and resources for CEF automated translation"), funded by the CEF Telecom programme (Connecting Europe Facility).

## References

Arcan, Mihael, Caoilfhionn Lane, Eoin Ó Droighneáin, and Paul Buitelaar. 2016. IRIS: English-Irish Machine Translation System. *LREC 2016, Proceedings of the Tenth International Conference on Language Resources and Evaluation*, pages 566–572.

Bojanowski, Piotr, Edouard Grave, Armand Joulin, and Tomas Mikolov. 2017. Enriching word vectors with subword information. *Transactions of the Association of Computational Linguistics*, 5(1):135–146.

Brown, Peter F., Jennifer C. Lai, and Robert L. Mercer. 1991. Aligning sentences in parallel corpora. In *Proceedings of the 29th annual meeting on Association for Computational Linguistics*, pages 169–176.

Buck, Christian, Kenneth Heafield, and Bas van Ooyen. 2014. N-gram Counts and Language Models from the Common Crawl. *LREC 2014, Proceedings of the Ninth International Conference on Language Resources and Evaluation*, pages 3579–3584.

Buck, Christian and Philipp Koehn. 2016. Findings of the WMT 2016 Bilingual Document Alignment

Shared Task. *WMT 2016, Proceedings of the First Conference on Machine Translation*, Volume 2: Shared Task Papers, pages 554–563.

Buck, Christian and Philipp Koehn. 2016. Quick and Reliable Document Alignment via TF/IDF-weighted Cosine Distance. *WMT 2016, Proceedings of the First Conference on Machine Translation*, Volume 2: Shared Task Papers, pages 672–678.

Dowling, Meghan, Lauren Cassidy, Eimear Maguire, Teresa Lynn, Ankit Srivastava, and John Judge. 2015. Tapadóir: Developing a statistical machine translation engine and associated resources for Irish. *LRL 2015, Proceedings of The Fourth LRL Workshop: "Language Technologies in support of Less-Resourced Languages"*, Poznan, Poland.

Joulin, Armand, Edouard Grave, Piotr Bojanowski, and Tomas Mikolov. 2017. Bag of tricks for efficient text classification. *ACL 2017, Proceedings of the 15th Conference of the European Chapter of the Association for Computational Linguistics: Volume 2, Short Papers*, pages 427–431.

Klein, Guillaume, Yoon Kim, Yuntian Deng, Jean Senellart, and Alexander M. Rush. 2017. Opennmt: Open-source toolkit for neural machine translation. *ACL 2017, Proceedings of ACL 2017 Conference Demo Papers*, Vancouver, Canada, pages 67-72.

Sánchez-Cartagena, Victor M., Marta Bañón, Sergio Ortiz-Rojas, and Gema Ramírez-Sánchez. 2018. Prompsit's submission to WMT 2018 Parallel Corpus Filtering shared task. *WMT 2018, Proceedings of the Third Conference on Machine Translation*, Volume 2: Shared Task Papers, pages 995–962.

Varga, Daniel, László Németh, Péter Halácsy, András Kornai, Viktor Trón, and Viktor Nagy. 2005. Parallel corpora for medium density languages. *RANLP 2005. Recent Advances in Natural Language Processing IV: Selected papers from RANLP 2005*, pages 590-596.

## Appendices

### Appendix A. Overview of corpora statistics

| domain/url<br><br>EN-FR | description | #doc. (EN) | #doc. (FR) | #doc. match Malign |
|---|---|---|---|---|
| https://e-justice.europa.eu | European e-justice portal | 2,581 | 1,973 | 1,642 |
| laws-lois.justice.gc.ca | Consolidated Acts and regulations | 5,062 | 5,062 | 3,355 |
| http://justice.gc.ca | Department of Justice | 25,402 | 5,952 | 2,732 |
| www.noscommunes.ca | House of commons | 382 | 382 | 381 |
| https://sencanada.ca | Senate | 136 | 136 | 136 |
| www.legifrance.gouv.fr | Government entity responsible for publishing legal texts online | 12,110 | 34,378 | 9,270 |
| www.oecd.org | Org. for Economic Co-operation and Developm. | 1,321 | 1,321 | 1,292 |

Table A.1. Overview of corpora statistics on document level for each scraped web-domain (EN-FR). Last column shows the number of aligned documents using Malign (threshold=0.1).

| domain/url<br><br>EN-GA | description | #doc. (EN) | #doc. (GA) | #matched doc. (Malign) |
|---|---|---|---|---|
| https://www.education.ie | Department of Education and Skills | 18,542 | 3,459 | 1,340 |
| www.courts.ie | Courts Service | 610 | 544 | 235 |

Table A.2. See Table A.1, but now for the EN-GA language-pair.

| domain/url<br><br>EN-FR | #unique aligned sent. (Hunalign) | #unique aligned sent. (Hunalign + Bicleaner) | #unique aligned sent. (Hunalign + Bicleaner +Topic model) |
|---|---|---|---|
| https://e-justice.europa.eu | 50,884 | 26,004 | 16,926 |
| laws-lois.justice.gc.ca | 66,346 | 30,163 | 21,416 |
| http://justice.gc.ca | 142,458 | 60,841 | 11,785 |
| www.noscommunes.ca | 1,042,797 | 581,358 | 13,090 |
| https://sencanada.ca | 123,570 | 70,657 | 2,846 |
| www.legifrance.gouv.fr | 25,321 | 13,266 | 11,624 |
| www.oecd.org | 21,511 | 4,431 | 2,158 |

Table A.3: Overview of corpora statistics for each scraped web-domain (EN-FR). Second column shows the number of resulting aligned sentences after alignment with Hunalign (no Hunalign threshold was set). Third column shows results after applying Bicleaner (Bicleaner threshold=0.7). Last column shows the number of Bicleaner-cleaned sentences labeled as 'legal' by our topic model.

| domain/url<br><br>EN-FR | #EN tokens in unique aligned sent. (Hunalign) | #EN tokens in unique aligned sent. (Hunalign + Bicleaner) | #EN tokens in unique aligned sent. (Hunalign + Bicleaner +Topic model) |
|---|---|---|---|
| https://e-justice.europa.eu | 1,376,827 | 690,768 | 496,644 |

| | | | |
|---|---|---|---|
| laws-lois.justice.gc.ca | 2,300,404 | 1,028,717 | 858,844 |
| http://justice.gc.ca | 3,571,748 | 1,369,891 | 281,943 |
| www.noscommunes.ca | 23,074,752 | 12,793,886 | 281,820 |
| https://sencanada.ca | 2.802.562 | 1,600,373 | 73,578 |
| www.legifrance.gouv.fr | 827,434 | 444,850 | 405,203 |
| www.oecd.org | 571,287 | 110,183 | 58,521 |

Table A.4: Overview of corpora statistics for each scraped web-domain (EN-FR). Columns show the number of EN tokens in the unique aligned sentences reported in Table A.3.

| domain/url<br><br>EN-GA | #unique aligned sent. (Hunalign) | #unique aligned sent. (Hunalign + Bicleaner) | #unique aligned sent. (Hunalign + Bicleaner +Topic model) |
|---|---|---|---|
| www.educationinireland.com | 164,620 | 92,245 | 30,953 |
| www.courts.ie | 3,308 | 2,033 | 743 |

Table A.5: See Table A.3, but now for the EN-GA language pair.

| domain/url<br><br>EN-GA | #EN tokens in unique aligned sent. (Hunalign) | #EN tokens in unique aligned sent. (Hunalign + Bicleaner) | #EN tokens in unique aligned sent. (Hunalign + Bicleaner +Topic model) |
|---|---|---|---|
| www.educationinireland.com | 4,293,616 | 2,615,973 | 961,459 |
| www.courts.ie | 78,148 | 50,827 | 21,062 |

Table A.6: Overview of corpora statistics for each scraped web-domain (EN-GA). Columns show the number of EN tokens in the unique aligned sentences reported in Table A.5.

## Appendix B. Gold standard statistics

| | |
|---|---|
| English Sentences | 723 |
| French sentences | 716 |
| 1-to-1 beads | 629 |
| Many-to-1 beads | 16 |
| 1-to-many beads | 18 |
| Many-to-many beads | 1 |
| **Total number of beads used for evaluation** | **664** |
| 1-to-0 beads | 35 |
| 0-to-1 beads | 32 |
| English sentences in partial links | 5 |
| French sentences in partial links | 5 |
| Total number of beads | 731 |

Table B.1: Gold standard statistics (EN-FR). Note that partial links involve two partially equivalent sentences that are not part of a bead; they are considered as a combination of a 0-to-1 bead and a 1-to-0 bead, hence they are ignored.

| | |
|---|---|
| English Sentences | 746 |
| Irish sentences | 778 |
| 1-to-1 beads | 631 |
| Many-to-1 beads | 18 |
| 1-to-many beads | 19 |
| Many-to-many beads | 3 |
| **Total number of beads used for evaluation** | **671** |
| 1-to-0 beads | 38 |
| 0-to-1 beads | 67 |
| English sentences in partial links | 13 |
| Irish sentences in partial links | 15 |
| Total number of beads | 776 |

Table B.2: Gold standard statistics (EN-GA).

## Appendix C. Baseline training data and test data

| Corpus | EN-FR | EN-GA |
|---|---|---|
| DCEP[23] | 3,728,978 | 46,418 |
| DGT[24] | 3,071,997 | 44,309 |
| ECDC[25] | 2,499 | |
| EAC[26] | 4,476 | |
| Eubookshop[27] | | 133,363 |
| **Total (cleaned)** | **4,258,861** | **139,404** |

Table C.1: Overview of the training data of our baseline engines. This data was also used for training of X>EN engines necessary for document alignment.

[23]https://wt-public.emm4u.eu/Resources/DCEP-2013/DCEP-Download-Page.html
[24]http://opus.nlpl.eu/DGT.php
[25]https://ec.europa.eu/jrc/en/language-technologies/ecdc-translation-memory
[26]https://ec.europa.eu/jrc/en/language-technologies/eac-translation-memory
[27]http://opus.nlpl.eu/EUbookshop-v2.php

| Corpus | EN-FR (full) | EN-FR (test sample) | EN-GA (full) | EN-GA (test sample) |
|---|---|---|---|---|
| JRC-Acquis | 814,167 | 2000 | | |
| EU-Const | 10,103 | 1000 | 10,027 | 1000 |
| Acts of the Oireachtas | | | 315,231 | 2000 |
| **Total** | **824,270** | **3000** | **325,258** | **3000** |

Table C2: Overview of the corpora used for the creation of the in-domain test sets

# Monolingual backtranslation in a medical speech translation system for diagnostic interviews - a NMT approach

**Jonathan Mutal**[1], **Pierrette Bouillon**[1], **Johanna Gerlach**[1], **Paula Estrella**[2], and **Hervé Spechbach**[3]

[1]FTI/TIM, University of Geneva, Switzerland
[2]FaMaF y FL, University of Córdoba, Argentina
[3]Hôpitaux Universitaires de Genève (HUG), Switzerland
{Jonathan.Mutal, Pierrette.Bouillon, Johanna.Gerlach}@unige.ch
paula.estrella@unc.edu.ar
herve.spechbach@hcuge.ch

## Abstract

BabelDr is a medical speech to speech translator, where the doctor has to approve the sentence that will be translated for the patient before translation; this step is done using monolingual backtranslation, which converts the speech recognition result into a core sentence. In this work, we model this step as a simplification task and propose to use neural networks to perform the backtranslation by generating and choosing the best core sentence. Results of a task-based evaluation show that neural networks outperform previous versions of the system.

## 1 Introduction

BabelDr[1] is a joint project between the Faculty of Translation and Interpreting of the University of Geneva and Geneva University Hospitals (HUG) (Bouillon et al., 2017; Boujon et al., 2017).

The aim of the project is to build a speech to speech translation system for emergency settings which meets three criteria: reliability, data security and portability to low-resourced target languages relevant for the HUG. To ensure reliability, the system is based on a set of manually pre-translated sentences (around 30'000 *core sentences*) defined with the help of doctors and classified by anatomic domains (e.g. head, chest, abdomen, etc.). The basic idea is that the doctor can speak freely and

the system will map the recognised utterance to the closest core sentence.

The translation from source recognition result to target language is done in two steps: 1) mapping of the source recognition result to a core sentence (*backtranslation*, Gao et al., 2006; Seligman and Dillinger, 2013) and 2) look-up of the (human) translation of the core sentence for the relevant target language.

Backtranslation is therefore an essential step in this type of architecture (see also Ehsani et al., 2008; Seligman and Dillinger, 2013). The doctor has to approve the backtranslation of his utterance, ensuring awareness of the exact meaning of the translation produced for the patient. Backtranslation can also be considered as a type of simplification task (Cardon, 2018). It translates the doctor's questions for the layman, reducing the vocabulary by 40%, removing medical jargon and making the meaning explicit both for the human translator and the patient. The following are examples of such lexical, syntactic and semantic simplification processes:

- Recognition result: *c'est chaud* (it is warm) → Backtranslation: *la peau est-elle chaude ?* (is the skin warm?)

- Recognition result: *où est-ce que se trouve la douleur* (where is the pain) → Backtranslation: *pouvez-vous me montrer avec le doigt où est la douleur ?* (can you show with your finger where the pain is?)

- Recognition result: *avez-vous un hématome* (do you have a hematoma) → Backtranslation: *avez-vous un bleu ?* (do you have a



[1]More information available at https://babeldr.unige.ch/

bruise?)

In the current version of the system, backtranslation is performed by rule-based methods and methods borrowed from information retrieval. In this paper, we investigate a backtranslation approach using neural machine translation (NMT) trained on the data generated from the existing grammar. Our aim is to see whether it is possible to bootstrap the NMT from the rule-based system and how it will perform in comparison with the existing strategies used in BabelDr.

Section 2 describes BabelDr and the different strategies used for backtranslation in the current system. We then explain how NMT was derived from the grammar to create different neural network versions (Section 3). Section 4 describes the task-based evaluation and Section 5 presents the results.

## 2 BabelDr versions

The current BabelDr application used at the HUG translates from French to Arabic, Albanian, Farsi, Spanish, Tigrinya and French Swiss Sign Language. It is a hybrid system which combines rule-based and tf-idf methods for backtranslation. In this section we describe these different methods and the system versions used in our study.

### 2.1 Version 1 - rule-based version

The rule-based version of the system relies on a manually written grammar, using a formalism based on Synchronous CFG (SCFG, Aho and Ullman, 1969). The grammar consists of a set of rules defining source language variation patterns which are mapped to core sentences (Gerlach et al., 2018). This grammar is compiled into a language model which can be used by Nuance[2] for speech recognition and parsing to core sentences. While this rule based approach works well for in coverage (IC) spoken utterances, i.e. utterances that are among the variations described in the grammar, it often fails for out-of-coverage (OOC) ones. For the abdominal domain (one out of 13 diagnostic domains), the grammar currently contains 1'797 rules which map 4'082 core sentences to 488 million variations.

### 2.2 Version 2 - tf-idf/DP version

The second version of the system uses a large vocabulary speech recogniser (Nuance Transcrip-

tion Engine) customised with data derived from the grammar. It then applies an approach based on tf-idf indexing and dynamic programming (DP) to match the recognition result to a core sentence (Rayner et al., 2017). This version is better suited for processing of OOC utterances, but remains imperfect, in particular because it relies on a bag of words approach.

### 2.3 Version 3 - hybrid version

The third version of the system, which is the currently deployed version, combines the rule-based method (Version 1) with the tf-idf/DP approach (Version 2) in order to benefit from the precision of the rules on IC sentences while ensuring robustness on OOC data. The results from the two methods are combined as follows: when the rule based recogniser confidence score is over a given threshold, Version 1 is used; when it is below the threshold, suggesting poor recognition, the tf-idf/DP result is used instead.

In the next sections we describe how we used NMT for backtranslation and present the experiments carried out to compare the different approaches.

## 3 NMT for backtranslation

As mentioned, backtranslation is seen here as a translation to a simplified language, where many variations of the same source sentence are translated into a predefined easy-to-understand core sentence. Even if simplification is a well studied process, only few studies apply machine translation and NMT (Wang et al., 2016). The main reason is the lack of aligned corpora as mentioned in (Suter et al., 2016), in particular in the medical domain and for French (Cardon, 2018). In this study, we propose to use data generated from the grammar to construct an aligned corpus and train a NMT system. The backtranslation is performed by NMT and the final result is chosen among the N-Best translations according to a heuristic (Section 3.3). In the next sections, we describe the generated corpus, explain how we trained the NMT system and introduce two BabelDr versions based on NMT.

### 3.1 Data set

For this experiment, we used the data generated from an early version of the SCFG, described in (Rayner et al., 2017). It consists of 221'819

---

[2]https://www.nuance.com

| Source variation | Backtranslation |
| --- | --- |
| votre ventre fait mal ? | avez-vous mal au ventre ? <br> (do you have stomach pain?) |
| ça vous soulage de rester couché | la douleur au ventre diminue-t-elle quand vous restez couché ? <br> (does the stomach pain decrease when you lie down?) |
| avez-vous des antécédents chirurgicaux au niveau de l'abdomen ? | avez-vous eu une opération du ventre ? <br> (have you had abdominal surgery?) |
| est ce que vous pourriez me montrer votre carte d'assuré ? | pouvez-vous me montrer la carte d'assurance ? <br> (could you show me your insurance card?) |

**Table 1:** Examples of aligned sentences derived from rules (source variations-backtranslation).

sentences from the abdominal diagnostic domain mapped to 2'517 different core sentences. Table 1 illustrates examples of the data.

Since we are interested in evaluating the complete set of core sentences, development and test data follow the same distribution as the training data, i.e. each subset contains an equal proportion of core sentences. Tables 2 and 3 summarise the number of sentences, tokens and vocabulary for each subset, for source variations and core sentences (target) respectively.

| Subset | #sentences | #tokens | #vocabulary |
| --- | --- | --- | --- |
| Train | 199k | 2M | 2132 |
| Dev | 12k | 124k | 1581 |
| Test | 10k | 103k | 1478 |

**Table 2:** Number of sentences, tokens and vocabulary for source variations.

| Subset | #sentences | #tokens | #vocabulary |
| --- | --- | --- | --- |
| Train | 199k | 1.5M | 880 |
| Dev | 12k | 99k | 838 |
| Test | 10k | 82k | 829 |

**Table 3:** Number of sentences, tokens and vocabulary for core sentences (target).

The source sentences have been lower cased and tokenized; then, Byte-pair encoding (Sennrich, 2016) was trained on the training data set and applied to training, development and test data.

### 3.2 NMT configuration

We used OpenNMT-tf (Klein et al., 2017, Open-NMT,) for training and decoding. OpenNMT is a framework mainly focused at developing encoder-decoder architectures.

As we can consider our task a low resource NMT (2M tokens in training data, Zoph et al., 2016), we had two alternatives to tackle this task: 1) follow (Zoph et al., 2016) and apply transfer learning or 2) choose an appropriate neural architecture in terms of size. We find 2) a better alternative because of the lack of medical corpora suitable for this application.

Transformer (Vaswani et al., 2017) is the state-of-art in most NMT tasks, but it is better suited to learn in high-resource conditions (Tran et al., 2018). Therefore, we decided to compare Transformer performance with an encoder-decoder architecture based on recurrent neural networks (RNN) (Kalchbrenner and Blunsom, 2013; Bahdanau et al., 2014; Loung et al., 2015).

**Transformer:** The model is composed of a 512 embedding size in the encoder and decoder. The architecture is described in (Vaswani et al., 2017). The parameters used were the default for this model[3].

**RNN:** The model is composed of 512 embedding size in the encoder and decoder. Encoder and decoder are each composed of two LSTM (Hochreiter et al., 2006) with an attention mechanism on the decoder side (Bahdanau et al., 2014; Loung et al., 2015). The model was trained with a dropout rate of 0.3 and a batch size of 64 examples.

Both models use early stopping in order to reduce the number of training steps by monitoring the performance on the development set. All the models are trained using ADAM optimiser (Kingma and Ba, 2014). The parameters were averaged from the last 10 checkpoints for each model.

---

[3]http://opennmt.net/OpenNMT-tf/model.html#catalog

| **Speech rec. result** | Avez-vous des animaux |
|---|---|
| **1-best NMT** | travaillez-vous avec des animaux ? (is core sentence = true) |
| **2-best NMT** | avez-vous des animaux ? (is core sentence = false) |
| **Result** | travaillez-vous avec des animaux ? |

**Figure 1:** Example of utterance where the 1-best NMT result is a core sentence and is therefore chosen as final result

| **Speech rec. result** | Avez-vous des nausées les vomissements |
|---|---|
| **1-best NMT** | vomissez-vous des boissons alcoolisées ? (is core sentence = false) |
| **2-best NMT** | vomissez-vous des nausées ? (is core sentence = false) |
| **Closest core to 1-best** | buvez-vous des boissons alcoolisées tous les jours ? (0.43) |
| **Closest core to 2-best** | avez-vous des nausées ? (0.84) |
| **Result** | avez-vous des nausées ? |

**Figure 2:** Example of utterance where neither of the NMT results is a core sentence and final result is selected based on cosine similarity.

### 3.3 N-Best sentence

The model was configured to generate $n$ candidates ($n = 1, 2, 3$ for this experiment); the best candidate is selected by keeping the first one which matches a core sentence. This case is illustrated in Figure 1. If none of the candidates are core sentences, the *word embedding similarity* selection heuristic from STS 2016 (see Agirre et al., 2016) is used to find the closest core sentence. In order to find the closest sentence, sentence embeddings (Arora et al., 2016) are computed using word embeddings learned by the decoder. Afterwards, the candidates (i.e. the $n$ results generated by NMT) are embedded to the same continuous space and cosine similarity is calculated to choose the closest core sentence. Figure 2 illustrates this case.

### 3.4 NMT Evaluation

We carried out an automatic evaluation to choose between the two neural MT architectures, adding N-Best sentence generation to each model. We measured system performance on the test data using two standard metrics: BLEU (Papineni et al., 2002) and TER (Snover et. al, 2006), as shown in Table 4.

| Model | N-Best | TER | BLEU |
|---|---|---|---|
| | 1-best | 0.8 | 97.84 |
| RNN | 2-best | 0.7 | 99.7 |
| | 3-best | 0.7 | 99.7 |
| | 1-best | 0.9 | 97.65 |
| Transformer | 2-best | 0.8 | 99.45 |
| | 3-best | 0.8 | 99.45 |

**Table 4:** Comparison between models with N-Best (N=1,2,3) sentences.

Table 4 shows that there was no significant difference between the results obtained with Transformer and with RNN. An intuitive explanation for this is that the sentences in our data set are rather short, with a mean sentence length of 10.37 words, and thus present no difficulties for the RNN approach. Furthermore, the amount of training data might not be suitable for a transformer architecture (Tran et al., 2018). We also observe that adding the 2nd best sentence improves the performance of the model while adding a 3rd best does not bring an improvement.

To carry out the next experiments, we chose RNN with 2-best sentences.

### 3.5 BabelDr NMT versions (Version 4 and 5)

Two new versions of BabelDr were built based on the neural architecture described in previous Sections.

**Version 4:** uses the same large vocabulary speech recogniser as Version 2, but instead of an approach based on tf-idf and dynamic programming (DP), it is based on a neural approach.

**Version 5:** is hybrid, following the same principle as Version 3 but using NMT instead of tdf-idf to generate the core sentences when the rule-based recogniser confidence score is below the threshold.

## 4 Task-based evaluation

### 4.1 Motivation

Our main research question is to see if it is possible to bootstrap a NMT system from the data generated with the rule-based system. To answer this, we will focus on the following sub-questions: 1)

| Version | Speech | | | Text | | |
|---|---|---|---|---|---|---|
| | IC | OOC | ALL | IC | OOC | ALL |
| Version 1 | 13.9 | 72.0 | 31.2 | 0 | 100 | 29.8 |
| Version 2 | 8.5 | 48.1 | 20.4 | 1.2 | 43.5 | 13.8 |
| Version 3 | 6.4 | 48.1 | 18.8 | – | – | – |
| Version 4 | 9.3 | 32.7 | 16.3 | 0.8 | 21.0 | 6.8 |
| Version 5 | 6.2 | 32.2 | 13.9 | – | – | – |

**Table 5:** SER for IC, OOC and ALL for in domain speech recognition results (Speech) and transcriptions (Text). No text results are provided for the hybrid versions (3 and 5), since transcriptions are independent from the speech recogniser confidence score threshold.

will the system be able to generate core sentences, 2) does a non core sentence indicate an out-of-domain (OOD) utterance, i.e. one that could not be associated with any of the core sentences, and 3) how will the system perform in comparison with the currently used approaches. In order to answer these questions, we used the different versions of the system (described in Sections 2 and 3.5) to process utterances collected during diagnostic interviews. These test data are the same as used in Rayner et al. (2017). Results for system Versions 1-3 are therefore taken from this publication.

### 4.2 Test Data

The test data are French utterances collected in an experiment where doctors and medical students used the system to diagnose two standardised patients (Bouillon et al., 2017). It includes 10 complete diagnostic interviews by 10 different speakers, for a total of 827 utterances. Each utterance was transcribed and annotated, where possible, with a corresponding core sentence. We excluded out-of-domain (OOD) utterances, which represent 110 items (14%). The remaining data can be split into IC (503 items), where transcriptions are among the variations described in the SCFG, and OOC (214 items), where the transcriptions are not among these variations, but match a core sentence closely enough to be considered synonymous.

### 4.3 Evaluation criteria

We want to compare the different versions at the task level, namely how many spoken utterances will result in a correct translation for the patient. Since the system relies on human pre-translation (Section 1), a correct core sentence is equivalent to a correct translation. We therefore measured the sentence error rate (SER), defined as the percentage of utterances for which the resulting core sentence is not identical to the annotated correct core sentence. As input utterances we used the speech recognition results from the large vocabulary recogniser (speech) and the transcriptions (text, which simulates the case where recognition is perfect). This metric and approach allows us to compare our results with those reported for system Versions 1-3 in Rayner et al. (2017).

## 5 Results

In order to answer our first research question, we calculated the proportion of non core sentences among the sentences generated by the NMT system. Considering all data (IC, OOC and OOD), these only amount to 2% on 2-Best and 5% on 1-Best. Nearly 50% of these non core sentences are translations of out of domain utterances. These results suggest that non core sentence backtranslations could serve as indicator for out of domain utterances, a fact that could be exploited in the BabelDr application to identify concepts not covered by the system.

Table 5 presents SER results on test data both on speech recognition results and on transcriptions. For spoken data, the NMT model (Version 4) outperforms all the previous versions on ALL data for the task, reducing the SER by 4 points in comparison with the best of the previous versions. A closer comparison of the two non-hybrid versions shows that Version 4 has a slightly higher error rate than Version 2 on IC utterances (9.3 vs 8.5), while it has a much lower error rate on OOC utterances (32.7 vs 48.1). These results could be explained by the different approaches: since tf-idf matches words and computes its scores based on grammar content, it has more chances of finding correct results for IC utterances than NMT, which generates a new sentence based on a semantic representation. On the other hand, NMT is better suited to handle OOC, since this semantic representation allows it to generalise.

As expected, the hybrid NMT version (Version 5) obtains similar performance to Version 4 on OOC and improves scores on IC data (6.2 vs 9.3), since as with the previous hybrid system (Version 3) the generally reliable high-confidence rule-based results replace potentially incorrect NMT results.

When using transcriptions as input, the proportion of errors for NMT is reduced by 9.5 SER points (16.3 to 6.8 on ALL data for Version 4), showing the negative impact of speech recognition errors on the result. A closer look at the data shows that most errors occur when the speech recognition result contains 1) words that are not in the training data, which often happens when words are recognised incorrectly by the large vocabulary recogniser, resulting in OOD items, or 2) words that appear in the grammar but are rare in the training data.

## 6 Conclusion

The results of this study show that for this backtranslation task, NMT outperforms previous versions of the system. It also shows the potential of NMT and hybrid architectures for simplification tasks.

For BabelDr, the neural network approach reduces the error by 4 SER points on spoken utterances and by 9.5 points on transcriptions, which simulate perfect speech recognition. Results also show that this approach has generated core sentences in all but 2% of cases (2-Best), suggesting that it can learn the simplified language. Non core sentences mostly indicate OOD utterances.

This study has several limitations. It uses only a subset of the sentences generated by the SCFG for training, thus allowing for words present in the rules, but missing from the training data; this is subject to further improvements by enlarging the training corpus.

Another limitation is that for this study we used an older version of the grammar. The latest version of the grammar not only includes more words (nearly 5000 for abdominal domain), core sentences and variations but also contains ambiguous rules. These rules allow multiple backtranslations for ambiguous utterances, for example *est-elle forte* (is it severe?) could translate to *la fièvre est-elle forte* (is the fever high?) or *la douleur au ventre est-elle forte ?* (is the abdominal pain se-

vere) depending on the context, where context can be defined as the utterances before, e.g. *avez-vous de la fièvre* (do you have a fever?) for the example above. Integrating context dependent processing is thus another area for improvement of the backtranslation process. One possibility for this could be to use document-level machine translation (Lesly et al., 2018) or add the context when translating (Agrawal et al., 2018).

A further aspect worth investigating is the size of the grammar: the current grammar extensively describes variations, necessary for grammar-based speech recognition, yet it is unclear whether such an extensive grammar is necessary for the generation of training data for the NMT approach, or whether a more compact grammar, combined with the NMT approach in a hybrid system, could achieve similar performance.

Finally, future work will also include a comparison of the NMT approach with state-of-the-art approaches for semantic text similarity (STS) tasks (Zhao and Vogel, 2002; Cer et al., 2017; Rychalska et al., 2016).

Despite these limitations, to the best of our knowledge, it is the first experiment to use NMT for backtranslation in fixed phrase translators and to test it on data from real diagnostic interviews.

## Acknowledgements

This project is financed by the "Fondation Privée des Hôpitaux Universitaires de Genève". We would also like to thank Nuance Inc for generously making their software available to us for research purposes.

## References

Agirre Eneko, Banea Carmen, Cer Daniel, Diab Mona, Gonzalez-Agirre Aitor, Mihalcea Rada, Rigau German and Wiebe Janyce. 2016. SemEval-2016 Task 1: Semantic Textual Similarity, Monolingual and Cross-Lingual Evaluation. *Proceedings of the 10th International Workshop on Semantic Evaluation (SemEval-2016)*. San Diego, California. 497–511.

Agrawal, Ruchit AND Turchi, Marco AND Negri, Matteo. 2018. *Proceedings of the 21st Annual Conference of the European Association for Machine Translation*: 28-30 May 2018, Universitat d'Alacant, Alacant, Spain, pp. 11-20.

Aho, Alfred and Ullman, Jeffrey. 1969. Properties of syntax directed translations. *Journal of Computer and System Sciences*. 3. 319–334. 10.1016/S0022-0000(69)80018-8.

Bahdanau, Dzmitry, Kyunghyun Cho, and Yoshua Bengio. 2014. Neural Machine Translation by Jointly Learning to Align and Translate. In Proceedings of the International Conference on Learning Representations (arXiv:1409.0473).

Bouillon P, Gerlach J, Spechbach H, Tsourakis N, Halimi. 2017. BabelDr vs Google Translate: a user study at Geneva University Hospitals (HUG). Proceedings of the 20th Annual Conference of the European Association for Machine Translation. Prague, Czech Republic. p 747-52.

Boujon V, Bouillon P, Spechbach H, Gerlach J, Strasly I. 2017 September 15-16. Can speech-enabled phraselators improve healthcare accessibility? A case study comparing BabelDr with MediBabble for anamnesis in emergency settings. Proceedings of the 1st Swiss Conference on Barrier-free Communication. Winterthur, Switzerland. p. 32-38. 2017. 2018 DOI 10.21256/zhaw-3000.

Cardon, Rémi. 2018. Approche lexicale de la simplification automatique de textes médicaux. *In: RJC 2018, 14-18 May 2018*. Rennes, France.

Daniel M. Cer, Mona T. Diab, Eneko Agirre, Iñigo Lopez-Gazpio and Lucia Specia. 2017. SemEval-2017 Task 1: Semantic Textual Similarity - Multilingual and Cross-lingual Focused Evaluation. *dblp computer science bibliography, https://dblp.org*. CoRR. arXiv. 1708.00055. http://arxiv.org/abs/1708.00055. Mon, 13 Aug 2018 16:45:59 +0200.

Ehsani, Farzad, Jim Kimzey, Elaine Zuber, Demitrios Master, and Karen Sudre. 2008. Speech to Speech Translation for Nurse Patient Interaction. *In: Coling 2008: Proceedings of the Workshop on Speech Processing for Safety Critical Translation and Pervasive Applications*. Manchester, England, August, 2008, pages 54-59.

Felix Hill, Kyunghyun Cho and Anna Korhonen 2016 Learning Distributed Representations of Sentences from Unlabelled Data. *CoRR*.abs/1602.03483 .http://arxiv.org/abs/1602.03483. arXiv. Mon, 13 Aug 2018. dblp computer science bibliography, https://dblp.org.

Gao Y, Gu L , Zhou B, Sarikaya R, Afify M, Kuo K, Zhu W, Deng Y, Prosser C, Zhang W,

Besacier L. IBM MASTOR SYSTEM: Multilingual automatic speech-to-speech translator. Proceedings of the First International Workshop on Medical Speech Translation, in conjunction with NAACL/HLT. 2006 June 4-9; New York, NY, USA. Madison, WI; Omnipress Inc; 2006.

Gerlach J, Spechbach H, Bouillon P. 2018 Creating an online translation platform to build target language resources for a medical phraselator. *Proceedings of the 40th Edition of the Translating and the Computer Conference (TC40)*. 2018 15-16 November; London, UK. 2018.

Hochreiter S and Schmidhuber J. 2006. Long Short-Term Memory *Neural Computation, 9(8):1735–1780, 1997*.

Kingma, D. P. and Ba, J. 2014. Adam: A method for stochastic optimization. *arXiv preprintarXiv:1412.6980*.

Ke M. Tran, Arianna Bisazza and Christof Monz. 2017. The Importance of Being Recurrent for Modeling Hierarchical Structure. *dblp computer science bibliography, https://dblp.org*. Mon, 13 Aug 2018 16:46:56 +0200.

Klein, Guillaume, Yoon Kim, Yuntian Deng, Jean Senellart, and Alexander M. Rush. 2017. Opennmt: Open-source toolkit for neural machine translation. *arXiv preprintarXiv:1701.02810*.

Lesly Miculicich Werlen and Dhananjay Ram and Nikolaos Pappas and James Henderson. 2018. Document-Level Neural Machine Translation with Hierarchical Attention Networks. *CoRR*.abs/1809.01576. dblp computer science bibliography, https://dblp.org.

Luong, Thang, Hieu Pham, and Christopher D. Manning. 2015. Effective Approaches to Attention-based Neural Machine Translation. *Proceedings of the 2015 Conference on Empirical Methods in Natural Language Processing*. 1412–1421.

Nal Kalchbrenner and Phil Blunsom. 2013. Recurrent Continuous Translation Models. *In Proceedings of the 2013 Conference on Empirical Methods in Natural Language Processing*, pages 1700–1709, Seattle,Washington, USA. Association for Computational Linguistics.

Papineni, Kishore, Salim Roukos, Todd Ward, and Wei-Jing Zhu. 2002. Bleu: a method for automatic eval-uation of machine translation. *In*

*Proceedings of the 40th annual meeting on association for computational linguistics,* pages 311–318. Association for Computational Linguistics.

Rayner M, Tsourakis N, Gerlach J. 2017. Lightweight Spoken Utterance Classification with CFG, tf-idf and Dynamic Programming. *In: Camelin N., Estève Y., Martín-Vide C. (eds) Statistical Language and Speech Processing. SLSP 2017.* Lecture Notes in Computer Science, vol 10583. Springer, Cham

Rychalska, B., Pakulska, K., Chodorowska, K., WojciechWalczak and Andruszkiewicz, P. 2016. Samsung Poland NLP team at SemEval-2016 task 1 : Necessity for diversity ; combining recursive autoencoders, wordnet and ensemble methods to measure semantic similarity. *In SemEval-2016, pp. 614–620* 497–511.

Sanjeev Arora, Yingyu Liang, and Tengyu. Ma. 2016. A simple but tough-to-beat baseline for sentence embeddings. *In ICLR 2017.*

Seligman M, Dillinger M. 2013. Automatic speech translation for healthcare: some internet and interface aspects. *Proceedings of the 10th International Conference on Terminology and Artificial Intelligence (TIA-13).* 2013 October 28-30; Paris, France. 2013.

Sennrich, Rico, Barry Haddow, and Alexandra Birch. 2016. Neural machine translation of rare words with subword units. *In Proceedings of the 54th Annual Meeting of the Association for Computational Linguistics, ACL 2016,* August 7-12, 2016, Berlin, Ger-many, Volume 1: Long Papers.

Snover, M., B. Dorr, R. Schwartz, L. Micciulla and J.Makhoul. 2006. A study of translation edit rate withtargeted human annotation. *Proceedings of the Association for Machine Translation in the Americas,* Vol. 200, No. 6.

Srivastava, Nitish, Geoffrey Hinton, Alex Krizhevsky, Ilya Sutskever, and Ruslan Salakhutdinov. 2014. Dropout: A Simple Way to Prevent Neural Networks from Overfitting. *Journal of Machine Learning Research 15: 1929–58.*

Suter, J., Ebling, S., Volk, M. 2016. Rule-based automatic text simplification for German. *KONVENS 2016.* Bochum, germany, 2016.

Vaswani, Ashish, Noam Shazeer, Niki Parmar, Jakob Uszkoreit, Llion Jones, Aidan N. Gomez, Lukasz Kaiser, and Illia Polosukhin. 2017. Attention Is All You Need. *In Advances in Neural Information Pro-cessing Systems.* ArXiv:1706.03762. (pp. 6000-6010).

Zhao, B. and Vogel, S. 2002. Adaptive parallel sentences mining from web bilingual news collection. *In IEEE Int Conf on Data Mining,* pp. 745–748.

Zoph, Barret and Yuret, Deniz and May, Jonathan and Knight, Kevin 2016. Transfer Learning for Low-Resource Neural Machine Translation. *Proceedings of the 2016 Conference on Empirical Methods in Natural Language Processing.* Austin, Texas Association for Computational Linguistics.

Wang, T., Chen, P., Rochford, J., Quiang J. 2016. Text Simplification using Neural machine translation. *Proceeding of AAAI-16, 4270-4271.*

# Improving Domain Adaptation for Machine Translation with Translation Pieces


**Catarina Silva**
Unbabel
catarina@unbabel.com



## Abstract

Neural Machine Translation has achieved impressive results in the last couple years, in particular when aided by domain adaptation methods. However, it has well known caveats, and can sometimes generate inadequate content that appears fluent, but does not convey the meaning of the original sentence. In particular, for scarce in-domain data, these models tend to overfit, performing poorly on any content that differs slightly from the domain data. In this paper, we apply a recent technique based on translation pieces and show that it can work as a way to improve and stabilize domain adaptation. We present human evaluation results, with gains as high as 20 MQM points for single domains, and consistent gains in a multiple subdomain scenario of 3 MQM points for several language pairs.


## 1 Introduction

Neural Machine Translation (NMT) is a state-of-the-art technique to do machine translation. While NMT has proved to be efficient translating texts between multiple languages (Sennrich et al, 2016a) (Wang et al, 2017) in general settings, the ability of NMT technology to adapt to new domain has not attracted much focus from the research community. On the other hand, domain adaptation is a fundamental element of many industrial applications in which in-domain data is often scarce. In one of the most popular scenarios,

large generic data is used to train an initial NMT system, obtaining a set of parameters that are then fine tuned on the much smaller in-domain corpus (Chu and Wang, 2018). The problem with this approach is that NMT often overfits to the target domain, which makes it less robust when it has to translate content which differs even slightly from the in-domain training data (Arthur et all, 2016) (Kaiser et al, 2017). Thus, the problem also holds when trying to generalize across more than one domain (Koehn and Knowles, 2017), where improving in one of the domains might sacrifice quality in others. In this paper, we present a possible solution to this issue, describing an application of the retrieved translation pieces (Zhang et al, 2018), which we show to help with cross-domain generalisation. We show that translation pieces improves the translation quality in a single domain, but also when combining multiple domains.

## 2 Experimental Setup

### 2.1 Neural Machine Translation

The aim of this work is to assess the impact of adding translation pieces to NMT models. For this purpose, we use the Marian framework[1] (Junczys-Dowmunt et al, 2018) to train models using the attention-based encoder–decoder architecture as described in Sennrich et al (2017).

For all experiments a standard preprocessing routine was applied, consisting of the following steps: entity replacement, tokenisation, truecasing and Byte-Pair Encoding (BPE) (Sennrich et al, 2016b) with 89,500 merge operations.

The process of entity replacement consists of identifying entities that should not be translated or that have a direct translation, usually defined



---

[1] https://marian-nmt.github.io/

as glossaries, and replacing them by placeholders that are put back in the text after translation. These placeholders are protected in the BPE step, so they are always considered as unique subwords.

## 2.2 Domain Adaptation

The domain adaptation process consists on a typical setting of training that uses a pretrained model:

- A model is trained with generic data and its best performing version is kept - using BLEU as the performance metric at validation;

- The generic model is passed as the `pretrained-model` flag in Marian;

- The initialized model is trained on in-domain data, with a lower validation frequency to achieve a validation per epoch .

Besides the validation frequency, for this experiment no other parameters were tuned in the model in the domain adaptation stage.

## 2.3 Translation Pieces Retrieval

For these experiments, we follow a process similar to the one proposed by Zhang et al (2018), where we assume we have a pool of pairs in our language pair – source and corresponding translation – that we can sample before-hand, from which we retrieve nearest neighbours with respect to the source sentences in our training data. Our retrieval process, unlike the base method, is based on sentence embeddings and not on a search engine. We then pick the retrieved sentences and compute a similarity measure that is used to score the pieces.

**Translation Memories Retrieval:** We get average sentence embeddings over all candidates and query sentences, through fastText word embeddings[2] (Joulin et al, 2016), and then run a nearest neighbour algorithm with FAISS (Johnson et al, 2017). This retrieves the neighbours by measuring the cosine similarity between the query embedding and candidate embeddings, as shown in Figure 1.

**Translation Pieces generation:** To get the related translation pieces, we first go through query and candidate sentences and get the unedited words, this is, equal words appearing in both on the same order. We then run an aligner on the candidate's source and target and get the target pieces

---

[2]English embeddings downloaded from wiki-news-300d-1M.vec.zip in https://fasttext.cc/docs/en/english-vectors.html

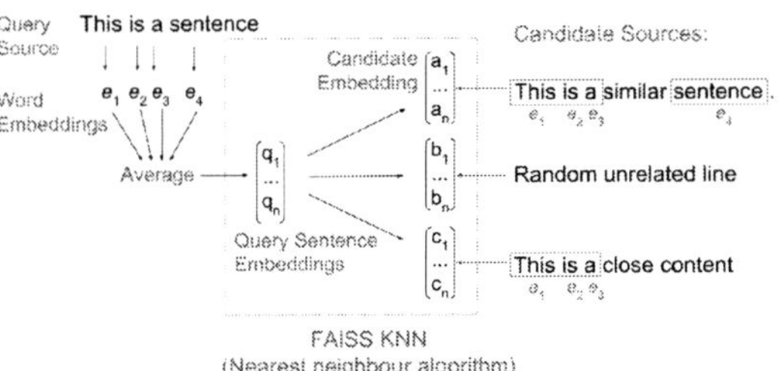


**Figure 1:** Procedure to obtain nearest neighbours with sentence embeddings

corresponding to the unedited regions. For these alignments, we used models trained with fast align (Dyer et al, 2013) based solely on generic data.

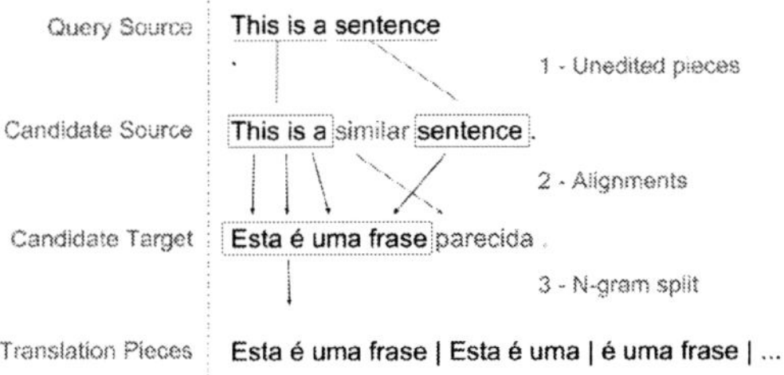


**Figure 2:** Process to obtain translation pieces with unedited words in nearest neighbours

We then merge the target regions obtained and generate as many translation pieces as possible, by breaking them into n-grams, up until a length of 4, as shown in Figure 2. Then, a score $s(X_q, X_c)$ is computed per sentence and associated with each generated piece, as shown in equation 1, where $ed$ stands for the edit distance between the candidate and query sentences. We use the scoring method from (Zhang et al, 2018), and pick the maximum score $s(u)$ from all sentences featuring the translation piece $u$, as shown in equation 2. To apply the pieces in the beam search for a word $w$, we use a factor $\lambda$ as an added weight, as shown in equation 3. For each hypothesis in the beam and each word, the set $G$ consists of all pieces ending in word $w$.

$$s(X_q, X_c) = 1 - \frac{ed(X_q, X_c)}{max(|X_q|, |X_c|)} \quad (1)$$

$$s(u) = \max_{\{1 < m < M, u \in X_c^m\}} s(X_q, X_c^m) \quad (2)$$

$$p_{beam}(w) = p_{beam}(w) + \lambda * \sum_{u \in G} (s(u)) \quad (3)$$

## 2.4 Implementation Details

The process of retrieving the translation pieces can be kept completely separate from the model. However, to integrate these in the generated translation, we require the model to be able to integrate these scores with its own.

Since in Marian, the produced scores from different scorers are combined at each time step $t$, before the beam is searched, we integrate the method with a new scorer module. This block can access the pieces and their scores for each sentence, and outputs the corresponding score delta for each word. It additionally allows for its weight to be used as the factor $\lambda$ of the original method.

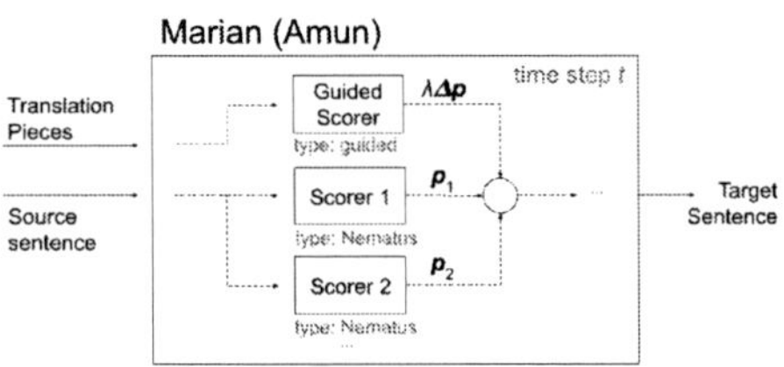


**Figure 3:** Amun implementation of translation pieces through a new scorer

Figure 3 provides a scheme of the implementation. Although we use only one scorer throughout the experiments presented, we show in this image a combination of several scorers of type `Nematus` to represent the possibilities of combining the implementation with other available features.

The combined scores will then be used in the beam search, with the effect of guiding the probabilities towards the translation pieces suggested. The factor $\lambda$ must then be tuned to avoid overusing the provided pieces. Additionally, in our implementation [3] we introduce an extra parameter to this scorer, a threshold for the similarity that will disregard low-similarity pieces.

## 2.5 Tuning process

As mentioned in the previous section, we have only two model parameters that control the translation pieces implementation - the weight $\lambda$ and a similarity threshold. To tune them, we run a grid search on both parameters, and keep the best performing pair as evaluated by a set of automatic

metrics in our validation set. For simplicity, this process is ran only at the end of the initial model training.

The chosen automatic metrics follow. We pick as main metric BLEU, since it is a standard metric in machine translation. We also pick OTEM (Over Translation Evaluation Metric) and UTEM (Under Translation Evaluation Metric), since they have shown strong correlation with human evaluation (Yang et al, 2018) (Malaviya et al, 2018). Moreover, we believe that one of the possible caveats of the translation pieces could be related to overusage of these pieces, and these metrics can help detect that.

# 3 Results

To understand the impact of the translation pieces method, we first pick three language pairs: EN→FR, EN→NL and EN→RO. We chose data from email customer support, which we will consider our domain, and use available translation memories as base for the translation pieces retrieval. This experiment focuses on the impact on one single domain, and its results are presented on section 3.1. We then run a second experiment for EN→FR, EN→DE, EN→ES, EN→IT and EN→PT, where we analyze the impact of the translation pieces when used to fine tune subdomains, which we present in section 3.2. Appendix A presents additional information on the generic models used to fine tune both experiments.

We present results on the previously mentioned metrics – BLEU, OTEM and UTEM. We also present human evaluation on a subset of the test set. For this purpose we compiled 15 documents, making up a sample of 150 to 200 lines of data per set. One professional linguist annotated the errors in the data for each language. This gave us a breakdown of the most common errors for each model, and also a Multidimensional Quality Metric (MQM) score (Lommel et al, 2014)[4].

We use for these experiments the model architecture described in Section 2.1, with the fine tuning process listed in Section 2.2. We then apply the translation pieces method as described in Sections 2.3 and 2.4. Finally, we use the tuning process mentioned in 2.5 to obtain thresholds. All results presented correspond to the domain adap-

---

[3] https://github.com/CatarinaSilva/marian/guided-translation-scoring. Currently available only for Amun for CPU, but will be developed in the future for GPU and marian-decoder

[4] A definition can be consulted in the following link; http://www.qt21.eu/mqm-definition/definition-2015-12-30.html

tation baseline and the evaluation result using the attained thresholds.

## 3.1 Domain Adaptation

For the first set of experiments we gathered the available in-domain lines, and queried our available Translation Memories for the same domain. We present the resulting number of lines for each language pair in table 1.

|  | Train | Dev | Test | TMs |
|---|---|---|---|---|
| $D_{EN \to FR}$ | 43.69K | 1004 | 1002 | 1852 |
| $D_{EN \to NL}$ | 82.71K | 1002 | 1001 | 1217 |
| $D_{EN \to RO}$ | 73.15K | 1000 | 1006 | 337 |

**Table 1:** Number of in-domain lines available for the training of models in each language pair

We ran the first experiment for the EN→FR language pair, a language pair with a strong baseline – around 65 BLEU points and 78 MQM points. The results can be seen in Table 2.

|  | BLEU | OTEM | UTEM | MQM |
|---|---|---|---|---|
| DA | **65.21** | **0.74** | **32.97** | 77.39 |
| DA + TPs | 64.31 | 0.77 | 35.22 | **82.58** |

**Table 2:** Comparison of domain adaptation (DA) with added translation pieces (DA + TPs) for EN-FR

It is possible to see that, even though the automatic metrics do not reflect that, and they seem to point to the existence of more over and under translation, the human evaluation score shows improvements over the baseline.

|  | Macro MQM | Micro MQM |
|---|---|---|
| DA | 78.2 | 77.39 |
| DA + TPs | **82.62** | **82.58** |

**Table 3:** Macro and Micro MQM of evaluated jobs for EN-FR

In Table 3 we show both the micro and macro MQM scores. The first presents the calculated value over the full analyzed set, similar to considering the full annotated data as one single document. The later presents an average of MQM scores for each document. We can see that both are very close to each other, which leads us to believe there are no particular outliers pulling the average up or down in the macro average.

The second experiment performed considered the EN→NL language pair, which has a weaker baseline, related both to a weaker baseline model

and to the lack of availability of the same amount of domain data.

|  | BLEU | OTEM | UTEM | MQM |
|---|---|---|---|---|
| DA | 35.05 | **2.21** | 59.96 | 48.23 |
| DA + TPs | **41.82** | 3.22 | **55.38** | **53.07** |

**Table 4:** Comparison of domain adaptation (DA) with added translation pieces (DA + TPs) for EN-NL

In this experiment both BLEU and UTEM improved significantly, as shown in Table 4, as well as the human evaluation metric. Aditionally, looking into the errors tagged by the linguists, we found that in particular errors concerning grammatical register and named entity errors decreased significantly.

|  | Macro MQM | Micro MQM |
|---|---|---|
| DA | 47.52 | 48.23 |
| DA + TPs | **56.32** | **53.07** |

**Table 5:** Macro and Micro MQM of evaluated jobs for EN-NL

Regarding micro and macro averages, we noticed a wider spread than for the previous language pair, with a few outliers in the distribution, for example the existence with jobs of negative MQM. This can happen typically when a job is small and has the presence of a few major or critical errors or when a job has a huge amount of errors. Figure 4 presents the distribution of documents for both models.

The results in Table 5 show that the macro average increased significantly more than the micro average. Through 4 we see that the worst-scoring jobs were pulled to higher MQM values, which explains this impact. The most visible example is the lowest scoring job, that went from a negative value to a positive one, with a difference of about 30 MQM points.

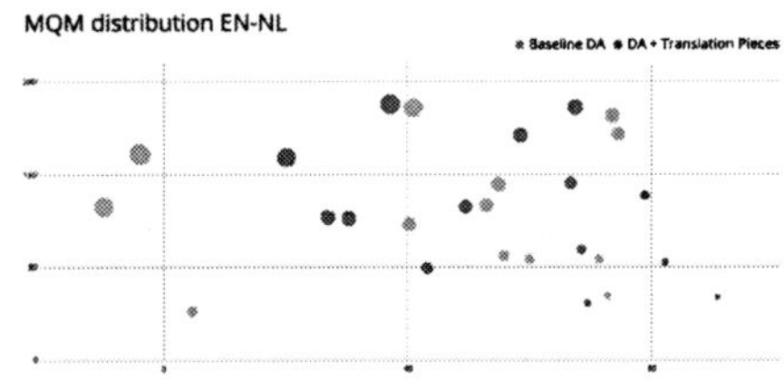


**Figure 4:** Distribution of MQM for EN→NL annotated jobs. The lighter dots are the jobs corresponding to the baseline, while the darker ones correspond to the model with translation pieces

The final language pair tested on this experiment was EN→RO, which is a language pair with lower resources, which leads to very low baselines, as we can see in tables 6 and 7.

|         | BLEU  | OTEM | UTEM  | MQM   |
|---------|-------|------|-------|-------|
| DA      | 64.91 | 1.01 | 38.58 | 43.94 |
| DA + TPs| **65.28** | **1.00** | **38.18** | **73.19** |

**Table 6:** Comparison of domain adaptation (DA) with added translation pieces (DA + TPs) for EN-RO

For this language pair we see improvements in all metrics, with the human evaluation score raising 15 points of macro and 30 points of micro MQM. It is visible that the micro and macro averages are very different, which is linked to the existence of a lot of small jobs that resulted in very low MQMs, pulling the macro average down. Figure 5 shows the distribution of jobs, where it is possible to see that for the translation pieces the distribution is skewed to higher values, with only one exception.

|          | Macro MQM | Micro MQM |
|----------|-----------|-----------|
| DA       | 16.25     | 43.94     |
| DA + TPs | **31.86** | **73.19** |

**Table 7:** Macro and Micro MQM of evaluated jobs for EN-RO

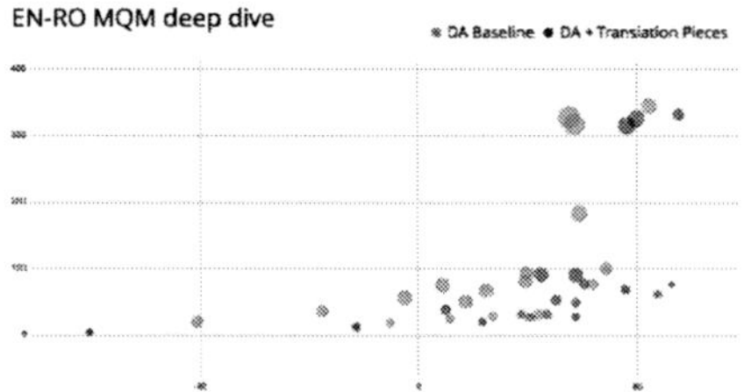


**Figure 5:** Distribution of MQM for EN→RO annotated jobs. The lighter dots are the jobs corresponding to the baseline, while the darker ones correspond to the model with translation pieces

Overall, for this experiment, the amount of jobs with less than 100 words had a big impact on macro MQMs, making it a bit hard to assess jobs comparatively or at a macro scale. However, all metrics suffered tremendous improvements, with significant drops in all errors, allowing us to clearly pick the translation pieces implementation over the baseline.

To summarize, for all language pairs, we see improvements in both macro and micro MQM, even when automatic metrics do not represent this improvement. We discuss this further in section 4.

## 3.2 Subdomain Distinction Impact

The second experiment aimed at comparing the usage of translation pieces of a particular domain to a direct adaptation in that particular subdomain. A subdomain can be seen as a smaller set of data inside the original domain that is more closely related. For example, if considering crisis data as a domain, more specific medical crisis data could be a subdomain inside of the first. In these, experiments, we keep the wide domain of email customer support, and consider different companies as subdomains.

For the first experiment, we reused the data from experiment 3.1, which we will consider as our subdomain (SD). We ran the domain adaptation process for it and for its parent domain (D) and ran the translation pieces code on top of both. The results are shown in Table 8. Interestingly, the baseline with the wider domain performs better in all automatic metrics, even though the human evaluation does not corroborate that.

|          | BLEU  | OTEM | UTEM  | MQM   |
|----------|-------|------|-------|-------|
| D        | **69.34** | **0.67** | **28.64** | 76.46 |
| D + TPs  | 68.14 | 1.55 | 31.37 | 81.07 |
| SD       | 65.21 | 0.74 | 32.97 | 77.39 |
| SD + TPs | 64.31 | 0.77 | 35.22 | **82.58** |

**Table 8:** Comparison of translation pieces on top of Domain Adaptation (D) and subdomain adaptation (SD) for EN→FR

In fact, the results show that using translation pieces directly on the subdomain performs better as measured by human evaluation. Additionally, using a wider domain with translation pieces already surpasses the baseline for the subdomain. We consider the latter result of great interest since, if it holds for other subdomains, it would mean that the same baseline model can perform better than several subdomain models. Table 9 discriminates the micro and macro scores for MQM, both supporting the previous observations.

We then completed this set of experiments by picking several subdomains inside a known domain and using translation pieces on each. These domains vary in size, but neither performed better when adapting directly on the subdomain than the wider domain model. The goal was to understand if the previous behaviour holds, that is, if we can make a domain model perform better in its

|         | Macro MQM | Micro MQM |
|---------|-----------|-----------|
| D       | 76.8      | 76.46     |
| D + TPs | 80.55     | 81.07     |
| SD      | 78.2      | 77.39     |
| SD + TPs | **82.62** | **82.58** |

**Table 9:** Macro and Micro MQM of evaluated jobs for a domain and subdomain in EN-FR

subdomains through translation pieces. Table 10 presents the average micro and macro MQM variation attained in each Language Pair. The break down of these results can be seen in appendix B.

|         | $\Delta$Macro-MQM | $\Delta$Micro-MQM |
|---------|-------------------|-------------------|
| EN→DE   | -0.74             | + 0.84            |
| EN→FR   | + 0.47            | + 1.77            |
| EN→ES   | + 2.92            | + 2.77            |
| EN→IT   | + 2.90            | + 1.85            |
| EN→PT   | + 3.78            | + 3.51            |

**Table 10:** Average difference across experiment subdomains for different language pairs: $\Delta = \text{MQM}_{TP} - MQM_{Base}$

The results show a positive trend over most language pairs. We consider this an encouraging result that seems to support our previous hypothesis. However, even though we seem to attain there are slight variations over different domains in the tested language pairs. We leave as future work a more thorough analysis of the baseline quality of our translation memories and its relation with these variations, as discussed in the next section.

## 4 Discussion

Overall the experiments show that the use of translation pieces brings benefit to domain adaptation. In particular, the results for subdomain distinction are very promising, opening an easier path for a wider model to improve over its contained subdomains. We further discuss some caveats and future work regarding these experiments.

We used BLEU, OTEM and UTEM as metrics for both tuning and evaluating the presented method. However, we see throughout several experiments that these metrics seem to either contradict or under represent the improvements seen with human evaluation. If this is the case, a possible caveat is that we are tuning our threshold with sub-optimal metrics.

We hypothesise that these metrics might suffer from the fact that they are single reference. This might clash with the fact that our domain data contains a high number of repetition on the source side, thus presenting a lot of different variations of the same translation. Since our test set is just a slice of this pool of jobs, we might be over-weighting a specific variation present in the test set of the sources, penalizing good variations produced by the different models.

We propose that in future work, the usage of multiple references in evaluation should be studied (Fomicheva and Specia, 2016) (Dreyer and Marcu, 2012). We believe this might lead to more reliable scores, and align better with human evaluation.

Another important factor that we do not present on these experiments is the quality of the translation pieces and its direct link to the quality of the results. We suspect that by having a better control of the quality of the pool of translation memories used, even if reducing its size, the performance of the method should improve even further, and at most should have as lower bound the quality of the baseline model.

In future work, we want to assess the quality of the used translation memories and compare the method in a scenario where we use only subdomains with available quality data. In this setting, the expected behavior would be for these subdomains to improve, without hurting other subdomains that might lack the same amount or quality of data. For this purpose, an analysis by professional linguists is necessary, both to produce a baseline value that can be related to the presented results, but also as a data selection procedure so that we can run experiments on gold data.

Finally, we want to extend the analysis to the reasons that cause the translation quality to improve with translation pieces. We suspect that the method is improving the translation of rare words, but also increasing the agreement and consistency of the translations, in particular with specific terminology. We plan to investigate this hypothesis to gain better understanding of this method.

## Acknowledgements

We would also like to thank the support provided by the European Union in the context of the PT2020 project: 038510. We would additionally like to thank André Martins and Maxim Khalilov from Unbabel AI and the Unbabel Quality Team for their help with the human evaluation.

## References

Arthur, Philip and Neubig, Graham and Nakamura, Satoshi 2016 Incorporating discrete translation lexicons into neural machine translation. In Proceedings of the 2016 Conference on Empirical Methods in Natural Language Processing 15571567 Association for Computational Linguistics

Chu, Chenhui and Wang, Rui 2018 In Proceedings of of the 27th International Conference on Computational Linguistics 1304-1319

Dreyer, Markus and Marcu, Daniel 2012 Hyter: Meaning-equivalent semantics for translation evaluation. *In 2012 Conference of the North American Chapter of the ACL: Human Language Technologies* 162171

Dyer, Chris and Chahuneau, Victor and Smith, Noah A. 2013 A simple, fast, and effective reparameterization of IBM Model 2 In Proc. NAACL

Fomicheva, Marina and Specia, Lucia 2016 Reference Bias in Monolingual Machine Translation Evaluation *Proceedings of the 54th Annual Meeting of the Association for Computational Linguistics (Volume 2: Short Papers)* 77–82 Association for Computational Linguistics https://www.aclweb.org/anthology/P16-2013

Johnson, Jeff and Douze, Matthijs and Jégou, Hervé 2017 Billion-scale similarity search with GPUs *CoRR* abs/1702.08734

Joulin, Armand and Grave, Edouard and Bojanowski, Piotr and Douze, Matthijs and Jégou, Hérve and Mikolov, Tomas 2016 FastText.zip: Compressing text classification models arXiv:1612.03651

Junczys-Dowmunt, Marcin and Grundkiewicz, Roman and Dwojak, Tomasz and Hoang, Hieu and Heafield, Kenneth and Neckermann, Tom and Seide, Frank and Germann, Ulrich and Fikri Aji, Alham and Bogoychev, Nikolay and Martins, André F. T. and Birch, Alexandra 2018 Marian: Fast Neural Machine Translation in C++ *Proceedings of ACL 2018, System Demonstrations* 116–121 Association for Computational Linguistics

Kaiser, Łukasz and Nachum, Ofir and Roy, Aurko and Bengio, Samy 2017 Learning to remember rare events

Koehn, Philipp and Knowles, Rebecca 2017 Six challenges for neural machine translation *In Proceedings of the First Workshop on Neural Machine Translation* 2839

Lommel, Arle and Uszkoreit, Hans and Burchardt, Aljoscha 2014 Multidimensional Quality Metrics ( MQM ): A Framework for Declaring and Describing Translation Quality Metrics

Malaviya, Chaitanya and Ferreira, Pedro and Martins, André F. T. 2018 Sparse and Constrained Attention for Neural Machine Translation *Proceedings of the 56th Annual Meeting of the Association for Computational Linguistics (Volume 2: Short Papers)* 370–376

Mikolov, Tomas and Grave, Edouard and Bojanowski, Piotr and Puhrsch, Christian and Joulin, Armand 2018 Advances in Pre-Training Distributed Word Representations *Proceedings of the International Conference on Language Resources and Evaluation (LREC 2018)*

Sánchez-Gijón, Pilar and Moorkens, Joss and Way, Andy 2019 Post-editing neural machine translation versus translation memory segments *Machine Translation* 1–29 Association for Computational Linguistics

Sennrich, Rico and Firat, Orhan and Cho, Kyunghyun and Birch, Alexandra and Haddow, Barry and Hitschler, Julian and Junczys-Dowmunt, Marcin and Läubli, Samuel and Miceli Barone, Antonio Valerio and Mokry, Jozef and Nadejde, Maria 2017 Nematus: a Toolkit for Neural Machine Translation *Proceedings of the Software Demonstrations of the 15th Conference of the European Chapter of the Association for Computational Linguistics* 65–68

Sennrich, Rico and Haddow, Barry and Birch, Alexandra 2016 Neural Machine Translation of Rare Words with Subword Units *Proceedings of the 54th Annual Meeting of the Association for Computational Linguistics (Volume 1: Long Papers)* 1715–1725 Association for Computational Linguistics https://www.aclweb.org/anthology/P16-1162

Sennrich, Rico and Haddow, Barry and Birch, Alexandra 2016 Edinburgh Neural Machine Translation Systems for WMT 16 *Proceedings of the First Conference on Machine Translation* 371–376 Association for Computational Linguistics https://www.aclweb.org/anthology/W16-2323

Wang, Yuguang and Cheng, Shanbo and Jiang, Liyang and Yang,Jiajun and Chen,Wei and Li, Muze and Shi, Lin and Wang, Yanfeng and Yang, Hongtao 2017 Sogou neural machine translation systems for wmt17 *In Proceedings of the Second Conference on Machine Translation* 410415

Yang, Jing and Zhang, Biao and Qin, Yue and Zhang, Xiangwen and Lin, Qian and Su, Jinsong 2018 Otem&Utem: Over- and Under-Translation Evaluation Metric for NMT *NLPCC*

Zhang, Jingyi and Utiyama, Masao and Sumita, Eiichro and Neubig, Graham and Nakamura, Satoshi 2018 Guiding Neural Machine Translation with Retrieved Translation Pieces *Proceedings of the 2018 Conference of the North American Chapter of the Association for Computational Linguistics: Human Language Technologies, Volume 1 (Long Papers)* 1325–1335 Association for Computational Linguistics https://www.aclweb.org/anthology/N18-1120

## Appendix A: Additional information on generic data

Below follows a list of datasets used to compile the generic models for the presented experiments in this work:

- Books, DGT, ECB, EMEA, EUbookshop, Europarl, EUConst, giga-fren, GlobalVoices, GNOME, JRC-Acquis, KDE4, MultiUN, News-Commentary, SETTIMES, Tanzil, Tatoeba, TED2013, Ubuntu and Wikipedia (from http://opus.nlpl.eu/)

- CommonCrawl (from https://www.statmt.org/wmt13/translation-task.html)

- Paracrawl (from https://paracrawl.eu/releases.html)

- Rapid Corpus of EU press releases (from https://www.statmt.org/wmt18/translation-task.html) – Rapid

These corpora do not hold the same amount of data for all language pairs. The specific sets can be consulted in the links provided. Tables 11 and 12 present the corpora used for each language pair.

| EN→ | FR | DE | ES | PT |
|---|---|---|---|---|
| EUbookshop | x | x | x | x |
| DGT | | x | | x |
| Europarl | x | x | x | x |
| JRC-Acquis | | x | | x |
| EMEA | | x | | x |
| ECB | | x | | x |
| MultiUN | x | x | x | |
| GNOME | | | | x |
| KDE4 | | | | x |
| GlobalVoices | | x | x | x |
| News-Commentary | x | x | x | |
| Books | | x | x | x |
| Rapid | | x | | |
| Ubuntu | | | | x |
| TED2013 | | x | x | x |
| Tanzil | | | | x |
| Wikipedia | | | x | x |
| Tatoeba | | | x | x |
| EUConst | x | | x | x |
| CommonCrawl | x | | | x |
| giga-fren v2 | x | | | |

Table 11: Used corpora for training of generic models

| EN→ | IT | NL | RO |
|---|---|---|---|
| EUbookshop | x | x | x |
| DGT | x | x | x |
| Europarl | x | x | x |
| JRC-Acquis | x | x | x |
| EMEA | x | x | x |
| ECB | x | x | |
| GNOME | x | | |
| KDE4 | x | | |
| GlobalVoices | x | | |
| News-Commentary | x | x | |
| Books | x | x | |
| Ubuntu | x | | |
| TED2013 | x | x | x |
| Tanzil | x | | |
| Wikipedia | | | x |
| Paracrawl | | | x |
| SETTIMES | | | x |

Table 12: Used corpora for training of generic models

Table 13 presents the resulting number of lines, after joining all datasets presnted in the aforementioned tables.

| | Train | Dev | Test |
|---|---|---|---|
| $EN \rightarrow FR$ | 32.42M | 1500 | 1500 |
| $EN \rightarrow DE$ | 18.38M | 1500 | 1500 |
| $EN \rightarrow ES$ | 35.97M | 1500 | 1500 |
| $EN \rightarrow IT$ | 13.97M | 1500 | 1500 |
| $EN \rightarrow PT$ | 14.03M | 1500 | 1500 |
| $EN \rightarrow NL$ | 13.38M | 1500 | 1500 |
| $EN \rightarrow RO$ | 6.97M | 1999 | 1999 |

Table 13: Number of lines used for training of generic models

# Appendix B: Break down of subdomain results

|          | Baseline | TPs   | Δ       |
|----------|----------|-------|---------|
| Domain A | 72.47    | 78.76 | + 6.29  |
| Domain B | 81.27    | 77.36 | - 3.91  |
| Domain C | 90.53    | 85.93 | -4.6    |
| Overall  | 81.42    | 80.68 | -0.74   |

**Table 14:** Macro MQM subdomain evaluation for EN→DE

|          | Baseline | TPs   | Δ       |
|----------|----------|-------|---------|
| Domain A | 67.92    | 76.41 | + 8.49  |
| Domain B | 79.61    | 78.93 | - 0.68  |
| Domain C | 89.35    | 84.07 | - 5.28  |
| Overall  | 78.96    | 79.80 | + 0.84  |

**Table 15:** Micro MQM subdomain evaluation for EN→DE

|          | Baseline | TPs   | Δ       |
|----------|----------|-------|---------|
| Domain A | 88.48    | 85.12 | - 3.36  |
| Domain B | 57.62    | 57.61 | - 0.01  |
| Domain C | 89.12    | 93.89 | + 4.77  |
| Overall  | 78.41    | 78,87 | + 0.47  |

**Table 16:** Macro MQM subdomain evaluation for EN→FR

|          | Baseline | TPs   | Δ       |
|----------|----------|-------|---------|
| Domain A | 87.24    | 86.38 | - 0.86  |
| Domain B | 60.62    | 60.02 | - 0.60  |
| Domain C | 86.16    | 92.93 | + 6.77  |
| Overall  | 78.01    | 79.78 | + 1.77  |

**Table 17:** Micro MQM subdomain evaluation for EN→FR

|          | Baseline | TPs   | Δ        |
|----------|----------|-------|----------|
| Domain A | 34.07    | 46.94 | + 12.87  |
| Domain B | 67.31    | 70.56 | + 3.25   |
| Domain C | 61.22    | 57.62 | - 3.6    |
| Domain D | 54.54    | 53.71 | - 0.83   |
| Overall  | 54.29    | 57.21 | + 2.92   |

**Table 18:** Macro MQM subdomain evaluation for EN→IT

|          | Baseline | TPs   | Δ        |
|----------|----------|-------|----------|
| Domain A | 34.36    | 45.88 | + 11.52  |
| Domain B | 61.04    | 64.0  | + 2.96   |
| Domain C | 59.62    | 58.46 | -1.16    |
| Domain D | 55.69    | 53.47 | -2.22    |
| Overall  | 52.33    | 55.45 | + 2.77   |

**Table 19:** Micro MQM subdomain evaluation for EN→IT
Micro MQM

|          | Baseline | TPs   | Δ       |
|----------|----------|-------|---------|
| Domain A | 67.09    | 66.07 | - 1.02  |
| Domain B | 52.62    | 60.20 | + 7.58  |
| Domain C | 49.92    | 52.07 | + 2.15  |
| Overall  | 56.54    | 59.45 | + 2.9   |

**Table 20:** Macro MQM subdomain evaluation for EN→ES

|          | Baseline | TPs   | Δ       |
|----------|----------|-------|---------|
| Domain A | 74.50    | 72.22 | - 2.28  |
| Domain B | 52.24    | 60.39 | + 8.15  |
| Domain C | 54.64    | 54.96 | + 0.32  |
| Overall  | 60.46    | 62.52 | + 1.85  |

**Table 21:** Micro MQM subdomain evaluation for EN→ES

|          | Baseline | TPs   | Δ        |
|----------|----------|-------|----------|
| Domain A | 71.45    | 72.90 | + 1.45   |
| Domain B | 60.45    | 64.89 | + 4.44   |
| Domain C | 88.65    | 87.79 | - 0.86   |
| Domain D | 58.48    | 68.55 | + 10.07  |
| Overall  | 69.76    | 73.53 | + 3.78   |

**Table 22:** Macro MQM subdomain evaluation for EN→PT

|          | Baseline | TPs   | Δ        |
|----------|----------|-------|----------|
| Domain A | 76.58    | 73.90 | - 2.68   |
| Domain B | 55.1     | 60.19 | + 5.09   |
| Domain C | 83.75    | 83.60 | - 0.15   |
| Domain D | 56.65    | 68.42 | + 11.77  |
| Overall  | 68.02    | 71.53 | + 3.51   |

**Table 23:** Micro MQM subdomain evaluation for EN→PT

# Raising the TM Threshold in Neural MT Post-Editing:
# a Case-Study on Two Datasets


**Anna Zaretskaya**
TransPerfect
Passeig de Gràcia, 11
08007 Barcelona, Spain
azaretskaya@translations.com



## Abstract

This study intends to determine whether replacing fuzzy TM matches by suggestions from neural machine translation (NMT) can decrease the post-editing effort. We compare the post-editing distance of TM fuzzy matches and of NMT suggestions based on two datasets. We found that in one of the datasets MT was consistently more useful than TM matches, but in the other dataset it was not. We argue that it is necessary to collect extensive data on PED in TM matches in order to be able to easily optimize the TM threshold for any given project.


## 1    Introduction

TransPerfect is a large language service provider (LSP) translating about two billion words each year with a strong focus on technology, including machine translation (MT). We provide a variety of different MT services, most of which involve MT post-editing (MTPE). In the past few years, we experienced a steady growth of the share of translations produced with MTPE workflows. This growth can be attributed to the implementation of proprietary neural MT technology (NMT), which has improved the average quality of MT, and consequently increased its benefits and acceptance among our linguist experts community. On average, switching from our previous statistical MT framework to the current neural one decreased the post-editing distance by 9.2%, which means an improvement in quality of approximately 29%.

Our MTPE workflow, similarly to the majority of LSPs, combines translation memory (TM) leverage and MT suggestions. We use the 75% TM threshold, which means that only TM matches of 75% and above are shown to the linguists as draft translations during post-editing, and the rest of the segments are pre-translated by an MT system. This study intends to investigate if the threshold has to be raised considering the increase in MT quality, and if so where the new threshold should lie. In other words, we want to know if the linguists' performance will increase if we use MT suggestions instead of the so-called high fuzzy matches (75-99%), and what it depends on.

We approached this task by measuring the post-editing distance (PED) between the TM matches and the final translation and comparing it to the PED between NMT suggestions and the same final translations. This will show whether the amount of editing that has to be applied to the TM fuzzy matches is greater or smaller than that of NMT output.

For this study we selected two different datasets, which are very similar in regards to their content but differ by language pair: English-Chinese and English-Spanish. This study is intended as an initial stage of a large-scale study that will allow us to draw broader conclusions and create best practices on establishing TM thresholds in NMT post-editing projects.

## 2    Background

There have been previous studies that compared MT and TM matches from the point of view of post-editing effort as well as linguists' perception. In one of them it was demonstrated that translators were more productive when editing MT suggestions (from a statistical MT system) than editing fuzzy TM matches from the range of 80-90% (Guerberof, 2009). In this experiment translators even produced better quality when editing MT suggestions compared to the quality of edited TM matches. One potential explanation for that was the fact that TM matches are valid sentences in the target language and they read naturally (therefore the errors are easier to miss) while MT errors are more obvious, because they often render sentences ungrammatical.

Two related studies (Moorkens and Way, 2016; Rico et al., 2018) also investigated the potential usefulness of MT suggestions compared to TM matches, concluding that having a reliable MT system and a way to predict its performance in many cases is more beneficial than TM leverage. O'Brien (2006) used eye-tracking techniques to study the cognitive load of post-editors and found that the cognitive activity when editing MT suggestions is similar to the activity observed when editing 80-90% fuzzy matches.

This has been confirmed by other studies on the topic, with evidence showing that, while there are still certain prejudices against MT, using MT suggestions instead of TMs increases translators' performance in certain scenarios. For example, it seems that translators are likely to choose MT suggestions over TM matches during post-editing more often if the origin of the suggestion is unknown (i.e. translators do not know whether it comes from MT or TM) (Sánchez-Gijón et al., 2018). Along the same lines, translators prefer to know whether translation suggestions comes from MT or TM, but they are actually more productive when they are not provided this information (Teixeira, 2014).

It is especially important to ask now more than ever, as we have observed a leap in MT quality in general with the spread of neural MT systems. While the abovementioned studies used statistical machine translation for the experiments, our prediction is that the advantage of MT suggestions over TM matches will be even stronger when neural MT is used. The most recently published study on the topic (Sanchez-Gijón et al., 2019) does use neural MT for the comparison. This experiment carried out on a small dataset follows the authors' previous studies that used SMT: apart from the edit distance, it considers the editing time and the subjective quality perception of the post-editors. The authors come to the conclusion that using NMT reduces the amount of editing, but does not improve the translators' productivity.

In general terms, the results of these and other related studies (He et al, 2010; Yamada, 2011) point to the fact that in many cases MT suggestions are more useful than TM matches, and therefore it is clear that we should ask ourselves whether the widely used TM threshold of 75% still holds. Nevertheless, the specific practical recommendations resulting from these studies are not defined, as they seem to depend on the specific scenario: the way MT quality is measured, how MT suggestions are presented to the user of the translation environment, and of course the specific characteristic of the MT engine. That is why in the long term, our goal is to establish a new universal TM threshold that would suit TransPerfect specific post-editing setup or, if this threshold varies depending on some conditions, identify these conditions and create a simple guideline for establishing a TM threshold on a project basis.

## 3    Experiment Data and Setup

The datasets used for this study included only translation units (TUs) that, at the moment of their translation, matched with the existing segments in the TMs. We retrieved the source segment, the target segment suggestions from the TM, and the final translation of the same segment. In addition, we produced an NMT suggestion for each of the source segments.

For each TU, we compared the target segment from the TM with the final translation and calculated the PED between them. We will refer to these values as *PED-TM*. We also compared the target produced by the NMT systems with the final translated segment to obtain the values of *PED-MT*.[1] PED is a standard MT quality metric used at TransPerfect and is very common in the translation industry in general. It evaluates the quality of MT from the point of view of the *post-editing effort*, in other words it shows how many changes the linguists make in the initial draft translation in order to produce final translation. It is based on the Levenshtein edit distance, is character-based, and is presented as a percentage of edited characters over all the characters in the sentence. Lower PED means that less post-editing effort required and thus better MT quality.

When talking about the amount of work involved in post-editing, it is common to distinguish technical, temporal and cognitive post-editing effort (Krings, 2001). Even though PED as a method of evaluating post-editing effort is limited only to the technical post-editing effort (i.e. it does not account for the cognitive load of the post-editors, or for the time needed to per-

---

[1] Even though we call it post-editing distance, in case of segments produced by MT there was no post-editing performed. The final translation used as a reference was not creating by post-editing the corresponding MT output. However, we make this assumption for simplicity of the calculation. We also acknowledge the fact that this way, the PED-MT values might be slightly higher than if the translation were produced by means of actual post-editing.

form post-editing), it allows to obtain objective data on the actual amount of editing needed to reach the final translation, and this is a critical factor in improving translators' performance (Plitt and Masselot, 2010; Federico et al., 2012).

### 3.1 Datasets

For this experiment we selected post-edited texts from past post-editing projects, two different accounts. Dataset *ENES* contained post-edited files from English into Spanish from the online fashion retail domain. The projects included in the study dated from the time period of January 2018 to March 2019 and were post-edited by 6 different linguists.

Dataset *ENZH* contained data from a different online fashion retail account, post-edited from English into Chinese by 21 different linguists in the time period of February 2018 to March 2019. The data in the two datasets comes from two different accounts, however, the content is very similar (short fashion product descriptions). We deliberately chose the same content type in order to minimize the impact of different content types on the results, but at the same time we were able to compare the results for two different language pairs.

From both datasets we gathered only the translation units (TUs) that are considered high fuzzy matches, i.e. at the time the file was analyzed against a TM, the leverage score of the segments was from 75% to 99% (both included). The number of TUs in the dataset ENES was 8183, with an average source segment length of 5.6 words. The number of TUs in the dataset ENZH was 7521 with an equal average of 5.6 words per source segment. We distributed the TUs in five groups by ranges of TM match scores, a break-down of all the TUs is shown in Table 1.

| TM range | # of TUs in ENES | # of TUs in ENZH |
|---|---|---|
| 75-79% | 3243 | 2801 |
| 80-84% | 1956 | 1811 |
| 85-89% | 1401 | 1446 |
| 90-94% | 420 | 361 |
| 95-99% | 1163 | 1102 |
| Total | 8183 | 7521 |

Table 1. Breakdown of TM match scores in the experiment data.

The biggest range in terms of segment count is the lowest range of 75-79%. In the ENES dataset, it constitutes 40% of all segments, and in the ENZH it constitutes 37% of all segments.

### 3.2 Neural Machine Translation

The MT systems used for the experiment were proprietary neural MT systems. Both systems are the ones that are currently used in the post-editing projects in the two accounts. The ENES system was a generic one, i.e. it was created using a generic training corpus and did not undergo any kind of customization using client data. The ENZH system had been customized using the client TM.

The average post-editing distance of the ENES system on the account content in general (on all segments that were actually post-edited in real projects) was 25.86%, and the average PE distance of this system measured on the dataset selected for this experiment was 30.30%. The average PE distance of the ENZH system on all the post-edited in the account was 23.09%, while the PE distance measured on our dataset was 15.17%.

## 4 Results

The results of the comparison of the PED-MT and PED-TM values for the two datasets were strikingly different. In dataset ENES, PED-MT was consistently higher than PED-TM (Figure 1).

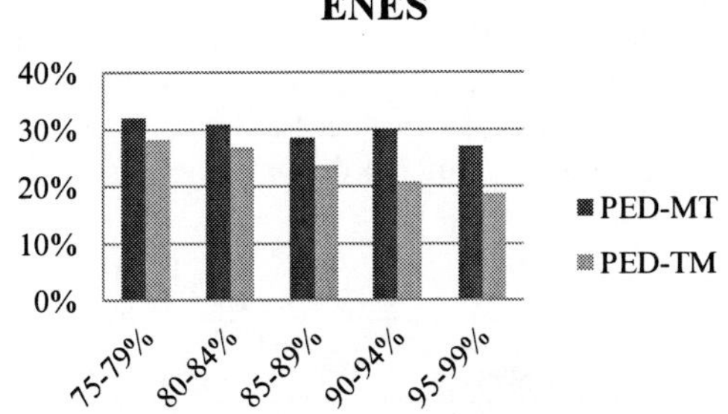


Figure 1. Comparison of PED-MT and PED-TM in different ranges of fuzzy matches in the ENES dataset.

The picture in the ENZH dataset was almost exactly the opposite: in all the TM ranges except for one we observe lower PED-MT and higher PED-TM (Figure 2).

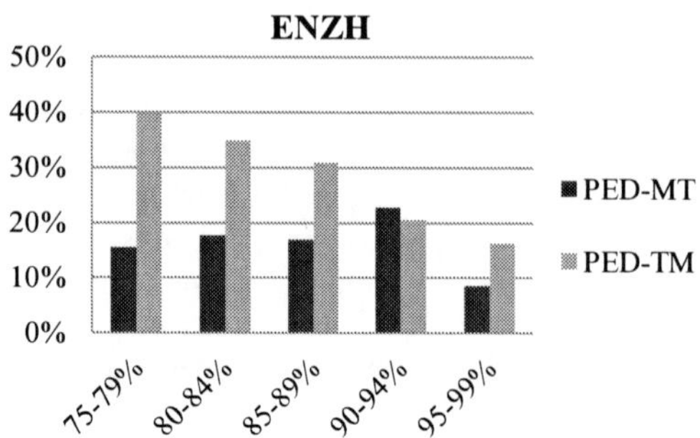


Figure 2. Post-editing distance in different ranges of fuzzy matches compared to the post-editing distance of MT segments.

This result was not unexpected, considering the difference in the performance of the two MT systems: the average PED-MT in the ENES dataset was significantly higher than PED-MT in the ENZH dataset. This is of course due to the system customization. We have seen that a customized system can improve the PED by up to 20% compared to a baseline generic system. In fact, we have confirmed this by calculating the PED-MT value on the same ENZH dataset, but using a generic NMT system, and the result was 31.31%, which is significantly higher that the PED-MT value of the customized system (16.61%).

In addition, almost a half of the MT segments in the ENZH dataset (42.5%) were exactly the same as the final translation, i.e. PED-MT was equal to 0% and these segments did not need any editing. (Table 2).

|  | **PED-MT = 0%** |
|---|---|
| **ENES** | 1200 (8.3%) |
| **ENZH** | 3378 (42.5%) |

Table 2. Number of segments with PED-MT equal to 0 in both datasets.

Based on these results, the ENZH account is, without a doubt, a good candidate for replacing fuzzy matches by NMT suggestions. In fact, we have received feedback from one of the post-editors working on the account, who confirmed our observations and pointed out the following:

*"Funny thing is for these files, fuzzy matches take much more time than MT, because the changes in high fuzzy matches need to be carefully identified, but some of the MT is perfect."*

Nevertheless, there was one TM range (90-94%) where TM matches had lower PED than MT suggestions. The analysis of the segments revealed one possible reason for this, which is the segment length. The average number of words in the seg-

ments of this TM match range was 10.54, which is significantly higher than the average for the dataset (5.6). Our assumption is that this MT system performs worse on longer segments.

We further investigated this assumption on the ENZH dataset. Table 3 shows the average PED-MT and the average segment length in each of the TM match ranges.

| **TM range** | **Avg. PED-MT** | **Avg. Length** |
|---|---|---|
| **75-79%** | 15.43% | 4.64 |
| **80-84%** | 17.63% | 5.62 |
| **85-89%** | 16.86% | 6.02 |
| **90-94%** | 22.79% | 10.54 |
| **95-99%** | 8.60% | 6.65 |

Table 3. Average PED-MT and average source segment length in different TM ranges in the ENZH dataset.

Even thought we observed only weak correlation between the segment length and PED-MT ($r$=0.32), there is a clear association as the range 90-94% seems to be an exception both in terms of segment length and PED-MT. The reason for that might be that the longer sentences are more challenging for MT to handle. In the retail product descriptions, longer sentences usually constitute a more creative part of a description, which requires substantial modifications in the target language in order for it to sound natural. Shorter sentences, on the other hand, are very straight forward, not creative, and only list the characteristics of the product that normally come from a limited set.

As expected, there was observed an association between the fuzzy match score and the PED-TM value: the correlation was stronger in the ENZH dataset ($r$=-0.40) and weaker in the ENES dataset ($r$=-0.20). This means that the higher the fuzzy match the less it needs to be edited. However, MT performs relatively similar in all fuzzy match ranges. This has an implication when choosing a new TM threshold: while some fuzzy matches require more editing than others, MT suggestions require the same amount of editing on average.

Another interesting observation was the difference in the average PED-TM in the two datasets: 25.37% in ENES and 32.24% in ENZH. This is due to the difference in writing systems and the way PED is calculated. The average number of characters in Chinese sentences is lower, and since the PED is calculated as a percentage on the total number of characters, the PED will always be higher. For this reason, if we base our TM threshold strategy uniquely on the PED we should treat the languages with character-based writing systems like Chinese and Japanese differently than European languages. This issue will be discussed in more detail in the following section.

## 5 Discussion

The difference in the results obtained for the two datasets demonstrate the importance of the initial high performance of the MT system that is needed in order to provide high-quality segments that will potentially replace fuzzy matches. The main difference between the two MT systems was the fact that one of them was generic and the other one was customized for the client content. NMT system customization with a large amount of high-quality data can significantly improve the system performance. An experiment that had been conducted at TransPerfect showed that a customization with additional 100 000 new translation units yields about 4% increase of the PE distance over the baseline system, and the quality grows exponentially when adding more data. Depending on the initial performance and the quality of the data, customization can boost the performance by up to 20% of PED.

This study has shown that, when the performance of the MT system is sufficiently good, replacing fuzzy matches (or at least some of them) reduces the overall post-editing distance, or in other words, the post-editing effort. The challenge lies in establishing the definition of the sufficiently good performance for this specific purpose.

We suggest that one simple approach is comparing the average PED of the MT system on the content type to the post-editing distance required to edit the TM matches, similar to what was done in this study. If we know the average PED-TM for each TM range, we will be able to determine if the MT output requires less or more editing than fuzzy matches, and if so we can raise the TM threshold to the corresponding TM range. For this we need, however, to determine if the average PED-TM values are consistent across all languages and content types. Thus, we have already mentioned that these values can depend on the writing system of the target language: in the TM match range of 75-80%, the average PED-TM in the ENES dataset was around 28% while in the ENZH it was approximately 40%. We need to carry out a large-scale comparison that would include other languages and content types in order to have a full picture of PED-TM.

Then, we will be able to compare it to the PED-MT in each specific case. For example, if we have an account where NMT is used for post-editing from English into Spanish, and we know that the average PED is 18%, we must be able to say with a high degree of certainty that this value is lower than the average PED-TM of TM matches between 75% and 79%, and only then we can raise the TM threshold to 80%. As mentioned in Section 3.1, in both our datasets, 75-79% fuzzy matches constituted about one third of all the TUs, so replacing them by NMT suggestions means improving the quality of approximately one third of all fuzzy matches in post-editing projects.

## 6 Conclusion and Future Work

This study was the first step in defining optimal TM threshold for MTPE projects with neural MT. Our hypothesis was that using NMT suggestions instead of TM fuzzy matches can reduce, at least in some cases, the post-editing effort. In order to confirm it, we have compared the PED of NMT suggestions with PED of TM fuzzy matches of different ranges. The results obtained in the two datasets were very different in two aspects. First, the general quality of the NMT systems used varied significantly. When the PED-MT values were low (meaning good MT performance), the MT suggestions required less editing than the TM matches, and so in this case we could see the benefits of replacing them by MT. However, when the general MT quality is lower (for example, when the MT system is generic and not customized for the content type), the TM matches continue to me the best source of draft translation.

Given these results, the next step in optimizing the MTPE workflow will consist in gathering data on the average PED of different ranges of TM matches in a wide variety languages and content types. This will allow us to compare the PED-MT with PED-TM for any given project.

Along with the post-editing distance, there are other metrics we use to measure post-editing effort, the most common being post-editing time. PE time and distance do not always correlate. Post-editing activity involves time spent on understanding the source segment and the MT/TM suggestion and assessing if the latter is usable. In fact, studies of linguists' behavior during post-editing have shown that they mostly spend time on contemplating the changes than executing them (Koehn, 2009). As part of future work, we are planning to compare the time required to edit NMT suggestions with the time it takes to edit TM fuzzy matches.

# References

Federico, Marcello, Cattelan, Alessandro and Trombetti, Marco, 2012. Measuring User Productivity in Machine Translation Enhanced Computer Assisted Translation. *Proceedings of the Tenth Conference of the Association for Machine Translation in the Americas (AMTA).*

Guerberof, Ana, 2009. Productivity and quality in MT post-editing. *MT Summit XII. The twelfth Machine Translation Summit.* Ottawa, Canada.

He, Yifan, Ma, Yanjun, Roturier, Johann, Way, Andy, and van Genabith, Josef, 2010. Improving the Post-Editing Experience Using Translation Recommendation: A User Study. *AMTA 2010 - 9th Conference of the Association for Machine Translation in the Americas.*

Koehn, Philipp, 2009. A process study of computer-aided translation. *Machine Translation* 23(4): 241-263.

Krings, Hans P., 2001. *Repairing Texts.* Kent State University Press, Ohio, USA.

Moorkens, Joss, and Way, Andy 2016. Comparing Translators Acceptability of TM and SMT Outputs. *Baltic J. Modern Computing*, 4(2):141-151.

O'Brien, Sharon, 2006. Eye-tracking and translation memory matches. *Perspectives: Studies in Translatology*, 14(3), 185-205.

Plitt, Mirko and Masselot, François, 2010. A Productivity Test of Statistical Machine Translation Post-Editing in a Typical Localisation Context. *The Prague Bulletin of Mathematical Linguistics*, 93, 7-16.

Rico, Celia, Sánchez-Gijón, Pilar, and Torres-Hostench, Olga, 2018. The Challenge of Machine Translation Post-editing: An Academic Perspective. *Trends in E-Tools and Resources for Translators and Interpreters*, Brill: 203-218.

Sánchez-Gijón, Pilar, Moorkens, Joss and Way, Andy. 2018. Perception vs. Acceptability of TM and SMT Output: What do translators prefer? *EAMT 2018, 21st Annual Conference of the European Association for Machine Translation*, Alicante, Spain, 331.

Sánchez-Gijón, Pilar, Moorkens, Joss and Way, Andy. 2019. Post-Editing Neural Machine Translation versus Translation Memory Segments. Machine Translation, 33(1-2), 31-59.

Teixeira, Carlos S.C., 2014. Perceived vs. measured performance in the post-editing of suggestions from machine translation and translation memories. *WPTP-3, Third Workshop on Post-Editing Technology and Practice.* Vancouver, Canada, 45-60.

Yamada, Masaru, 2011. *Revising text: An empirical investigation of revision and the effects of integrating a TM and MT system into the translation process* (Doctoral thesis). Rikkyo University.

# Incremental Adaptation of NMT for
# Professional Post-editors: A User Study


**Miguel Domingo**[1] and **Mercedes García-Martínez**[2] and **Álvaro Peris**[1] and **Alexandre Helle**[2]
and **Amando Estela**[2] and **Laurent Bié**[2] and **Francisco Casacuberta**[1] and **Manuel Herranz**[2]

[1]PRHLT Research Center - Universitat Politècnica de València
{midobal, lvapeab, fcn}@prhlt.upv.es
[2]Pangeanic / B.I Europa - PangeaMT Technologies Division
{m.garcia, a.helle, a.estela, l.bie, m.herranz}@pangeanic.com



## Abstract

A common use of machine translation in the industry is providing initial translation hypotheses, which are later supervised and post-edited by a human expert. During this revision process, new bilingual data are continuously generated. Machine translation systems can benefit from these new data, incrementally updating the underlying models under an online learning paradigm. We conducted a user study on this scenario, for a neural machine translation system. The experimentation was carried out by professional translators, with a vast experience in machine translation post-editing. The results showed a reduction in the required amount of human effort needed when post-editing the outputs of the system, improvements in the translation quality and a positive perception of the adaptive system by the users.


## 1 Introduction

Translation post-editing is a common use case of machine translation (MT) in the industrial environment. Post-editing consists of the supervision by a human agent of outputs generated by an MT system, who corrects the errors made by the MT system. As MT systems are continuously improving their capabilities, translation post-editing has acquired major relevance in the translation market (Arenas, 2008; Hu and Cadwell, 2016). As a byproduct of this process, new data are continuously generated. These data have valuable properties: they are domain-specific training samples,

which can be leveraged for adapting the system towards a given domain or post-editor. Moreover, an adaptive system can learn from its mistakes. In other words, it can avoid making the same errors again.

A typical way of profiting from these post-edits consists in updating the system following an online learning paradigm: as the user validates a post-edit, the system is incrementally updated, by taking into account this sample. Hence, when the system generates the next translation, it will consider the previous user post-edits. It is expected that better translations (or more suited to the human post-editor preferences) will be produced.

In this paper, we evaluate this strategy in an industrial scenario. We study the enhancements brought about by an adaptive system via online learning, and the effects on the post-editing process of data generated by a neural machine translation (NMT) system. To that end, we firstly evaluate our system under laboratory conditions. Next, we conduct the evaluation of the system on a production environment. This experiment involved professional translators, who regularly rely on MT post-editing in their workflow. The results show improvements of adaptive systems in terms of productivity and translation quality.

## 2 Related work

Translation post-editing has been a widely adopted practice in the industry for a long time (e.g., Vasconcellos and León, 1985). As MT technology advanced and improved, the post-editing process gained more relevance and many user studies have demonstrated its capabilities (Aziz et al., 2012; Bentivogli et al., 2016; Castilho et al., 2017; Green et al., 2013a).

Adapting an MT system from user post-edits via

online learning techniques has also attracted the attention of researchers and industry parallel to the rise of the post-editing protocol. Many advances in this direction were achieved during the CasMaCat (Alabau et al., 2013) and MateCat (Federico et al., 2014) projects, which adapted phrase-based statistical machine translation systems incrementally from user post-edits.

Following recent breakthroughs in NMT technology, some works studied the construction of adaptive systems via online learning in this post-editing scenario. Turchi et al. (2017) and Peris et al. (2017) proposed to adapt an NMT system with post-edited samples to a new domain via online learning. Other works aimed to refine these adaptation techniques: Wuebker et al. (2018) applied sparse updates; Kothur et al. (2018) introduced a dictionary of translations for dealing with the novel words included in the new domain. However, in all these works, the users were simulated, due to the economical costs of involving humans within experiments.

User studies on online adaptation from post-edits have been conducted, mainly for phrase-based statistical machine translation systems (Alabau et al., 2016; Bentivogli et al., 2016; Denkowski et al., 2014; Green et al., 2013b). Regarding the NMT technology, several user studies have been recently conducted, analyzing different MT technologies (Koponen et al., 2019; Jia et al., 2019) or protocols (Daems and Macken, 2019). The closest work to ours was developed by Karimova et al. (2018), who showed savings in human effort, due to the effect of online learning. But in contrast to our work, the individuals used in Karimova et al. (2018) were students, whereas we conducted the study using professional, experienced translators.

## 3 Online learning from NMT post-edits

NMT relies on the statistical formalization of MT (Brown et al., 1990). The goal is to obtain, given a source sentence $\mathbf{x}$, its most likely translation $\hat{\mathbf{y}}$:

$$\hat{\mathbf{y}} = \arg\max_{\mathbf{y}} \Pr(\mathbf{y} \mid \mathbf{x}) \tag{1}$$

This probability is directly modeled by a neural network with parameters $\boldsymbol{\Theta}$:

$$\hat{\mathbf{y}} = \arg\max_{\mathbf{y}} \log p(\mathbf{y} \mid \mathbf{x}; \boldsymbol{\Theta}) \tag{2}$$

This neural network usually follows an encoder–decoder architecture, featuring recurrent (Bahdanau et al., 2015; Sutskever et al., 2014) or convolutional networks (Gehring et al., 2017) or attention mechanisms (Vaswani et al., 2017). The parameters of the model are typically estimated jointly on large parallel corpora, via stochastic gradient descent (SGD; Robbins and Monro, 1951; Rumelhart et al., 1986). At decoding time, the system obtains the most likely translation by means of a beam search method.

### 3.1 Adaption from post-edits via online learning

During the usage of the MT system, we can leverage the post-edited samples for continuously adapting the system on the fly, as soon as a sentence has been post-edited. This procedure is described in Algorithm 1: for each sentence to be translated $(\mathbf{x})$, the system produces a translation hypothesis $\hat{\mathbf{y}}$. The user post-edits this sentence, obtaining a corrected version of it $(\mathbf{y})$. Right after this post-editing process, and before translating the next sample, the NMT system is updated, taking into account $\mathbf{x}$ and $\mathbf{y}$.

---

**Input** : $\boldsymbol{\Theta}_1$ (initial NMT system),
$\{\mathbf{x}_n\}_{n=1}^{n=N}$ (source sentences)

1 **begin**
2     $n \leftarrow 1$
3     **while** $n \leq N$ **do**
4        $\hat{\mathbf{y}}_n \leftarrow \text{Translate}(\mathbf{x}_n, \boldsymbol{\Theta}_n)$
5        $\mathbf{y}_n \leftarrow \text{Post-edit}(\mathbf{x}_n, \hat{\mathbf{y}}_n)$
6        $\boldsymbol{\Theta}_{n+1} \leftarrow \text{Update}((\mathbf{x}_n, \mathbf{y}_n), \boldsymbol{\Theta}_n)$
7        $n \leftarrow n + 1$

**Algorithm 1:** Adaptation via online learning during NMT post-editing.

---

This adaptation of the NMT model can be performed following the same method used in regular training: SGD.

## 4 Experimental framework

We now describe the experimental conditions arranged in our study: the translation systems and environment, the main features of the tasks under study and the evaluation criteria considered.

### 4.1 NMT systems

Our NMT system was a recurrent encoder–decoder with an additive attention mechanism (Bahdanau et al., 2015), built with OpenNMT-py (Klein et al., 2017). We used long short-term memory units

(Gers et al., 2000) and we set all model dimensions to 512. The system was trained using Adam (Kingma and Ba, 2014) with a fixed learning rate of 0.0002 (Wu et al., 2016) and a batch size of 60. We applied label smoothing of 0.1 (Szegedy et al., 2015). At the inference time, we used a beam search with a beam size of 6. We applied joint byte pair encoding to all corpora (Sennrich et al., 2016), using 32, 000 merge operations.

The adaptive systems were built considering the findings from Peris and Casacuberta (2019), and conducting an evaluation on a development set. For each new post-edited sample, we performed two plain SGD updates, with a fixed learning rate of 0.05.

### 4.2 Translation environment

In order to assess the benefits of the adaptive system, we started by conducting an experiment with simulated users in a laboratory setting. This study is frequently carried out within the literature (e.g., Ortiz-Martínez, 2016), due to the economical costs of involving humans within experiments. Following common practices, we used the reference sentences as translation post-edits. Therefore, in the static scenario, we assessed the quality of the system using the references. In the adaptive scenario, we translated each source sentence and applied online learning with the corresponding reference.

Once we studied the behavior of the system under simulated conditions, we conducted the experiment with the real users. They were three professional translators, with an average of four years of experience, who regularly make use of MT in their workflow.

The experiment was conducted using SDL Trados Studio as the translation environment. This software is widely used in the translation industry, and all the participants use it in their daily work. Fig. 1 shows a screenshot of the SDL Trados Studio interface.

Our NMT system was deployed as a server, which delivered the translations to SDL Trados Studio and performed the adaptation using the post-edits. This system is compatible with all OpenNMT-py models and it is publicly available[1]. We also developed a plugin that connected SDL Trados Studio with our systems.

### 4.3 Tasks and evaluation

We evaluated our systems on a real task from our production scenario. This task consisted in a small corpus belonging to a medico-technical domain (description of medical equipments), and was conformed by two documents of 150 sentences each, containing 1.7 and 2.7 thousand words respectively. The translation direction was from English to Spanish. Since we lacked an in-domain corpus, we trained a general system with the data from the translation task from WMT'13 (Bojar et al., 2013), consisting in 15 million parallel segments. Next, we applied the FDA data selection technique (Biçici and Yuret, 2015) for selecting related instances from our general corpus and a medical (UFAL, Bojar et al., 2017) and technological[2] ones. We selected 8 million additional segments, which were used for fine-tuning the general system.

The effects of adaptivity were assessed according to the post-editing time and to two common MT metrics: (h)BLEU (Papineni et al., 2002) and (h)TER (Snover et al., 2006). For ensuring consistent BLEU scores, we used sacreBLEU (Post, 2018). Since we computed per-sentence BLEU scores, we used exponential BLEU smoothing (Chen and Cherry, 2014). In order to determine whether two systems presented statistically significant differences, we applied approximate randomization tests (Riezler and Maxwell, 2005), with 10, 000 repetitions and a $p$-value of 0.05.

## 5 Results

As introduced in the previous section, we first analyzed the adaptation process in a simulated environment. Next, we studied and discussed the results obtained in the user trials.

### 5.1 Adaptation with simulated users

Table 1 shows the results in terms of translation quality of a static system, compared with an adaptive one, updated using the reference samples. The results obtained on this synthetic setup support the usefulness of the adaptation via online learning: in all cases, the adaptive system achieved better TER and BLEU than the static one. These differences were statistically significant in all cases but one. We observed important gains in terms of TER (5.5

---

[1] https://github.com/midobal/OpenNMT-py/tree/OnlineLearning

[2] https://metashare.metanet4u.eu/go2/qtleapcorpus

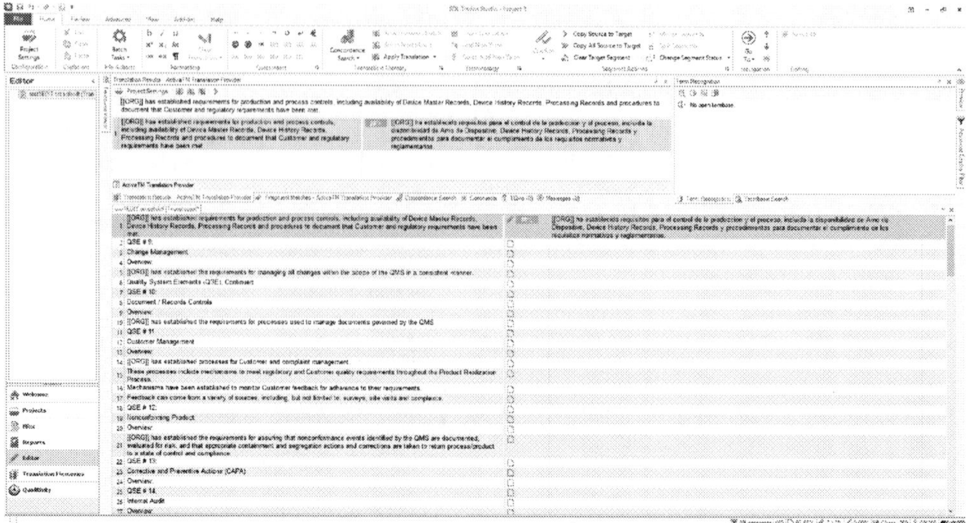

**Figure 1:** User Interface from SDL Trados Studio. From top to bottom, the first row and the leftmost column correspond to the user menus. On the next row, the middle column contains information about the segment that is being translated: on the left, the source sentence and, on the right, the MT translation. The right column displays the content of the terminological dictionary (if any). The document that is being translated appears on the bottom row: on the left, the original document and, on the right, the user post-edits.

and $1.1$ points), which suggests a lower human effort required to for post-edit these samples. We also experimented with a larger document ($1,500$ sentences), belonging to the same domain. The adaptation to this larger document was more effective: we observed gains of $10.4$ TER points and $13.6$ BLEU points.

| Test | System | TER [↓] | BLEU [↑] |
|------|--------|---------|----------|
| T1 | Static | 54.0 | 26.9 |
|    | Adaptive | 48.5$^{\dagger}$ | 32.0$^{\dagger}$ |
| T2 | Static | 56.1 | 23.4 |
|    | Adaptive | 55.0 | 26.3$^{\dagger}$ |

**Table 1:** Results of the simulated experiments. Static systems stand for conventional post-editing, without adaptation. Adaptive systems refer to post-editing in an environment with online learning. TER and BLEU were computed against the reference sentences. $^{\dagger}$ indicates statistically significant differences between the static and the adaptive systems.

Additionally to the assessment of the system in terms of translation quality, we need to satisfy an adequate latency, including decoding and updating times. Our NMT system was deployed in a CPU server, equipped with an Intel(R) Xeon(R) CPU E5-2686 v4 at 2.30GHz and 16GB of RAM. On average, generating a translation took the system $0.23$ seconds and each update took $0.45$ seconds. These low latencies allow a correct usage of the system, as the flow of thoughts of the user remains uninterrupted (Nielsen, 1993).

## 5.2 Adaptation with human post-editors

| User | Static | Adaptive |
|------|--------|----------|
| User 1 | T1 | T2 |
| User 2 | T2 | T1 |
| User 3 | T1 | T2 |

**Table 2:** Distribution of users (1, 2 and 3), test sets (T1 and T2) and scenarios (Static and Adaptive).

Once we tested our system in a simulated environment, we moved on to the experimentation with human post-editors. Three professional translators were involved in the experiment. For the adaptive test, all post-editors started the task with the same system, which was adapted to each user using their own post-edits. Therefore, at the end of the online learning process, each post-editor obtained a tailored system. For the static experiment, the initial NMT system remained fixed along the complete process. In order to avoid the influence of translating the same text multiple times, each participant post-edited a different test set under each scenario (static and adaptive), as shown in Table 2.

The main results of this experiment are shown in Table 3. These numbers are averages over the results obtained by the different post-editors. The

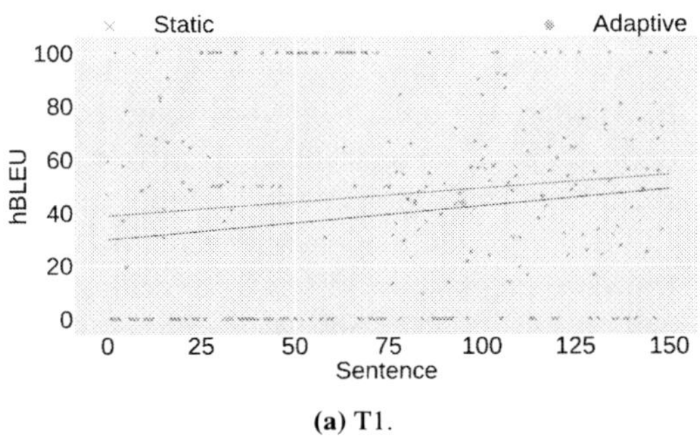
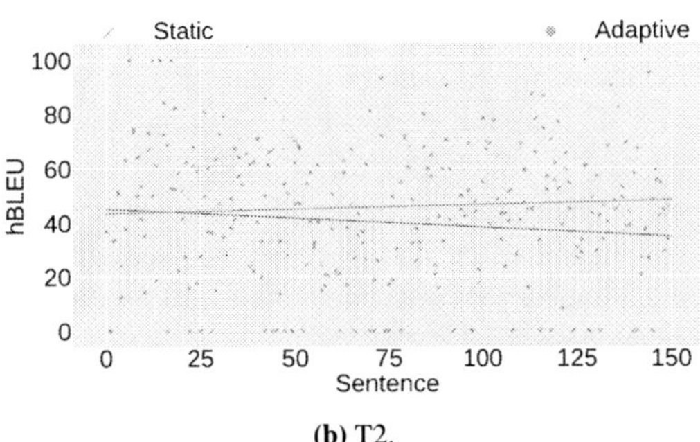





**Figure 2:** hBLEU per sentence of static and adaptive systems for both test sets (T1 and T2). Individual sentence scores are plotted for each system, static (red crosses) and adaptive (blue dots). The sentences were processed sequentially, hence, we can observe the progress of the system with its usage. To this end, we show a fit of the scores of each system, in dashed red and solid blue lines, for static and adaptive systems, respectively.

large reduction of post-editing time per sentence for the set T1 is especially relevant (an average of 7.5 seconds per sentence). In the test set T2, the post-editing time of the adaptive system was also slightly lower than the static system one, but only by 0.7 seconds.

| Test | System | Time (s) | hTER [↓] | hBLEU [↑] |
|---|---|---|---|---|
| T1 | Static | 37.9 | 39.5 | 47.3 |
|  | Adaptive | 30.4 | 34.2 | 55.1[†] |
| T2 | Static | 45.8 | 38.4 | 45.7 |
|  | Adaptive | 45.1 | 34.2[†] | 50.5[†] |

**Table 3:** Results of the user experiments. Static systems stand for conventional post-editing, without adaptation. Adaptive systems refer to post-editing in an environment with online learning. Time corresponds to the average post-editing time per sentence, in seconds. hTER and hBLEU refer to the TER and BLEU of the system hypothesis computed against the post-edited sentences. [†] indicates statistically significant differences between the static and the adaptive systems.

In terms of translation quality, adaptive systems performed much better than static ones, as reflected by the significant improvements in terms of hTER (5.3 and 4.2 points) and hBLEU (7.8 and 4.8 points). These results show that adaptive systems generated more correct translations, as they required less post-edits from the user.

In order to gain additional insights into the adaptation process, we studied the evolution of the hBLEU during the post-editing process. To this end, Fig. 2 compares the hBLEU per sentence of static and adaptive systems, for both test sets. Since the sentences were processed sequentially, we study the progress of the systems along its usage: for observing these trends, we computed a linear fit of the scores of each system via the least squares method.

In Fig. 2a, we observe that for the test split T1, the adaptive system consistently produced slightly better hypotheses than the static one, but there was no clear evidence on the effects of online learning. Both systems behaved similarly: the hBLEU values were gradually increased, which suggests either that the test document was increasingly easy to translate or that the user felt more comfortable with the style and translations provided by the system. Therefore, they applied less post-edits to the final sentences.

In the case of T2 (Fig. 2b), we observe a degradation on the hBLEU of the static system, as the post-editing process advances. This degradation is prevented by the adaptive system, in which the hBLEU is even slightly increased. The effects of the adaptation are noticeable from the 30th sentence onwards.

Finally, it is interesting to compare the simulated experiment against this one. We observed that, in terms of automatic metrics, the system yielded much better results when evaluating against post-edits, rather than against reference sentences (compare the "Static" rows from Table 3 and Table 1, respectively). This suggests that the translation hypotheses provided by the system were useful to the human users, as they produced similar post-edited samples. It is also worth to point out that the adaptation process was, in most cases, slightly less effective in the simulated experiment.

## 5.3  User perceptions and opinions

After finishing each experiment, the participants answered a questionnaire regarding the post-editing task they had just performed. In this survey, we asked the users about their level of satisfaction of the translations they produced, whether they preferred to perform post-editing or translating from scratch and their opinions on the automatic translations provided, in terms of grammar, style and overall quality. We also requested for them to give their feedback on the task, as an open-answer question.

The users were generally satisfied with the translations they generated. In all cases, they preferred to perform this translation task via post-editing rather than translating from scratch. Two of them preferred to perform this translation from scratch in less than a $25\%$ of the sentences. The other post-editor preferred to translate from scratch around a $50\%$ of the sentences. In all cases, they are keen to perform translation post-editing in the future. These perceptions on the MT utility are slightly better than those reported by Daems and Macken (2019). We believe that these differences are due to the background in translation post-editing that our users had: they perform translation post-editing as their regular way of work; therefore, they perceptions toward this methodology are generally favorable.

Regarding the translation quality offered by the NMT system, their general opinion is that the system produced translations of average quality. The strongest attribute of the translations was their grammatical accuracy. The style and overall quality was perceived in some cases below the average, depending on the user and the experimental condition.

In order to avoid biases, the users did not know whether the experiment they performed featured a static or an adaptive system. Once they finished both experiments, they were asked to identify the adaptive systems. All users guessed correctly which one was the adaptive system.

Regarding their general opinions, they all observed how corrections applied on one segment were generally reflected in the following segment, especially corrections related to product names, grammatical structures and lexical aspects. This mostly reduced upcoming corrections to changes in the style. Overall, their perception was that the static system produced less fluent translations, and that the machine translation was very good in most cases, but useless in a few ones.

The post-editors reported a couple of minor issues regarding the NMT system: in a few cases, they noticed that a domain-specific term was "forgotten" by the system, being wrongly translated. In addition, the users noticed in some cases, the occurrence of some made-up words (e.g., "absolvido"). This problem was probably caused by an incorrect segmentation of a word, via the byte pair encoding process. In order to deploy natural and effective translation systems, these problems need to be addressed.

## 6 Conclusions and future work

We conducted an evaluation of an adaptive NMT system in a post-editing scenario. The system leveraged the data generated during the post-editing process for adapting its underlying models. After testing the system in a laboratory setting, we conducted an experiment involving three professional translators, who regularly make use of MT post-editing. We observed reductions in post-editing times and significant improvements in terms of hTER and hBLEU, due to online learning. The users were pleased with the system. They noticed that corrections applied on a given segment generally were reflected on the successive ones, making the post-editing process more effective and less tedious.

As future work, we should address some of the concerns noticed by the post-editors, namely, the degradation of domain-specific terms and the incorrect generation of words due to subwords. To that end, we should study and analyze the hypotheses produced by the adaptive system and the post-edits performed by the users, similarly as Koponen et al. (2019). Moreover, we want to integrate our adaptive systems together with other translation tools, such as translation memories or terminological dictionaries, with the aim of fostering the productivity of the post-editing process. With this feature-rich system, we would like to conduct additional experiments involving more diverse languages and domains, using domain-specialized NMT systems, testing other models (e.g., Transformer, Vaswani et al., 2017) and involving a larger number of professional post-editors. Finally, we also intend to implement the interactive–predictive machine translation protocol (Lam et al., 2018; Peris and Casacuberta, 2019) in our translation environment, and compare it with the regular post-editing process.

**Acknowledgements**

The research leading to these results has received funding from the Spanish Centre for Technological and Industrial Development (Centro para el Desarrollo Tecnológico Industrial) (CDTI) and the European Union through Programa Operativo de Crecimiento Inteligente (Project IDI-20170964). We gratefully acknowledge the support of NVIDIA Corporation with the donation of a GPU used for part of this research, and the translators and project managers from Pangeanic for their help with the user study.

**References**

Alabau, V., Bonk, R., Buck, C., Carl, M., Casacuberta, F., García-Martínez, M., González-Rubio, J., Koehn, P., Leiva, L. A., Mesa-Lao, B., Ortiz-Martínez, D., Saint-Amand, H., Sanchis-Trilles, G., and Tsoukala, C. (2013). CASMACAT: An open source workbench for advanced computer aided translation. *The Prague Bulletin of Mathematical Linguistics*, 100:101–112.

Alabau, V., Carl, M., Casacuberta, F., Garca-Martnez, M., Gonzlez-Rubio, J., Mesa-Lao, B., Ortiz-Martnez, D., Schaeffer, M., and Sanchis-Trilles, G. (2016). *New Directions in Empirical Translation Process Research*, chapter Learning Advanced Post-editing, pages 95–110. New Frontiers in Translation Studies.

Arenas, A. G. (2008). Productivity and quality in the post-editing of outputs from translation memories and machine translation. *Localisation Focus*, 7(1):11–21.

Aziz, W., Castilho, S., and Specia, L. (2012). Pet: a tool for post-editing and assessing machine translation. In *In proceedings of The International Conference on Language Resources and Evaluation*, pages 3982–3987.

Bahdanau, D., Cho, K., and Bengio, Y. (2015). Neural machine translation by jointly learning to align and translate. *arXiv:1409.0473*.

Bentivogli, L., Bertoldi, N., Cettolo, M., Federico, M., Negri, M., and Turchi, M. (2016). On the evaluation of adaptive machine translation for human post-editing. *IEEE/ACM Transactions on Audio, Speech and Language Processing*, 24(2):388–399.

Biçici, E. and Yuret, D. (2015). Optimizing instance selection for statistical machine translation with feature decay algorithms. *IEEE/ACM Transactions on Audio, Speech and Language Processing*, 23(2):339–350.

Bojar, O., Buck, C., Callison-Burch, C., Haddow, B., Koehn, P., Monz, C., Post, M., Saint-Amand, H., Soricut, R., and Specia, L., editors (2013). *Proceedings of the Eighth Workshop on Statistical Machine Translation*. Association for Computational Linguistics.

Bojar, O., Haddow, B., , D. M., Sudarikov, R., Tamchyna, A., and Vari, D. (2017). Report on building translation systems for public health domain (deliverable D1.1). Technical Report H2020-ICT-2014-1-644402, Technical report, Health in my Language (HimL).

Brown, P. F., Cocke, J., Pietra, S. A. D., Pietra, V. J. D., Jelinek, F., Lafferty, J. D., Mercer, R. L., and Roossin, P. S. (1990). A statistical approach to machine translation. *Computational Linguistics*, 16:79–85.

Castilho, S., Moorkens, J., Gaspari, F., Calixto, I., Tinsley, J., and Way, A. (2017). Is neural machine translation the new state of the art? *The Prague Bulletin of Mathematical Linguistics*, 108(1):109–120.

Chen, B. and Cherry, C. (2014). A systematic comparison of smoothing techniques for sentence-level bleu. In *Proceedings of the Ninth Workshop on Statistical Machine Translation*, pages 362–367.

Daems, J. and Macken, L. (2019). Interactive adaptive smt versus interactive adaptive nmt: a user experience evaluation. *Machine Translation*, pages 1–18.

Denkowski, M., Dyer, C., and Lavie, A. (2014). Learning from post-editing: Online model adaptation for statistical machine translation. In *Proceedings of the 14th Conference of the European Chapter of the Association for Computational Linguistics*, pages 395–404.

Federico, M., Bertoldi, N., Cettolo, M., Negri, M., Turchi, M., Trombetti, M., Cattelan, A., Farina, A., Lupinetti, D., Martines, A., Massidda, A., Schwenk, H., Barrault, L., Blain, F., Koehn, P., Buck, C., and Germann, U. (2014). The matecat tool. In *Proceedings of the 25th International Conference on Computational Linguistics: System Demonstrations*, pages 129–132.

Gehring, J., Auli, M., Grangier, D., Yarats, D., and

Dauphin, Y. N. (2017). Convolutional sequence to sequence learning. *arXiv:1705.03122*.

Gers, F. A., Schmidhuber, J., and Cummins, F. (2000). Learning to forget: Continual prediction with LSTM. *Neural computation*, 12(10):2451–2471.

Green, S., Heer, J., and Manning, C. D. (2013a). The efficacy of human post-editing for language translation. In *Proceedings of the SIGCHI Conference on Human Factors in Computing Systems*, pages 439–448.

Green, S., Wang, S., Cer, D., and Manning, C. D. (2013b). Fast and adaptive online training of feature-rich translation models. In *Proceedings of the 51st Annual Meeting of the Association for Computational Linguistics*, volume 1, pages 311–321.

Hu, K. and Cadwell, P. (2016). A comparative study of post-editing guidelines. In *Proceedings of the 19th Annual Conference of the European Association for Machine Translation*, pages 34206–353.

Jia, Y., Carl, M., and Wang, X. (2019). Post-editing neural machine translation versus phrase-based machine translation for english–chinese. *Machine Translation*, pages 1–21.

Karimova, S., Simianer, P., and Riezler, S. (2018). A user-study on online adaptation of neural machine translation to human post-edits. *Machine Translation*, 32(4):309–324.

Kingma, D. P. and Ba, J. (2014). Adam: A method for stochastic optimization. *arXiv preprint arXiv:1412.6980*.

Klein, G., Kim, Y., Deng, Y., Senellart, J., and Rush, A. M. (2017). OpenNMT: Open-source toolkit for neural machine translation. In *Proceedings of the Association for the Computational Linguistics*, pages 67–72.

Koponen, M., Salmi, L., and Nikulin, M. (2019). A product and process analysis of post-editor corrections on neural, statistical and rule-based machine translation output. *Machine Translation*, pages 1–30.

Kothur, S. S. R., Knowles, R., and Koehn, P. (2018). Document-level adaptation for neural machine translation. In *Proceedings of the 2nd Workshop on Neural Machine Translation and Generation*, pages 64–73.

Lam, T. K., Kreutzer, J., and Riezler, S. (2018). A reinforcement learning approach to interactive-predictive neural machine translation. In *Proceedings of the European Association for Machine Translation conference*, pages 169–178.

Nielsen, J. (1993). *Usability Engineering*. Morgan Kaufmann Publishers Inc.

Ortiz-Martínez, D. (2016). Online learning for statistical machine translation. *Computational Linguistics*, 42(1):121–161.

Papineni, K., Roukos, S., Ward, T., and Zhu, W.-J. (2002). BLEU: a method for automatic evaluation of machine translation. In *Proceedings of the Annual Meeting of the Association for Computational Linguistics*, pages 311–318.

Peris, Á. and Casacuberta, F. (2019). Online learning for effort reduction in interactive neural machine translation. *Computer Speech & Language. In Press*.

Peris, Á., Cebrián, L., and Casacuberta, F. (2017). Online learning for neural machine translation post-editing. *arXiv:1706.03196*.

Post, M. (2018). A call for clarity in reporting bleu scores. In *Proceedings of the Third Conference on Machine Translation: Research Papers*, pages 186–191.

Riezler, S. and Maxwell, J. T. (2005). On some pitfalls in automatic evaluation and significance testing for mt. In *Proceedings of the ACL workshop on intrinsic and extrinsic evaluation measures for machine translation and/or summarization*, pages 57–64.

Robbins, H. and Monro, S. (1951). A stochastic approximation method. *The Annals of Mathematical Statistics*, pages 400–407.

Rumelhart, D. E., Hinton, G. E., and Williams, R. J. (1986). Learning representations by back-propagating errors. *nature*, 323(6088):533.

Sennrich, R., Haddow, B., and Birch, A. (2016). Neural machine translation of rare words with subword units. In *Proceedings of the Annual Meeting of the Association for Computational Linguistics*, pages 1715–1725.

Snover, M., Dorr, B., Schwartz, R., Micciulla, L., and Makhoul, J. (2006). A study of translation edit rate with targeted human annotation. In *Proceedings of the Association for Machine Translation in the Americas*, pages 223–231.

Sutskever, I., Vinyals, O., and Le, Q. V. (2014). Sequence to sequence learning with neural networks. In *Proceedings of the Advances in Neural Information Processing Systems*, volume 27, pages 3104–3112.

Szegedy, C., Liu, W., Jia, Y., Sermanet, P., Reed, S., Anguelov, D., Erhan, D., Vanhoucke, V., and Rabinovich, A. (2015). Going deeper with convolutions. In *Proceedings of the IEEE Conference on Computer Vision and Pattern Recognition*, pages 1–9.

Turchi, M., Negri, M., Farajian, M. A., and Federico, M. (2017). Continuous learning from human post-edits for neural machine translation. *The Prague Bulletin of Mathematical Linguistics*, 108(1):233–244.

Vasconcellos, M. and León, M. (1985). SPANAM and ENGSPAN: machine translation at the pan american health organization. *Computational Linguistics*, 11(2-3).

Vaswani, A., Shazeer, N., Parmar, N., Uszkoreit, J., Jones, L., Gomez, A. N., Kaiser, Ł., and Polosukhin, I. (2017). Attention is all you need. In *Advances in Neural Information Processing Systems*, pages 5998–6008.

Wu, Y., Schuster, M., Chen, Z., Le, Q. V., Norouzi, M., Macherey, W., Krikun, M., Cao, Y., Gao, Q., Macherey, K., Klingner, J., Shah, A., Johnson, M., Liu, X., Kaiser, Ł., Gouws, S., Kato, Y., Kudo, T., Kazawa, H., Stevens, K., Kurian, G., Patil, N., Wang, W., Young, C., Smith, J., Riesa, J., Rudnick, A., Vinyals, O., Corrado, G., Hughes, M., and Dean, J. (2016). Google's neural machine translation system: Bridging the gap between human and machine translation. *arXiv:1609.08144*.

Wuebker, J., Simianer, P., and DeNero, J. (2018). Compact personalized models for neural machine translation. In *Proceedings of the 2018 Conference on Empirical Methods in Natural Language Processing*, pages 881–886.

# When less is more in Neural Quality Estimation of Machine Translation. An industry case study


**Dimitar Shterionov**[*] **Félix do Carmo**[*] **Joss Moorkens**[*] **Eric Paquin**[*]
**Dag Schmidtke**[†] **Declan Groves**[†] **Andy Way**[*]
[*]ADAPT Centre / Dublin City University, Dublin Ireland,
{firstname.lastname}@adaptcentre.ie
[†]Microsoft E+D Global, Ireland, [dags,degroves]@microsoft.com



## Abstract

Quality estimation (QE) of machine translation (MT), the task of predicting the quality of an MT output without human references, is particularly suitable in dynamic translation workflows, where translations need to be assessed continuously with no specific reference provided. In this paper, we investigate sentence-level neural QE and its applicability in an industry usecase. We assess six QE approaches, which we divide into two-phase and one-phase approaches, based on quality and cost. Our evaluation shows that while two-phase systems perform best in terms of the predicted QE scores, their computational costs suggest that alternatives should be considered for large-scale translation production.


## 1 Introduction

Quality estimation (QE) (Specia et al., 2009) is the process of predicting the quality of a machine translation (MT) system without human intervention or reference translations. QE can be applied at word-, sentence-, or document-level. In the case of document- and sentence-level, the task is typically to predict a score that corresponds to a target evaluation criteria or metric (e.g., BLEU (Papineni et al., 2002), TER (Snover et al., 2006), etc.), i.e. it is a regression task. In this work, we investigate sentence-level QE, estimating TER scores.

QE has been the focus of multiple WMT shared tasks. In such tasks the common evaluation criteria are metrics that score the quality of the estimates, such as Pearson's $r$ or Root Mean Square

Error (RMSE). However, in a commercial setting, it is important to set a balance between performance and efficiency. Furthermore, a QE solution for industry needs to be generalizable and as language-independent as possible. Feature-based methods have ranked highly in such tasks. However, neural methods have recently not only outperformed feature-based ones, from a quality perspective, but they also provide a more generalizable and language-independent solution. In our work, we first assess the predictive capabilities of neural QE (NQE) systems applied on MT data from the IT software domain, i.e. UI strings, for the English→German and English→Spanish language pairs. We then focus on the efficiency aspect. We further compare the performance of QE systems from a business perspective, i.e. using industry-established metrics.

Our contribution is two-fold: the analysis and comparison of NQE approaches, and the implementation of a new efficient method that scores on a par with the others. The use of QE in commercial setting has been discussed in previous work (Astudillo et al., 2018), but there are, to our knowledge, no published results of tests as extensive as ours of the application of QE to commercial data.

## 2 State-of-the-art

The state-of-the-art in QE was most recently presented at WMT 2018 (Specia et al., 2018a).

**Traditional versus Neural QE** In traditional feature-based QE approaches, the input is first processed and QE features are extracted. Then, these features are used to train a regression or classification model. For sentence-level QE there are 17 features that have been established as standard (Specia et al., 2013), which can be classified as blackbox (or system-independent) or glass-box (system-dependent).

In contrast to traditional QE systems, NQE systems process source and target text in an end-to-end fashion, using neural networks (NN). It is not necessary to explicitly define QE features to feed to the NQE system. Similar to the encoder-decoder approach for MT (Sutskever et al., 2014; Cho et al., 2014; Bahdanau et al., 2015), NQE systems use one or multiple encoders to compress the input information in a context vector and use this vector to predict a quality score; the context vector implicitly encodes features used to learn estimates.

**One-phase and two-phase approaches** We classify QE in two groups: one-phase and two-phase approaches. The former have a unified architecture and are trained to generate estimates in an end-to-end fashion, with no distinct intermediate stages. The latter employ two phases in training and in testing, typically involving two networks that are trained separately; the first one targets decomposing the input (a source sentence and its MT) into features, which are then used as input for the second network to compute a QE score.

**NQE Systems** The top-scoring systems in the segment-level task at WMT 2018 were QEBrain (Wang et al., 2018) and UNQE (Li et al., 2018), both two-phase systems.

*QEBrain* is an extension of the 'Neural Bilingual Expert model' (Fan et al., 2018) with extra features. The first phase extracts high latent semantic and alignment information between the source and the translation output. Based on Transformer (Vaswani et al., 2017), this network builds a conditional language model – the neural bilingual expert. It is complemented with an error-prediction model which identifies possible mismatches of words. In the second phase, the features of these two models are used in a bi-LSTM model to output the QE score.

The *POSTECH* architecture (Kim et al., 2017) consists of a *word predictor* model and an *estimator* model. The predictor model is used to extract QE feature vectors (QEFVs) which are employed to train the estimator: a logistic regression model based on a summary representation of the QEFVs.

*deepQuest* (Ive et al., 2018) implements two types of architectures: (i) BiRNN (a one-phase approach) and (ii) POSTECH (a two-phase approach). The BiRNN architecture employs two bidirectional RNNs (with GRU units) whose outputs are combined through an attention mechanism. The resulting vector representation is used to produce an estimate of quality. Similarly, the *deepQuest* implementation of POSTECH uses a bidirectional RNN to compute QEFVs.

The first-phase models of systems like QEBrain and POSTECH are typically trained on parallel data. One-phase systems, such as the *deepQuest* BiRNN, are trained only on QE data: source, MT output, and a score.

## 3 SiameseQE

Siamese NNs were proposed initially for the problems of signature verification (Bromley et al., 1993) and fingerprint recognition (Baldi and Chauvin, 1993). The model consists of two (or more) identical networks, encoding different inputs. The two networks share the same configuration with mirrored weights. Siamese NNs have also been applied to address the task of text similarity (Yih et al., 2011; Mueller and Thyagarajan, 2016) and image recognition (Koch et al., 2015).

With the aim of providing an efficient QE system, we implemented our SiameseQE with one LSTM-based RNN that encodes both source and MT sentences in so called *left* and *right* passes, respectively. The encoded representations – the RNN outputs – of both sentences are used to compute a distance score which is optimised through an MSELoss with respect to the expected TER score. We use Euclidean distance in our implementation. Given that we build on a single RNN, we use joint vocabulary so that we could train without mismatch of tokens.

We also explored three types of networks: (i) with no attention; (ii) with Soft Dot Attention (Luong et al., 2015) and (iii) with word-by-word attention, as defined in Rocktäschel et al. (2015).

Ueffing et al. (2018) presented a Siamese NN system for QE with two LSTM RNNs with tied weights, using cosine similarity. Their application identified quality levels of automatically generated product titles. We aim to further optimise the performance via a single RNN (with LSTM units) and by implementing attention mechanisms.

## 4 Use-case and data

Our use-case is QE of the translations of software UI strings from Microsoft products. The domain is, therefore, technical/IT. To train our QE systems we used proprietary Microsoft data collected from post-edits scored using TER. The language pairs are English-German (EN-DE) and English-Spanish (EN-ES). We also used parallel data from Europarl (Koehn, 2005) and from Microsoft for two-phase systems, abbreviated as EU and MS respectively. In Table 1 we present details of the QE and the extra parallel training data.

To train the one-phase systems, only the QE data was used. To train the two-phase systems (POSTECH systems and QEBrain) for EN-DE and EN-ES we used parallel data (EU or MS) for the feature-extraction part of the model, i.e. for the first phase, and the provided QE data for the QE score computation model, i.e. the second phase. We trained one POSTECH system per language pair on EU data, and another on the MS parallel data sets. The evaluation of these four systems (two per language) led to the conclusion that there were no advantages in the use of the EU data, so for the experiments with the QEBrain system we used only MS parallel data.

| QEdata | EN-DE | EN-ES | Extra data | EN-DE | EN-ES |
|---|---|---|---|---|---|
| Train | 67 718 | 46 217 | EU | 1 863 144 | 1 850 469 |
| Dev | 7 524 | 5 136 | MS | 1 741 218 | 1 581 875 |
| Test | 32 898 | 34 623 | | | |

**Table 1:** Number of sentences in the QE data sets and number of parallel sentences of extra data used to train the feature-extraction part of the two-phase systems.

## 5 Experimental setup

We experimented with three different systems: *deepQuest*, *QEBrain* and *SiameseQE*. While the first two systems have been developed over an extensive period of time, have undergone significant empirical evaluations, and have achieved high rankings in WMT QE shared tasks, the last one is developed by our team for maximum efficiency.

### 5.1 Hardware and software setup

We trained our models on two GPU-powered machines: one with *2 × nVidia TitanX, 64GB RAM and an Intel(R) Core(TM) i7-5960X* CPU; and another with *4 × nVidia GTX 1080Ti, 128GB RAM and an Intel(R) Core(TM) i7-7820X* CPU. Each model is trained and evaluated using one GPU, with the exception of the *QEBrain* ones, which required a lot of computational power and for which we used 4 GPUs to train one model in parallel, as recommended. For fair comparison, we mir-

rored the software and configurations on the two machines using Anaconda3 virtual environments.

### 5.2 Systems hyperparameters

**deepQuest BiRNN and POSTECH**. We used the EU and MS parallel data (see Table 1) to train the POSTECH models for EN-DE and EN-ES. We used the default vocabulary size of 30 000 tokens. Sentences were clipped after length 70. The mini-batch size was set to 70.

**QEBrain** We used the following settings for the *Expert model:* max-vocab-size=49999; num-train-steps=75000; embedding-size=512; num-nits=512; num-layers=2; batch-size=512; infer-batch-size=24; metrics=BLEU; src-max-len=70; tgt-max-len=70; num-gpus=4; For the *QE model:* num-train-steps=50000; rnn-units=128; rnn-layers=1; qe-batch-size=10; infer-batch-size=10; metrics=pearson.

**SiameseQE** We used the following options: *Vocabulary:* joint; *size:* EN-DE 62 468, EN-ES 41 729; *batch size:* 64; *RNN type:* bidirectional, LSTM; *RNN units:* 64; *layers:* 2; *embedding size:* 256; *learning optimizer:* Adam (Kingma and Ba, 2014); *learning rate:* 0.001.

## 6 Evaluation

### 6.1 Business impact

We compared the performance of the NQE systems according to Microsoft's business metrics, developed to maximise the use of MT output. As a baseline we used a non-neural QE system based on 33 features (referred to as "33features").

The following evaluation focuses only on strings above 10 words, with TER scores below 0.3, indicative of good quality. The metrics we used are:

**AUC - area under the curve**: a metric of the capacity of classification of the model;

**Throughput**: the percentage of words, out of all translated words, that is approved for publication at an optimal QE threshold. Note that, when calculated as a percentage of MTed words, these values are much higher, since a large percentage of words (up to as much as 55%) is not MTed: they are recycled from translation memories, excluded due to length restrictions, or due to the fact that they belong to high-impact strings (e.g. marketing).

**Gain**: the difference between the percentage of volume approved (below the maximum low quality admitted) by a non-QE system, and the throughput of the QE system.

**Precision**: these values are measured as ratios of words that are associated with correct TER scores, within a fine-grained optimal QE score threshold.

**Distance to ideal (DtI)**: the distance between throughput scores and the respective value for an ideal QE system (a system with 100% precision, 100% recall), as estimated by Microsoft. The ideal values for throughput are: 15.49% for German and 29.32% for Spanish.

The scores in these metrics are summarised in Table 2 and Table 3.

| System | AUC ↑ | Thr. ↑ | Gain ↑ | Prec. ↑ | DtI ↓ |
|---|---|---|---|---|---|
| BiRNN | 0.7475 | 12.63% | 2.83% | 36.97% | 2.86% |
| POST. EU | 0.7154 | 12.38% | 2.58% | 36.74% | 3.11% |
| POST. MS. | 0.7047 | 11.95% | 2.15% | 34.50% | 3.54% |
| QEBrain | **0.8091** | **13.35%** | **3.55%** | **40.33%** | **2.14%** |
| S. NoATT | 0.6004 | 10.39% | 0.59% | 26.64% | 5.10% |
| S. DotATT | 0.7342 | 12.57% | 2.77% | 37.39% | 2.92% |
| S. w2wATT | 0.6698 | 12.43% | 2.63% | 35.67% | 3.06% |
| 33features | 0.6639 | 11.10% | 1.30% | 29.24% | 4.39% |

**Table 2:** Business evaluation scores of QE systems for EN-DE (best scores marked in bold).

| System | AUC ↑ | Thr. ↑ | Gain ↑ | Prec. ↑ | DtI ↓ |
|---|---|---|---|---|---|
| BiRNN | 0.6683 | 21.77% | 5.02% | 63.42% | 7.55% |
| Post. EU | 0.6401 | 21.01% | 4.26% | 62.10% | 8.31% |
| Post. MS | 0.6708 | 21.92% | 5.16% | 63.61% | 7.40% |
| QEBrain | **0.7259** | **22.82%** | **6.06%** | **65.38%** | **6.50%** |
| S. NoATT | 0.5359 | 16.65% | -0.11% | 54.95% | 12.67% |
| S. DotATT | 0.6557 | 21.87% | 5.12% | 63.62% | 7.45% |
| S. w2wATT | 0.6008 | 21.36% | 4.60% | 62.71% | 7.96% |
| 33features | 0.6617 | 21.63% | 4.88% | 63.14% | 7.69% |

**Table 3:** Business evaluation scores of QE systems for EN-ES (best scores marked in bold).

An interesting observation in these tables is the fact that, although all systems were configured in the same way (with the exception of the vocabulary sizes determined by the available data), the scores can be clearly grouped by language pairs:

- For throughput, gain and precision, all systems trained with Spanish data achieve better scores than any system trained with German data. For example, Spanish systems show throughput values of between 22.82% and 16.65%, but the German systems are all below 13.35%.
- However, regarding distance to the ideal QE system, all German-trained systems are better than the Spanish ones: the distance to the ideal values for German is between 2.14% and 5.10%, while for Spanish it is 6.5% or more.

This clear separation between languages shows the impact of fine-tuning and optimising metrics, for different types of data and language.

The ranking of systems for German data shows that QEBrain performs best according to all metrics. The BiRNN system takes second place in all metrics except precision, in which the usually third system, SiameseDotATT, replaces it. The system that scores consistently lowest is the SiameseNoATT, followed by the 33features system.

The ranking of systems trained with Spanish data is very similar to the German ranking, with a few exceptions. QEBrain is confirmed as the best system according to all metrics. The second-best system according to most metrics (except precision) is the Postech MS system, instead of BiRNN. The SiameseDotATT ranks third for most metrics, except precision. In all metrics, the 33features system outperforms three systems (SiameseW2wATT, Postech EU and SiameseNoATT), and in terms of AUC, it also outperforms the SiameseDotATT system.

## 6.2 Model performance

We also evaluated the systems' performance with standard metrics used for the evaluation of QE systems: Pearson correlation coefficient (*Pearson r*), RMSE and MAE. *Pearson r* is a measurement of the strength of the linear dependency between two variables. Both RMSE and MAE are measures of the differences between predicted and expected values.

Previous work has noted that in order to avoid the biases and limitations of each metric, it is necessary to consider them jointly (Specia et al., 2018b). We define Equation (1) to combine these metrics and derive a rank score (denoted by $\omega$), where $\bar{r}$, $\overline{MAE}$ and $\overline{RMSE}$ are the arithmetic means of the sets of scores for each of the respective metrics.

$$\omega_i = \left(0.5 + \frac{0.5 \times r_i}{\bar{r}}\right) - \left(\frac{MAE_i}{\overline{MAE}} + \frac{RMSE_i}{\overline{RMSE}}\right)/2 \quad (1)$$

The intuition is to allow ascending metrics to subsume descending ones and normalize over the set of all tested systems, thus generating a ranking score that takes into account not only the individual metrics and their combination, but also the distribution of these metrics' scores over all investigated systems. This method takes into account not only the ranking of the systems according to each metric, but also the distances within each metric.

The performance scores of all models are presented in Table 4 and Table 5 for EN-DE and EN-ES, respectively.

| System | Pearson ↑ | MAE ↓ | RMSE ↓ | ω ↑ | Rank |
|---|---|---|---|---|---|
| BiRNN | 0.4811 | 0.2107 | 0.2819 | 0.3169 | 2 |
| Post. EU | 0.4102 | 0.2194 | 0.2838 | 0.1883 | 6 |
| Post. MS | 0.4255 | 0.2153 | 0.2770 | 0.2312 | 5 |
| QEBrain | 0.6232 | 0.1753 | 0.2416 | 0.6726 | 1 |
| S. NoATT | 0.2535 | 0.2555 | 0.3176 | -0.1803 | 7 |
| S. DotATT | 0.4277 | 0.2132 | 0.2755 | 0.2416 | 4 |
| S. w2wATT | 0.2869 | 0.2545 | 0.3609 | -0.1990 | 8 |
| 33features | 0.4585 | 0.2124 | 0.2729 | 0.2938 | 3 |

**Table 4:** Performance and rank scores for experiments on EN-DE.

| System | Pearson ↑ | MAE ↓ | RMSE ↓ | ω ↑ | Rank |
|---|---|---|---|---|---|
| BiRNN | 0.3599 | 0.2226 | 0.2914 | 0.0930 | 2 |
| Post. EU | 0.3055 | 0.2534 | 0.3214 | -0.1036 | 6 |
| Post. MS | 0.3636 | 0.2292 | 0.2975 | 0.0747 | 3 |
| QEBrain | 0.5235 | 0.1856 | 0.2455 | 0.4940 | 1 |
| S. NoATT | 0.1115 | 0.2216 | 0.2750 | -0.2530 | 7 |
| S. DotATT | 0.3206 | 0.2297 | 0.2898 | 0.0212 | 5 |
| S. w2wATT | 0.2993 | 0.3084 | 0.4237 | -0.3975 | 8 |
| 33features | 0.3650 | 0.2349 | 0.2935 | 0.0712 | 4 |

**Table 5:** Performance and rank scores for experiments on EN-ES.

These are the most important observations regarding the different system performance scores:

• QEBrain is clearly the best-performing system. It ranks first across all metrics by quite some distance to the other systems.

• BiRNN ranks second in both language pairs, although its ranks per metric are very different. In German, it ranks second in terms of Pearson's $r$ score and MAE, but it is only fifth for RMSE; in Spanish, it is the third system (for MAE only) or fourth system in each metric rank. However, its consistent scores make it second-best.

• The next best-ranked systems are either the POSTECH MS or the Siamese DotATTN.

• The baseline system ("33features") has very good scores for German (second best for RMSE, and third in the other scores). In Spanish, it reaches second position for Pearson's $r$, but ranks lower for the other metrics.

The rank and scores of the Siamese NoATT system called our attention:

• In Spanish, this system ranks quite highly according to MAE and RMSE (it is the second-best system according to these metrics), but it scores very poorly according to Pearson's $r$. In the case of EN-ES, the variance in this system's predictions is very low, but so is the mean: $\sigma^2 = 0.0012$, $\mu = 0.2909$; and the max and min values are $max = 0.4435$, $min = 0.2159$. The error measurement based on the mean difference between predicted and expected values will also be low, as there will not be extreme differences per assessed pair. However, Pearson's $r$ takes this into account and, as seen from Table 5, gives such a system a lower score. This further supports the claim that, although widely used in QE research, these three metrics should not be considered independently.

• In the case of EN-DE, the variance, mean, min and max values are broader and thus cover the distribution of TER scores more realistically.

Our ranking method balanced these disparate results, making this system rank low, as expected, in the global ranking for both language pairs.

### 6.3 Cost of the different systems

Table 6 shows training times, and Table 7 inference times, i.e., the time for the model to generate TER scores for the given input. These tables also show adjusted values for cost, as described next.

The first three systems (BiRNN, POSTECH EU and POSTECH MS) were trained on a TitanX machine, while the last four were trained on a GTX 1080Ti system. To compensate for the speed difference of these machines and obtain realistic comparative times, we ran the BiRNN model on the GTX 1080Ti machine and we calculated a speed coefficient. We also took into account that QE-Brain was trained in parallel on 4 GPUs, using TensorFlow's *in-graph* replication. To further account for this, we multiplied the time consumed for training the expert model by 4.

The ranking according to GPU costs shows how the total cost of QEBrain significantly exceeds all others: by a factor of approximately 4 for the second slowest system, by a factor of 95 for the fastest EN-DE system and a factor of 62 for the fastest EN-ES system. The biggest share of the consumed time of two-phase systems is during phase 1, when systems are learning word-level features from parallel data. The most cost-effective systems are one-phase: Siamese systems and Deep-Quest BiRNN. In fact, all one-phase systems train more than 10 times faster than the fastest two-phase system. Also, since they can run on a single GPU, one-phase systems can train different models in parallel, on multi-GPU machines.

In terms of inference (prediction of the TER scores for unseen data), presented in Table 7, we notice similar trends in the time consumption for all systems, with only one exception; the deep-Quest systems perform the quickest. There are

| System | GPU | Original time (m) | | | | | | Adjusted time (m) GPU speed coef. = 0.45 | | | | | |
|---|---|---|---|---|---|---|---|---|---|---|---|---|---|
| | | EN-DE | | | EN-ES | | | EN-DE | | | EN-ES | | |
| | | I | II | Tot. | I | II | Tot. | I | II | Tot. | I | II | Tot. |
| BiRNN | T | – | – | 265 | – | – | 152 | – | – | 119 | – | – | 68 |
| Post. EU | T | 1 770 | 262 | 2 032 | 1 859 | 159 | 2 018 | 797 | 118 | 915 | 837 | 72 | 908 |
| Post. MS | T | 1 118 | 160 | 1 268 | 1 752 | 154 | 1 906 | 503 | 72 | 575 | 788 | 69 | 858 |
| QEBrain | G | 859 | 107 | 966 | 863 | 91 | 954 | 3 436 | 107 | 3 543 | 3 452 | 91 | 3 543 |
| S. NoATT | G | – | – | 37 | – | – | 86 | – | – | 37 | – | – | 86 |
| S. DotATT | G | – | – | 102 | – | – | 80 | – | – | 102 | – | – | 80 |
| S. w2wATT | G | – | – | 75 | – | – | 62 | – | – | 75 | – | – | 62 |

**Table 6:** Training time in minutes for phase 1, phase 2 and total, denoted as **I**, **II** and **Tot.** respectively. Training time for single-phase systems is only marked as total for readability.

| System | GPU | Original time (s) | | | | Adjusted time (s) speed coef. = 0.45 | | | |
|---|---|---|---|---|---|---|---|---|---|
| | | EN-DE | | EN-ES | | EN-DE | | EN-ES | |
| | | val. | test | val. | test | val. | test | val. | test |
| BiRNN | T | 15 | 62 | 10 | 71 | 7 | 28 | 5 | 32 |
| Post. EU | T | 56 | 213 | 40 | 242 | 25 | 96 | 18 | 109 |
| Post. MS | T | 56 | 209 | 40 | 244 | 25 | 94 | 18 | 110 |
| QEBrain | G | 42 | 163 | 30 | 195 | 43 | 163 | 30 | 195 |
| S. NoATT | G | 29 | 136 | 20 | 144 | 29 | 136 | 20 | 144 |
| S. DotATT | G | 32 | 146 | 22 | 157 | 32 | 146 | 22 | 157 |
| S. w2wATT | G | 32 | 148 | 22 | 161 | 32 | 148 | 22 | 161 |

**Table 7:** Inference time (in seconds) for the validation and the test sets. Number of sentence pairs for the validation set for EN-DE and EN-ES: 7525, 5136 respectively; for the test set for EN-DE and EN-ES: 32898, 34623 respectively.

several factors that play a role here, one of which is the batch size. In the experiments for the Siamese networks we invoke per-sentence inference, i.e., the batch size during test is equal to 1.

In a commercial setting, latency is critical, as it is essential that a deployed QE model does not introduce any additional latency into the workflow. A factor in favour of the one-phase systems is memory consumption. While typically two-phase systems would consume almost 100% of the GPU memory, the one-phase systems with our configuration would only consume between 70% – 90%. This would suggest that, by adapting the training hyperparameters of the one-phase systems to maximally utilise the GPU hardware, one can expect that either one model can be trained faster, or multiple models can be trained on the same GPU, e.g., by adapting the batch or vocabulary size. We also ought to note the size of models and additional files stored on the disk as an extra cost worth considering, one which is optimal for SiameseQE systems.

While the numbers in the previous rankings are in favour of the two-phase systems, we suggest that these rankings should be considered in combination with costs of implementation and use of such systems. We also point out that other business fac-

tors must be taken into account when evaluating such systems. For example, two-phase systems require more training data, which may not be easily available, or of sufficiently high quality. In addition, other computing resources increase the cost of ownership or rental of equipment, or the maintenance and optimisation cost for such systems. All these issues should be addressed in future research.

## 7 Conclusion – discussion of results and future work

This paper investigates NQE applied to industry data. We tested existing deepQuest (BiRNN and POSTECH) and QEBrain systems and the newly-introduced SiameseQE (no attention, Soft Dot attention and word-to-word attention). We conducted a series of experiments to test the performance of these systems on data provided by Microsoft and with additional training data.

Our evaluation shows that the QEBrain system outperforms all others, but is by far the most computationally expensive. An important outcome of our work is the observation that simpler, one-phase systems like BiRNN and Siamese networks show very promising results with low computational costs and easy implementations. In addition, the Siamese NN systems evidence reasonable room for improvement. Using attention yields much better results.We should also note that the baseline system – a statistical QE system – performs quite well. This suggests that statistical, feature-based systems can potentially be integrated into new hybrid approaches.

**Acknowledgements** The ADAPT Centre for Digital Content Technology is funded under the SFI Research Centres Programme (Grant 13/RC/2106) and is co-funded under the ERD Fund. Félix do Carmo collaborates under an Horizon 2020 programme: EDGE COFUND Marie Skodowska-Curie Grant Agreement no. 713567.

We would also like to thank F. Blain for the useful comments.

# References


Astudillo, Ramón Fernández, João Graça, and André Martins. 2018. Translation Quality Estimation and Automatic Post-Editing - Workshop Proceedings. In *The 13th Conference of The Association for Machine Translation in the Americas (AMTA2018)*, Boston, USA.

Bahdanau, Dzmitry, Kyunghyun Cho, and Yoshua Bengio. 2015. Neural machine translation by jointly learning to align and translate. In *Proceedings of the 6th International Conference on Learning Representations (ICLR 2015)*, San Diego, CA, USA. 15pp.

Baldi, Pierre and Yves Chauvin. 1993. Neural networks for fingerprint recognition. *Neural Computation*, 5(3):402–418.

Bromley, Jane, Isabelle Guyon, Yann LeCun, Eduard Säckinger, and Roopak Shah. 1993. Signature verification using a "siamese" time delay neural network. In *Proceedings of the 6th International Conference on Neural Information Processing Systems*, NIPS'93, pages 737–744, San Francisco, CA, USA. Morgan Kaufmann Publishers Inc.

Cho, Kyunghyun, Bart van Merriënboer, Çalar Gülçehre, Dzmitry Bahdanau, Fethi Bougares, Holger Schwenk, and Yoshua Bengio. 2014. Learning phrase representations using RNN encoder–decoder for statistical machine translation. In *Proceedings of the 2014 Conference on Empirical Methods in Natural Language Processing*, pages 1724–1734, Doha, Qatar.

Fan, Kai, Bo Li, Fengming Zhou, and Jiayi Wang. 2018. "bilingual expert" can find translation errors. *CoRR*, abs/1807.09433.

Ive, Julia, Frédéric Blain, and Lucia Specia. 2018. DeepQuest: a framework for neural-based Quality Estimation. *Proceedings of COLING 2018, the 27th International Conference on Computational Linguistics, Sante Fe, New Mexico, USA*, pages 3146–3157.

Kim, Hyun, Jong-Hyeok Lee, and Seung-Hoon Na. 2017. Predictor-estimator using multilevel task learning with stack propagation for neural quality estimation. In *Proceedings of the Second Conference on Machine Translation, WMT 2017, Copenhagen, Denmark, September 7-8, 2017*, pages 562–568.

Kingma, Diederik P. and Jimmy Ba. 2014. Adam: A method for stochastic optimization. *CoRR*, abs/1412.6980.

Koch, Gregory, Richard Zemel, and Ruslan Salakhutdinov. 2015. Siamese neural networks for one-shot image recognition. In *Proceedings of the 32nd International Conference on Machine Learning (JMLR: W&CP 2015)*, Lille, France.

Koehn, Philipp. 2005. Europarl: A Parallel Corpus for Statistical Machine Translation. In *Conference Proceedings: the 10th Machine Translation Summit (MTSummit 2005)*, pages 79–86, Phuket, Thailand.

Li, Maoxi, Qingyu Xiang, Zhiming Chen, and Mingwen Wang. 2018. A unified neural network for quality estimation of machine translation. *IEICE Transactions*, 101-D(9):2417–2421.

Luong, Thang, Hieu Pham, and Christopher D. Manning. 2015. Effective approaches to attention-based neural machine translation. In *Proceedings of the 2015 Conference on Empirical Methods in Natural Language Processing, (EMNLP 2015)*, pages 1412–1421, Lisbon, Portugal.

Mueller, Jonas and Aditya Thyagarajan. 2016. Siamese recurrent architectures for learning sentence similarity. In *Proceedings of the Thirtieth AAAI Conference on Artificial Intelligence*, AAAI'16, pages 2786–2792, Phoenix, Arizona, USA.

Papineni, Kishore, Salim Roukos, Todd Ward, and Wei-Jing Zhu. 2002. BLEU: A Method for Automatic Evaluation of Machine Translation. In *Proceedings of the 40th Annual Meeting on Association for Computational Linguistics*, pages 311–318, Philadelphia, Pennsylvania, USA.

Rocktäschel, Tim, Edward Grefenstette, Karl Moritz Hermann, Tomás Kociský, and Phil Blunsom. 2015. Reasoning about entailment with neural attention. *CoRR*, abs/1509.06664.

Snover, Matthew, Bonnie Dorr, Richard Schwartz, Linnea Micciulla, and John Makhoul. 2006. A study of translation edit rate with targeted human annotation. In *Proceedings of the 7th Conference of the. Association for Machine Translation of the Americas. Visions for the Future of Machine Translation (AMTA 2006)*, pages 223–231, Cambridge, Massachusetts, USA.

Specia, Lucia, Nicola Cancedda, Marc Dymetman, Marco Turchi, and Nello Cristianini. 2009. Estimating the sentence-level quality of machine translation systems. In *Proceedings of the 13th Annual Conference of the European Association for Machine Translation (EAMT 2009)*, pages 28–35, Barcelona, Spain.

Specia, Lucia, Kashif Shah, José G. C. de Souza, and Trevor Cohn. 2013. Quest - A translation quality estimation framework. In *51st Annual Meeting of the Association for Computational Linguistics, (ACL 2013), Proceedings of the Conference System Demonstrations*, pages 79–84, Sofia, Bulgaria.

Specia, Lucia, Frédéric Blain, Varvara Logacheva, Ramón Fernández Astudillo, and André F. T. Martins. 2018a. Findings of the WMT 2018 shared task on quality estimation. In *Proceedings of the Third Conference on Machine Translation: Shared Task Papers, (WMT 2018)*, pages 689–709, Belgium, Brussels.

Specia, Lucia, Carolina Scarton, and Gustavo Henrique Paetzold. 2018b. *Quality Estimation for Machine Translation*. Synthesis Lectures on Human Language Technologies. Morgan & Claypool Publishers.

Sutskever, Ilya, Oriol Vinyals, and Quoc V. Le. 2014. Sequence to sequence learning with neural networks. In *Proceedings of Advances in Neural Information Processing Systems 27: Annual Conference on Neural Information Processing Systems (NIPS 2014)*, pages 3104–3112, Montreal, Quebec, Canada.

Ueffing, Nicola, José GC de Souza, and Gregor Leusch. 2018. Quality estimation for automatically generated titles of ecommerce browse pages. In *Proceedings of the 2018 Conference of the North American Chapter of the Association for Computational Linguistics: Human Language Technologies, (NAACL-HLT 2018)*, pages 52–59, New Orleans, Louisiana, USA.

Vaswani, Ashish, Noam Shazeer, Niki Parmar, Jakob Uszkoreit, Llion Jones, Aidan N Gomez, Łukasz Kaiser, and Illia Polosukhin. 2017. Attention is all you need. In *Advances in Neural Information Processing Systems 30: Annual Conference on Neural Information Processing Systems (NIPS 2017)*, pages 5998–6008, Long Beach, CA, USA.

Wang, Jiayi, Kai Fan, Bo Li, Fengming Zhou, Boxing Chen, Yangbin Shi, and Luo Si. 2018. Alibaba submission for wmt18 quality estimation task. In *Proceedings of the Third Conference on Machine Translation (WMT 2018)*, pages 822–828, Belgium, Brussels, October. Association for Computational Linguistics.

Yih, Wen-tau, Kristina Toutanova, John C. Platt, and Christopher Meek. 2011. Learning discriminative projections for text similarity measures. In *Proceedings of the Fifteenth Conference on Computational Natural Language Learning (CoNLL 2011)*, pages 247–256, Portland, Oregon.

# Author Index


Šics, Valters, 179

Ajausks, Ēriks, 1
Alonso, Juan, 125
Alvarez, Sergi, 49
Arcan, Mihael, 125
Artma, Tambet, 116
Aziz, Wilker, 122

Bērziņš, Aivars, 1
Badia, Toni, 49
Bawden, Rachel, 122
Bentivogli, Luisa, 73
Bernardinello, Giorgio, 174
Bernardini, Silvia, 73
Bié, Laurent, 114, 219
Bienfait, David, 116
Birch, Alexandra, 122
Bouillon, Pierrette, 149, 196
Brabers, Joris, 186

Casacuberta, Francisco, 219
Casas, Noe, 125
Castilho, Sheila, 179
Chen, Long-Huei, 101
Cresceri, Diego, 36

Defauw, Arne, 186
Depraetere, Heidi, 110, 116
Do Campo Bayón, María, 30
Do Carmo, Félix, 228
Domingo, Miguel, 219

Esplà, Miquel, 118
Esplà-Gomis, Miquel, 122
Estela, Amando, 114, 219
Estrella, Paula, 196
Everaert, Frederic, 110, 116, 186

Farah, Eduardo, 110
Ferraresi, Adriano, 73
Forcada, Mikel, 118, 122

García-Martínez, Mercedes, 114, 219

Gaspari, Federico, 179
Gaspari, Federico , 112
Gerlach, Johanna, 196
Groves, Declan, 159, 228
Gupta, Rohit, 142

Haddow, Barry, 122
Haelterman, Johan, 116
Heinisch, Barbara, 42
Helle, Alex, 179
Helle, Alexandre, 109, 114, 219
Herranz, Manuel, 109, 114, 179, 219
Hiraoka, Yusuke, 64
Hoang, Hieu, 118

Ive, Julia, 110
Iwai, Ritsuko, 23

Kageura, Kyo, 101
Katariina Teder , Laura, 116
Kauliņš, Kaspars, 1
Kawahara, Daisuke, 23
Khalilov, Maxim, 110
Kosmaczewska, Kasia, 167
Kumada, Takatsune, 23
Kurohashi, Sadao, 23

Lambert, Patrik, 142
Lesznyák, Ágnes, 16
Li, Chaofeng, 95
Liu, Chao-Hong, 120
Liu, Jessie, 95
Liyanapathirana, Jeevanthi, 149
Lušicky, Vesna, 42

Maroti, Christine, 110
Martins, André, 120
Masoud, Maraim, 125
Mazur, Marek, 179
Meļņika, Jūlija, 1
Mesa-Lao, Bartolomé, 149
Miceli Barone , Antonio Valerio, 122
Moorkens, Joss, 228

Morozova, Daria, 88
Murgolo, Elena, 36
Mutal, Jonathan, 196

Naskar, Sudip, 8
Nunziatini, Mara, 57

O'Dowd, Tony, 179
Oliver, Antoni, 49
Ovchinnikova, Irina, 88

Pérez-Ortiz, Juan Antonio, 122
Pal, Santanu, 8
Pals, Liming, 95
Paquin, Eric, 228
Pasricha, Nivranshu, 125
Patel, Raj, 142
Peris, Álvaro, 219
Pinnis, Mārcis, 179
Popovic, Maja, 80
Premoli, Valeria, 36

Qian, Ming, 95

Raja Chakravarthi, Bharathi, 125
Ramírez-Sánchez, Gema, 118, 179
Resende, Natália, 179
Roturier, Johann, 134

Sánchez-Cartagena, Víctor, 122, 179
Sánchez-Gijón, Pilar, 30
Sánchez-Martínez, Felipe, 122
Sāmīte, Indra, 1
Saartee, Piret, 116
Scansani, Randy, 73
Schlatter, Brian, 134
Schmidtke, Dag, 159, 228

Scholte, Kim, 186
Secker, Andrew, 122
Shterionov, Dimitar, 228
Sics, Valters, 116
Silva, Catarina, 120, 204
Silva, David, 134
Skadiņa, Inguna, 1
Spechbach, Hervé, 196
Specia, Lucia, 110
Szoc, Sara, 110, 186

Tammsaar, Katri, 116
Tinsley, John, 142
Tito, Ivan, 122
Torregrosa, Daniel, 125
Train, Matt, 167
Tukeyev, Ualsher, 123

Vali, Ingmar, 116
Van den Bogaert, Joachim, 110, 116, 186
van der Kreeft, Peggy, 122
van Genabith, Josef, 8
Van Winckel , Koen, 116
Van Winckel, Koen, 110, 186
Vanallemeersch, Tom, 110, 116, 186
Vasiļevskis, Artūrs, 116
Vasiļjevs, Andrejs, 1
Vela, Mihaela, 8
Ventura, Artur, 110

Way, Andy, 112, 120, 179, 228

Yamada, Masaru, 64

Zampieri, Marcos, 8
Zaretskaya, Anna, 213
Zhumanov, Zhandos, 123

**Association for Computational Linguistics**
209 N. Eighth Street
Stroudsburg, Pennsylvania 18360

ISBN 978-1-5108-9293-4